The East German leadership
1946–1973

MANCHESTER
UNIVERSITY PRESS

The East German leadership 1946–1973

Conflict and crisis

Peter Grieder

Manchester University Press

Manchester and New York

distributed exclusively in the USA by St. Martin's Press

Published by Manchester University Press
Oxford Road, Manchester M13 9NR, UK
and Room 400, 175 Fifth Avenue, New York, NY 10010, USA
http://www.man.ac.uk/mup

Distributed exclusively in the USA by
St. Martin's Press, Inc., 175 Fifth Avenue, New York,
NY 10010, USA

Distributed exclusively in Canada by
UBC Press, University of British Columbia, 6344 Memorial Road,
Vancouver, BC, Canada V6T 1Z2

British Library Cataloguing-in-Publication Data
A catalogue record for this book is available from the British Library

Library of Congress Cataloging-in-Publication Data applied for

ISBN 0 7190 5498 2 *hardback*

First published 1999

06 05 04 03 02 01 00 99   10 9 8 7 6 5 4 3 2 1

Typeset in Monotype Sabon
by Servis Filmsetting Ltd, Manchester
Printed in Great Britain
by Bookcraft (Bath) Ltd, Midsomer Norton

Contents

Acknowledgements

First of all I would like to thank my doctoral supervisor, Mr Timothy Garton Ash of St Antony's College, Oxford. Without his encouragement, expertise, sound advice and constructive criticism, this book might never have been written. As a supervisor, he was everything one could hope for, combining flexibility with high expectations. Professor Mary Fulbrook also provided invaluable support, reading through the text and suggesting a range of improvements.

I owe a special debt of gratitude to the archivists at the central party archive of the SED in Berlin, notably Frau Nestler, Frau Räuber, Dr Inge Pardon, Herr Lange, Herr Bergmann and Frau Müller. I would also like to thank Herr Förster and Frau Schulz for their assistance at the archives of the former ministry for state security.

Herr Georg Tetmeyer helped me to improve my German in 1991 and for this I will always be grateful. Dr Wilfriede Otto provided indispensable advice during my visits to Berlin, directing me to relevant sources and reading through my work. I would also like to thank Dr Stefan Wolle of the Humboldt University for his assistance in 1992 and Dr Dirk Spilker for his expertise and stimulating conversation. Finally, I am indebted to my two research students Alan McDougall and Josie McLellan for drawing my attention to new publications.

The many interviews I conducted with former SED leaders and policymakers were a source of great inspiration. Their testimony enriched my work and furthered my understanding of SED high politics. I would like to thank all of them for their time, particularly Karl Schirdewan, Wolfgang Berger, Alfred Neumann, Gerhard Schürer, Kurt Hager and Herbert Wolf.

I owe a particular debt to Trinity College, Cambridge for awarding me a pre-research linguistic studentship and financing three research trips to Berlin. The British Academy provided me with a three-year major state studentship for which I am extremely grateful. Without the financial generosity of the *Deutscher Akademischer Austauschdienst* (DAAD) and the German Historical Institute in London, I would not have been able to spend a year in Germany. I would also like to thank Magdalen College, Oxford for providing me with the ideal environment to complete this book. Finally, I owe a special debt of gratitude to Vanessa Graham and the other staff at Manchester University Press. Without their patience and support, this book would not have been possible.

Foreign words and abbreviations

Abgrenzung   Honecker's policy of disassociating the GDR from any notion of a shared German culture with the FRG after 1971

apparatchik   an official in the Communist Party administration

APZ   *Aus Politik und Zeitgeschichte*. A supplement to the weekly *Das Parlament*

BBC   British Broadcasting Corporation

Bezirk   a district of East Germany after 1952 (there were fourteen in total) (see also entry for *Land*)

bloc parties   'bourgeois' parties allied to the SED

BStU   Bundesbeauftragte für die *Stasi* Unterlagen (*Stasi* archive)

Bundestag   West German parliament

BzG   *Beiträge zur Geschichte der Arbeiterbewegung*

CC   central committee

CDU   Christlich-Demokratische Union (Christian Democratic Union)

CIA   Central Intelligence Agency (of the USA)

Comecon   Council for Mutual Economic Assistance

Cominform   Information bureau for the Communist Parties of Eastern Europe

CP   Communist Party

CPC   Communist Party of Czechoslovakia

CPCC   central party control commission

CPSU   Communist Party of the Soviet Union (see also KPdSU)

CS   central secretariat

CSSR   Czechoslovakian Soviet Socialist Republic

CSU   Christlich-Soziale Union (Christian Social Union)

CWIHP   *Cold War International History Project*

DA   *Deutschland Archiv*

DDR   Deutsche Demokratische Republik (German Democratic Republic; see GDR)

DEFA   Deutsche Film AG (German Film Company)

Deutschlandpolitik   policy on relations between the two German states

DFD   Demokratischer Frauenbund Deutschlands (Democratic Women's Federation of Germany)

DGB Deutsche Gewerkschaftsbund (West German Trade Union Federation)

DWK Deutsche Wirtschaftskommission (German Economic Commission)

East Germany see GDR

ESS Economic System of Socialism

FAZ *Frankfurter Allgemeine Zeitung*

FDGB Freier Deutscher Gewerkschaftsbund (Free German Trade Union Federation)

FDJ Freie Deutsche Jugend (Free German Youth)

FDP Freie Demokratische Partei (Free Democratic Party)

FRG Federal Republic of Germany (also called West Germany)

GDR German Democratic Republic (also called East Germany)

JCH *Journal of Contemporary History*

Jugendweihe GDR ceremony in which fourteen year olds were given adult social status

KGB Komitet Gosudarstvennoi Bezopasnosti (Committee of State Security of the USSR)

KJV Kommunistischer Jugendverband (Communist Youth Association)

KPD Kommunistische Partei Deutschlands (Communist Party of Germany)

KPdSU Kommunistische Partei der Sowjetunion (Communist Party of the Soviet Union or CPSU)

Kreis a local authority of East Germany after 1952 (there were 217 in total)

Land a state in eastern Germany until 1952 (see also entry for *Bezirk*)

LDPD or **LDP** Liberal-Demokratische Partei Deutschlands (Liberal Democratic Party of Germany)

LPG Landwirtschaftliche Produktionsgenossenschaft (agricultural production co-operative)

mass organizations 'organizations for the masses'; e.g. the FDJ and FDGB

MfS Ministerium für Staatssicherheit (ministry for state security or *Stasi)*

NATO North Atlantic Treaty Organization

National Front A united front of anti-fascist parties and mass organizations under the direction of the SED. The organization had committees at district, local and neighbourhood level. During general and local government elections, it submitted a joint list of candidates and single electoral programme

ND *Neues Deutschland* (the daily newspaper of the SED)

NEP New Economic Policy

NES New Economic System

NKFD Nationalkomitee Freies Deutschland (National Committee For a Free Germany)

NL Nachlaß (unpublished collections of documents pertaining to individual SED leaders)

NPD Nationaldemokratische Partei Deutschlands (National Democratic Party of Germany)

NSDAP Nationalsozialistische Deutsche Arbeiterpartei (National Socialist Party of Germany or Nazi Party)

NVA   Nationale Volksarmee (National People's Army)
NW   *Neuer Weg*
Ostpolitik   West German policy of rapprochement towards the Soviet bloc and particularly towards the GDR
Party of the new type   party based on the CPSU model
PB   politburo
PCI   Communist Party of Italy
PDS   Partei des Democratischen Sozialismus (Party of Democratic Socialism)
PE   party executive
POC   *Problems of Communism*
PUWP   Polish United Workers' Party
Reichstag   the German parliament before 1945
Reichswehr   the German army, 1919–35
RIAS   Radio in the American Sector (of Berlin)
SAPMO-BArch, BPA   Stiftung Archiv der Parteien und Massenorganisationen der DDR im Bundesarchiv, Berlin Parteiarchiv (Foundation for the archive of the parties and mass organizations of the GDR in the Federal archive, Berlin party archive)
SAPMO-BArch, ZPA   Stiftung Archiv der Parteien und Massenorganisationen der DDR im Bundesarchiv, Zentrales Parteiarchiv (Foundation for the archive of the parties and mass organizations of the GDR in the Federal archive, central party archive)
SBZ   Sowjetische Besatzungszone (Soviet occupation zone)
SED   Sozialistische Einheitspartei Deutschlands (Socialist Unity Party of Germany)
SMAD   Sowjetische Militäradministration in Deutschland (Soviet Military Administration in Germany)
SPD   Sozialdemokratische Partei Deutschlands (Social Democratic Party of Germany)
Stasi   Staatssicherheitsdienst (East German ministry for state security or MfS)
TR   *Tägliche Rundschau* (newspaper of the Soviet occupation forces in Germany)
UN   United Nations
USA   United States of America
USPD   Unabhängige Sozialistische Partei Deutschlands (Independent Socialist Party of Germany)
USSR   Union of Soviet Socialist Republics
VfZ   *Vierteljahrshefte für Zeitgeschichte*
Volkskammer   East German parliament
VVN   Vereinigung der Verfolgten des Naziregimes (Association of those persecuted by the Nazi regime)
West Germany   see FRG
Westpolitik   Policy of the GDR towards the West, particularly towards West Germany
ZK   Zentralkomitee (central committee or CC)

Introduction

East Germany was a dictatorship. Moreover, it was a *totalitarian* dictatorship. This means that the ruling Socialist Unity Party of Germany (SED) attempted – though not always successfully – to control all areas of public life and society.[1] In the pages that follow, I use the word Stalinist to describe the nature of this regime. Stalinism is best defined in a narrow and a broad sense. In the narrow sense, it designates a form of despotic rule characterized by purges, arbitrary terror, and personality cult. The Soviet leader, Nikita Khrushchev, mitigated its worst excesses when he introduced 'de-Stalinization' at the twentieth congress of the Communist Party of the Soviet Union (CPSU) in 1956. In the broad sense, however, it describes the socio-political system the USSR exported to East-Central Europe after the Second World War. Its defining feature was the hierarchical, hegemonic control of the communist party over every aspect of society, aided and abetted by an all-pervasive secret police.[2] Stalinism, then, was a form of communist totalitarianism. It survived in East Germany (also called the German Democratic Republic or GDR) – albeit with certain modifications – until the revolution of 1989.

As reunited Germany tries to come to terms with the legacy of the German Democratic Republic, historians are left with the task of reassessing forty-four years of SED rule. Studies of high politics are an essential part of this process because power in the Stalinist state was concentrated in the communist party leadership – that is to say the politburo and central committee. After more than forty years it is now possible to shed light on this clandestine, hermetically sealed world. The end of the Cold War has presented historians with a treasure trove of new primary source material as archives in countries once behind the Iron Curtain are opened up for the first time. Histories written before 1989[3] were necessarily dependent on censored party literature and the memoirs of communists who fled to the West. Although these accounts require revision, they remain a valuable supplement to the primary sources. This book aims to provide an empirical, in-depth study of conflict in the SED leadership between 1946 (when the party was founded) and 1973, when its first leader, Walter Ulbricht, died. It is based on new primary source material from three Berlin archives: the central party archive of the SED, the archive of the former ministry for state security, and the Berlin district party archive. I also conducted more than twenty interviews with former SED functionaries, some of whom were members of the politburo and central committee.

The party was to communists what the medieval church was to catholics – the source of all truth and redemption. To engage in 'factionalism' was to violate the first commandment of Stalinist politics: that 'the party was always right'. Any deviation from the official line was interpreted as an attack on party unity and a distraction from the fight against capitalism. 'Objectively', such people were 'counter-revolutionaries' who were giving succour to the class enemy. Demoted, ostracized and persecuted, they were required to recant in a public ritual known as 'self-criticism'. The ultimate sanction was excommunication, even execution. Conflict, then, was taboo for a communist leadership which regarded the main-tenance of party discipline as a fundamental article of faith. The aim of this book is to explode this taboo and penetrate the public image of a monolithic regime.

Before giving an account of the primary sources upon which this study is based it is necessary to say something about the archives themselves. In 1992, the central party archive, which also housed the archive of the Berlin district party leadership, was part of the Institute for the History of the Labour Movement (formerly the Institute for Marxist–Leninism) administered by the SED's succes-sor party, the Party of Democratic Socialism (PDS). On arrival there was little way of ascertaining precisely what was available because there was only a limited catalogue, something which was later rectified. Access to new files and file indexes often seemed to depend on building up good personal relationships with key archivists. Daily attendance and constant dialogue with the administration was really the only way of maintaining progress. One must, of course, bear in mind a range of mitigating circumstances. In 1992 the archive – like the rest of former East Germany – was making the difficult transition to democracy. In early spring, the entire building was overrun by police in search of the elusive order to shoot refugees trying to escape to the West. The behind-the-scenes legal battle over who should control the archive created an air of uncertainty which culmi-nated in its being shut down at the end of November 1992. It reopened again as part of the 'Foundation for the archive of the parties and mass organizations of the GDR in the Federal archive' in January 1993. When I next visited in the spring and summer of 1994, the situation had become more stable.

I was lucky to gain access to the archive of the former ministry for state secur-ity (the *Staatssicherheitsdienst*, or *Stasi* as it is commonly known). In 1992 there was a seven month waiting list and applicants were dependent on the commend-able efforts of archivists searching for relevant material. The estimated 180 kilo-metres of documents will take years to classify and the overstretched staff were inundated with applications, not only from academics, but from the thousands of former East German citizens who wanted to read their *Stasi* files. I was even-tually given some invaluable material relating to conflict in the SED leadership during the 1950s.

Most of the material cited in this book was found in the central party archive of the former SED. Before 1989 the historian could merely peruse the published, and therefore heavily edited, versions of party executive and central committee debates (the party executive, which existed between 1946 and 1950, convened once a month; its successor, the central committee, on a quarterly basis). Now, however, the stenographic verbatim minutes of their discussions are available. Uncensored and more lively than previously assumed, they are the most useful source for discerning differences of opinion in the SED leadership. They are supplemented by records of attendance, agenda and approved resolutions.

The politburo, set up in 1950, was the nerve-centre of power in the SED state and, like its predecessor, the central secretariat, met at least once a week. With one notable exception,[4] there are no stenographic verbatim minutes of their meetings. There are, however, records of attendance, the weekly agenda and approved resolutions. These were crucial in tracing the development of policy on specific issues. They sometimes hint at the existence of disagreement on key questions and are occasionally accompanied by handwritten notes of the discussion. After 1952 they were supplemented by so-called *Arbeitsprotokollen* (literally 'working records'), containing a variety of material discussed at weekly politburo meetings. These might be draft reports, resolutions and speeches, policy statements, and even the private correspondence of SED leaders. Draft documents were sometimes altered, even rejected, enabling one to identify issues of conflict. Members of the politburo and central committee also sat on various commissions whose task it was to elaborate party policy in specific areas. The stenographic verbatim transcripts of their deliberations are now available for study.

The central party control commission was the SED's internal police force – judge and jury of leading functionaries accused of deviating from the party line. Its records were not made available until 1993 and some of the highly sensitive personal material is still subject to the thirty-year rule (not allowing files to be opened until thirty years after the deaths of the individuals concerned). Restrictions on files pertaining to political matters have, however, been lifted. Particularly useful were the stenographic verbatim transcripts of central party control commission interrogations. There were also statements from disgraced party leaders and the testimonies of those closely associated with them. The retrospective and denunciatory nature of some of the evidence renders it unreliable.

The party kept confidential files on all its functionaries (known as 'cadre files'), regardless of status. Although some remain closed (like those of the central party control commission, many are subject to the thirty-year rule), a considerable number were declassified between 1993 and 1994. They contain a variety of material ranging from personal and official correspondence to records of an individual's political career.

Particularly interesting were the so-called *Nachlässe* of certain SED leaders. These are miscellaneous collections of private correspondence, speeches, policy

statements, communiqués, draft resolutions and other working materials. Some
contained detailed handwritten notes of politburo and central committee discussions as well as stenographic and shorthand accounts of conversations with
Soviet leaders. Members of the politburo also administered departments in the
party bureaucracy (for example 'propaganda and agitation' or 'international
relations') and documents not kept in the *Nachlässe* were often preserved here
instead. These collections (known as *Büros* or 'offices') contain a wealth of interesting material, ranging from personal and official correspondence to policy
directives and records of discussions with political leaders.

Some politburo members played an important role in the Berlin district party
leadership, the records of which enabled me to gain a more profound insight into
communist high politics in East Germany. The speeches of SED leaders to Berlin
party activists at key moments were occasionally useful in illuminating the dif-
fering perceptions of party leaders on certain issues. The *Stasi* was kept informed
of power struggles in the upper echelons of the SED. Records I consulted from
the former ministry for state security contained typed-up minutes of politburo
discussions, statements from purged SED leaders, as well as testimonies and
denunciations of those closely associated with them. Many of these documents,
however, were also stored at the central party archive.

Extensive use was made of printed primary source material. It was SED practice to publish stenographic verbatim minutes of its party congresses and conferences. The former were held every four to five years, the latter on an *ad hoc*
basis in between. Not all traces of conflict were airbrushed out of the records.
Members of the politburo also wrote articles for party newspapers and journals
such as *Neues Deutschland, Einheit* and *Neuer Weg*. These were invaluable in
delineating different shades of opinion in the SED leadership. Party executive,
central committee and politburo reports were sometimes published in the SED
press or as separate booklets. I also consulted contemporary German newspapers and periodicals to provide additional information pertaining to the conflicts under study.

The pitfalls of political bias, distorted memory and self-justification notwith-
standing, memoirs written before 1989[5] are still of some use in reconstructing a
history of conflict in the East German leadership. Accounts recently published
include those of Rudolf Herrnstadt (politburo critic of Walter Ulbricht in the
early 1950s), Erich Honecker (Ulbricht's successor as party leader), Carl-Heinz
Janson (a leading economics functionary in the apparatus of the central committee), Günter Mittag (member of the politburo responsible for the GDR's
economy from the early 1960s) and Karl Schirdewan (number two in the SED
hierarchy, purged for 'revisionist' tendencies in 1958).[6]

According to Voltaire 'history is a pack of tricks we play upon the dead'. The
adage is not so easily applied to contemporary history because many of the par-
ticipants are still alive. Rich in detail and flavour, their testimony is a diminish-
ing, yet largely untapped resource. In the corridors of power, conversations were
rarely recorded and important decisions frequently made over the telephone or

at the hunting lodge. While interviews are no substitute for the careful study of archival manuscripts, they are a valuable supplement to it. They supply a wealth of additional information and vivid detail, shed new light on the written evidence and fill important gaps in the historian's knowledge. Conversely they can be crude attempts at self-justification and the historian must beware of the colouring of retrospect. The archives offer huge reservoirs of historical facts but not the personal perspectives to interpret them. Unless this 'unwritten history' is taken into account it will be lost forever.

A history of conflict in the East German leadership can only be written with Soviet positions clearly in view. The SED, after all, was ultimately subject to and dependent on the Kremlin, even if it enjoyed more room for manoeuvre than previously believed. I therefore consulted Soviet primary sources accessible in Germany: for example, *Tägliche Rundschau* (the newspaper of the Soviet occupation forces), the stenographic verbatim minutes of the CPSU central committee plenum in July 1953[7] and published excerpts of documents recently discovered in Russian archives. The bulletin of the Washington based *Cold War International History Project* was particularly useful. Account was also taken of the small but growing Western literature on Soviet actions in Germany as well as of Russian memoirs and publications translated into English or German.[8] For a number of reasons I did not visit archives in the former USSR, although limited use was made of material stored at the Moscow Center for the Preservation of Contemporary Documentation (TsKhSD). At the time of writing the situation in Moscow was uncertain and the central committee archives only open for the period to 1953. It was possible to make substantial and original (if not completely comprehensive) contributions to the debate without consulting these archives, especially since Soviet positions are often reflected in the East German sources. There is a vast amount of new material in Berlin, and since this study is primarily concerned with SED high politics, this is where most of the relevant documents are kept. It should also be pointed out that remarkably little has yet been discovered in the Soviet archives relating to the conflicts discussed here.

This book is a study of 'hawks' and 'doves', of 'reformers' and 'hard-liners'. It poses the question of whether there were alternative policies on offer that could have been adopted at four crisis points in the history of the SED. Could East Germany have pursued a different path to the one eventually taken? The chapters that follow provide detailed case-studies of the Stalinization process in the SED between 1946 and 1953, the Zaisser–Herrnstadt opposition of 1950–53, the anti-Ulbricht opposition of 1956–58 and the causes of Ulbricht's downfall in 1971.

Notes

1 Although this is not the place to enter into comparative debates about the German Democratic Republic (GDR) and the Third Reich, both these dictatorships can be described as totalitarian. In fact, the former was probably *more* totalitarian than the

latter in that it built up a larger state security apparatus and exercised a greater degree of control over the economy. In most other respects, however, the two regimes were very different. For a fuller discussion of this last point, see M. Fulbrook, *Anatomy of a dictatorship. Inside the GDR, 1949–1989* (Oxford, 1995), pp. 283–6.

2 See also H. Weber, *Aufbau und Fall einer Diktatur. Kritische Beiträge zur Geschichte der DDR* (Köln, 1991), p. 203; H. Weber, 'Die DDR-Geschichtswissenschaft im Umbruch? Aufgaben der Historiker bei der Bewältigung der stalinistischen Vergangenheit', *DA*, 7 (1990), 1058–70; p. 1062.

3 Prime examples are K. W. Fricke, *Warten auf Gerechtigkeit. Kommunistische Säuberungen und Rehabilitierungen. Bericht und Dokumentation* (Köln, 1971); K. W. Fricke, *Opposition und Widerstand in der DDR. Ein politischer Report* (Köln, 1984); M. Jänicke, *Der dritte Weg. Die antistalinistische Opposition gegen Ulbricht seit 1953* (Köln, 1964); H. Lippmann, *Honecker. Porträt eines Nachfolgers* (Köln, 1971); P. C. Ludz, *Parteielite im Wandel. Funktionsaufbau, Sozialstruktur und Ideologie der SED-Führung* (Köln–Opladen, 1968); P. C. Ludz, *The German Democratic Republic from the sixties to the seventies. A socio-political analysis* (Cambridge, MA, 1970); F. Oldenburg, *Konflikt und Konfliktregelung in der Parteiführung der SED 1945/46–1972* (Köln, 1972); C. Stern, *Porträt einer bolschewistischen Partei. Entwicklung, Funktion und Situation der SED* (Köln–West Berlin, 1957); C. Stern, *Ulbricht. Eine politische Biographie* (Köln–West Berlin, 1963); F. T. Stößel, *Positionen und Strömungen in der KPD/SED 1945–54* (Köln, 1985). Other informative books in English include: D. Childs, *The GDR: Moscow's German ally* (London, 1983, 1988); M. Fulbrook, *The Fontana history of Germany 1918–1990. The divided nation* (London, 1991); M. McCauley, *Marxism-Leninism in the German Democratic Republic. The Socialist Unity Party (SED)* (London, 1979); M. McCauley, *The German Democratic Republic since 1945* (London, 1983).

4 A PB meeting called on 26 October 1971 to discuss Ulbricht's antipathy towards Honecker and the new party line.

5 Examples include: H. Brandt, *Ein Traum, der nicht entführbar ist. Mein Weg zwischen Ost und West* (München, 1967); E. W. Gniffke, *Jahre mit Ulbricht* (Köln, 1966 edn); W. Leonhard, *Die Revolution entlässt ihre Kinder*, (Köln–West Berlin, 1955 edn); F. Schenk, *Im Vorzimmer der Diktatur. 12 Jahre Pankow* (Köln–West Berlin, 1962 edn).

6 N. Stulz Herrnstadt (ed.), R. Herrnstadt, *Das Herrnstadt-Dokument. Das Politbüro der SED und die Geschichte des 17. Juni 1953* (Reinbek bei Hamburg, 1990). Herrnstadt, who died in 1966, wrote this account in the mid-1950s. Confiscated by the *Stasi*, it could only be published after the collapse of the GDR; A. Andert, W. Herzberg, *Der Sturz. Honecker im Kreuzverhör* (Berlin–Weimar, 1991); K. Janson, *Totengräber der DDR. Wie Günter Mittag den SED-Staat ruinierte* (Düsseldorf, Wien, New York, 1991); G. Mittag, *Um jeden Preis. Im Spannungsfeld zweier Systeme* (Berlin-Weimar, 1991); K. Schirdewan, *Aufstand gegen Ulbricht. Im Kampf um politische Kurskorrektur, gegen stalinistische, dogmatische Politik* (Berlin, 1994). Others include: W. Harich, *Keine Schwierigkeiten mit der Wahrheit* (Berlin, 1993); W. Janka, *Schwierigkeiten mit der Wahrheit* (Reinbek bei Hamburg, 1989); H. Wolf, *Hatte die DDR je eine Chance?* (Hamburg, 1991); F. Dahlem, 'Nachgelassenes. Ausgelassenes. Über einen Prozess und die Schwierigkeiten seiner richtigen Beurteilung', *BzG*, 1 (1990), 17–25. Dahlem died in 1981. This extract was censored from his memoirs by the SED; W. Otto 'Ernst Wollweber: Aus Erinnerungen. Ein Porträt Walter Ulbrichts', *BzG*, 3 (1990), 350–78. Wollweber (1953–55 state secretary, 1955–57 minister for state

security) died in 1967. He dictated this document to his wife Erika in October 1964. Ten years later she handed it to party leader Erich Honecker.

7 V. Knoll, L. Kölm (ed. and translated), *Der Fall Berija. Protokoll einer Abrechnung. Das Plenum des ZK der KPdSU Juli 1953. Stenographischer Bericht* (Berlin, 1993).

8 W. S. Semjonow, *Von Stalin bis Gorbatschow. Ein halbes Jahrhundert in diplomatischer Mission 1939–1991* (Berlin, 1995); P. Sudoplatov, A. Sudoplatov, J. L. Schecter, L. P. Schecter, *Special tasks. The memoirs of an unwanted witness – a Soviet spymaster* (London, 1995); V. Falin, *Politische Erinnerungen* (München, 1993); A. Resis (ed.), *Molotov remembers. Inside Kremlin politics. Conversations with Felix Chuyev* (Chicago, 1993); J. Schecter, V. Luchkov (ed.), *Khrushchev remembers. The glasnost tapes* (Boston, 1990); A. Gromyko, *Memories* (London, 1989).

1

The Stalinization of the SED 1946–53

When it was founded, the Socialist Unity Party of Germany (SED) did not present itself as a Leninist party committed to Sovietization but as a Marxist party committed to parliamentary democracy. Originally a compromise between communist and social democrat traditions, it was soon transformed into a highly centralized, hierarchical organization based on the model of the Communist Party of the Soviet Union (CPSU) and swearing allegiance to Marxist–Leninist ideology as interpreted by Stalin. The doctrine of 'democratic centralism' was adopted, the central secretariat and party executive abolished and power concentrated in a small politburo and central committee. 'Social democracy' was vilified and the principle of parity between former social democrats and communists disbanded. 'Party discipline' (enforced by control commissions functioning as a kind of internal police force) became the main weapon of Stalinist power consolidation. Those suspected of deviating from the party line were purged from its ranks. Only three of the original fourteen members of the central secretariat (Wilhelm Pieck, Walter Ulbricht and Otto Grotewohl) continued to serve in the politburo after 1950. This 'revolution from above' entailed a return to the Communist Party of Germany (KPD) model of Weimar. Once again the 'apparatus' was the fountain-head of power: The 'party of the new type' was really the party of the old type in new clothes.

Stalinization was a dual process. Not only did the SED undergo internal Bolshevization, it became an hegemonic elite dominating all other institutions. On 17 October 1949, Ulbricht issued guidelines compelling all government bodies to submit their proposals to the politburo for prior approval.[1] When the SED adopted Loius Fürnberg's song 'The party is always right' in 1950, there could be no doubting its dictatorial intentions.

The motives behind Stalinization and the forced merger of the two socialist parties were essentially the same – the communists feared social democracy more than any other political force. The Social Democratic Party of Germany (SPD), after all, was destroyed, and the 'bourgeois' parties merely co-opted. Stalinization proceeded by stealth between 1946 and 1947.[2] It was officially proclaimed in 1948, accelerating with the onset of the Cold War and Yugoslavia's refusal to accept Stalin's *Diktat*. By 1953 the process was complete.

There were three aspects to this metamorphosis and each will be examined in turn. First, the defeat of Anton Ackermann and his 'special German way to socialism'; second, the ostracism of the former social democrats; third, the purge of Paul Merker and Franz Dahlem who had spent the war in the West.

The defeat of Ackermann and the 'special German way to socialism'

Stalinization entailed embracing the Soviet system, yet the SED had once sworn to uphold 'a special German way to socialism'[3] – a commitment articulated by Anton Ackermann in the name of the KPD in February 1946.[4]

Anton Ackermann was born as Eugen Hanisch to a poor family in the Erzgebirge in 1905. After completing school he found employment in the hosiery industry. At the age of fourteen he entered the Free Socialist Youth and a year later the Communist Youth Association. He held a number of offices in these organizations before joining the KPD in 1926.[5] Two years later he graduated from the Lenin School in Moscow. By 1932 he was working for the German section of the Comintern.

After 1933, Hanisch – now renamed 'Willi' – worked illegally for the KPD in Berlin. He experienced at first hand how Stalin's defamation of the social democrats aided Hitler's consolidation of power and was filled with hope when, in 1935, the seventh world congress of the Comintern began revising policy towards the SPD. The failure, however, to condemn unequivocally the sectarianism of the early 1930s came as a bitter blow.[6] Elected to the KPD's politburo and central committee at its Brussels' conference in 1935 (from now on he was called Anton Ackermann), he instigated a radical reform of the party's youth policy. A year later in Prague the 'non-partisan' Free German Youth movement was founded.[7] In early 1937, after a short period in Paris, he announced the KPD's policy of establishing a 'democratic People's Republic' along Spanish lines. This entailed combining radical socio-economic reform with traditional 'bourgeois liberalism'.[8] He then fought in the Spanish Civil War as a member of the International Brigades before returning to Paris in 1938.[9]

In 1940, Soviet agents smuggled him back to the USSR through occupied Belgium, Holland and Norway.[10] After working for Radio Moscow and editing a newspaper for German prisoners-of-war, he helped found the National Committee for a Free Germany in 1943. As head of its radio station, Ackermann worked with a broad coalition of anti-Nazi forces. Serving on the KPD politburo's policy commission in February 1944, he strongly advised broadening the party's 'progressive' appeal.[11] In October 1944 he drafted a programme for the democratic reconstruction of Germany[12] and the following February wrote an article recommending different paths of development for the countries of East-Central Europe.[13] Georgi Dimitrov, leader of the Bulgarian communists, could

conceive of only two possible successors to Pieck as KPD chairman: Walter
Ulbricht and Anton Ackermann.[14]

Landing in Saxony with a group of 'Moscow émigrés' in June 1945,
Ackermann declared the need for 'broad-based initiative from below'.[15] Ulbricht,
however, disbanded the voluntary anti-fascist committees.[16] The KPD programme promulgated on 11 June was mainly Ackermann's work.[17] It rejected the
Soviet model, embraced private enterprise and propagated 'anti-fascist parliamentary democracy'. While Ackermann defended it as a genuinely new set of
policies,[18] Ulbricht alluded to a secret agenda.[19] In early 1946, the latter apparently defended a resolution declaring the liability of all persons who had not
actively resisted Nazi persecution of the Jews and other national groups.
Vladimir Semyonov (deputy political adviser to the head of the Soviet Military
Administration in Germany) claims to have annulled the directive on the grounds
that it threatened the 'anti-fascist democratic' course being pursued in the Soviet
zone.[20] Concern also seems to have been caused by Ulbricht's prejudices against
'bourgeois' politicians and his lack of tact when dealing with the intelligentsia.[21]

In January 1946 Ackermann is said to have supported proposals for a ballot
before unification of the two socialist parties.[22] On 2 March he apparently condemned past communist failures: 'sectarianism', 'dogmatism', 'apeing of the
Soviet example' and 'neglect of the national question'.[23] At the fifteenth party
congress of the KPD on 19 April, he heralded the SED as an 'independent' party
pledged to adapt Marxism to specific German conditions.[24] Popular among
former social democrats in the central secretariat,[25] he became the party's head
of ideology with special responsibility for culture, education and political
instruction.

In February 1946 Ackermann asked whether the working class could, given
the total collapse of 'bourgeois' state institutions, attain power through peaceful and parliamentary means rather than through violent revolution. The question was answered in the affirmative, thus banishing an old KPD dogma.

> If the young (*neue*) democratic state develops as a new instrument of power in the
> hands of reactionary forces, then the peaceful transition to socialism cannot take
> place. If, however, the anti-fascist democratic Republic becomes a state of all
> working people under the leadership of the working class, then the peaceful road
> to socialism is certainly possible, insofar as the use of force against the (completely
> lawful and legitimate) claim of the working class to all power is impossible.[26]

Enshrined in the SED's founding charter, the 'democratic way to socialism'[27] was
interpreted in two divergent ways. Some saw it as a special German road to
Sovietization. Others cherished a vision of a qualitatively different socio-political system to that existing in the USSR. Walter Ulbricht, Paul Wandel and Fred
Oelßner subscribed to the former view, Ackermann and his supporters to the
latter.[28]

The dichotomy is discernible in the minutes of the party executive which met
monthly between 1946 and 1948. At its sixth session (24–25 October 1946),

Ackermann argued that the lessons of the Russian revolution could not be mechanically applied to Germany. The SED needed to take account, not only of Lenin and Stalin, but of socialists such as Georgi Plekhanov, August Bebel, Karl Liebknecht, Karl Kautsky and Rudolf Hilferding.[29] Unlike their Russian comrades, the German working class constituted a majority of the population and could therefore win power through the ballot box.[30] It was highly significant, he declared, that the party's statement of principles eschewed the term 'dictatorship of the proletariat'.[31]

> When we use the term 'political power of the working class' and not 'dictatorship of the proletariat', that means that we do not regard the same forms of working class rule in Russia as necessary or possible . . . In Germany the possibilities not only of coming to power but also of exercising that power through democratic means are incomparably better than they were in Russia.[32]

Clearly, Ackermann regarded the 'special German way to socialism' not just as a method of obtaining power but as a means of exercising it. Wandel took issue with this, arguing that there could be no difference between German and Soviet perceptions of socialism.

> . . . the dictatorship of the proletariat in the Soviet Union is in essence rule of the working class, and here the rule of the working class, whether the people like it or not . . . will be a dictatorship . . . in the sense that Marx and, after him Lenin and Stalin, essentially understood it . . . The road in the Soviet Union is also democratic, because it is based on the will of the overwhelming (*gewaltigen*) majority of the people. . . .[33]

Ackermann, however, refused to concede on this issue. In his closing speech he insisted that socialism in Germany would be fundamentally different from the Soviet system. The SED, unlike the Bolsheviks, would govern through the democratic process.[34]

Addressing a symposium for education and political instruction on 29 March 1947, Ackermann reiterated this position. An electoral takeover of power would avoid civil war, encourage 'democratic', 'progressive' and 'humanitarian' impulses and facilitate 'new forms of working class rule'.[35] Wolfgang Leonhard testifies to Ackermann's sincerity in advocating a separate road to socialism without recourse to the Soviet model.[36] His account is corroborated by former social democrats who later fled to the West.[37] In July 1946 Ackermann apparently appealed for courage and flexibility when applying Marxism to a changing situation.[38]

Not only was the 'special German way to socialism' popular in the SED rank and file, it was also endorsed by the majority of former communists.[39] Ackermann himself was renowned in the party and, according to Kurt Hager, would have been the ideal successor to Ulbricht.[40] When the latter came last in the leadership elections at the second party congress in September 1947, the results were not even published.[41] In the general population, however, the 'special German way to socialism' received a setback as early as October 1946. In free elections to the zone's state parliaments and local authorities in that month, the SED won 47.5 per cent of the popular vote, making it the largest party but with no absolute majority. In Berlin, the SED won a mere 19.8 per cent.[42]

Controversy has raged for decades over whether Stalin aimed for a Germany united under communism, a democratic, capitalist but neutral Germany or a separate communist GDR. In the long run he had undoubtedly set his sights on the first objective. When Yugoslav and Bulgarian leaders visited Moscow in the spring of 1946, Stalin is reported as saying: 'All of Germany must be ours, that is, Soviet, communist.'[43] Interviewed in 1972 by his biographer, Felix Chuyev, Stalin's foreign minister and loyal lieutenant, Vyacheslav Molotov, testified that the aim had been to extend communism to the country as a whole, albeit in stages.[44] His testimony is corroborated by Daniel Melnikov, an adviser to the Soviet dictator on German affairs.[45] An indication of what would eventually be expected from the SED in a reunited German state was its conversion to Stalinism in 1948.

In the medium term, however, the Soviets advocated the creation of a united, 'democratic' and 'peace-loving' German state on the basis of the Potsdam Agreement. According to Semyonov, this entailed reviving the structure of the Weimar Republic and destroying the 'roots' of militarism and Nazism.[46] Before leaving Moscow for Berlin in early 1945, members of the KPD initiative groups were informed that their task was to complete the 'bourgeois-democratic revolution' of 1848. All talk of socialism was condemned as 'pure demagogy'.[47] On 4 June 1945, Stalin is recorded as telling Pieck and Ulbricht that in the 'medium-term' there would be a 'bourgeois-democratic government in Germany'.[48]

Such a polity was not, as a recent book argues, compatible with the Western idea of democracy.[49] The far-reaching socio-economic reforms enacted in the Soviet zone after 1945 imposed draconian restrictions on capitalism, yet were seen by the Soviets as the corollary to reunification. The vision at this stage seems to have been of a freely elected, left-wing government for the country as a whole, radically implementing the stipulations in the Potsdam Agreement regarding demilitarization, denazification, decartelization and land reform. These were regarded by the communists as essential if the sources of war in Germany – monopoly capitalism and the Junker landowners – were to be destroyed. Stalin and the SED believed that they would do well in free elections and that the days of capitalism were numbered.[50] The 'special German way to socialism' was based on this illusion and served as the link between Stalin's medium-term and long-term agendas. After Ulbricht's return from a meeting with Stalin in February 1946, Pieck noted: 'parliamentary traditions in the West/pursue a democratic road to workers' power/not dictatorship.'[51] If the SED could win a nationwide free election, Germany would be reunited by the communists and their allies. This was exactly what Stalin wanted. On 4 June 1945, he had instructed Pieck and Ulbricht to 'secure the unity of Germany via a united KPD [and a] united central committee'.[52]

Although this 'democratic' and 'peace-loving' Germany would not have been a communist state in the Soviet sense, it would have acted as the springboard from which the SED could seize absolute power in future. In 1944 Stalin had dismissed any *immediate* prospect of a Soviet Germany, telling the exiled Polish leader Stanislaw Mikolajczyk: 'Communism fits Germany like a saddle fits a cow.'[53] A cautious approach therefore had to be adopted. The following June he apparently moderated SED proposals for land reform in the eastern zone.[54] At the Moscow foreign ministers' conference in March–April 1947, the Soviets endorsed a decentralized political structure for Germany based on the Weimar model.[55] The USSR's immediate interests were served by obtaining a peace treaty, generous reparations, a stake in the heavy industry of the Ruhr and economic assistance from the West. Any precipitous action by Moscow to Stalinize the whole of Germany would have alienated the Western Allies and placed these things in jeopardy.

Because of these considerations, the USSR treated the Soviet zone as a special case among its satellites. When the East European Communist Parties met at Szklarska Poreba to found the Cominform between 22 and 27 September 1947, the SED was not invited.[56] In Moscow on 18 December 1948, Stalin chided the SED leadership[57] for contemplating socialism in a divided country,[58] emphasizing the need to pursue 'reunification', 'peace' and 'democracy'.[59] Back in Berlin a few days later, Pieck reiterated the position: 'Cautious policies necessary – opportunist policies – zig-zag road to socialism . . . Fight for German reunification and peace.'[60] He then explained the strategy in the party's newspaper, *Neues Deutschland*: there would be no transition to 'People's Democracy' and no separate state in the east. Instead, 'the struggle for German unity and a just peace treaty' was defined as the top priority.[61]

Although regarded as the least favourable scenario, the option of a separate GDR was never ruled out. Stalin had already recognized the possibility of partition in 1945. During the meeting with Stalin on 4 June, Pieck noted: 'Perspective – there will be two Germanies – despite the unity of the Allies.'[62] The Yugoslav communist Milovan Djilas recalls Stalin saying in January 1948: 'The West will make Western Germany their own, and we shall turn Eastern Germany into our own state.'[63] But if this had been the overriding aim, Stalin would never have dismantled so much industry in his zone after 1945. Soviet policy hastened the division of Germany even though this was not its prime objective. The best example of this is the Berlin Blockade of 1948–49. Originally intended to coerce the Western Powers into abandoning their plans to establish their own currency and divide Germany economically, it ended up achieving precisely the opposite result.[64]

Stalin agreed only reluctantly – five months after the Federal Republic of Germany was founded in May 1949 – to the establishment of the German Democratic Republic on 7 October. Even then, the SED received only associate membership of the Cominform. The GDR did not participate on an equal basis with the other East European states in major diplomatic initiatives, and the USSR did not establish full diplomatic relations with it until after Stalin's death.[65] Six days after the GDR was founded, Stalin sent a congratulation telegram which did not mention the word 'socialism', but instead referred to his goal of establishing a 'united, independent, democratic [and] peace-loving Germany'.[66]

It is against this background that we must view different shades of opinion in the SED leadership. Ulbricht, by forcing the pace of Stalinization, became an uncompromising protagonist of German division.[67] Espousing the motto 'it must look democratic but we must control everything',[68] he set about establishing an SED dictatorship. In September 1946 he proposed allowing the mass organizations to participate in the local elections as a way of bolstering SED support.[69] Addressing the federal executive of the Free German Trade Union Federation (FDGB) in April 1946, he proposed the speedy nationalization of industry as a way of pre-empting a central German administration.[70] Following the failure of the London foreign ministers' conference in December 1947, he officially announced the transition to 'People's Democracy'. This entailed purging the 'bourgeois' parties of opposition elements and consolidating the SED's 'leading role'.[71] Three days before it was founded, Ulbricht promised that the GDR would never be relinquished.[72]

His staunchest supporter in this regard was Colonel Sergei I. Tiul'panov, head of the propaganda (later information) department of the Soviet Military Administration in Germany (SMAD). New evidence from Russian archives reveals the extent of Soviet disquiet about his stewardship of German affairs. As early as October 1946, he was being accused of committing 'serious errors' and showing a 'lack of discipine'.[73] By this time, he had already rejected the 'special German way to socialism'.[74] In March 1948 Semyonov apparently expressed concern that, together with Ulbricht, Tiul'panov was 'exceeding' Stalin's agenda.[75] A month later, Tiul'panov predicted that the 'People's Democracies' would become one-party states.[76] A committee of investigation at the end of April 1948 criticized him for failing to understand the 'historical perspective of Germany's development', for trying to introduce socialism in the eastern zone, for neglecting the 'bourgeois' parties and for interfering too much in the day-to-day politics of the SED. Four months later an envoy of the Soviet army's political administration, Lieutenant Colonel G. Konstantinovskii, informed Moscow that Tiul'panov was continuing to commit these excesses. As a result, he said, many officers erroneously believed that the eastern zone was becoming a 'socialist republic'.[77] Tiul'panov was removed from his position shortly before the creation of the GDR in October 1949.

Ackermann emphasized different issues to Ulbricht. At the eleventh session of the party executive on 22 May 1947 (summoned to debate the failure of the Moscow foreign ministers' conference the previous month) he criticized the SED for concentrating on peripheral 'organizational questions' and neglecting the all-German perspective. Without national reunification, he declared, there was no hope of alleviating socio-economic hardship. While Ackermann called on the Allies to set aside their differences and find solutions to the German question,[78] Ulbricht stressed 'ideological tasks' and inveighed against 'reactionary influences'.[79]

Erich Gniffke, a former social democrat member of the central secretariat who fled to the West, testifies to Ackermann's genuine desire for national reunification on the basis of 'parliamentary democracy'.[80] On 7 May 1947 the Bavarian premier, Hans Ehard, called a conference of state prime ministers in Munich with a view to promoting inter-German dialogue. Ulbricht opposed the initiative, dismissing Ehard as 'an American agent'.[81] Ackermann, however, favoured participation, as did the majority of central secretariat members.[82] Despite being overruled, Ulbricht succeeded in aborting the talks once they got under way on 6 June.[83]

In a speech to the party executive in August 1947, Ackermann warned that the SED was fast losing popular support. The trend, he warned, would continue unless the party 'changed its behaviour' and began addressing the needs of working people.[84] At the second party congress in September 1947, Ulbricht advocated transforming the SED into a 'party of the new type'.[85] Ackermann, by contrast, is said to have protested against the enlargement of the central secretariat, predicting its replacement by a small politburo.[86] He declared that he would rather be deported to Siberia than allow Ulbricht to proceed in this way.[87] In a speech to mark the thirtieth anniversary of the Bolshevik revolution, Ackermann apparently paid tribute to German social democracy before 1918, saying that the SED's task was to build on the tradition of August Bebel.[88] A major landmark was the Cominform's decision to excommunicate Josip Tito.[89] When the central secretariat debated the issue on 2 July 1948, it condemned the Yugoslav communists and undertook to convert the SED into a 'party of the new type'.[90] According to Gniffke, Ulbricht took the initiative in proposing the resolution, while Ackermann remained silent throughout.[91]

Ackermann was also responsible for cultural policy in the Soviet zone. As early as January 1946, he had written to Tiul'panov urgently requesting the withdrawal of two Soviet films which he described as excessively militaristic. Such films, he said, made the ideological work of eliminating militarism harder.[92] Many German artists in the zone were totally opposed to any kind of government interference or censorship. In May 1948, Ackermann noted that even Marxist painters could not be relied upon to apply 'a healthy realism' in their work. Unusually for a communist, however, he thought the best thing to do was to permit them to continue their work for the time being. It would be counterproductive, he felt, to try to bring order to the chaos that contemporary art represented.[93] He was also upset by the failure of the party to win adherents in the universities, and blamed this on SED students 'cutting themselves off from the rest in a sectarian way'.[94]

Between 7 and 9 September 1948, Ulbricht addressed a symposium at the department of culture, education and political instruction. Substituting for Ackermann, he launched an attack on 'West European' tendencies and described the Soviet system as the only possible form of socialism. Dissenting intellectuals were warned that the police were heavily armed and well organized: 'Perhaps this argument is more effective than your ideological arguments.' His insistence that things had to change and his attack on 'degenerate' culture can be read as an implicit criticism of Ackermann's work.[95]

Although the Stalinist morality of party discipline was ultimately more important to Ackermann than 'socialism with a democratic face' it is simplistic to characterize his capitulation in the fall of 1948 as naked opportunism. Despite being subjected to considerable psychological pressure, he did not immediately surrender all the positions he had defended in 1946. When Ulbricht attacked the 'special German way to socialism' at a meeting of the party executive in July 1948, Ackermann tried to salvage what he could. Although conceding the case for a 'party of the new type', he denied that the 'special German way to socialism' was a tactical manoeuvre. Unlike Russia, he argued, the countries of Eastern Europe could still proceed to socialism by more democratic means.[96] He was subsequently criticized by Grotewohl for placing too much emphasis on distinguishing rather than common characteristics.[97]

Addressing the next session of this body on 15–16 September, he expressed unease about the change of course.

> I ask the question whether the false theory of a special German way to socialism is identical with the question of the possibility of a democratic road to socialism . . . On this point I have not yet decided, here I have certain doubts . . . It is still an open question whether we have the right to describe this revolutionary road to socialism as a democratic way.[98]

When Wandel defended the Soviet model as a 'new form of democracy', Ackermann pointed out that it lacked 'a legal framework'.[99] Insisting that socialism could only be conceived through bitter class struggle, Ulbricht lambasted the non-Soviet road and called for the 'total elimination of capitalist elements'.[100]

Oelßner and Wandel attacked Ackermann for failing to condemn the 'special German way to socialism' in more unequivocal terms.[101] Ulbricht tried to deny that it had ever been official KPD policy.[102] On 24 September 1948, Ackermann relented and published the ignominious article required of him.

> This theory of a special German way to socialism has turned out to be absolutely false and dangerous . . . Wherever people are fighting for peace, democracy and socialism in the world, the Soviet Union is the basis for this fight . . . this theory opened up a split, through which nationalism and anti-Bolshevism could penetrate even the ranks of our party.[103]

Ackermann's surrender, even if it was under duress, meant that opposition lower down in the party was no longer represented in the leadership. The process of internal Stalinization was ratified by the first party conference in January 1949. Severed both from the working class it claimed to represent and from its own rank and file, Lenin's 'Jacobins tied to the proletariat' had become 'Jacobins tied to the Soviet Union'.

Neither did Ackermann countenance flight to the West. There were two reasons for this. First, his misgivings about Sovietization were eclipsed by a much stronger hatred of capitalism. Second, the Manichaean struggle between two world systems left no room for third alternatives.[104] Federalism (soon to be the basis of democracy in Bonn) was dismissed as a threat to national unity and a 'regional refuge' for representatives of 'finance-capital' wishing to circumvent all-German land reforms and other 'democratization' measures'.[105]

Grotewohl initially opposed demands that Ackermann engage in public self-criticism,[106] and, at the first party conference, called for his re-election to the leadership.[107] Pieck too was concerned to preserve his dignity, pointing out that he did not need to say 'pater peccavi'.[108] Although he was relegated to candidate-status, Ackermann remained in the politburo until 1953. He continued to oppose Soviet measures which he regarded as inappropriate to German conditions.[109]

In an extract from reminiscences written during the 1960s, Ackermann was bitter about the system he had embraced: 'The individual is weak against a very obedient and submissive apparatus. Moral-political superiority is of no help against that. To fight openly . . . means liquidation sooner or later, and without any benefit to the cause (*die Sache*).'[110] After Ulbricht's downfall, Ackermann wrote to Honecker complaining that the 'special German way to socialism' was being air-brushed out of party history.[111] In 1973, the SED leader telephoned to apologize for the way the party had castigated him twenty-five years earlier. This had been necessary, he said, to deter former social democrats from opposing the SED's transformation into a 'party of the new type'.[112] Ackermann died a few months later without achieving full rehabilitation.

The defeat of the former social democrats

It was a mixture of Soviet compulsion and self-deception which led many social democrats to join the SED in April 1946. On 4 February Grotewohl told the polit-ical adviser to the British commander in chief that 'not only was the strongest pressure being brought to bear on them personally (he spoke of being tickled by Russian bayonets) . . . their organization in the provinces had been completely undermined . . . there was no point in resisting . . . the "iron curtain" . . . had come to stay.'[113]

In a letter of 16 March, the veteran SPD leader Otto Buchwitz gave four reasons why he supported immediate unification with the KPD. First, most communist leaders understood that after twelve years of Nazi tyranny another dictatorship was impossible. Second, it was time to embrace 'revolutionary socialism' after the failure of Weimar reformism. Third, the West was intent on restoring a 'bourgeois-capitalist' order while in Russia the foundations of socialism had already been laid. Fourth, despite the pressure on the SPD, Moscow was not interested in imposing the Soviet system on Germany. If the working class united, Russian troops would withdraw, safe in the knowledge that peace and security were assured.[114]

Ernst Thape, vice-president of Saxony, believed that by joining the SED he could help allay Soviet suspicions about social democracy. Since former social democrats would constitute well over half its membership, the new party could be fashioned in their image. The Kremlin, he believed, would realize its interests were best served by accepting this situation.[115] Gniffke was chiefly concerned to assist his fellow east Germans and, like Thape, believed the new party would reflect the aspirations of ex-social democrats.[116] By February 1946 Grotewohl was resigned to the inevitability of unification and felt the SPD leadership should stand by its rank and file. If the working class remained divided there was a danger of it repeating the experience of 1918–33.[117] Another factor was the alleged willingness of the first head of SMAD, Marshal Georgi K. Zhukov,[118] to remove Ulbricht in advance of the merger, thereby increasing Grotewohl's chances of becoming party leader.[119]

The former social democrats constituted a discernible but by no means static group in the leadership. Racked by personal and political tension, it crumbled under the pressure of Stalinization during the summer and fall of 1948. In September 1946 Tiul'panov compiled a report for a CPSU commission evaluating the state of the SED and undertaking an assessment of the former social democrat leaders. Grotewohl – 'the central figure after Pieck' – was described as someone who enjoyed the respect of both social democrats and communists: 'All of his behaviour demonstrates that he sides with Marxist positions quickly and firmly.' Max Fechner, 'the second social democrat', was seen as 'rather an amorphous figure, not much of a battler'. As for the others, particularly Helmut Lehmann and Erich Gniffke, 'one can rely on them with considerably less certainty'. In the provinces there was only one figure to be counted on: Otto Buchwitz.[120]

At a party executive meeting during the same month, Grotewohl conceded that, in the SED as a whole, the process of fusion had yet to be consummated. Striking cultural differences remained; for example, the social democrats use of the polite *Sie* for 'you', against the communists preference for the informal *Du*.[121] On the political level, two main tendencies could be discerned: 'Sectarianism' on the left and sympathy for the West German SPD on the right.[122] According to Tiul'panov, the former was encouraged by Hermann Matern (one of Ulbricht's closest supporters) and constituted a 'dangerous problem'. Meanwhile former social democrats dreamt of the day when they would be able 'to drop out of the SED'.[123] These diverging attitudes often led to factionalism.[124] Despite the merger 'there is still a sense that two distinct groups exist . . . Both social democrats and communists keep their cards. And when you talk to them, they pull out their old membership cards and say: "I am a former communist and member of the SED."'[125] In conversation with a colleague on 20 December 1946, Fechner said that the central secretariat consisted of two groups which disagreed on many fundamental issues. Grotewohl, by attempting to mediate between them, had lost his influence and his reputation. Fechner was convinced that the SPD would soon be refounded and that, when this happened, not only the former social democrats but a majority of ex-communists would join.[126]

For a time in early 1947 Stalin seemed prepared to consider such a move as a quid pro quo for the establishment of the SED in the West. He thereby hoped to split the SPD in the other zones and overcome the opposition of their leader, Kurt Schumacher, to all-German negotiations. The possibility was discussed with SED leaders on 23 December 1946,[127] with Thuringian leaders in April 1947[128] and at a meeting of the party executive in May.[129] At the Moscow foreign ministers' conference in March, Molotov had pushed for a decree allowing all parties to unite at national level.[130] A month later Tiul'panov allegedly told Gniffke that the task of refounding the SPD might fall to him.[131]

The former social democrats in the central secretariat (with the exception of Otto Grotewohl and Friedrich Ebert) convened for a meeting in Fechner's house at the end of May 1948. Concluding that the two socialist traditions divided the party from top to bottom and that the SED experiment had failed, they swore to limit the influence of Ulbricht who was becoming party leader by stealth.[132] Within a matter of weeks, however, the group had disintegrated.

The campaign against ex-social democrats in the SED was officially launched by Ulbricht at a party executive meeting in June 1948.[133] War was declared on so called 'Schumacher agents', accused of infiltrating the party and sabotaging its operations.[134] In July it was decided to purge the SED of 'enemy' and 'degenerate' elements.[135] By the autumn of 1948 it was more dangerous to be a former member of the SPD than an active Nazi.[136] Those with misgivings about Stalinization were purged, imprisoned, sometimes even shot.[137]

Gniffke was the only member of the central secretariat to flee the Soviet zone. Born in 1895 as son of a worker, he was trained as a merchant before becoming a correspondent. He joined the SPD in 1913 and, after six years as a company secretary, became secretary of Brunswick's General Free Employees' Union in 1926. During the 1920s he led the region's anti-Nazi 'iron front' with his close friend Otto Grotewohl. Following Hitler's ascension to power, he was instrumental in organizing a resistance group while also running a business selling kitchen appliances. Subsequent to his release from seven months' imprisonment between 1938 and 1939, he resumed his resistance activities before helping to refound the SPD after the war. In April 1946 he became a member of the SED and was elected to serve on its highest body. Gniffke defected to West Germany in October 1948 and later rejoined the social democrats. He died in 1964.

When Ulbricht proclaimed his support for Stalinization at the second party congress in September 1947, Gniffke countered: 'We need neither a Social Democratic nor a Communist Party in our zone!'[138] On 12 March 1948, Gniffke was delegated the task of making a speech to commemorate the one-hundredth anniversary of the Communist Manifesto. Declaring it the SED's task to continue the tradition of Karl Marx, Friedrich Engels, August Bebel and Karl Liebknecht, he eschewed Lenin and Stalin and praised pre-1914 social democracy.[139] Tiul'panov, who used his own speech to pour scorn on SPD reformism, forbade publication of Gniffke's remarks.[140] In the central secretariat on 2 July 1948, Gniffke voted against the SED's conversion into a 'party of the new type'.[141] Later in the same month when the party executive launched its offensive against social democracy, he maintained that former members of the KPD also had something to learn from the past.[142]

Rejecting the Stalinist model, Gniffke instead favoured a 'Socialist People's Party'[143] in which a diverse membership reflected the interests of the majority of the working population. In such a party, he declared, members would decide for themselves what they meant by socialism, Marxist–Leninism would be one of a plurality of ideologies and the Soviet Union would be an ally rather than master.[144] In his farewell letter to the SED on 28 October 1948, Gniffke wrote: 'Today I resign from the "party of the new type", or rather from Ulbricht's KPD of 1932.'[145]

As general secretary of the German national council (on which all parties were represented), Gniffke was charged with the task of organizing a referendum on the country's reunification. In his inaugural address on 20 May 1948, Gniffke attempted to answer four questions posed by the British. First, on what conditions did the German people desire unity? Answer: These would be decided in free democratic elections. Second, would Germany grant its citizens the fundamental democratic rights of assembly and association or would she be a one-party state? Answer: Germany would be neither a one-party state nor a one-man dictatorship but a free democratic republic. Third, would the German people be able to elect their government by secret ballot without fear and compulsion, or would the elections be rigged by an incumbent party? Answer: Observers would ensure the election of parliament by secret ballot. Fourth, would citizens rights be respected and upheld or would they be sacrificed to an all-powerful totalitarian state? Answer: No party would be able to overthrow democracy and establish a totalitarian regime. Germany would be a welfare state in which the working people were granted a position appropriate to their importance and numerical strength.[146] In his farewell letter to the SED, Gniffke condemned Ulbricht's Sovietization project and endorsed Germany's reunification as a 'bourgeois democracy'.[147]

At an extraordinary meeting of the party executive called to rubber-stamp Gniffke's expulsion from the SED on 30 October 1948, former social democrats lost their final chance to oppose Stalinization.[148] In a deliberate move to gag a free debate on the issue, Grotewohl was billed to speak first. His failure to utter a word in defence of his one-time friend was a bitter blow to any Gniffke sympathisers present as was his veiled threat to any member who failed to vote for the resolution.[149]

The discussion was brief and Gniffke condemned *in absentia*. The party executive unanimously approved the resolution without reading Gniffke's letter of resignation and before the central secretariat had discussed his complaint that mutual distrust was poisoning intra-party life.[150] The session revealed that ex-social democrats were no longer a discernible force in the SED leadership. Apart from Grotewohl, none of them spoke in the debate. Yet, with the exception of Fechner, they were all present.[151] On the same day Käthe Kern allegedly told her chauffeur that 'although the Gniffke case was regrettable, it was true that the former social democrats in the central secretariat were being pushed up against a wall.'[152]

When Ernst Thape defected in November 1948 he accused the SED of dividing the working class, jeopardizing national reunification and discrediting socialism. Nation had to come before party, he declared, and without democracy socialism was doomed.[153] Friedrich Ebert also considered fleeing to the West where his mother and son awaited him. But he abandoned his plans after a fourteen-day visit to Moscow and Leningrad. On his return, Ebert was appointed mayor of east Berlin.[154] The man whose father had saved Germany from Bolshevism in 1918–19 helped make eastern Germany safe for communism after 1945.

Initially, Grotewohl warned against the party becoming a 'bureaucratic apparatus'[155] and supported the 'special German way to socialism'.[156] Allied occupation, he argued, rendered revolution unrealistic.[157] As for Soviet communism, it would become less dictatorial as external threats to its security diminished.[158] By mid-1948, however, Grotewohl had repudiated his social democrat past[159] and embraced Stalinization. In his closing speech to the eleventh meeting of the party executive in June 1948, he coined the euphemism 'orientation to the east' to describe this process.[160] At the first party conference in January 1949, he attacked reformism and endorsed the SED's conversion to a 'party of the new type'.[161] He apparently hoped to become general secretary in the new politburo[162] and mediate a lasting peace between Soviet Russia and a reunited Germany.[163] This was the same man who had once proclaimed democracy an 'historical necessity'[164] and opposed the creation of a united workers' party in the east.[165]

Despite his capitulation, however, Grotewohl's language continued to be more moderate than Ulbricht's. In a veiled attack on the latter in July 1949, Grotewohl criticized the use of 'dictatorial police methods', insisting that 'weaknesses and deficiencies' could only be overcome by 'comradely discussion and education'.[166] Six months earlier he had criticized a widespread tendency to underestimate the importance of the bloc parties.[167] According to Grotewohl's personal aide, Fritz Stempel, he was also concerned to prevent a 'formalistic' application of Leninism to German conditions.[168]

Grotewohl also had different priorities to Ulbricht on the question of national reunification. While the former tended to emphasize Stalin's medium-term agenda, the latter seemed to prefer a separate state in the east. In January 1948 the party executive called for a referendum to establish a united, indivisible German republic in which the regions enjoyed the same rights as under the Weimar constitution.[169] Dismissing claims that this was merely a tactical manoeuvre, Grotewohl welcomed the initiative as a realistic offer capable of being accepted by the Allies and other political parties. He declared the need to devise policies relevant to the country as a whole and called for political and economic measures to prevent any further separation from the western zones. Pouring scorn on suggestions that the SED advocated an over-centralized totalitarian state, he blamed the party itself for fuelling the fear of Bolshevism in

Germany.[170] Gniffke's contention that the resolution was a challenge to Ulbricht's *Deutschlandpolitik*[171] is borne out by the evidence. Already in May 1947 Ulbricht had demanded 'other methods of democracy, different from those of Weimar'.[172] On 7 August 1948, Grotewohl told the German national council that a republican constitution had to reflect an independent German point of view and could not therefore be written by the Allies. Based on 'progressive' and 'democratic' principles, it had to be a compromise acceptable to all Germans, be they on the right or left of the political spectrum.[173] His remarks were subsequently criticized in a conversation between Ulbricht, Pieck and Semyonov on 16 August.[174]

In early 1949, in response to Stalin's urgings the previous December, the SED launched its campaign for the establishment of a unified German state. Addressing the first party conference in January 1949, Grotewohl disparaged the tendency to neglect the national question and endorsed a constitution for Germany based on the Weimar model. Socialism could not be built, he said, until three main objectives had been achieved: reunification, a peace treaty and a 'democratic government' for the nation as a whole. 'Not even the most perfect East Germany', he said, could fulfil the task that a 'united, progressive, peace-loving and democratic Germany' could fulfil: that of ensuring a permanent peace in Europe. This, he insisted, was not a tactical but a strategic task of the party.[175]

His vision, like Stalin's, seems to have been of a competitive, multi-party system predicated on a radical interpretation of the stipulations in the Potsdam Agreement regarding demilitarization, denazification, decartelization and land reform.[176] Already in 1946, Grotewohl had called for the establishment of a 'real democracy', combining traditional 'bourgeois' freedoms with profound socio-economic transformation. 'Economic annihilation of the enemy', he declared, was what distinguished 'real democracy' from formal, parliamentary government in the West.[177]

Fechner and Ulbricht were jointly responsible for administering local government in the Soviet zone. The former attempted to develop the social democratic tradition of decentralization and, in December 1947, advocated strengthening the independence of the municipalities. 'Whatever can be done better locally, should be done locally', he said.[178] Ulbricht, by contrast, favoured centralizing the decision-making process as part of the SED's conversion to a 'party of the new type'. When these two concepts collided in May 1948, Ulbricht told his colleagues that self-administration was an anachronism soon to be replaced by 'democratic centralism'.[179] His two-year economic plan approved by the party executive a month later inaugurated the command economy and substantially reduced local and municipal power.[180] State particularism, he declared, impeded successful execution of the new tasks.[181] Ignominiously defeated and under pressure from Tiul'panov,[182] Fechner submitted to the communist tradition of party discipline, the perpetuation of which he had warned against in February 1946.[183]

Lehmann, together with Ackermann, had drafted the founding charter of the SED containing the pledge to pursue a democratic way to socialism.[184] It reserved the right, however, to resort to 'revolutionary means' should the 'bourgeoisie violate the basic principles of democracy'.[185] In September 1948, Lehmann invoked this proviso to explain why he no longer supported the parliamentary road.[186] Four months later, in a letter to the delegates of the first party conference, he condemned the treachery of the class enemy and endorsed Stalinization.[187] A sick man, he lacked the stamina to resist.[188] Evidence of initial doubts, however, can be discerned from his speech to the party executive the previous July. Taking issue with Grotewohl, he partly justified his social democrat past and declared that state power could only be won by peaceful means and with the support of the masses.[189] Endorsing the 'party of the new type' in November 1948, Lehmann felt it necessary to warn against blind emulation of the Soviet example.[190]

Weary from years of persecution by the Nazis, the former social democrats lacked the courage and the will to withstand the assault of their false brothers in the SED. Initially, Otto Meier attempted to counter-balance the massive condemnation of post 1918 social democracy with a half-hearted critique of the KPD. While conceding the SPD's penchant for 'revisionism', he criticized the communists for favouring the immediate transition to socialism. The lesson for post 1945, he said, was to build a 'transition state' in which the forces of capitalism could still operate. His remarks should be contrasted with Ulbricht's plea for the total elimination of 'capitalist elements'.[191] August Karsten went even further and voted against the SED's conversion into a 'party of the new type'.[192] Within a matter of weeks, however, they had both capitulated.[193] In the harsh climate of Stalinization, opposition was hardly an option. The former social democrats in the central secretariat were left with a stark choice: defect or collaborate. Defection was not only dangerous, it meant conceding defeat, bowing out of politics, losing material privileges and parting with loved ones. There was also disapproval of the 'restoration' being carried out in the western zones and animosity towards Kurt Schumacher's SPD. All these factors help explain why so many former social democrats converted to Marxist–Leninism after 1948.

Otto Buchwitz had been a fierce advocate of socialist unity in 1946 and two years later he supported the Stalinization process.[194] In January 1949 he promised that the central party control commission (of which he had just been appointed co-chairman) would not operate as an internal police force instilling fear and repressing dissent. 'Intra-party democracy', he declared, 'shall and will remain'.[195] Within two years, however, Buchwitz had become seriously disillusioned. Addressing the eighth central committee plenum in February 1952, he launched an astonishing attack on the democratic deficit in the GDR. The SED, he declared, was suffocating democracy by concentrating too much power in itself. It was ignoring the wishes of its membership, infringing the rights of the bloc parties and forcing potential allies to flee the Republic. Discerning a basic lack of 'humanity' both within the party and in the way it interacted with the population, Buchwitz condemned violations of human rights and abuses of civil liberties. Remote and dictatorial functionaries, he complained, were destroying the achievements of those who knew how to communicate with the masses.[196] Ulbricht's closest supporter in the leadership, Hermann Matern, refused to acknowledge these concerns, dismissing them as a manifestation of personal disaffection.[197]

When Pieck, Grotewohl, Ulbricht and Oelßner travelled to Moscow for discussions between 12 and 24 December 1948 the question of what to do with the former social democrats was discussed. Karsten was short-listed to lose his place on the central secretariat and Fechner's future was also cast in doubt. It was decided to create a new politburo consisting of seven members and two candidate members,[198] thereby neutralizing the central secretariat which unofficially ceased to function on 21 February 1949.[199] The principle of parity between communists and former social democrats was abandoned and a 5:4 ratio adopted until the third party congress in July 1950. Thereafter, the only former social democrats in an expanded politburo of nine members and six candidate members were Otto Grotewohl, Friedrich Ebert and Erich Mückenberger.

For a time after the foundation of the SED the atmosphere in the party executive was relatively open and former social democrats could make their views heard. In October 1946, for example, Richard Weimann (a co-founder of the eastern SPD) described the 'dictatorship of the proletariat' as a 'fatal' concept which was inflicting 'extraordinary damage' on the party. Socialism, he declared, could only be built by democratic means and this meant winning over not just the working class but other sections of the population as well. Attributing the victory of the social democrats in Berlin to their emphasis on human rights and democracy, he demanded that the word 'dictatorship' be banned from the SED's vocabulary.[200] Willi Jesse from Mecklenburg, was the first and only member of the executive with a social democrat background to be arrested in 1946. Accused of fostering links with the SPD, he was imprisoned without trial before being deported to Siberia in 1950. After four years hard labour he returned to live in West Germany.[201]

The situation changed dramatically with the SED's conversion to a 'party of the new type'. In 1949, a Soviet military tribunal condemned Max Fank, a member of the first party executive, to twenty-five years' forced labour for establishing contact with the 'eastern bureau'[202] of the SPD. He was released in January 1954. Another victim was concentration camp survivor Paul Szillat, elected to the SED executive by the first and second party congresses. Despite having campaigned hard for fusion with the KPD, he was arrested in 1950 and given an eight year gaol sentence for engaging in 'social democratic activities'. Pardoned in 1956, he died two years later as a result of the damage caused to his health. Stanislaw Trabalski from Saxony, elected to the party executive in 1946 and 1947, was accused of 'incitement to defect' and convicted to eight years' imprisonment in 1950. He was released six years later.[203]

The purge of former social democrats continued unabated during the early 1950s.[204] In 1992, Alfred Neumann testified that when he was appointed deputy mayor of Berlin, Ebert initially refused all contact with him, fearing that he was being put under surveillance. It was only after Neumann had made prolonged attempts to win his confidence that the two allegedly became close friends.[205] Fritz Uschner, candidate member of the central committee and SED leader in Magdeburg, was expelled from the party in May 1953. He was accused of laying himself open to class enemy manipulation by indulging in alcohol abuse and leading an immoral life-style.[206] Interviewed in 1992, his son Manfred claimed that the real reasons lay in his social democrat past. In Magdeburg, where social democracy had been the dominant political force for decades, Uschner allegedly opposed the anti-Tito campaign, continued to espouse the Ackermann thesis, expressed misgivings about the SED's conversion to a 'party of the new type' and rejected the 1952 decision to begin the 'accelerated construction of socialism'. The denunciation of his chauffeur, a former Nazi turned communist, was apparently instrumental in purging Uschner and his Magdeburg comrades.[207] The draconian nature of the punishment would seem to lend some credibility to this account. Most striking of all, however, was the case of Max Fechner. A member of the central committee and minister of justice, he went to gaol for defending the constitutional right to strike in the wake of the June 1953 uprising.[208]

The corollary to the defeat of the 'special German way to socialism' was the purge of the former social democrats. By the early 1950s they had been smashed as a discernible current in the leadership. At the end of 1953 the SED celebrated 'thirty-five years of the KPD', thereby presenting itself as the heir to the communist tradition.[209] The ghost of social democracy, however, refused to be exorcized and continued to stalk the corridors of power.[210]

The purge of Merker and Dahlem

SED functionaries who had spent the war in the West were especially distrusted by those who had emigrated to the Soviet Union. Paul Merker and Franz Dahlem were the two representatives of this group in the politburo. Both were purged in connection with the trials of the communist leaders Laszlo Rajk[211] in Hungary, Traycho Kostov[212] in Bulgaria and Rudolf Slansky[213] in Czechoslovakia.

Born in 1894 and a waiter by profession, Merker joined the Independent Socialist Party of Germany (USPD) in 1918 and the Communist Party of Germany (KPD) a year later. A member of the Prussian parliament between 1924 and 1932, he was elected to the KPD central committee in 1926 and to the politburo in 1928. Responsible for trade union affairs, he was accused of 'left-wing deviation' and expelled from the leadership in 1930. The motto of the German communists before 1933 'Soviet Russia is our example and our solution' does not seem to have been his guiding principle. He was apparently fond of quoting Rosa Luxemburg, a critic of Lenin, who foresaw the degeneration of Soviet power in Russia.[214] Many years later, as a prisoner of the GDR's ministry of state security, Merker told a cell-mate about his relationship to KPD leader Ernst Thälmann: 'I advised him often. He sometimes had a different opinion to me and concretely implemented all Comintern directives, although that was not always right because German conditions often required a different tactic.'[215] During the war, Merker criticized the KPD's programme of 1930 for failing to call on the people to defend democracy.[216]

An autodidact intellectual, Merker first emigrated to France and then to Mexico, where he founded the Free Germany movement. The fact that he preferred South America to Moscow says a lot about his relationship with the CPSU. As co-editor of the newspaper *Freies Deutschland*, he opposed Kremlin propaganda asserting the collective war guilt of the German people.[217] Contradicting Stalinist practice, he also supported the idea of independent workers' councils in industry. 'After all', he was reported as arguing, 'the factories belong to the workers.'[218]

In 1936 Merker allegedly criticized Ulbricht's 'unproductive and apelike imitation' of Comintern directives.[219] According to Ackermann's retrospective and denunciatory testimony to the central party control commission in August 1950, Merker had strongly opposed the Hitler–Stalin Pact of 1939. 'It is always the same', Merker is quoted as saying 'what communists in other countries build up is shattered again by Soviet foreign policy.'[220] In a central committee resolution of 24 August 1950, he was accused of 'showing no understanding for the German–Soviet Pact', displaying 'insufficient trust towards the Soviet Union as the leading progressive force' and 'imagining that the aim of the American, English and French imperialists was to free the masses from fascism'.[221] If Merker really did believe that World War Two had forged a permanent bond of friendship between the Allies,[222] he could not have been the only communist to do so. However, while other communists in Mexico characterized the abortive military coup against Hitler in June 1944 as an attempt by Germany to join forces with the West against the Soviet Union, Merker was allegedly more positive in his assessment.[223] Addressing the first congress of the Free Germany movement in Mexico, he apparently rejected 'mistaken slogans about the immediate realization of socialism', insisting that 'the decision over the type of social system . . . should be left to the popular masses themselves.'[224]

Exiled with other KPD leaders in Paris in 1938, Merker advocated an anti-Nazi People's Front representing a broad church of political opinions. Ulbricht, by contrast, rejected anti-fascists who did not also condemn Leon Trotsky and Nikolai L. Bukharin. The novelist and chairman of the German People's Front committee, Heinrich Mann, refused to work with Ulbricht whom he regarded as an incorrigible dogmatist. Consequently, Pieck ordered Ulbricht to Moscow and Merker successfully carried out his task of persuading Mann to continue co-operating with the KPD. The latter was a 'democratic socialist' whose vision of a non-capitalist society could neither be described as social-democratic nor communist.[225] Merker seemed to him to offer the best chance of this vision being realized. In January 1946, Mann penned him the following lines: 'Really, Germany would be fortunate with Paul Merker as Chancellor. I am thinking less of you, who would have a difficult life, than of the country, its internal development and relationship to the world.'[226]

Ostensibly, Merker was purged and imprisoned because of his links with Noel Field, an American communist falsely accused of working for the CIA.[227] This was, however, only part of the explanation. According to former KPD leader, Ruth Fischer, Merker had clashed with German communists during the war over the responsibility of 'Stalinist policies' for Hitler's rise to power: 'The Merker case', she wrote, 'illuminates a well hidden tension within the German Communist Party which could later become important. . . .'[228] In 1949 she was more explicit, crediting Merker with representing a 'relatively mild version of Stalinism': 'It is known that he is no special friend of hangman methods and that he has a dangerous tendency to seek more independence for the German Communist Party. Merker is therefore seen by many German communists as the liberal successor to Ulbricht, capable of introducing a new regime in the party.'[229] Fischer's testimony was corroborated by Herbert Wehner, who told RIAS (Radio in the American Sector of Berlin) that Merker was suspected of subscribing to a brand of communism that 'did not simply entail putting one's own country at the disposal of a foreign power'.[230]

Although Merker went along with Stalinization, he does seem to have harboured misgivings. Behind him were the years in Mexico, where he had been obliged to work without recourse to the Kremlin. In his own words, 'prior consultation with the distant comrades in Moscow was impossible and . . . perhaps also made little sense because over there they were faced with completely different questions.'[231] Democracy as practised by the Free Germany movement – for example the extensive if not total freedom of the press – was anathema to the Soviet model.[232] After 1946 it becomes difficult to document the evolution of his views on such subjects. The fact that he was so rarely invited to SMAD headquarters suggests he was not held in very high esteem by the Soviets.[233] By 1953 at the latest, he had come to see the system for what it was – the dictatorship of a small oligarchy buttressed by a huge party apparatus. During a prison interrogation, Merker was recorded as saying:

> Democracy in the central committee is only formally implemented. Only a few members decide. I experienced and went along with this all too frequently. I often did not think things through to the end and draw the right conclusions . . . The central committee and politburo consist of about seventy-five members. But only the party chairmen, general secretary and a few other confidants decide internal affairs.

Merker compared the party apparatus to a huge machine 'which had its levers in every factory and in every small administrative cell.' The leading functionaries of the party were able to pull these levers as and when they saw fit.[234]

Merker's views on the national question are also difficult to ascertain. Former social democrats in the SED who later fled to the West recall Merker's support for the 'special German way to socialism'[235] – an idea which presupposed the country's unification on the basis of free elections. According to Gniffke, Merker supported SED participation in the Munich conference of May 1947.[236]

Apparently, he was also unhappy about the designation of the Oder–Neisse Line as Germany's postwar border with Poland,[237] only upholding the party's position out of respect for the Potsdam Agreement.[238] Asked by a fellow prisoner (who had been given the task of mending his cell-window) whether Germany could have followed a different road after 1945, Merker replied that the Soviets were determined to impose their own social system and that those with a different vision were therefore doomed to failure.[239]

As state secretary in the ministry of agriculture, Merker was confronted with the excesses of the Soviet occupation forces. In January 1948, at a conference of SED functionaries, Merker condemned abuses such as the arbitrary requisitioning of sheep and cattle. 'Our comrades', he complained, 'allow themselves to be chased into a fox-hole by every lieutenant . . . Not once has there been any proper resistance to such things . . . That is surely an impossible situation . . . after all, at the end of the day it is our livestock . . . unless we speak out clearly and unambiguously . . . we can gain no ground because no one will have any faith in us.' The party had lost the confidence of the farmers, he said, and the only way to win it back was to stop interfering in their affairs. It was also time to eradicate 'schematism' from the SED's work and to enhance the role of the bloc parties in the decision-making process.[240] Addressing an SED farmer's conference in January 1949, Ulbricht adopted a very different tone.

> When our comrade Stalin helps us with food and tractors, then it is clear that the farmers and workers should ask: how is that possible? What kind of country is that which helps Germany . . . whose troops a few years ago committed the greatest crimes against the Soviet people? . . . Stalin has kept his word and supported the national unity of Germany. It is high time that we talk about that instead of, as is sometimes the case, talking about every possible side issue without sufficiently showing the big connections.[241]

In December 1949 the SED politburo published a book paying homage to the Soviet dictator on his seventieth birthday. Amidst a plethora of Stalin quotations, Merker staked out his position on the agricultural question. Recalling the many injustices done to small and medium-sized farmers – for example the long prison sentences imposed on those failing to deliver up their food for distribution – he called for methods of persuasion rather than compulsion.[242] In 1950, Merker was accused of retarding the 'democratization of village life' by threatening new farmers with expropriation if they did not manage their affairs properly. Among other things, he was also censured for failing to popularize the work of Trogin Lysenko,[243] a Soviet agrarian-biologist later exposed as a charlatan.

It is difficult to say with any certainty whether ultimate responsibility for the purge of Merker lay with Ulbricht or Moscow. At first, the general secretary was probably a willing executor of Soviet directives. On 18 October 1949, the politburo decided to screen all SED leaders who had emigrated to Britain or America during the war.[244] In the same month, Ulbricht endorsed Matern's plan to establish a commission to investigate Field's contacts with German communists.[245]

After being isolated in the leadership,[246] Merker was expelled from the party in August 1950.[247] A day before his arrest on 2 December 1952 (his name had recently been mentioned at the Slansky trial), Matern told the politburo: 'The unmasking and rendering harmless of agents like Merker is of the greatest importance for the party today. In the period of socialist construction, the party cannot tolerate any deviation, any divided opinions (*doppelte Meinungen*) in its ranks.'[248]

After Stalin's death, Lavrentii P. Beria's execution, the proclamation of the New Course and the acquittal of Noel Field in March 1954, Ulbricht continued to pursue his personal vendetta. Merker's interrogators were now German, not Russian. On 30 May 1955 he was brought before the GDR supreme court and condemned to another eight years in prison. The trial could not have been held for propaganda reasons because it was conducted in secret and received no press coverage. Looking back in 1968, Merker was in no doubt about Ulbricht's responsibility: 'This certainly happened on [his] instructions. Only he could have had any interest in my conviction. No one else had the power to enforce it.'[249] When Merker was released in January 1956, Ulbricht tried to prevent his rehabilitation.[250]

Unlike his Hungarian and Czechoslovakian counterparts (who were tortured until they confessed to the false charges levelled against them) Merker apparently refused to co-operate with attempts to frame him as an 'imperialist agent'. A week before being arrested in December 1952, he denied any involvement in the 'Slansky plot'.[251] In a letter to Pieck shortly after his release he wrote:

> During all my years in prison, despite complete isolation, despite constant threats, accusations and insults of the worst kind, [despite] the ever increasing hatred of the interrogators and the severity of my . . . unconstitutional imprisonment, I defended myself with all my strength against the expressed intentions of Beria's representatives and their German subordinates, to make me the vehicle and central figure of a big political show trial.[252]

That Ulbricht was preparing such a trial can no longer be disputed. One of the prospective defendants, Leo Bauer, recalled being informed in August 1950 by the state secretary of the ministry for state security (MfS or *Stasi*), Erich Mielke, that it was scheduled for February 1951 at the latest. Some weeks later, another of Mielke's officials stressed the personal role of Ulbricht in the whole affair.[253] Bauer's testimony is supported by the deputy chairman of the KPD and member of the West German parliament, Kurt Müller, who was arrested in 1950: 'Mielke declared quite openly: "you surely understand that in Germany we need a big trial to educate the party and the masses. We need a trial like that of Rajk in Hungary . . ." He explained to me that this trial, to which factory delegations would be invited, really had to begin in eight to nine months.'[254] Merker's resistance might have helped ensure that it never took place. Writing to Pieck on 14 April 1956, he alleged: 'The fact that the struggle I was forced to wage under such difficult conditions . . . helped hinder the Berlin representatives from arranging

[such] a trial, helps me to bear the effects of this struggle on my health and personal life more easily.'[255]

Other leading 'western émigrés' purged in 1950[256] also denied the charges
against them.[257] However, like the communist resistance-fighters in Germany,[258]
they were a heterogeneous political group. In 1940, emigrants in Switzerland like
Bruno Goldhammer had dismissed the SPD as a spent force and characterized
the 'fight for democracy' as obsolete. Instead, they had campaigned for the 'dictatorship of the proletariat', insisting that 'radical slogans' were required to win
over the working class.[259] This was in sharp contrast to Merker in Mexico, who
had warned against any immediate transition to communism in the postwar
period. Claims that all purged 'western émigrés' opposed Sovietization[260] cannot
be corroborated. In December 1948, Lex Ende enthusiastically supported the
SED's conversion to a 'Bolshevik-type' party.[261]

As with Slansky in Czechoslovakia, there was a strong anti-Semitic element
in the purge of Merker.[262] Although not himself Jewish, he had used his position
during World War Two to defend the Jews from persecution. This was exploited
by Merker's interrogators to allege espionage in the service of 'Western imperialism'.

> The Soviet interrogators and their German assistants declared over and over again,
> that it was incomprehensible to them, that a non-Jew, like myself, should speak up
> for the Jews . . . for them, my actions on behalf of the Jewish people, during a time
> of the most terrible persecution . . . were sufficient proof that I was an imperialist
> agent and an enemy of the working class . . . During the period of investigation and
> during the trial at the Supreme Court I decisively rejected these defamatory accu-
> sations . . . [263]

In contrast to Ulbricht, Merker favoured facing up to the Nazi past, particularly
with regard to the Jews.[264] In May 1953, the central committee passed a resolution in which 'the complete unmasking of Merker as an agent of US imperialism' was attributed to 'the unmasking of the role of the Zionists as a centre of
imperialist espionage.'[265] When he was prosecuted in 1955, it was under article
six of the GDR constitution, which outlawed war-mongering and incitement to
racial hatred.[266]

Two accepted wisdoms can therefore be questioned: first that Merker failed
to resist attempts to frame him as the 'German Slansky', and second that
Ulbricht was responsible for ensuring that there were no show-trials or executions of SED leaders between 1949 and 1953.[267] The fact that Merker repeatedly
appealed to Pieck[268] rather than Ulbricht for redress is significant. It not only
highlights his poor relationship with Ulbricht but also that he regarded Pieck as
a potential ally in his struggle for rehabilitation. According to one witness, the
Ulbricht–Pieck relationship had always been strained.[269] It is therefore likely that
Merker was trying to play one off against the other. Unfortunately for him,
however, Pieck had lost power to Ulbricht by 1950 and merely retained some
limited influence. Nonetheless, the evidence shows that he used his position to

protect Merker. When Matern sacked the latter as a waiter in 1951[270] (on the grounds that customers could not eat *Bockwurst* served up by an enemy of the working class) Pieck wrote to Ulbricht asking for an investigation.[271] His efforts to obtain permission for Merker to publish the next volume of his book *Deutschland: Sein oder nicht Sein?*[272] were unsuccessful,[273] but he did manage to persuade the politburo to permit him to work as a translator just three months before he was arrested.[274]

The purge of Merker and other 'western émigrés' was a cause of tension at the second central committee plenum in August 1950. Attempts to link the accused with 'crimes' committed *after* 1945 were rebuffed by Pieck,[275] who was subsequently criticized by Ulbricht.[276] The East German president, however, was bent on a damage-limitation exercise.

> The situation of the Germans in emigration during the Hitler regime was extraordinarily difficult. We must never lose sight of that. Now, when in this difficult situation some people did not live up to expectations (*sich nicht bewährt haben*), then that is a blot on the reputation of the German emigration, but it does not belittle its great work in the Hitler period. One cannot conclude that the entire German emigration was corrupted (*versumpft*) and in the hands of the enemy . . . I want to say that at least.[277]

While Pieck was clearly uncomfortable with the purge, calling it 'a very embarrassing subject',[278] Ulbricht was determined to increase the political temperature with a clarion call for a witch-hunt in the party and state apparatuses: 'In Weimar, agents are organizing the abduction of certain representatives of the technical intelligentsia . . . how many agents are there in the secretariat, in the office of the VVN [Association of those persecuted by the Nazi regime]?'[279] What is going on in the various trade union leaderships?'[280] He even justified purging party functionaries on grounds of suspicion alone, before there was sufficient evidence against them.[281]

Although the resolution to expel Merker and others was passed unanimously, some central committee members were clearly suppressing doubts. The only female member of the politburo, Elli Schmidt, came nearest to defending one of the purge victims. Despite pressure from Matern, she expressed misgivings about the severity of the punishment meted out to Maria Weiterer.[282] Neither could the straitjacket of party discipline conceal the uneasiness of other former 'western émigrés' present. Kurt Hager, who spent the duration of the war in Britain and in 1992 maintained that he had lived through the early 1950s in constant fear of arrest,[283] made the distinction between 'deliberate treason' and 'carelessness'[284] – a dichotomy hardline Stalinists never acknowledged. Nonetheless, he believed the allegations against Merker in 1950[285] and even wrote the introduction to the German edition of the minutes of the Rajk trial in October 1949.[286] By contrast, Erich Mielke demanded that the party be more severe in its condemnation of the purge victims. The manner in which he poured derision on the accused and his implication that Pieck's attitude was too nonchalant exposed him as one of Ulbricht's main stooges in the Stalinist witch-hunts of the early 1950s.[287]

On 29 August 1950, the politburo unilaterally inserted a passage into the central committee resolution condemning disagreement in the SED leadership over how to deal with the 'western émigrés'. The party executive was accused of not being vigilant enough. Up until the third party congress a month earlier, there had apparently been 'conciliatory tendencies in the leadership towards party functionaries who had committed serious errors in the past'.[288]

The other member of the SED leadership who had spent the war in the West was Franz Dahlem. Born in Lorraine in 1892 as son of a railway worker, financial difficulties forced him to leave school early and begin a commercial training. Sacked for engaging in trade union activity, Dahlem joined the SPD in 1913. A year later he was chairman of the Socialist Youth movement in Cologne. During his time as a soldier and member of the USPD, he distributed Spartacist and anti-war propaganda on the German front. When malaria put him out of action for ten months, he used the time to study Marxist literature. In 1918 he led a soldiers' mutiny, played a central role in the revolution in Allenstein and joined the action committee of the workers' and soldiers' council in Cologne.[289]

Dahlem joined the KPD in 1920. Three years later, collaborating with the French communists, he helped organize the general strike in the Ruhr. During the 1920s, Dahlem was apparently instrumental in purging the party of 'Trotskyists' and other 'enemy' groups.[290] A member of the Prussian parliament between 1920 and 1924, he was elected to the central committee in 1927, a year later to the politburo and the *Reichstag*. In 1934, after a brief spell working underground in Berlin, Dahlem fled to Prague to escape Nazi persecution. He then helped formulate the People's Front policy at the Brussels conference of the KPD. Between 1937 and 1938, Dahlem gained a popular reputation as political head of the International Brigades in Spain. He then took over from Ulbricht as leader of the German communists in Paris.[291] Like Merker, Dahlem seems to have harboured misgivings about the Hitler–Stalin Pact of 1939. Following his arrest in September of that year, he submitted a statement appealing for an alliance between France, the Soviet Union and a 'new, free Germany.'[292] Had he followed Moscow's request and emigrated to the Soviet Union,[293] he might not have survived the war.[294] Instead, he opted for internment in the French concentration camp at Vernet. Here he continued to engage in communist activity until 1941. Handed over to the Gestapo in August 1942, he spent eight months in prison before being transferred to Mauthausen where he played a key role in the resistance. After the camp's liberation by American troops, he travelled to Moscow before returning to Berlin in May 1945.

In the SED leadership during the late 1940s, Dahlem enjoyed as much influence as Ulbricht. As cadre-chief, he built a formidable power base by appointing former Spanish Civil War veterans to key positions.[295] Not only was he responsible for relations with other Communist Parties, he controlled the activities of the SED in West Germany. The VVN was also under his auspices. Of all the 'pairs' in the central secretariat, the Gniffke–Dahlem relationship was one of the least problematic.[296]

Like Merker, Dahlem was an accomplice rather than an opponent of Stalinization. On 2 February 1950, he announced the transformation of all non-party organizations into 'assistant bodies' of the SED.[297] However, even within the parameters of the Stalinist consensus which existed in the politburo after 1949, there was ample room for political conflict. The Ulbricht–Dahlem power struggle had begun before 1933 and the latter was widely regarded as an alternative leader.[298]

In February 1946, Dahlem had written an article setting out his views on internal party democracy. Although refusing to condemn the principle of 'democratic centralism', special emphasis was laid on the need for rank-and-file participation in the decision-making process. SED leaders, elected by secret ballot, would have to win majority support among the membership.[299] Addressing communist delegates on the eve of the merger with the social democrats, Dahlem returned to this theme. Again, he did not explicitly reject the KPD model. However, in contrast to Ulbricht, he stressed the need for 'initiative from below', insisting that 'party discipline' could only be effective if the leadership enjoyed the trust of the grass roots. In the SED, he declared, the 'golden rule', would be 'the will of the party membership'.[300]

Initially, Dahlem appears to have accepted the 1946 compromise in good faith. If Gniffke is to be believed, he also advocated dissolving the British Communist Party, regarding it as an obstacle to working class unity after Labour's victory at the polls.[301] As far as the SED is concerned, Dahlem is said to have agreed that it should be a 'party of the masses' and not a 'communist cadre party'.[302] His own description of it in September 1946 as a 'genuine people's party'[303] would seem to bear this out. Another witness testified to Dahlem's genuine support for the 'special German way to socialism'.[304] Despite endorsing the restructuring of the SED along Soviet lines, he continued to emphasize the rights of the ordinary rank and file. In July 1948, he defined the priority as the safeguarding of internal party democracy. 'Free discussion' and the 'democratic election of leaders', he believed, were not incompatible with the SED's conversion to a 'party of the new type'.[305]

After 1949, Dahlem became increasingly concerned that the party was being damaged by sectarian and dictatorial practices.[306] In January 1952, as attempts were being made to win allies against the Schuman Plan and the General Treaty,[307] Dahlem met with colleagues to discuss tactics. The SED, he declared, was misinterpreting its 'leading role' by interfering too much in the activities of the National Front. The latter should develop its own initiatives, independent of the central committee departments. Before the SED could establish 'healthy' relations with other parties, it had to put its own house in order. What was required was nothing less than the 'complete reorganization of the whole apparatus' and an end to 'dictatorial', 'high-handed', 'bureaucratic' and 'arrogant' behaviour at all levels. Functionaries refusing to change their attitude had to be removed from their posts.[308]

The decision to begin the 'accelerated construction of socialism' in July 1952 plunged the GDR into a near fatal existential crisis. Increased repression, economic downturn and a mass exodus to the West persuaded Dahlem to distance himself from the worst excesses of the Ulbricht course.[309] On 15 April 1953, the CPSU politburo advised East Berlin to moderate its policies.[310] Ulbricht retaliated by simultaneously raising factory work norms and expelling Dahlem from the central committee.[311] After the popular uprising of 17 June 1953, Dahlem wrote the leadership a ninety-nine page letter demanding that the party implement decisive changes to win the trust of the population.[312] These included the election of a new politburo,[313] and the expulsion of 'bootlickers' from Ulbricht's central committee secretariat.[314] His proposals apparently resembled those of Zaisser and Herrnstadt,[315] purged from the leadership in July 1953.[316]

But Dahlem's biggest disagreement with Ulbricht concerned policy towards West Germany (also called the Federal Republic or FRG).[317] At the third central committee plenum in October 1950, he indirectly criticized the general secretary for underestimating the importance of a Soviet offer to establish an all-German constituent council.[318] The council, to be composed in equal measure of politicians from the GDR and the Federal Republic, was presented as a first step on the road to national reunification and the formation of a provisional government.

Addressing a district delegates' conference in Magdeburg on 28 September 1952, Dahlem complained that the SED was neglecting 'the struggle for a peace treaty and German unification'.[319] His attempts to instigate a more active *Deutschlandpolitik*, however, foundered on Ulbricht's determination to concentrate on domestic issues. According to Semyonov, the latter severely damaged the party's work in West Germany by deploying leading KPD cadres to work in the East.[320]

In March 1951, Dahlem was involved in trying to organize an 'international conference for the peaceful solution of the German question'.[321] In January 1952, he discussed the need to prepare for all-German elections by improving assessment of various forces in the West.[322] To forge a popular movement against the Schuman Plan and the General Treaty,[323] he argued, it was necessary to further enlist the help of 'bourgeois' politicians and enhance the role of the National Front.[324] Allies in the Federal Republic were needed too, and for this reason he sent a special emissary to explore the possibility of rapprochement with the CDU (Christian Democratic Union) and FDP (Free Democratic Party).[325] Dahlem also joined the presidium of the German peace council and attended the 'congress of nations' at Vienna in December 1952.[326] In early 1953, Dahlem allegedly walked out of a central committee secretariat meeting after Ulbricht had angrily rejected his proposal to establish contact with liberal politicians in West Germany.[327]

It is sometimes argued that Dahlem had a more realistic view of conditions in the Federal Republic than Ulbricht.[328] The evidence, however, seems to suggest that the opposite was true. Dahlem's support for a policy of rapprochement was based on the illusion that Konrad Adenauer's days were numbered. In September 1952, he attributed the first official meeting between a delegation of the *Volkskammer* (the East German parliament) and the president of the *Bundestag* (the West German parliament) to pressure from the 'peace-loving population' in the FRG: 'Every day brings new proof that the forces of the camp for world peace are advancing and that the forces of the imperialist camp are retreating.'[329] At the tenth central committee plenum three months later, he discerned the beginnings of a popular revolt against the 'US occupation' in West Germany and described the KPD's aim of establishing a 'government of national reunification' as feasible.[330] Ulbricht, however, was less interested in the all-German perspective, which he rightly feared as a threat to the GDR's existence. Instead, he collaborated with Adenauer and the Allies in dividing the country. Ulbricht's *Deutschlandpolitik* was also *Realpolitik*

At a politburo meeting on 18 October 1949, Ulbricht succeeded in dealing his arch rival a decisive blow. In a clear sign that Dahlem's days in the leadership were numbered, a resolution was passed sanctioning an investigation of all top SED functionaries who had spent more than three months in American, British, French or Yugoslav captivity.[331] For Dahlem, imprisoned in France between 1939 and 1941, this was a bad omen. Significantly, he was also relieved of responsibility for cadres, control over this decisive area being transferred to Ulbricht.[332]

Dahlem's western commission was abolished in early 1951 and its functions divided up among the departments of the central committee. Shortly thereafter a new commission was established, this time with Ulbricht as chairman.[333] On 20 December 1952, the central committee approved a resolution drawing 'lessons' from the Slansky trial in Prague. Although Dahlem's name had not been mentioned at the trial,[334] an investigation was launched into the alleged 'capitulation' of German communists in Paris following the outbreak of World War Two.[335] On 21 February 1953, Ulbricht dissolved the VVN.[336] At the end of the month, Dahlem made his last speech as a member of the SED leadership when he addressed delegates in Erfurt over 'the present situation in the struggle for a peace treaty and the establishment of German unity'.[337] On 17 March the politburo suspended him from all his functions and instructed the central party control commission to investigate his contacts with Noel Field. Dahlem's opposition to the resolution that effectively stripped him of power was tempered by a naive faith that the investigation would be conducted fairly.[338] However, the decision of 17 March was only a prelude. On 6 May, he was expelled from all leadership bodies.[339] Accused of 'blindness in the face of imperialist infiltration', his political death sentence was effectively pronounced at the thirteenth central committee plenum later in the month.[340]

Two years earlier, Dahlem had been chosen to be one of the main defendants in an East German show-trial. Leading members of the KPD were expected to testify that he had worked for the Gestapo before becoming an agent of 'US imperialism'.[341] Stalin died in March 1953, but in Berlin preparations for the trial continued.[342] When the Soviet Union instigated a thaw in its foreign and domestic policies,[343] Ulbricht ignored the Kremlin's advice to do likewise. Dahlem appealed to the CPSU for assistance but was informed that his 'case' was an internal matter for the SED.[344] In May 1953, the central committee condemned 'insufficient evaluation' of the Slansky trial within party ranks and appealed for vigilance against increased enemy activity during the period of socialist construction.[345] There can be little doubt of Ulbricht's intention to make Dahlem play the 'German Slansky'.[346]

Dahlem vigorously resisted Ulbricht's campaign to destroy him in the spring and early summer of 1953. Summoned to appear before the politburo on 6 May,[347] he launched a massive attack on Matern who, as chairman of the central party control commission, was conducting the case against him. Six days later Dahlem was compelled to appear again, this time to account for his attempts to win over the minister for state security, Wilhelm Zaisser.[348]

Remarks attributed to Dahlem during a conversation with Grotewohl accuse Ulbricht of spinning a plot to frame him as the 'German Slansky'.[349] Complaining that he was being denied 'the most basic means of defence', he demanded that Matern be brought to account for his abuses.[350] Dahlem was deprived of the opportunity to defend himself before the central committee[351] because this would have exposed the charges levelled against him as bogus. Although the resolution was passed unanimously, there were apparently doubters present. In 1992, Kurt Hager regretted not defending his former comrade from the Spanish Civil War days but insisted that this would have meant expulsion from the party, perhaps even arrest. He also spurned the concept of Stalinism as an invention of Western propaganda.[352] Dahlem's woes were exacerbated later that summer when his son Robert was accused of participating in the June uprising and expelled from the SED. Arrested by the *Stasi* in 1954, he then fled to West Berlin to ask for political asylum.[353]

The purges of Merker and Dahlem were carried out in an atmosphere of paranoia flowing from the highly charged international situation in the early 1950s. In a letter to the central committee some years later, former politburo member Rudolf Herrnstadt referred to the 'witch-hunt' psychology gripping the SED leadership at this time.[354] Fear and mutual suspicion seem to have engulfed all its members. After being purged, Dahlem allegedly accused Ulbricht and Matern of trying to destroy him by collaborating with the class enemy in the West.[355] The latter is even supposed to have named 'imperialist agents' sitting in the central committee.[356] Ackermann apparently tried to implicate Matern in the 'Slansky conspiracy'[357] and, according to Honecker, the general secretary himself was in danger.[358]

Notes

1 SAPMO-BArch, ZPA, J IV 2/3/057. Official minutes from meeting of Ulbricht's 'small secretariat', 17.10.49. 'Richtlinien über die Fertigstellung von Vorlagen und wichtigen Materialien für die Regierung und Regierungsstellen zur Entscheidung

durch die zuständigen Organe des Parteivorstandes sowie über die Kontrolle der Durchführung dieser Entscheidungen.'

2 See H. Weber, 'Die Wandlung der SED und ihre Rolle im Parteiensystem 1945 bis 1950', *DA*, 2 (1993), 255–65.

3 The other East European Communist Parties (CPs) also pledged themselves to independent roads to socialism in the immediate postwar period. Josip Tito did so in the name of Yugoslavia, Wladyslaw Gomulka in the name of Poland.

4 A. Ackermann, 'Gibt es einen besonderen deutschen Weg zum Sozialismus?', *Einheit*, 1 (February 1946), 22–32.

5 G. Dietrich, 'Ein Mitbürger der Vergangenheit, Gegenwart und Zukunft. Anton Ackermann', *BzG*, 1 (1991), 107–15; p. 107.

6 *Ibid.*, p. 108.

7 O. Pfefferkorn, 'Anton Ackermann. Shdanows Schatten', *SBZ-Archiv*, 17 (5.9.53), 263–4; p. 263. See also D. Borkowski, *Erich Honecker. Statthalter Moskaus oder deutscher Patriot?* (München, 1987), pp. 142–3.

8 A. Sywottek, *Deutsche Volksdemokratie. Studie zur politischen Konzeption der KPD 1935–46* (Düsseldorf, 1971), pp. 74–9.

9 Pfefferkorn, 'Anton Ackermann', p. 263.

10 *Ibid.*

11 A. Fischer, *Sowjetische Deutschlandpolitik im Zweiten Weltkrieg 1941–1945* (Stuttgart, 1975), p. 86.

12 Entwurf eines Aktionsprogramms des Blocks der kämpferischen Demokratie'. See H. Laschitza, *Kämpferische Demokratie gegen den Faschismus. Die programmatische Vorbereitung auf die antifaschistisch-demokratische Umwälzung in Deutschland durch die Parteiführung der KPD* (Berlin, 1969).

13 W. Leonhard, *Die Revolution entlässt ihre Kinder* (Köln, 1992), p. 518.

14 S. Neumann, 'Die Tragödie des Gehorsams', *Die Weltbühne*, 34 (1990), 1080–2; p. 1081.

15 SAPMO-BArch, ZPA, NL 109/10. Cited in Dietrich, 'Ein Mitbürger der Vergangenheit, Gegenwart und Zukunft', p. 109.

16 Leonhard, *Die Revolution entlässt ihre Kinder*, pp. 469–79

17 G. Benser, *Die KPD im Jahre der Befreiung. Vorbereitung und Aufbau der legalen kommunistischen Massenpartei (Jahreswende 1944/1945 bis Herbst 1945)* (Berlin, 1985), p. 139. The programme, officially approved by Stalin, was written by Ackermann in Moscow on the night of 5–6 June 1945.

18 A. Ackermann, 'Wohin soll der Weg gehen?', *Deutsche Volkszeitung* (14.6.45). Cited in Dietrich, 'Ein Mitbürger der Vergangenheit, Gegenwart und Zukunft', p. 109.

19 Leonhard, *Die Revolution entlässt ihre Kinder*, p. 486. Asked to explain how KPD policies differed from those of other parties, Ulbricht apparently retorted: 'You'll see soon enough, comrade! Just wait a bit!'

20 W. S. Semjonow, *Von Stalin bis Gorbatschow. Ein halbes Jahrhundert in diplomatischer Mission 1939–1991* (Berlin, 1995), pp. 244–5.

21 *Ibid.*, p. 226.

22 E. Gniffke, *Jahre mit Ulbricht* (Köln, 1990), p. 129.

23 *Ibid.*, p. 192.

24 Cited in Leonhard, *Die Revolution entlässt ihre Kinder*, pp. 537–8.

25 Gniffke, *Jahre mit Ulbricht*, p. 181.

26 Ackermann, 'Gibt es einen besonderen deutschen Weg zum Sozialismus?', p. 30.

27 'Grundsätze und Ziele der Sozialistischen Einheitspartei Deutschlands', *Einheit*, 2 (March, 1946), 2–4; p. 4.

28 This view is corroborated by Hans Mahle, one of two surviving members of the 'Ulbricht group' flown from Moscow to Germany in May 1945 (interviewed in 'Messengers from Moscow', BBC2 television documentary directed and produced by Daniel Wolf, 19.2.95). Mahle was stripped of all his functions in 1951.

29 SAPMO-BArch, ZPA, IV 2/1/10. Ackermann's speech to 6 PE meeting, 24.–25.10.46. This excerpt can also be found in the private papers of Fred Oelßner, SAPMO-BArch, ZPA, NL 215/105.

30 SAPMO-BArch, ZPA, IV 2/1/10.

31 See 'Grundsätze und Ziele', p. 4.

32 SAPMO-BArch, ZPA, IV 2/1/10.

33 *Ibid.* Wandel was a close associate of Pieck, having served as his political secretary in Moscow.

34 SAPMO-BArch, ZPA, IV 2/1/11.

35 SAPMO-BArch, ZPA, NL 109/15. Ackermann's speech entitled 'Our road to socialism'.

36 Leonhard, *Die Revolution entlässt ihre Kinder*, p. 520. Leonhard spent the duration of the war in the USSR, returning to Berlin with the 'Ulbricht Group' in April 1945. He worked in the apparatus of the CS until 1948 when he fled to Yugoslavia to escape Stalinization. He lived in West Germany after 1950. A close associate of Ackermann.

37 B. W. Bouvrier, H. P. Schultz, '. . . *die SPD aber aufgehört hat zu existieren'. Sozialdemokraten unter sowjetischer Besatzung* (Bonn, 1991). See interview with 'M. H.', 24 June 1974, pp. 123–46; p. 130.

38 Gniffke, *Jahre mit Ulbricht*, p. 192.

39 Leonhard, *Die Revolution entlässt ihre Kinder*, p. 521. Also see Tiul'panov's report to a commission of CPSU CC dated 16.9.46. Cited in N. Naimark, 'The Soviet occupation: Moscow's man in (East) Berlin', *CWIHP Bulletin*, 4 (Fall, 1994), 34, 45–8; p. 46: 'neither the communists nor the social democrats understand the new forms shaping the struggle for power, the movement towards socialism. They do not understand that the SED is not a tactical manoeuvre, but the situation by which they can achieve . . . that which was accomplished in our country by different means. They do not speak about the dictatorship of the proletariat, but about democracy. [Still,] they have no understanding of the nature of the struggle after World War II.' Tiul'panov, head of the propaganda (later information) administration of SMAD, dominated political life in the Soviet zone.

40 Interview with Kurt Hager, 1.12.92.

41 Gniffke, *Jahre mit Ulbricht*, p. 255. In September 1946, Tiul'panov noted: 'they [members of the SED] don't like Ulbricht; they do not like him for his harshness.' Cited in Naimark, 'The Soviet occupation', p. 47.

42 H. Weber, *DDR. Grundriß der Geschichte, 1945–1990* (Hannover, 1991), pp. 24, 286.

43 M. Djilas, *Conversations with Stalin* (London, 1962), p. 139. Milovan Djilas, a leading member of the Yugoslav CP, was a frequent guest at the Kremlin between 1944 and 1948.

44 Cited in 'Messengers from Moscow'.

45 *Ibid.* See also the testimony of ambassador Vladimir Yerofeyev, an official in the European affairs department of the Soviet foreign ministry. 'Working for Molotov', seminar at Corpus Christi College, Cambridge University, 27.6.95.

46 Semjonow, *Von Stalin bis Gorbatschow*, pp. 200–1.

47 Leonhard, *Die Revolution entlässt ihre Kinder*, p. 400.

48 SAPMO-BArch, ZPA, NL 36/629. Pieck's notes from conversation with Stalin on 4 June 1945 in Moscow.

49 W. Loth, *Stalins ungeliebtes Kind. Warum Moskau die DDR nicht wollte* (Berlin, 1994).

50 For more details, see Dirk Spilker's doctoral dissertation, 'The Socialist Unity Party of Germany (SED) and the German Question, 1944–53' (University of Oxford, 1998).

51 SAPMO-BArch, ZPA, NL 36/631. In April 1945, Stalin had allegedly told Tito: 'Today socialism is possible even under the English monarchy. Revolution is no longer necessary everywhere.' Djilas, *Conversations with Stalin*, p. 104.

52 SAPMO-BArch, ZPA, NL 36/629. Pieck's notes from conversation with Stalin on 4 June 1945 in Moscow.

53 Cited in A. McElvoy, *The saddled cow. East Germany's life and legacy* (London, 1993), p. 2.

54 Semjonow, *Von Stalin bis Gorbatschow*, pp. 237–9.

55 *Ibid.*, pp. 251–2. See also Loth, *Stalins ungeliebtes Kind*, pp. 85–6.

56 Gniffke, *Jahre mit Ulbricht*, p. 264.

57 Pieck, Grotewohl, Ulbricht and Oelßner were in Moscow between 12–24 December 1948.

58 The SED delegation went to Moscow with proposals to 'intensify the class struggle' and force the pace of socialization. SAPMO-BArch, ZPA, NL 36/695, 'Antwort auf die Fragen zur Besprechung am 18.12.48'.

59 SAPMO-BArch, ZPA, NL 36/695. Pieck's notes of conversation between Stalin and SED leaders in Moscow, 18.12.48. A day later, the Bulgarian leader Georgi Dimitrov defined 'People's Democracy' as 'a system of the Soviet type' (Dimitrov to congress of Bulgarian CP, 19.12.48. Cited in Loth, *Stalin's ungeliebtes Kind*, p. 148). Stalin kept open the option of forming a 'provisional German government' in the east should a separate state be founded in the west.

60 SAPMO-BArch, ZPA, NL 36/695. Pieck's report on meeting with Stalin to CS, 27.12.48.

61 Wilhelm Pieck über die Politik der SED. Unterredung des Parteivorsitzenden mit einem Vertreter des "Neuen Deutschland"', *ND* (30.12.48), 1.

62 SAPMO-BArch, ZPA, NL 36/629. Pieck's notes from conversation with Stalin on 4 June 1945 in Moscow.

63 Djilas, *Conversations with Stalin*, pp. 138–9. Stalin was receiving delegations from Yugoslavia and Bulgaria.

64 C. Kennedy-Pipe, *Stalin's Cold War. Soviet strategies in Europe, 1943 to 1956* (Manchester, 1995), pp. 136–7.

65 J. Gaddis, *We now know. Rethinking Cold War history* (Oxford, 1997), p. 127.

66 Loth, *Stalins ungeliebtes Kind*, p. 161.

67 See F. T. Stößel's analysis of Ulbricht's speeches in *Positionen und Strömungen in der KPD/SED 1945–54*, (Köln, 1985), pp. 235–40. See also SAPMO-BArch, ZPA, J IV 2/202/4. Gniffke's valedictory letter to SED, 28.10.48.

68 Leonhard, *Die Revolution entlässt ihre Kinder*, p. 440.

69 Gniffke, *Jahre mit Ulbricht*, pp. 207–8.

70 Loth, *Stalins ungeliebtes Kind*, p. 59.

71 Ulbricht had already propagated the virtues of 'People's Democracy' in March 1947. See W. Ulbricht, 'Die geschichtliche Rolle der SED', *NW*, 3/4 (1947), 4–5. Cited in Stößel, *Positionen und Strömungen*, pp. 163–4.

72 SAPMO-BArch, ZPA, IV 2/1/37. Ulbricht's interjection during Gerhart Eisler's speech to PE, 4.10.49.

73 N. Naimark, *The Russians in Germany. A history of the Soviet zone of occupation 1945–1949* (London, 1995), p. 336.

74 SAPMO-BArch, ZPA, IV 2/1/52. Ackermann's speech to PE, 15–16 September 1948.

75 Gniffke, *Jahre mit Ulbricht*, p. 298.

76 SAPMO-BArch, ZPA, NL 109/20. Lecture in April 1948 entitled 'People's Democracy'.

77 Naimark, *The Russians in Germany*, pp. 341–6. See also Semjonow, *Von Stalin bis Gorbatschow*, pp. 262–3.

78 SAPMO-BArch, ZPA, IV 2/1/20.

79 *Ibid.*

80 Gniffke, *Jahre mit Ulbricht*, p. 233.

81 *Ibid.*, pp. 236–7. See also Leonhard, *Die Revolution entlässt ihre Kinder*, p. 568.

82 Gniffke, *Jahre mit Ulbricht*, p. 237.

83 Ulbricht instructed the eastern delegation to cry off if its agenda was not adopted. For more detail see *ibid.*, pp. 242–3 and Loth, *Stalins ungeliebtes Kind*, pp. 89–90.

84 SAPMO-BArch, ZPA, IV 2/1/24.

85 Cited in Stößel, *Positionen und Strömungen*, p. 296.

86 Gniffke, *Jahre mit Ulbricht*, pp. 257–8.

87 SAPMO-BArch, ZPA, J IV 2/202/4. Gniffke's farewell letter to the SED, 28.10.48.

88 SAPMO-BArch, ZPA, IV 2/1/057. Grotewohl's speech to extraordinary session of PE, 30.10.48. Ackermann's speech, with minor alterations, was subsequently delivered by Gniffke.

89 On 28 June 1948, the Yugoslav communists were expelled for defying Stalin and pursuing an independent road to socialism.

90 SAPMO-BArch, ZPA, IV 2/2.1/214. The process was expedited by the 11, 12 and 13 meetings of the PE between June and September 1948.

91 Gniffke, *Jahre mit Ulbricht*, p. 325. Gniffke's designation of 3 July 1948 as the day of the debate is refuted by the official minutes. See also Ulbricht's closing speech to 12 PE meeting, 28.–29.7.48, SAPMO-BArch, ZPA, IV 2/1/50 and Ulbricht's report to 13 PE meeting, 15.–16.9.48, 'The theoretical and practical significance of the Cominform resolution concerning the situation in the Yugoslavian Communist Party', SAPMO-BArch, ZPA, IV 2/1/52.

92 Naimark, *The Russians in Germany*, p. 420.

93 *Ibid.*, p. 432.

94 *Ibid*, pp. 445–6.

95 Cited in S. Prokop, 'Ackermann-Legende?', *Die Weltbühne*, 27 (1990), 850–3; p. 851. In the art journal, he claimed, 'representatives of progress' were 'being stifled by a group of expressionists'. In the field of music: 'What kind of African-American music must we listen to today? It is such a mixture that it is difficult to tell whether the music, or better noise, comes from the jungle or a plant of [Henry] Ford.' *Ibid.*, pp. 851–2.

96 SAPMO-BArch, ZPA, IV 2/1/50.

97 *Ibid.*

98 SAPMO-BArch, ZPA, IV 2/1/52.

99 *Ibid.*

100 *Ibid.*

101 *Ibid.*

102 *Ibid.* Ulbricht's interjection during Grotewohl's closing speech to PE, September 1948.

103 A. Ackermann 'Über den einzig möglichen Weg zum Sozialismus', *ND* (24.9.48), 2.

104 SAPMO-BArch, ZPA, NL 109/24. Draft of a composition for *ND*, December 1948: 'Where does the SPD stand and where is it going?'

105 SAPMO-BArch, ZPA, NL 109/14. Draft of a speech delivered in Weimar, 4.12.46: 'The political and cultural tasks of the new democracy'.

106 SAPMO-BArch, ZPA, IV 2/1/52. Grotewohl's interjection during Oelßner's speech to PE, September 1948. See also Grotewohl's closing speech at this session.

107 O. Grotewohl, 'Die Politik der Partei und die Entwicklung der SED zu einer Partei neuen Typus', *Protokoll der Verhandlungen der I. Parteikonferenz der Sozialistischen Einheitspartei Deutschlands* (Berlin, 1949), 327–97; pp. 374–5. When it was his turn to address the conference, Ackermann thanked Grotewohl for his support. See SAPMO-BArch, ZPA, NL 109/86.

108 SAPMO-BArch, ZPA, IV 2/1/52. Pieck's interjection during Oelßner's speech to 13 PE meeting, September 1948.

109 SAPMO-BArch, ZPA, NL 90/699. Typed-up record of Fritz Ebert's remarks to a PB meeting, 6.6.53.

110 SAPMO-BArch, ZPA, EA 1291.

111 SAPMO-BArch, ZPA, NL 109/58. Undated draft of a letter written in 1972 or 1973. Ackermann condemned the party's falsification of history both before and after 1945.

112 Prokop, 'Ackermann-Legende?', p. 852.

113 Letter from C. Steel (office of political adviser to commander-in-chief in Germany) to British foreign office, 7.2.46. Cited in R. Steininger (ed.), *Quellen zur Geschichte des Parlamentarismus und der Politischen Parteien. Die Ruhrfrage 1945/46 und die Entstehung des Landes Nordrhein-Westfalen. Britische, Französische und Amerikanische Akten* (Düsseldorf, 1988), pp. 78–9.

114 F. Zimmermann, 'Brief von Otto Buchwitz an Berliner SPD-Funktionäre, 16. März 1946', *BzG*, 2 (1991), 235–8; pp. 237–8.

115 From Thape's resignation letter of 29 November 1948 published in A. Malycha, 'Sozialdemokraten in der SED: Der "Fall" Ernst Thape', *BzG*, 3 (1993), 77–90; pp. 84–5.

116 Gniffke, *Jahre mit Ulbricht*, p. 149.

117 *Ibid.*, p. 144.

118 Replaced by Colonel General V. D. Sokolovskii in March 1946.

119 SAPMO-BArch, ZPA, J IV 2/202/4. Gniffke's valedictory letter to SED, 28.10.48.

120 From Tiul'panov's report at the meeting of the CC commission of the CPSU to evaluate the activities of the propaganda administration of SMAD, 16.9.46. Cited in Naimark, 'The Soviet occupation', p. 47.

121 SAPMO-BArch, ZPA, IV 2/1/8. Grotewohl's speech to PE, 18.–19.9.46.

122 *Ibid.*

123 From Tiul'panov's report at the meeting of the CC commission of the CPSU to evaluate the activities of the propaganda administration of SMAD, 16.9.46. Cited in Naimark, 'The Soviet occupation', p. 46.

124 SAPMO-BArch, ZPA, IV 2/1/8. Grotewohl's speech to PE, 18.–19.9.46.

125 From Tiul'panov's report at the meeting of the CC commission of the CPSU to evaluate the activities of the propaganda administration of SMAD, 16.9.46. Cited in
Naimark, 'The Soviet occupation', p. 46.

126 SAPMO-BArch, ZPA, NL 36/663. Conversation between Fechner and Konitzer
(former SPD politician in charge of the central health administration) on 20.12.46 as
reported by the latter on 14.1.47. Another document with the same date accused
Konitzer, who was arrested in July 1947, of fostering 'conspiratorial' contacts with
the LDP and SPD. SAPMO-BArch, ZPA, NL 36/663.

127 SAPMO-BArch, ZPA, NL 36/734.

128 G. Braun, ' "Regierungsangelegenheiten" in Thüringen im Spannungsfeld von sowjetischer Deutschlandpolitik und SED-Kalkülen 1947', BzG, 34 (1992), 67–91; p. 79.

129 SAPMO-BArch, ZPA, IV 2/1/20. On 11 July 1947, Tiul'panov retrospectively criticized 'wavering in the party executive over authorization of the SPD in the eastern
zone'. SAPMO-BArch, ZPA, NL 36/734.

130 Loth, Stalins ungeliebtes Kind, p. 80.

131 SAPMO-BArch, ZPA, NL 90/99. Gniffke's unpublished manuscript for the
Frankfurter Rundschau, March 1950. See also Gniffke, Jahre mit Ulbricht, p. 229.

132 Gniffke, Jahre mit Ulbricht, pp. 306–8.

133 SAPMO-BArch, ZPA, IV 2/1/48. Unofficially, the campaign had already begun. See
the complaint of former social democrat Otto Meier against Honecker at a CS
meeting on 4.2.47. According to the minutes: 'The office of the CS is instructed to
express the CS's disapproval to Erich Honecker over his behaviour towards Meier'.
SAPMO-BArch, ZPA, IV 2/2.1/63.

134 Ulbricht continued his attacks at subsequent PE meetings. See, for example,
Ulbricht's report and closing speech to 13 PE meeting, 15.–16.9.48, SAPMO-BArch,
ZPA, IV 2/1/52.

135 SAPMO-BArch, ZPA, IV 2/1/50. Dahlem's report to 12 PE meeting, 29.–30.7.48:
'Anweisungen für die organisatorische Festigung der Partei und ihre Säuberung von
feindlichen und entarteten Elementen.' Ulbricht remarked that the purge had been
justified in great detail.

136 See Thape's resignation letter of 9 November 1948 published in Malycha,
'Sozialdemokraten in der SED', pp. 85–6. According to an internal party analysis in
1954 former National Socialists accounted for 25.4 per cent of the SED membership.
In the districts of Halle and Erfurt every third comrade was a former Nazi. In local,
factory and district leaderships they often constituted the majority. In the words of
the Berlin historian Armin Mitter: 'The NSDAP represented nothing less than a cadre-
reservoir.' 'Für ehrliche Zusammenarbeit', Der Spiegel, 19 (9.5.94), 84–91; p. 91.

137 For more detail see K. W. Fricke, Opposition und Widerstand in der DDR. Ein poli-
tischer Report (Köln, 1984), pp. 34–7. See also K. W. Fricke, Warten auf
Gerechtigkeit. Kommunistische Säuberungen und Rehabilitierungen. Bericht und
Dokumentation (Köln, 1971), pp. 69–73, 75, 77.

138 Gniffke's speech to 2 party congress of SED in Protokoll der Verhandlungen des II.
Parteitages der Sozialistischen Einheitspartei Deutschlands (Berlin-Ost, 1947), pp.
112–13. See also SAPMO-BArch, ZPA, NL 90/99, Gniffke's unpublished manuscript
for the Frankfurter Rundschau, March 1950.

139 SAPMO-BArch, ZPA, IV 2/11/v746. Gniffke's speech '100 years Communist
Manifesto' delivered in the House of Soviet Culture, 12.3.48.

140 Gniffke, *Jahre mit Ulbricht*, p. 294.
141 *Ibid.*, p. 325. Confirmed some months later in W. Ulbricht, 'Die Bedeutung des Briefes des Informbüros für die SED', *ND* (17.7.49), 4.
142 SAPMO-BArch, ZPA, IV 2/1/50. Gniffke's speech to 12 PE meeting, 28.–29. 7. 48.
143 SAPMO-BArch, ZPA, J IV 2/202/4. Gniffke's valedictory letter to SED, 28.10.48.
144 SAPMO-BArch, ZPA, NL 36/666. Gniffke's article in *Freiheit* (15.9.48), 'Kritik und Selbstkritik in der Partei. Eine wegweisende Klarstellung von Erich W. Gniffke'. In a stinging rebuttal ten days later, Gniffke was accused of neutralizing the party's class character, negating its leading role and disregarding the Soviet example. See E. Gniffke, 'Eine notwendige Aufklärung von Hans Marum, *Pressedienst* (25.9.48).
145 SAPMO-BArch, ZPA, J IV 2/202/4.
146 SAPMO-BArch, ZPA, NL 90/99. Gniffke's unpublished manuscript for the *Frankfurter Rundschau*, March 1950. See also Gniffke, *Jahre mit Ulbricht*, p. 305.
147 SAPMO-BArch, ZPA, J IV 2/202/4.
148 According to Wandel, some were unhappy with the decision to expel Gniffke from the party. Interview with Paul Wandel, 30.11.92.
149 SAPMO-BArch, ZPA, IV 2/1/57. Grotewohl's speech to PE.
150 Cited in *ibid.*
151 SAPMO-BArch, ZPA, IV 2/1/58. Register of attendance.
152 SAPMO-BArch, ZPA, IV 2/11/v746. Memo dated 4.11.48.
153 See Thape's resignation letter of 29 November 1948 published in Malycha, 'Sozialdemokraten in der SED', pp. 83–8.
154 O. Pfefferkorn, 'Fritz Ebert. "Der Oper-Bürgermeister" in Ostberlin', *SBZ-Archiv*, 9 (5.5.53), 137–8; p. 137.
155 SAPMO-BArch, ZPA. IV 2/1/8. Grotewohl's speech to 5 PE meeting, 18.–19. 9. 46.
156 See Stößel, *Positionen und Strömungen*, pp. 230–3. In November 1946, Grotewohl spoke of the need for 'economic alleviation' if the SED was to 'guarantee democracy' by winning over 'the majority' of the working population. Cited in *ibid.*, p. 234. See also interview with the former social democrat and CC secretary, 'S. F.' on 21.3.74 in Bouvrier, Schulz '. . . *die SPD aber aufgehört hat zu existieren*', pp. 51–8, 63–4.
157 Grotewohl cited in *ND*, 23.4.47, Stößel, *Positionen und Strömungen*, p. 166.
158 SAPMO-BArch, ZPA, NL 215/105. Excerpt from Grotewohl's speech to 6 PE meeting, 24.–25.10.46.
159 SAPMO-BArch, ZPA, IV 2/1/50. Grotewohl's report to 12 PE meeting, 28.–29. 7.48: 'The November revolution and lessons to be drawn from the history of the German labour movement'.
160 SAPMO-BArch, ZPA, IV 2/1/48.
161 Grotewohl, 'Die Politik der Partei', pp. 365–74.
162 Grotewohl in conversation with Gniffke, June 1948 Gniffke, *Jahre mit Ulbricht*, p. 312.
163 'Otto Grotewohl', *Der Spiegel*, 40 (30.9.64), p. 72.
164 Grotewohl's speech from September 1945, cited in Gniffke, *Jahre mit Ulbricht*, p. 324.
165 A. Malycha, ' "Hier stehe ich, ich kann nicht anders!" Rede Otto Grotewohls am 11. November 1945', *BzG*, 2 (1992), 167–84.
166 O. Grotewohl, 'Ein Jahr auf dem Wege zu einer Partei neuen Typus', *ND* (17.7.49), 4.
167 Grotewohl, 'Die Politik der Partei', p. 375.
168 F. Stempel, 'Erinnerung an Otto Grotewohl. Zu dessen 100. Geburtstag am 11. März 1994', *Utopie Kreativ*, 41/42 (March–April, 1994), 154–65; p. 156.

169 SAPMO-BArch, ZPA, IV 2/1/39. Resolution approved by 6 PE meeting, 14.–15.1.48.

170 SAPMO-BArch, ZPA, IV 2/1/42. Grotewohl's report to 8 PE meeting, 20.3.48: 'The tasks of the party after the second German national congress for unity and a just peace'.

171 SAPMO-BArch, ZPA, NL 90/99. Gniffke's unpublished manuscript for the *Frankfurter Rundschau*, March 1950.

172 SAPMO-BArch, ZPA, IV 2/1/20. Ulbricht's speech to PE, 22.5.47.

173 *Deutschlands Stimme*, 8.8.48. Cited in Loth, *Stalins ungeliebtes Kind*, p. 140.

174 SAPMO-BArch, ZPA, NL 36/735. Pieck's notes from conversation on 16.8.48. Cited in Loth, *Stalins ungeliebtes Kind*, p. 140.

175 Grotewohl, 'Die Politik der Partei', pp. 327–97.

176 SAPMO-BArch, ZPA, IV 2/1/39. Grotewohl's speech to 6 PE meeting, 14.–15. 1. 48.

177 SAPMO-BArch, ZPA, IV 2/1/10. Grotewohl's speech to 6 PE meeting, 24.–25.10.46.

178 Cited in A. Malycha, 'Sozialdemokratische Vorstellungen in der SED in den Jahren 1946–1948', *BzG*, 3 (1990), 339–49; p. 347. Fechner was addressing a meeting of the local government advisory committee in Alexisbad.

179 Gniffke, *Jahre mit Ulbricht*, p. 306.

180 SAPMO-BArch, ZPA, IV 2/1/48. Ulbricht's report to 11 PE meeting: 'The economic plan for 1948 and the two-year plan for 1949–50 to re-establish and develop the peacetime economy of the Soviet occupation zone'.

181 Cited in Malycha, 'Sozialdemokratische Vorstellungen', p. 347. Ulbricht was addressing the first 'political conference' of the SED staged in Werder between 23–24 July 1948.

182 Gniffke, *Jahre mit Ulbricht*, pp. 311, 317.

183 M. Fechner, 'Erfahrungen aus der Aktionseinheit', *Einheit*, 1 (February, 1946), 4–6; p. 6.

184 SAPMO-BArch, ZPA, IV 2/1/52. Lehmann's speech to 13 PE meeting, 15.–16.9.48. See also H. Lehmann, 'Von der Demokratie zum Sozialismus', *Einheit*, 1 (February, 1946), 20–2. Lehmann's guidelines for municipal government drawn up in December 1945 recommended devolving power to the communes, regions and provinces. See SAPMO-BArch, ZPA, NL 101/15.

185 'Grundsätze und Ziele', p. 4.

186 SAPMO-BArch, ZPA, IV 2/1/52. Lehmann's speech to 13 PE meeting, 15.–16.9.48.

187 SAPMO-BArch, ZPA, IV 2/2.022/9. Lehmann's letter to the 1 party conference excusing his non-attendance on grounds of ill health, 24.1.49.

188 Gniffke, *Jahre mit Ulbricht*, p. 318.

189 SAPMO-BArch, ZPA, IV 2/1/50. Lehmann's speech to 12 PE meeting, 28.–29.7.48.

190 H. Lehmann, 'Lehren der Vergangenheit für die Gegenwart', *ND* (4.11.48), 4.

191 SAPMO-BArch, ZPA, IV 2/1/50. Meier's speech to 12 PE meeting, 28.–29.7.48. See also Ulbricht's speech to 13 PE meeting, 15.–16.9.48, SAPMO-BArch, ZPA, IV 2/1/52.

192 Gniffke, *Jahre mit Ulbricht*, p. 325. CS resolution of 2.7.48, see SAPMO-BArch, ZPA, IV 2/2.1/214.

193 Karsten resigned from the CS due to ill health in January 1949 and was given responsibility for animal livestock in the government of Brandenburg. SAPMO-BArch, ZPA, IV 2/1/59–60.

194 SAPMO-BArch, ZPA, IV 2/1/50. See Buchwitz's speech to 12 PE meeting, 28.–29.7.48. Endorsing the party purge, Buchwitz conceded that the attitude of many towards the USSR was inappropriate.

195 Buchwitz's speech to 1 party conference, 25.–28.1.49 in *Protokoll der Verhandlungen der I. Parteikonferenz der Sozialistischen Einheitspartei Deutschlands*, (Berlin-Ost, 1949) pp. 402–7; p. 407.

196 SAPMO-BArch, ZPA, IV 2/1/101. Buchwitz's speech to 8 CC plenum, 21.–23.2.52.

197 SAPMO-BArch, ZPA, IV 2/1/102. Matern's speech to 8 CC plenum.

198 SAPMO-BArch, ZPA, NL 36/695.

199 See M. Kaiser, 'Die Zentrale der Diktatur – organisatorische Weichenstellungen, Strukturen und Kompetenzen der SED-Führung in der SBZ/DDR 1946 bis 1952'. Cited in J. Kocka (ed.) *Historische DDR-Forschung. Aufsätze und Studien* (Berlin, 1993), pp. 57–86; pp. 72–3.

200 SAPMO-BArch, ZPA, IV 2/1/10. Weimann's speech to 6 PE meeting, 24.–25.10.46.

201 Fricke, *Warten auf Gerechtigkeit*, p. 70. Also see F. Oldenburg, *Konflikt und Konfliktregelung in der Parteiführung der SED 1945/46–1972* (Köln, 1972), p. 18.

202 An agency set up by the SPD to monitor the persecution of social democrats and other abuses in the Soviet zone.

203 Fricke, *Warten auf Gerechtigkeit*, p. 71. Also see Oldenburg, *Konflikt und Konfliktregelung*, p. 23.

204 In September 1953 Ulbricht claimed that there were about 400,000 former social democrats in the SED. This compares to approximately 679,000 at the time of unification. Given that no more than 50,000 could have died in this short period of time, we are left with a total of 229,000 who either resigned from the party or were expelled from its ranks. See Fricke, *Warten auf Gerechtigkeit*, p. 77. See also Fricke, *Opposition und Widerstand in der DDR*, pp. 42–5.

205 Interview with Alfred Neumann, 16.10.92.

206 Resolution of 13 CC plenum, 14.5.53 evaluating the lessons to be learned from the Rudolf Slansky trial in Czechoslovakia. Published in Fricke, *Warten auf Gerechtigkeit*, pp. 192–201; p. 200. See also SAPMO-BArch, ZPA, IV 2/1/169, PB resolution of 9.10.56 rescinding Fritz Uschner's expulsion from the SED.

207 Interview with Manfred Uschner, 8.12.92. Manfred Uschner was later employed in the CC and became a private aide to PB member Hermann Axen. In the 1970s and 1980s he was a senior figure in talks between the SED and the West German SPD.

208 See Chapter 2: Opposition, June–July 1953.

209 Cited in Malycha, 'Sozialdemokratische Vorstellungen', p. 341.

210 For more detail, see H. J. Spanger, *Die SED und der Sozialdemokratismus. Ideologische Abgrenzung in der DDR* (Köln, 1982).

211 Laszlo Rajk was the most popular man in the Hungarian leadership. Interior minister after the war, he had fought in Spain during the 1930s and spent virtually no time in Moscow. After a show trial in September 1949, he was executed as an 'agent of imperialism'.

212 Vice-premier and former secretary of the Bulgarian CP during its years underground. Executed for treason after a show trial in 1949–50.

213 After Klement Gottwald, Rudolf Slansky was the most powerful man in the Czechoslovak CP. Slansky was a Jew and had spent the war in Moscow. After the most infamous of the East European show trials in November 1952, he was executed as an 'imperialist agent'.

214 SAPMO-BArch, ZPA, NL 102/29. Excerpt from an article in *Der Spiegel*, 19.12.56: 'Harich – Schlag ins Genick'. Luxemburg predicted that the repression of political life in Russia would lead to the bureaucratic dictatorship of a small clique.

215 BStU, UA 192/56. Record of Merker's remarks, 14.2.53.

216 P. Merker, *Deutschland. Sein oder Nicht Sein?*, vol 1 (Mexico, 1944), p. 212.

217 SAPMO-BArch, ZPA, NL 102/29. Excerpts from an article in *Der Spiegel*, 19.12.56: 'Harich – Schlag ins Genick'.

218 *Ibid*. For more detail on Merker's war-time conflict with Moscow, see W. Kießling, 'Im Widerstreit mit Moskau: Paul Merker und die Bewegung Freies Deutschland in Mexico', *BzG*, 3 (1992), 29–42.

219 SAPMO-BArch, ZPA, IV 2/4/106. Chairman of the Federal committee for all-German questions, Herbert Wehner, interviewed by RIAS on 11.9.50 at 22:45. A former communist and close associate of Merker, Wehner went on to become deputy-chairman of the West German SPD.

220 SAPMO-BArch, ZPA, IV 2/4/117. Ackermann's written testimony to the CPCC, Berlin, 29.8.50: 'Concerning anti-Soviet remarks of Paul Merker'. Ackermann was closely associated with Merker in Paris during the late 1930s.

221 SAPMO-BArch, ZPA, IV 2/2/106. PB meeting 29.8.50, 'Statement of the CC and CPCC of the Socialist Unity Party of Germany concerning contacts between former German political emigrants and the head of the unitarian service committee, Noel H. Field.'

222 SAPMO-BArch, ZPA, IV 2/4/117. Johann Schmidt's testimony to the CPCC, Berlin, 19.8.52: 'Short report on Paul Merker'. Schmidt was a close associate of Merker during the war years.

223 SAPMO-BArch, ZPA, IV 2/4/112, 'André Simone's report to the CPCC on the CC's resolution to expel Merker'.

224 W. Janka, *Spuren eines Lebens* (Berlin, 1991), p. 191. Janka was a close associate of Merker in Mexico and after the war in Germany.

225 W. Kießling, 'Zweikampf oder die Abstinenz von Demokratie. Memorial für Paul Merker (1. Februar 1894 bis 13. Mai 1969)', *Utopie Kreativ* (January–February 1994), 114–23; pp. 114–17.

226 Heinrich Mann's letter to Paul Merker, 23.1.46. Cited in W. Kießling *Allemania Libre in Mexico. Band 2: Texte und Dokumente zur Geschichte des antifaschistischen Exils (1941–46)* (East Berlin, 1974), p. 426.

227 Noel Field worked for the unitarian service committee during World War Two and in this capacity provided safe havens for persecuted communists in Europe. Arrested in connection with the Rajk trial in Hungary, he was accused of being an 'imperialist agent' and made the key witness in the East European show trials. Communists associated with Field during their time in Western emigration were purged. Field himself was released in 1954, innocent of the charges levelled against him.

228 SAPMO-BArch, ZPA, NL 36/666. R. Fischer, 'Agenten in Deutschland' (article published in the *Morning Mercury*, November 1946).

229 Cited in 'Säuberung. Neun befühlen ihren Hals', *Der Spiegel*, 36 (6.9.50), 5–6; p. 5. The quotation comes from an interview Fischer gave to Zürich's *Weltwoche* in January 1949.

230 SAPMO-BArch, ZPA, IV 2/4/106. Chairman of the Federal committee for all-German questions, Herbert Wehner, interviewed by RIAS (Radio in the American Sector), on 11.9.50 at 22:45.

231 Cited in W. Kießling, 'Paul Merker und der "Sozialismus der dummen Kerls"', *ND* (1.12.92), 14.

232 Kießling, 'Zweikampf oder die Abstinenz von Demokratie', p. 118.

233 Gniffke, *Jahre mit Ulbricht*, p. 223.

234 BStU, UA 192/56.

235 Interview with CC secretary 'S. F.' on 21.3.74 in Bouvrier, Schulz, '. . . *die SPD aber aufgehört hat zu existieren'*, pp. 51–88; pp. 63–4.

236 Gniffke, *Jahre mit Ulbricht*, pp. 236–7.

237 The GDR and Poland signed an accord recognizing the Oder–Neisse line as the border between their two countries on 6.7.50.

238 Interview with Wolfgang Kießling, 15.9.92.

239 Cited in Kießling, 'Zweikampf oder die Abstinenz von Demokratie', p. 116. The prisoner was a social democrat by the name of Hermann Kreutzer.

240 SAPMO-BArch, ZPA, IV 2/1.01/75. Merker's speech to agricultural conference, 16.1.48.

241 SAPMO-BArch, ZPA, IV 2/1.01/106. Ulbricht's report to SED farmer's conference, 19.–20.2.49 in Halle: 'The new tasks in agriculture'.

242 *Unserem Freund und Lehrer. J. W. Stalin zum 70. Geburtstag* (Berlin, 1949), pp. 266–7.

243 SAPMO-BArch, ZPA, IV 2/4/288. 'Collection of material against former state secretary Paul Merker', 11.10.50. An eleven-point indictment by the central commission for state control.

244 SAPMO-BArch, ZPA, IV 2/2/51. PB meeting 18.10.49. All staff at 'Radio Berlin' who had spent the war in English exile were summarily dismissed.

245 SAPMO-BArch, ZPA, IV 2/4/106. Ulbricht's memo to Matern, 25.10.49.

246 Kießling, 'Zweikampf oder die Abstinenz von Demokratie', p. 117.

247 SAPMO-BArch, ZPA, IV 2/2/106. PB meeting 29.8.50: 'Schlußredaktion des Dokuments des Zentralkomitees über die Unterstützung des Agenten Field durch Parteifunktionäre'.

248 Cited in Kießling, 'Paul Merker und "der Sozialismus der dummen Kerls"', p. 14.

249 *Ibid*. Paul Merker interviewed by Wolfgang Kießling, 1968.

250 See Chapter 3: Merker or Dahlem: A 'German Gomulka' in waiting?

251 SAPMO-BArch, ZPA, NL 102/27, Merker's letter to Pieck, 30.11.52. See also SAPMO-BArch, ZPA, NL 102/27, Merker's letter to Pieck, 26.11.52.

252 SAPMO-BArch, ZPA, NL 102/27, Merker's letter to Pieck, 14.4.56.

253 L. Bauer, '"Die Partei hat immer recht". Bemerkungen zum geplanten deutschen Rajkprozeß (1950)', *APZ*, B27 (4.7.56), 405–19; p. 409. See also the testimony of two other prospective defendants Erica Wallach and Gitta Bauer. Cited in P. Brandt, J. Schumacher, G. Schwarzrock, K. Sühl, *Karrieren eines Außenseiters. Leo Bauer zwischen Kommunismus und Sozialdemokratie 1912 bis 1972* (Berlin and Bonn, 1983), pp. 196–7.

254 Müller's letter to Grotewohl, 31.5.56. Published in H. Weber, 'Kurt Müller, Ein historisches Dokument aus dem Jahre 1956. Brief an den DDR-Ministerpräsidenten Otto Grotewohl', *APZ*, B11 (9.3.90), 16–29; p. 19. See also 'Ich bin kein Lump, Herr Mielke!', *Der Spiegel*, 5 (30.1.57), 30–7. Another of the prospective defendants, Hans Schrecker, was ordered to incriminate up to thirty people, many of them party members with a Jewish background. See Schrecker's written report to Karl Schirdewan, 1956, cited in: W. Otto, '"Genossen, ich verstehe nicht . . ." Die Geschichte von Hans Schrecker und die Jagd nach einer "Slansky-Verschwörerbände" in der DDR', *Horch und Guck*, 5 (1993), 25–30; p. 29.

255 SAPMO-BArch, ZPA, NL 102/27. Merker's letter to Pieck, 14.4.56.

256 The others being Maria Weiterer (head of the women's section in the PE and member of *Deutsche Frauenbund* [DFD]) Leo Bauer (chief editor of Radio Germany), Willi Kreikemeyer (general director of the *Deutsche Reichsbahn*), Bruno Goldhammer (sectional head in the Office of Information), Walter Beling (member of the CS, 1948–49) and Lex Ende (chief editor of *ND)*.

257 On 29 August 1950, the PB felt it necessary to unilaterally alter the resolution adopted by the CC four days previously: 'During the investigation it became clear that a number of former émigrés of the party were not helping to clear things up (*die Zusammenhänge einwandfrei zu klären*). That applies particularly to Bruno Goldhammer, Willi Kreykemeier, Maria Weiterer and also, to a certain extent, Walter Beling.' SAPMO-BArch, ZPA, IV 2/2/106, PB meeting 29.8.50: 'Schlußredaktion des Dokuments über die Unterstützung des Agenten Field durch Parteifunktionäre'.

258 According to Leonhard, communist resistance fighters in Germany were more likely to support an independent, antifascist socialist movement than those who emigrated to Moscow. See Leonhard, *Die Revolution entlässt ihre Kinder*, p. 479. Many of their representatives in the SED leadership, however, (e.g. Honecker, Neumann) were diehard Stalinists and enthusiastic supporters of Walter Ulbricht. No evidence was found to support the assertion of one historian that they aspired to a 'democratic' party based on the ideas of Liebknecht, Thälmann and Luxemburg. See U. Arens, *Die andere Freiheit. Die Freiheit in Theorie und Praxis der Sozialistischen Einheitspartei Deutschlands* (München, 1976), p. 86.

259 SAPMO-BArch, ZPA, IV 2/4/114. 'Swiss sector. Short report over political differences during the war', by Bertz (émigré in France and Switzerland), Berlin, 2.8.45.

260 L. Bauer, ' "Die Partei hat immer recht" ', p. 411.

261 SAPMO-BArch, ZPA, IV 2/1.01/104. Stenographic record of discussion with newspaper editors in Berlin and the Soviet zone before the 1 party conference, 1.12.48.

262 For more details, see J. Herf, 'East German communists and the Jewish question: The case of Paul Merker', *JCH*, 29 (1994), 627–61.

263 SAPMO-BArch, ZPA, IV 2/11/v801. Merker's letter to CPCC, 1.6.56. For more detail on the anti-Semitic element of the purges, see P. O'Doherty, 'The GDR in the context of Stalinist show trials and anti-Semitism in Eastern Europe, 1948–54', *German History*, 3 (October 1992), pp. 302–17 and M. Kessler (ed.), *Antisemitismus und Arbeiterbewegung. Entwicklungslinien im 20. Jahrhundert* (Bonn, 1993).

264 For more detail, see J. Herf, *Divided memory. The Nazi past in the two Germanys* (London, 1997).

265 Resolution of 13 CC plenum, 14.–15.5.53: 'Über die Auswertung des Beschlusses des ZK der SED zu den Lehren aus dem Prozeß gegen das Verschwörerzentrum Slansky', *ND* (20.5.53), 3–4; p. 3.

266 W. Kießling, ' "Ich wehrte mich gegen die Beschuldigung, ein Agent zu sein" ', *ND* (17.–18.8.91), 13.

267 This latter myth is especially prevalent among former members of the SED elite. Among those who still subscribe to it are Wandel (interviewed, 30.11.92), Hager (interviewed, 1.12.92) and Gerhard Schürer (former Head of the state planning commission and PB member in the Honecker era, interviewed 5.11.92). See also Brandt et al., *Karrieren eines Außenseiters*, pp. 196–9.

268 SAPMO-BArch, ZPA, IV 2/4/117, Merker's letter to Pieck, 24.8.50. SAPMO-BArch, ZPA, IV 2/11/v801, Merker's letter to Pieck, 22.4.51. See also SAPMO-BArch, ZPA, NL 102/27, Merker's letters to Pieck of 26.11.52, 30.11.52, 14.4.56 and 24.8.56.

269 Interview with Wandel, 30.11.92.
270 SAPMO-BArch, ZPA, IV 2/11/v801. Memo from CC secretariat to Schön and Ulbricht, 1.6.51.
271 SAPMO-BArch, ZPA, IV 2/11/v801. Pieck's letter to Ulbricht, 26.4.51.
272 SAPMO-BArch, ZPA, IV 2/11/v801. In his letter to Pieck of 22.4.51, Merker had asked that he be allowed to proceed with this work, the first volume of which had been published in 1944.
273 SAPMO-BArch, ZPA, IV 2/11/v801. Memo from CC secretariat to Schön and Ulbricht, 1.6.51.
274 SAPMO-BArch, ZPA, NL 102/27. Pieck's letter to Merker, 28.8.52.
275 SAPMO-BArch, ZPA, IV 2/1/86. Pieck's intervention during Fritz Lange's speech to 2 CC plenum, 24.8.50.
276 SAPMO-BArch, ZPA, IV 2/1/86. Ulbricht's intervention at 2 CC plenum.
277 SAPMO-BArch, ZPA, IV 2/1/86. Pieck's speech to 2 CC plenum.
278 SAPMO-BArch, ZPA, IV 2/1/86. Pieck's closing speech to 2 CC plenum.
279 The 'Vereinigung der Verfolgten des Naziregimes' [Association of those persecuted by the Nazi regime] was founded on 22 February 1947 as a broad church of former antifascist resistance fighters persecuted on grounds of race, religion and political affiliation. Initially independent, it soon became a satellite of the SED. Home to a large number of 'western émigrés', it was also Dahlem's power base. Three years later Dahlem followed Merker into political oblivion.
280 SAPMO-BArch, ZPA, IV 2/1/86. Ulbricht's speech to 2 CC plenum.
281 *Ibid.*
282 SAPMO-BArch, ZPA, IV 2/1/86. Schmidt's speech to 2 CC plenum. According to Ulbricht, Weiterer had defended Noel Field during interrogations by the CPCC (Ulbricht's speech to 2 CC plenum, SAPMO-BArch, ZPA, IV 2/1/86).
283 Interview with Hager, 1.12.92.
284 SAPMO-BArch, ZPA, IV 2/1/86.
285 Interview with Hager, 1.12.92.
286 *Ibid.* Confirmed in Weber, 'Kurt Müller', p. 20.
287 SAPMO-BArch, ZPA, IV 2/1/86. Mielke's speech to 2 CC plenum.
288 SAPMO-BArch, ZPA, IV 2/2/106. PB meeting, 29.8.50: 'Schlußredaktion des Dokuments des Zentralkomitees über die Unterstützung des Agenten Field durch Parteifunktionäre'. The CC document was entitled: 'Statement of the SED's CC and CPCC regarding the contacts of former German political emigrants to the head of the unitarian service committee Noel Field.'
289 O. Pfefferkorn, 'Franz Dahlem. Der letzte Revolutionär', *SBZ-Archiv*, 6 (20.3.53), 85–6; p. 85.
290 Report in the *TR* to mark Dahlem's sixtieth birthday in 1952. Cited in *ibid.*
291 Pfefferkorn, 'Franz Dahlem', p. 85.
292 *Ibid.* His detailed statement was handed to the head prefect in Paris. See also resolution of 13 CC plenum, 14.–15.5.53: 'Über die Auswertung', p. 3; Matern's report to 13 CC plenum 'Über die Durchführung des Beschlusses des ZK der SED "Lehren aus dem Prozeß gegen das Verschwörerzentrum Slansky"', *ND* (19.5.53), 3–4; p. 3.
293 Matern's report to 4 party congress of the SED, 30.3.–6.4.54. Excerpts published in Fricke, *Warten auf Gerechtigkeit*, pp. 211–20; pp. 215–16. See also 'Fäden zum Strick', *Der Spiegel*, 22 (27.5.53), 13–14; p. 14.

294 Under the terms of the Pact, German communists who had sought sanctuary in Russia were handed over to the Gestapo. Others were murdered in Soviet emigration. This did not prevent Ulbricht from accusing Dahlem of capitulating to French imperialism and 'liquidating' the communist emigration in Paris. See Matern's report to 13 CC plenum, 14.–15.5.53, 'Über die Durchführung', p. 3.

295 Stößel, *Positionen und Strömungen*, p. 174. Also see Pfefferkorn, 'Franz Dahlem', p. 85.

296 Gniffke, *Jahre mit Ulbricht*, pp. 181, 203.

297 'Der Weg einer Tarnorganisation. Zur Auflösung der VVN in der Sowjetzone', *SBZ-Archiv*, 6 (20.3.53), 86–7; p. 86.

298 E. Richert, *Die DDR-Elite oder unsere Partner von Morgen?* (Reinbek bei Hamburg, 1968), p. 100.

299 F. Dahlem, 'Zur Frage der innerparteilichen Demokratie', *Einheit*, 1 (February 1946), pp. 17–20.

300 Dahlem's speech to 15 party congress of KPD, 19.–20.4.46. Cited in Stößel, *Positionen und Strömungen*, pp. 168–9.

301 SAPMO-BArch, ZPA, J IV 2/202/4, Gniffke's valedictory letter to SED, 28.10.48.

302 Gniffke, *Jahre mit Ulbricht*, p. 175.

303 F. Dahlem, 'Vom Wesen und von den Aufgaben der SED', *NW*, 6 (1946), 2. Cited in Stößel, *Positionen und Strömungen*, p. 170. His characterization of the SED in May 1946 as a 'state-building party' destined to lead in 'all areas of democratic reconstruction' was not a plea for Stalinist hegemony. Rather, it was an expression of his belief that power could be obtained and exercised through the democratic system. Cited in H. Weber, 'Die Wandlung der SED', p. 263. Dahlem was addressing the 2 PE meeting.

304 Interview with 'S. F.', 21.3.74 in Bouvrier, Schulz, ' . . . *die SPD aber aufgehört hat zu existieren'*, pp. 51–88; pp. 63–4.

305 SAPMO-BArch, ZPA, IV 2/1/50. Dahlem's report to 12 PE meeting, 29.–30.7.48: 'Anweisungen für die organisatorische Festigung der Partei und ihre Säuberung von feindlichen und entarteten Elementen.'

306 According to a report in *Der Spiegel*, Dahlem blamed Ulbricht for the SED's unpopularity and attempted to take advantage of his absence at Dimitrov's funeral in July 1949 to replace him as deputy chairman. 'Dreimal gleiche Treue. Glückhafter Beginn', *Der Spiegel*, 3 (21.7.49), 6–7; p. 6.

307 SAPMO-BArch, ZPA, IV 2/2/189. PB meeting, 29.1.52. Point 4 of the agenda: 'Campaign against the Schuman Plan and General Treaty etc.': 'Approval is given to the report on the continuation and broadening of the campaign against implementation of the Schuman Plan and the General Treaty and for all-German consultations over elections to a national assembly.'

308 SAPMO-BArch, ZPA, 2/4/110. Record of a conversation between Dahlem, Koenen, Seigewasser, Vesper, Zorn and Grützner, 30.1.52 (continuation of an earlier conversation held on 19.1.52).

309 H. Brandt, *Ein Traum, der nicht entführbar ist. Mein Weg zwischen Ost und West* (München, 1967), p. 182. Brandt was a member of the SED's district leadership in Berlin. He subsequently fled to the West.

310 W. Osten, 'Die Deutschlandpolitik der Sowjetunion in den Jahren 1952/53', *Osteuropa*, 1 (January 1964), 1–13; p. 6.

311 *Ibid*. See also Loth, *Stalins ungeliebtes Kind*, pp. 197–8.

312 SAPMO-BArch, ZPA, IV 2/4/391. Dahlem's letter to the leadership, 19.7.53, p. 91. Cited by Matern during CPCC interrogation of Rudolf Herrnstadt, 13.11.53. A copy of the original has not been found.

313 Rudolf Herrnstadt's letter to W. S. Semyonov, 28.11.62. Published in N. Stulz-Herrnstadt (ed.), R. Herrnstadt, *Das Herrnstadt-Dokument. Das Politbüro der SED und die Geschichte des 17. Juni 1953* (Reinbek bei Hamburg, 1990), pp. 264–78; p. 223.

314 SAPMO-BArch, ZPA, IV 2/4/391. Cited during the interrogation of Rudolf Herrnstadt by the CPCC, 13.11.53. After 1950, Ulbricht packed this body with his own supporters and used it to undermine the PB.

315 SAPMO-BArch, ZPA, IV 2/4/391. Conversation between Matern and Mewis during a session of the CPCC, 3.12.53.

316 See Chapter 2.

317 The possibility that he opposed the Oder–Neisse Line as Germany's postwar border with Poland cannot be ruled out. See Dürmayer's report on Dahlem, 3.6.53, SAPMO-BArch, ZPA, J IV 2/202/4. Dürmayer was a close associate of Dahlem during the 1930s and 1940s. In his report he recalled the latter's opposition to a passage in a VVN resolution pledging to fight all attempts to revise postwar borders in 1948. The testimony is rendered unreliable by its denunciatory nature.

318 SAPMO-BArch, ZPA, IV 2/1/89. Dahlem's speech to 3 CC plenum, 26.–27.10.50. This initiative emanated from the conference of East European leaders held in Prague (20.–21.10.50). It was rejected by the Adenauer government in West Germany.

319 F. Dahlem, ' "Die Generallinie der Partei durchführen, heißt täglicher Kampf um Friedensvertrag und Einheit Deutschlands". Kritischer Diskussionsrede auf der Bezirksdelegiertenkonferenz Magdeburg am 28. September 1952', *NW*, 21 (November 1952), 5–6.

320 Semjonow, *Von Stalin bis Gorbatschow*, p. 226.

321 SAPMO-BArch, ZPA, IV 2/4/278.

322 SAPMO-BArch, ZPA, 2/4/110. Record of a conversation between Dahlem, Koenen, Seigewasser, Vesper, Zorn and Grützner, 30.1.52 (continuation of an earlier conversation held on 19.1.52).

323 SAPMO-BArch, ZPA, IV 2/2/189. PB meeting, 29.1.52.

324 SAPMO-BArch, ZPA, IV 2/4/110. Record of a conversation between Dahlem, Koenen, Seigewasser, Vesper, Zorn and Grützner, 30.1.52 (continuation of an earlier conversation held on 19.1.52).

325 'Fäden zum Strick', *Der Spiegel*, 22 (27.5.53), 13–14. The emissary was Karlheinz Reinecke, former editor of the National Front newspaper *Deutschlands Stimme*. Disguised as a journalist, he conducted informal interviews with liberal and christian democrat politicians, some of whom were members of the *Bundestag*. Ulbricht used the fact that he began working for the CIA in August 1952 to accuse Dahlem of 'blindness in the face of imperialist infiltration'.

326 Pfefferkorn, 'Franz Dahlem', p. 86.

327 Interview with Karl Schirdewan, 23.11.92. See also K. Schirdewan, *Aufstand gegen Ulbricht. Im Kampf um politische Kurskorrektur, gegen stalinistische, dogmatische Politik* (Berlin, 1994), p. 40. Schirdewan, a member of the CC secretariat, had worked closely with Dahlem while head of the western commission.

328 C. Stern, *Ulbricht. A political biography* (London, 1965), pp. 119–20. E. Richert, *Das zweite Deutschland. Ein Staat, der nicht darf* (Frankfurt, Hamburg, 1966), p. 43. See also Richert, *Die DDR-Elite*, p. 100.

329 Dahlem, 'Die Generallinie der Partei', p. 6.

330 F. Dahlem, ' "Die realen Perspektiven der Erhaltung des Friedens." Aus der Diskussionsrede auf der 10. Tagung des Zentralkomitees der SED', *NW*, 24 (December 1952), 6–7.

331 SAPMO-BArch, ZPA, IV 2/2/51. PB meeting, 18.10.49.

332 *Ibid.*

333 Stößel, *Positionen und Strömungen*, p. 527.

334 Otto, ' "Genossen, ich verstehe nicht . . ." ', pp. 28–9.

335 W. Jakob, 'Der Fall Dahlem', *SBZ-Archiv*, 10 (25.5.53), 145–7; p. 145. The resolution was published on 4 January 1953.

336 *Ibid.*, p. 146.

337 *Ibid.*

338 SAPMO-BArch, ZPA, NL 90/699. 'Beschluß des Politbüros des Zentralkomitees der SED vom 17.3.1953'. According to Grotewohl, Dahlem agreed to the investigation but protested against being suspended from all his functions.

339 SAPMO-BArch, ZPA, J IV 2/2/279. PB meeting, 6.5.53.

340 'Über die Auswertung', p. 3.

341 SAPMO-BArch, ZPA, J IV 2/202/5. Testimony of Fritz Sperling (leading figure in the West German KPD) to CPCC, 5.6.56; Müller's letter to Grotewohl, 31.5.56, published in Weber, 'Kurt Müller', p. 29. See also 'Ich bin kein Lump, Herr Mielke', p. 34.

342 Bruno Haid (later deputy state prosecutor of the GDR), interviewed by the German historian Wilfriede Otto. Cited in Otto, ' "Genossen, ich verstehe nicht . . ." ', p. 29.

343 See Chapter 2: Conflict, 1950 – May 1953.

344 SAPMO-BArch, ZPA, J IV 2/2/275. PB meeting, 14.4.53.

345 'Über die Auswertung', p. 3.

346 An impression shared by contemporaries. See Brandt, *Ein Traum*, pp. 202, 204.

347 SAPMO-BArch, ZPA, J IV 2/2/279. PB meeting, 6.5.53.

348 SAPMO-BArch, ZPA, J IV 2/2/280. PB meeting, 12.5.53.

349 SAPMO-BArch, ZPA, NL 90/699. Grotewohl's handwritten notes of a conversation with Dahlem.

350 *Ibid.* See also extracts of Dahlem's letter read to 15 CC plenum, 24.–26.7.53, SAPMO-BArch, ZPA, IV 2/1/119.

351 SAPMO-BArch, ZPA, IV 2/1/116. Resolution of 13 CC plenum, 13.–14.5.53.

352 Interview with Hager, 1.12.92.

353 SAPMO-BArch, ZPA, IV 2/11/v5280/2. *Der Kurier*, 19.10.54.

354 SAPMO-BArch, ZPA, NL 90/303. Herrnstadt's letter to SED CC, 25.5.57.

355 SAPMO-BArch, ZPA, IV 2/4/391. Matern during CPCC's interrogation of Dahlem's nephew, Karl Mewis, 3.12.53.

356 N. Stulz-Herrnstadt, *Das Herrnstadt-Dokument*, p. 158.

357 SAPMO-BArch, ZPA, IV 2/4/391. Herrnstadt's remarks during his interrogation by the CPCC, 13.11.53.

358 Honecker interviewed in R. Andert, W. Herzberg, *Der Sturz. Erich Honecker in Kreuzverhör* (Berlin and Weimar, 1990), p. 232.

2

The Zaisser–Herrnstadt opposition 1950–53

During the late 1940s, Ulbricht had become known as 'the motor' of the SED.[1] In July 1950, the central committee unanimously elected him general secretary.[2] Over the next three years he moulded the fledgling 'party of the new type' into an instrument of his own dictatorial power, building up a compliant apparatus which dominated every aspect of East German society. Ulbricht's sectarianism, however, was rejected by some members of the politburo who waged a tenacious campaign to bring him to account. The staunchest of his critics were Wilhelm Zaisser and Rudolf Herrnstadt.

The proclamation of the New Course at the Kremlin's behest in June 1953 was designed to lead the GDR out of its existential crisis and prepare the ground for German reunification on terms favourable to the Soviets. Instead it unleashed a popular uprising, confirming Tocqueville's adage: 'The most dangerous moment for a bad government is when it seeks to mend its ways.' Only Soviet tanks could quell the unrest and prevent the collapse of communist rule. Ulbricht's invention of the Zaisser–Herrnstadt conspiracy enabled him to circumscribe the New Course, defeat his opponents and consolidate his own embattled position.

Conflict, 1950–May 1953

According to some historians, the so-called 'Zaisser–Herrnstadt opposition' was simply a Machiavellian power struggle waged for the sole purpose of unseating Walter Ulbricht as general secretary.[3] The historical evidence, however, shows that there was more to it than that. The opposition of Wilhelm Zaisser and Rudolf Herrnstadt was based on a genuine critique of certain Stalinist excesses perpetrated by Ulbricht in the early 1950s. If Zaisser and Herrnstadt were the most vocal of his critics, they were occasionally supported by other members of the politburo, such as Anton Ackermann, Hans Jendretzky, Heinrich Rau, Fred Oelßner and Elli Schmidt.

Wilhelm Zaisser was born in 1893. A school teacher by profession, he was converted to communism while serving in the Ukraine as a German reserve officer in 1918. After joining the KPD he played a central role in the Ruhr region, leading its 'red army' in 1920 and helping to organize the strikes against the French occupation three years later. In 1924 he matriculated at a military academy in Moscow before being deployed as an intelligence expert in China where he helped organize the Canton uprising. As the legendary 'General Gomez' and chief of staff of the International Brigades in Spain, he worked with a broad coalition of republican forces. According to one Spanish Civil War veteran, Zaisser was deeply disturbed by 'the degeneration of humanistic socialism under the thumb of the party bureaucracy'.[4] Fluent in Russian, French, Spanish and English, he then moved to the Soviet Union where he worked as a translator before heading the German section of the anti-fascist school in Krasnogorsk. Zaisser was one of the school's most successful teachers, renowned for his ability to work with people of different political persuasions.[5] Back in Germany after the war, he served as police chief in Saxony-Anhalt before becoming the state's interior minister. Here he seems to have won the respect of the other parties and mass organizations.[6] The president of Saxony's parliament (a former social democrat who later fled to the West) remembered Zaisser as a 'straightforward' politician opposed to the 'biased dictatorship of Moscow'.[7] Five months after being appointed East German minister for state security in February 1950, he was elected to the politburo and central committee. Zaisser's meteoric rise was due to the support of his patrons in Russia, whom he had served as a Soviet citizen and member of the CPSU for a quarter of a century.

Rudolf Herrnstadt was born in Prussia in 1903 and studied law at Heidelberg University[8] before choosing a career in journalism. After joining the KPD in 1929, he worked in Prague, Warsaw and Moscow as a correspondent for the *Berliner Tageblatt*. Fluent in Russian, Polish and German, he carried out espionage activities for the West European section of Red Army secret intelligence between 1933 and 1939. He then fled to the Soviet Union where he helped found the National Committee for a Free Germany, editing its newspaper *Freies Deutschland*. Like Zaisser, he was granted Soviet citizenship and membership of the CPSU. In 1944, when the KPD's working commission met to discuss strategy for postwar Germany, Herrnstadt was criticized for underestimating the revolutionary potential of the German people.[9] Back in Berlin after the war, he ran the *Berliner Zeitung* before being appointed editor-in-chief of the SED daily, *Neues Deutschland*, in 1949. A year later he was elected to the politburo and central committee.

The 'Zaisser–Herrnstadt opposition' was not an opportunistic creation of 1953. Its roots may be traced back to 1950 and earlier. At a conference of east German newspaper editors in December 1948, Herrnstadt was taken to task for implying that the SED should remain independent of the CPSU. 'We are not creating the Bolshevik party', he had insisted, 'but a very specific German party of the new type under certain historical conditions.'[10] He had also called on communists to adopt a more sensitive and understanding approach towards former members of the SPD.[11] In May 1950, Ulbricht's wife Lotte launched an attack on *Neues Deutschland* for publishing articles that contradicted party resolutions.[12]

From the very beginning Zaisser and Herrnstadt's relationship with Ulbricht was one of mutual distrust. Although all three had spent the war in Moscow, Zaisser and Herrnstadt differed from Ulbricht in that they were not creatures of the KPD apparatus. Looking back in 1948–49, Herrnstadt was remarkably frank about the severity of his conflicts with other Soviet émigrés.[13] He was particularly scathing about Ulbricht, whom he dismissed as a 'half Bolshevik'.[14] In 1945, when the others returned to Berlin, Zaisser stayed behind in Krasnogorsk. 'I am not a member of the Pieckwieck Club', he is reported as saying: 'these comrades do not regard me as German, because I have always worked for the Soviet Union.' As one of them later testified, neither did he have much confidence in their ability to govern.[15]

Ulbricht personified the type of *apparatchik* whom Zaisser and Herrnstadt profoundly distrusted, a distrust exacerbated by Ulbricht's authoritarian leadership style. Apparently, Zaisser had already criticized these methods in Moscow during the war.[16] After being elected to the leadership, both men experienced at first hand how the general secretary suppressed free debate, arrogated power to himself and his inner circle and used the central committee secretariat[17] to undermine politburo resolutions.[18] Zaisser and Herrnstadt were not alone in their attempts to rein in Ulbricht's personality cult. In a letter to Pieck of 28 November 1951, Heinrich Rau protested at the manner in which the secretariat usurped the politburo by censoring his speech on economic affairs.[19] It is significant that Rau appealed to Pieck rather than Ulbricht for redress because, according to Vladimir Semyonov, Ulbricht's relations with the East German president were not what they should have been.[20] Neither could Fred Oelßner contain his indignation at the constant violation of the norms of collective leadership.[21]

Heinz Lippmann, a private aide to Erich Honecker, the chief of the Free German Youth (FDJ), provides further examples of Ulbricht's dictatorial leadership style. The most remarkable was his failure to consult the politburo before hastily approving the 'service for Germany corps' (a form of labour youth service) in July 1952. He also withheld the fact that the camps were equipped with Soviet heavy weaponry. When Ulbricht went away on vacation, the politburo sent a delegation to inspect the camps. It discovered such appalling conditions that a full investigation by the central party control commission was proposed. Zaisser, Schmidt, Jendretzky and Rau were particularly outspoken in their criticism. So overwhelming was the evidence of maladministration that even Ulbricht's supporters voted for the motion. Zaisser extended the attack to the directors of the society for sports and technology and the government committee for sports and physical culture. As a result, both these organizations were removed from Honecker's jurisdiction. The damning report was presented to Ulbricht on his return, only to be thrown into the wastebasket with the comment 'that's the way the Russian comrades wanted it.'[22] In the absence of any institutional checks and balances, the general secretary effectively abolished collective leadership in favour of one-man rule.

Between 1950 and 1953, Zaisser and Herrnstadt were persistent critics of this arbitrary regime. On 23 October 1951 (in Ulbricht's absence) Zaisser registered his objections to the politburo's 'style of working' and demanded a debate on the issue as soon as possible.[23] Ulbricht's return the following week ensured that it did not take place. Zaisser brought the matter up again on 5 February 1952. This time a politburo commission (consisting of Zaisser, Herrnstadt, Ulbricht and Oelßner) was established to study the problem and propose remedies.[24] In March 1952, Zaisser compiled the commission's final report. Its conclusions were a thorough indictment of Ulbricht's personal regime.[25] The adoption of a resolution safeguarding the politburo's collective authority seems to have had little effect.[26] In a statement to the central party control commission over a year later, Herrnstadt described Ulbricht's leadership style as a 'peculiarly Prussian form of sectarianism'.[27]

The question of Ulbricht's personality cult is related to the purges which rocked the SED elite between 1950 and 1953. As we have seen, Ulbricht used the show trials in Hungary and Czechoslovakia to consolidate his grip on power. New evidence suggests that Zaisser and Herrnstadt harboured misgivings about the charges levelled at Slansky and his alleged German accomplices. Zaisser was apparently unconvinced of Dahlem's guilt,[28] which might explain why the latter attempted to mobilize him as an ally.[29] If Ulbricht is to be believed, the minister for state security did not firmly rebuff these advances.[30] Two weeks after his own expulsion from the leadership in July 1953, Zaisser was accused of disputing the allegations against Slansky (with whom he had been closely associated in Moscow).[31] Herrnstadt too seems to have harboured doubts about the Dahlem case.[32] Other members of the politburo who may have been uneasy were Grotewohl,[33] Jendretzky[34] and Rau.[35] Pieck, being treated by doctors inside the USSR, did not participate in the campaign against Dahlem (whose pleading letters were intercepted on the grounds that the president was too ill to occupy himself with such matters).[36]

As a Jew, Herrnstadt had every reason to be fearful of the Slansky trial. New evidence has emerged that in early 1953 attempts were made to smear him as a 'Jewish agent'.[37] The West German newspaper *Die Zeit* even alleged that Herrnstadt was under investigation by the central party control commission for collaborating with the *Reichswehr* during the 1930s.[38]

But Zaisser and Herrnstadt did not confine their criticism to Ulbricht's dictatorial behaviour in the politburo. They also disagreed with the way the SED exercised its 'leading role' in society. As general secretary, Ulbricht headed the party organization. In this most centralized of political systems, the apeing of his methods by lower ranking party officials severely damaged the SED's standing with its own members and with the East German population at large. As Herrnstadt put it in January 1952: 'The party organization is guilty, from top to bottom. And the further up one goes the more guilty it gets!'[39] Two months later, Zaisser expressed these concerns more clearly:

> Instead of making the effort to consult and persuade, decisions are decreed and imposed (*angeordnet und kommandiert*). This method is damaging . . . and will

become very dangerous if it causes many of those in the middle ranks of the party apparatus who enthusiastically imitate this method, to force through and implement false decisions.[40]

By virtue of their respective positions as minister for state security and chief editor of *Neues Deutschland*, Zaisser and Herrnstadt were especially well placed to gauge the political mood in the party and country. For Herrnstadt, the SED's entire approach to government was flawed, underpinned as it was by methods of compulsion rather than persuasion. Already at a politburo meeting in October 1950, he had noted the need for a 'new party apparatus'.[41] A year later, he wrote an article lambasting the FDGB for failing to represent the interests of the workers. 'If the trade unions become a salvation army', he declared, 'they should sing in the street, not practise politics in the factories'. The party itself, in his view, was chiefly to blame for this situation.[42]

In early 1952, using *Neues Deutschland* as his mouthpiece, Herrnstadt declared war on 'dictatorial' party functionaries guilty of 'stifling the initiative of the masses' (as a result, Ernst Lohagen, SED leader in Saxony, was expelled from the central committee).[43] East German 'democracy', he wrote, was 'underdeveloped' when measured against the statutes of the party and laws of the republic.[44] At the eighth central committee plenum in February of that year, Herrnstadt dismissed concerns that the 'achievements' of the SED were being eclipsed by the wave of criticism from below: 'Everyone of us needs criticism, must demand it, must worry when it fails to materialize . . . He must see it as the indispensable help (*unerlässliche Hilfe*) that society and the party owe him.'[45] Ulbricht, however, withheld his full support, accusing Herrnstadt of waging an essentially negative campaign.[46] Herrnstadt wanted to reinvigorate the communes and district councils which had atrophied during the period of Stalinization. He also expressed anxiety that the bureaucracy might provoke strike action by imposing unacceptable factory work norms.[47] Ulbricht ignored these concerns and blocked implementation of the plenum resolutions.[48]

Herrnstadt, however, continued his crusade under a different guise. In the autumn of 1952, he redefined 'social democracy' as a form of theoretical dogmatism which prevented SED functionaries from tackling the real needs of working people.[49] This infuriated party propagandists such as Oelßner and Hager who now stood accused of parroting empty phrases which cemented the rift with the masses.[50]

Zaisser and Herrnstadt were also concerned by the SED's mistreatment of the bloc parties. Already in early 1949, Herrnstadt had been taken to task for arguing that the SED should 'march side by side' rather than 'ahead' of its 'bourgeois' partners.[51] He seemed to reiterate this position at a politburo meeting in January 1950.[52] Addressing the sixth central committee plenum in June 1951, Herrnstadt condemned the marginalization of the bloc parties and contested the view that their ranks were full of 'reactionaries'. The 'patriotic bourgeoisie', he insisted, 'were the natural allies of the SED against the American and German imperialists.'[53] This point of view was supported by Hans Jendretzky, who blamed communist 'sectarianism' for poor relations with other 'democratic forces'.[54] If we can believe the testimony of Hanna Wolf, a key Ulbricht supporter Zaisser spoke in a similar vein during the spring of 1953. Like the 'dictatorship of the bourgeoisie', he is reported as saying, the 'dictatorship of the proletariat' could permit other parties a share in power. The latter was indistinguishable from the 'anti-fascist democratic order' and did not have to be based exactly on the Soviet model.[55]

Zaisser must take ultimate responsibility for the serious crimes committed by the ministry for state security (MfS or *Stasi*) in the early 1950s. Until the uprising of 17 June 1953, however, the *Stasi* only employed around four thousand people[56] and was not yet the sprawling, all-pervasive apparatus of later years. In March 1952, Zaisser drew up proposals suggesting ways it could improve its work. The fact that the MfS had failed to win the full trust of the 'progressive population', he argued, could be attributed to three factors. First, its lack of contact with the masses; second, the arrogant behaviour of some of its officials; and third, its violations of 'democratic legality'. These 'serious deficiencies', he declared, were compounded by the inadequate training of staff. To remedy the situation, Zaisser instructed his employees to foster closer links with the people and respect the laws of the republic.[57] Herrnstadt later recalled Zaisser's concern that the ministry was not operating as it should have been.[58] According to him, Zaisser was 'the complete opposite of a dictator'[59], and this might explain why he was so ineffectual in his job. Nonetheless, the possibility that he helped ensure there were no show trials of purged SED leaders between 1950 and 1953 cannot be ruled out.

The growing rift with the population was exacerbated in July 1952 when the second party conference of the SED proclaimed the 'accelerated construction of socialism'. This entailed deliberately ostracizing the middle classes by prescribing a campaign against the private sector in trade and industry. The regime also inaugurated a ruthless collectivization campaign, forcing independent farmers into production co-operatives. Those who refused to join were subjected to state-enforced delivery quotas, causing many to leave for the West. Work norms were increased and consumer stocks reduced as priority was given to heavy industry. Reparations and Soviet-decreed militarization put an additional burden on the East German economy. In the political sphere, the traditional German *Länder* were abolished, the personality cult pushed to new extremes and the state apparatus (like the party before it) restructured according to Leninist principles. Increased control was established over the non-communist parties and the number of political trials and purges proliferated. Furthermore, the teaching of religion in schools was forbidden, students and teachers loyal to the Church were demoted and politically conspicuous priests arrested. Artists were forced to subscribe to 'socialist realism' and attempts were made to foist 'the leading role of the party' on educational institutions. An extremely brutal system of criminal justice intensified the 'class struggle', with even minor violations of the law, such as anti-regime statements or black-market purchases, punishable with long prison sentences. The imposition of this crash course in Sovietization united East

Germans against the SED, unleashed dangerous social tensions and deepened divisions with the West.

It was Ulbricht who persuaded Stalin to agree to this recasting of priorities. In March 1952, the SED politburo had approved an agenda for the second party conference which concentrated on 'the new tasks in the struggle for a peace treaty, German unification and national reconstruction.'[60] 'Socialism' had not even been mentioned. This was because, on 10 March, Stalin had made his famous offer of German reunification to the Western Powers. But once the Allies had rejected these overtures, Ulbricht took advantage of the situation to canvass his own programme. On 2 July 1952, with the full support of the politburo, he wrote to the Soviet dictator saying that it was time to begin building 'socialism' in the GDR.[61] On 8 July, just one day before the SED party conference, Stalin granted his consent.[62] Twenty-four hours later in Berlin, Ulbricht was given a rapturous reception when he announced the new agenda to astonished delegates. Stalin, however, seems to have been less than enthusiastic. In his telegram to the conference, he eschewed the term 'socialism' altogether and confined himself to wishing the party 'new successes' in the 'historical task of creating a united, independent, democratic and peace-loving Germany'.[63] Furthermore, Soviet officials broke with tradition and stayed away from the conference proceedings.[64]

Shortly thereafter, Semyonov claims to have written Stalin a personal letter criticizing Ulbricht for copying Soviet methods and ignoring the special conditions of the GDR.[65] Instead of rejecting the letter, Stalin allegedly invited Semyonov to join other members of the CPSU politburo at his dacha in October 1952. Here he undertook a character assessment of the SED leader. Ulbricht, he is reported as saying, was a loyal and trustworthy communist. Nonetheless, he was weak in the field of theory and 'when he laid his fist on the table it was sometimes bigger than his head.' It was a mark of the Soviet dictator's concern that he instructed Semyonov to help Ulbricht overcome these weaknesses.[66]

Zaisser and Herrnstadt, like the rest of the politburo, endorsed the radical swing to the left in July 1952.[67] As the country plunged deeper into crisis, however, Herrnstadt began urging moderation in certain areas. Although he was more active than Zaisser in this respect, the latter broadly sympathized with his aims.[68] Herrnstadt proposed that the SED finance a national programme of reconstruction to alleviate the plight of the workers. The plan, to be managed by district authorities, contained measures to raise living standards, mechanize plant, improve health and safety, cut bureaucracy, expand social provision and facilitate cultural awareness. Its declared aim was to unleash a popular movement for socio-economic and cultural regeneration.[69] Ulbricht, however, was unsympathetic and the project atrophied. Supported by Rau, Herrnstadt attempted to salvage what he could by promoting a house-building programme. But Ulbricht shelved this project too, on the grounds that all available funds were needed for heavy industry.[70] Throughout these months, Herrnstadt continued his crusade against dictatorial party functionaries and called for closer consultation with factory employees. Although he persuaded the politburo to establish a central committee commission to examine the decline in worker's wages, its findings were never reported.[71] Apparently, Oelßner was also concerned to point up the interests of the working class during this period.[72]

Neither was Herrnstadt blind to the interests of other social groups, apparently advocating a less repressive stance towards the intelligentsia and middle classes.[73] In early 1953, Ulbricht disregarded Soviet advice and began forcing the pace of collectivization.[74] The result was an unprecedented exodus of farmers to the West. Alarmed by this development, Herrnstadt raised the matter in the politburo. The general secretary, however, was vehemently opposed to any change of policy: 'I am not the representative of the big landowners', he is reported as saying.[75]

In a statement to the central party control commission one month before being expelled from the SED, Herrnstadt gave this summary of his disagreements with Ulbricht.

> Comrade Ulbricht underestimates the possibility that a dramatic improvement can be made by correcting certain aspects of our approach towards the working class and the other sections of working people in town and country; by establishing the right organizational forms for the development of patriotic initiative; and above all by satisfying the legitimate need of the working people to see that work has an impact on their living conditions.

Without such changes, Herrnstadt maintained, the SED and KPD could never attract the kind of mass support enjoyed by the communist parties in France and Italy.[76] Since he was desperately trying to avert expulsion from the party at this stage, he had little interest in exaggerating his differences with the SED general secretary.

By early 1953, the situation in the GDR was approaching a state of civil war. Fifteen to twenty thousand East Germans a month were fleeing the country. In February or March of that year, 'a group of functionaries connected to the SED central committee and GDR government' compiled a report analysing the situation in the country and warning of dire consequences if existing policies were continued.[77] Ulbricht, however, dismissed their concerns and resorted to increased repression against the East German population. Else Zaisser, wife of the politburo member and minister for education at the time, later recalled some of the worst excesses. There was, for example, the party's constant interference in the affairs of government, which had even resulted in ministerial decrees being annulled without the knowledge of ministers. Then there were Ulbricht's rabid measures in the field of education, all of which she had tried to resist: the sudden termination of transport subsidies for poor children; the replacement of the traditional twelve-class secondary school with its Soviet equivalent; the closing of christian children's homes; the mass expulsions of 'politically unreliable' students and teachers.[78]

At the end of 1952, Ulbricht appealed to the Soviets for financial and material aid. The request went unanswered. Grotewohl tried again at Stalin's funeral in

March 1953 and at the beginning of April there was another appeal. On 15 April, Moscow sent a negative reply and advised the SED to adopt a softer line.[79] At the same time, the Soviet deputy planning chief, Nikitin, arrived in the GDR with news that the Kremlin was planning a 'New Course'.[80] He recommended that the party moderate its economic policies with a view to improving living standards. Ulbricht, however, decided to ignore these warnings. Already on 9 April he had authorized the council of ministers to withdraw food-rationing cards for two million people.[81] On 1 May Hans Jendretzky wrote a speech based on the Soviet and British prime minister's proposals to ease international tensions.[82] Although the draft was formally approved by Herrnstadt, it was condemned by Ulbricht for failing to mention the construction of socialism in the GDR.[83] Two weeks later, the central committee increased factory work norms by 10 per cent,[84] stoking the fires of discontent still further.

Throughout the period 1948 to 1953, Herrnstadt never lost sight of the goal of national reunification. In December 1948 he attempted to extol the all-German perspective by maintaining that the emphasis of the class struggle was in the western zones.[85] Herrnstadt recognized that the GDR was a temporary entity and that in the long run 'socialism in half a country' was doomed to failure. As he put it in October 1951: 'We have one leg over the mountain. If we don't drag the other one over too, we will lose everything.'[86]

At the third central committee plenum in October 1950, Herrnstadt warmly welcomed the recently proclaimed 'Prague resolutions', which proposed an all-German constituent council as a first step on the road to forming a provisional government. He also endorsed the fact that the Soviet offer eschewed the term 'German Democratic Republic' in the interests of creating a climate conducive to negotiations. Following the line laid down in Prague, he advised the SED to concentrate its attacks on the 'American imperialists' instead of the federal government in Bonn. Significantly, he censured those in the party who refused to countenance concessions: 'Many of us would do well to free themselves from the undialectical idea that the future united, democratic Germany will simply be an enlarged copy of the present German Democratic Republic.'[87]

Ackermann criticized the party's tendency to concentrate on domestic issues at the expense of the struggle for peace and reunification. Like Herrnstadt, he rejected the idea that a reunified Germany could be a replica of the GDR. He also refused to rule out the possibility of negotiations with Konrad Adenauer, on the grounds that his government was supported by the majority of West Germans. The SED, he declared, should avoid setting preconditions which might impede moves towards rapprochement.[88] Ulbricht, however, only paid lip service to the Prague resolutions.[89] Following their announcement on 20 and 21 October 1950, Grotewohl began to steal the limelight and the general secretary was forced to take a back seat.

Stalin made his offer a month after the three Western Powers had met in New York to lay the foundations for an integrated security system to include the Federal Republic. He feared the consequences of a remilitarized West Germany and wanted to prevent its entry into a Western military alliance.[90] At some point between 1951 and 1952, Pieck and Grotewohl apparently told the leader of the Italian Socialists, Pietro Nenni that 'policies being pursued by the Soviet government were ones which would call for great sacrifice from them and that they might soon be forced into a position in Germany comparable to that of Nenni in Italy, by which they presumably meant that of a left-wing minority in a parliamentary system.'[91] As can be seen from this third hand testimony, others later put their own interpretation on Pieck and Grotewohl's alleged remarks, thereby distorting their actual significance. Stalin may well have been prepared to sacrifice the GDR and the SED's monopoly on power, but only if Germany was reunited as a 'democratic' and 'peace-loving' state on the basis of the Potsdam Agreement. According to the Soviet interpretation, this meant ensuring that Germany was led by a government committed to the dismantling of monopoly capitalism. Moreover, the proposed all-German constituent council had to be composed equally of representatives from the GDR and Federal Republic (with those from the former being nominated by the SED), thus over-representing the smaller East Germany and ensuring that it could block any measures which did not suit its agenda. Finally, the proposals foresaw the establishment of an all-German provisional government *before* the holding of free elections, thereby allowing the communists to influence their outcome.

As we have seen, Herrnstadt harboured misgivings about Ulbricht's policies towards West Germany. Addressing the fifth central committee plenum in March 1951, he criticized party leaders for underestimating the struggle for 'peace and national unity'.[92] In his closing speech, Ulbricht barely mentioned the fact that the SED was about to embark on a referendum to foil remilitarization and facilitate the signing of a peace treaty.[93] Grotewohl, however, supported Herrnstadt in his attempts to make this the central issue.[94] Addressing the central committee three months later, Herrnstadt blamed the sectarianism of the SED for inhibiting the 'peace movement' in Germany.[95]

In October 1951, Herrnstadt dismissed the idea that the GDR could ever become a 'People's Democracy' like its East European allies. 'People's Democracy', he declared, would lead to socialism. The task of the GDR, however, was very different: to build an 'anti-fascist-democratic' order in preparation for a 'united, democratic Fatherland'.[96] If one compares these comments with those of Ulbricht as early as 1947,[97] a fundamental difference of opinion may be discerned. Writing to Stalin on 2 July 1952, Ulbricht described East Germany as a 'People's Democracy' ready for the transition to socialism.[98] In a politburo meeting on 6 June 1953, Herrnstadt recalled his anxiety that the resolutions of the second party conference might jeopardize attempts to find a peaceful solution to the German question.[99] As the 'accelerated construction of socialism' reached its climax in May 1953, Herrnstadt criticized the National Front for failing to mobilize the masses in favour of national reunification.[100]

On 10 March 1952, Stalin sent a 'note' to the Western Powers offering to sign a peace treaty with a reunited Germany. The country would now be permitted its own defence forces. Instead of being condemned to total neutrality she would only be forbidden from joining military alliances against those Powers who had defeated her in World War Two. Demands for denazification, reparations and 'economic democratization' were also dropped, although they had been included in the original drafts[101] and would probably have been brought up later in negotiations. Potential stumbling blocks included a ban on parties and organizations 'hostile to peace and democracy' (open to broad interpretation) and a commitment to the Oder–Neisse Line as the country's eastern border. An all-German government would be established to negotiate the peace treaty, but there was no mention of free elections, reflecting the low priority accorded to them by the USSR. The stated aim of the offer was to create conditions 'conducive to the development of Germany as a united, independent, democratic and peace-loving state in accordance with the Potsdam decisions'.[102]

The idea for the March 1952 note came from the Soviet foreign ministry. According to deputy Soviet foreign minister Andrei Gromyko, such an initiative would 'strengthen the struggle for peace and against remilitarization of West Germany' and 'help advocates of Germany's unity and of peace to unmask the three Western Powers' aggressive intentions'.[103] Writing to Stalin on 28 January 1952, Gromyko declared that the time had come 'to support the democratic forces in Germany in their struggle for reunification and a speedy conclusion of a peace treaty'.[104]

In response to Western objections, Stalin issued a second note on 9 April, declaring himself in favour of all-German free elections supervised by a Four Power commission. This time he did not insist on German representation. Western demands for UN supervision, however, were rejected, thereby ensuring that elections in the GDR would be run by the SED. The Soviet control commission then instructed the GDR foreign ministry to draw up plans for separate elections in both parts of Germany to a national assembly.[105] These elections would not, of course, have been free and fair. Those staged in the GDR in 1950 had proscribed competition between parties, yet were described by communist propaganda as the most democratic ever held in Germany. The communists clearly intended to mobilize the GDR mass organizations to bolster SED support. Significantly, the draft electoral law drawn up by the *Volkskammer* (the East German parliament) in 1952 contained a number of safeguards to ensure that the SED retained power.[106]

Stalin's offer seems to have been prompted by the imminent integration of the Federal Republic into an anti-communist military alliance (the European Defence Community). On 26 and 27 May the Bonn and Paris Treaties were due to be signed, setting in motion plans to integrate its armed forces into a unified West European army. In return, the West would grant virtual sovereignty to the government in Bonn. Stalin's offer was designed to prevent all this happening and advance the cause of socialism in Germany. Clearly, Stalin did not envisage negotiating with the conservative government of Konrad Adenauer. Instead he hoped to galvanize the Left and other pro-reunification forces in the Federal Republic to elect a new government willing to negotiate with the Soviets. At a minimum, Stalin could win a spectacular propaganda victory and increase support for the communists by posing as the champion of German reunification. At the maximum, Stalin hoped to achieve his medium-term objective of a united, 'democratic' and 'peace-loving' Germany with draconian restrictions on monopoly capitalism. This view is supported by Daniel Melnikov, who claims to have been one of the note's authors.[107]

The Western Powers rejected the Soviet offer on 25 March. But before Stalin made his offer of 'free elections' on 9 April, he told the SED to 'organize [its] own state' and begin building an East German army. Meeting with Pieck, Ulbricht and Grotewohl on 7 April, he is recorded as saying that: 'Irrespective of any proposals that we can make on the German question the Western Powers will not agree with them . . . It would be a mistake to think that a compromise might emerge or that the Americans will agree with the draft of a peace treaty . . . the Americans need their army in West Germany to hold Western Europe in their hands.'[108]

The Western Powers also rejected Stalin's offer of 9 April, insisting on UN supervision of elections and Germany's freedom to join military alliances. On 26 and 27 May 1952, Adenauer signed the Bonn and Paris Treaties. The 'battle of the notes' continued throughout the summer, but it took on an increasingly perfunctory character. The third Soviet note of May 1952 insisted that in working out a peace treaty with Germany, both its provisional government and the four occupation powers be guided by the conditions of the Potsdam Agreement.[109] The fourth Soviet note of 23 August set out very clearly the conditions under which it would allow 'free elections' to take place.

> As regards the inspection of Germany with the aim of determining the existence of conditions for the holding of all-German free elections, it is self-evident that the first task is to determine to what extent the decisions of the Potsdam Conference are being fulfilled. The realization of these decisions constitutes the condition for really free all-German elections and the formation of an all-German government representing the will of the German people.[110]

By this time, of course, Stalin had allowed Ulbricht to proclaim the 'accelerated construction of socialism' in the GDR.

In spite of this, the Soviet leadership did not give up all hope of achieving its aims in Germany. Stalin's medium-term agenda was referred to again by the deputy Soviet prime minister, Georgi Malenkov, at the fourteenth party congress of the CPSU in October 1952: 'In accordance with the Potsdam Agreement, the Soviet Union is tirelessly pursuing policies aimed at the speedy conclusion of a peace treaty . . . the withdrawal of all occupation troops . . . and the creation of a united, independent, peace-loving and democratic Germany.'[111] Stalin used the same language in a congratulation telegram to Grotewohl marking the third anniversary of the GDR. Significantly, the word 'socialism' did not appear at all, despite the resolutions of the second party conference three months earlier.[112]

How did the SED leadership react to these Soviet initiatives? Although it was consulted about and accepted Stalin's plan, it had reasons to fear the possible consequences. East German officials vainly sought Soviet reassurance that the proposed conclusion of a peace treaty was merely a tactical diversion to complicate the planned transfer of power to Bonn by the West.[113] The future of the SED's monopoly on power would have been placed in doubt had the Western Powers decided to explore Stalin's offer. After all, a united, 'democratic' and 'peace-loving' Germany would not have been an exact replica of the GDR.

The SED, of course, tried to put a brave face on things. On 25 March 1952, the politburo met to discuss a plan of action and reached the following conclusion: 'The answer to the question of what a united Germany will look like is: However the German people decide. All-German democratic elections will inevitably lead to the fall of Adenauer because in West Germany too the patriotic and democratic forces are gaining strength daily.'[114] The same meeting approved a letter from the district SED leadership in East Berlin to social democrats in the western part of the city, calling for mutual co-operation in the event of all-German elections to a National Assembly.[115]

Different shades of opinion were concealed behind the optimistic facade of 25 March. Ulbricht seems to have adopted a lukewarm position to the Stalin note and, in any case, had already derided the idea of a neutral Germany in 1950.[116] During March and early April, it was Grotewohl who dominated the pages of *Neues Deutschland*.[117] For a few weeks in March 1952, Ulbricht did not appear at all and then only as deputy prime minister. It was only after the second Soviet note of 9 April that he was referred to again as general secretary.[118] Interviewed in 1992, Kurt Hager insisted that the SED had been willing to sacrifice its monopoly on power in return for 'proper enforcement of the Potsdam Agreement'.[119] Oelßner regarded reunification as impossible unless both sides made concessions. A coming-together of the two German states, he declared, did not necessarily mean dismantling the economic structure of the GDR. Since the communist system had permitted a degree of private enterprise after 1945 it was capable of co-existing for a time with capitalist forces in the West.[120] In his speech to the fifteenth central committee plenum in July 1953, he conceded that policy towards West Germany had been a source of considerable conflict in the politburo.[121]

New documents contain the testimonies of five of Zaisser's former private aides which allege that the minister for state security seriously believed in the prospect of all-German free elections during the spring and early summer of 1952 – elections he admitted the SED would lose. The Soviet Union, he is quoted as saying, was primarily interested in maintaining world peace and might, therefore, consider making far-reaching concessions to expedite German reunification.[122] The problem with this evidence is that it was submitted in August 1953 at a time when the SED was denouncing Zaisser and Herrnstadt as 'enemies of the people'. Zaisser himself denied making the remarks during an interrogation by the central party control commission a month later.[123]

The evidence points to the existence of significant conflict in the SED leadership between 1950 and May 1953.[124] Ulbricht's adherence to a particularly sectarian form of Stalinist politics and the consequences of this for national reunification and the SED's credibility as the leading force in East German society brought him into conflict with a number of politburo colleagues. Zaisser and Herrnstadt were the most persistent of his critics and would be made to pay dearly in the months ahead.

Opposition, June–July 1953

On 22 April 1953, Vladmir Semyonov, political adviser to the Soviet control commission, was recalled to Moscow for consultations. Here he organized the drafting of various memoranda on the German question within the Soviet foreign ministry's 'third European department' (Germany and Austria). Molotov's foreign ministry officials wanted to seize the initiative by making a new offer to the West on reunification and extending economic aid to East Germany. This entailed a proposal to establish a provisional government composed of the two German parliaments, to be followed by 'free elections' and the withdrawal of all occupation troops. To bolster the international position of the GDR, they suggested transforming the Soviet control commission into a high commission on German affairs and upgrading the East German and Soviet missions in Moscow and Berlin to the status of embassies.[125]

According to one foreign ministry document, the aim was to 'increase the influence of the Soviet Union in the German population', prevent the 'militarization and fascistization' of the Federal Republic, revoke the Bonn and Paris Treaties and 'strengthen the movement of democratic forces for the reunification of Germany'.[126] In an internal statement of 5 May, Semyonov defined the objective as the establishment of a 'democratic and peace-loving Germany' on the basis of the Potsdam Agreement.[127]

While Molotov was drawing up proposals to strengthen East Germany in preparation for eventual reunification on terms favourable to the Soviets, Lavrentii Beria was allegedly preparing to abandon the GDR altogether.[128] In 1993 Pavel Sudoplatov, head of the 'bureau for special tasks' in Beria's interior ministry, testified to the latter's plan to exchange German unity for an extended reparations programme of ten billion dollars. East Germany, Beria reasoned, was a burden on Soviet economic resources. Rather than the Kremlin funding an illusory project to construct socialism in the GDR, a reunited Germany could help rebuild the Soviet Union.[129] This would explain his close interest in an analysis of the SPD's position on the national question conducted by the Soviet advisory committee on German affairs during the spring of 1953.[130]

Apart from Sudoplatov, only Zoya Rybkina, head of the ministry's German section, knew about the alleged plan. Molotov, one of Beria's main rivals in the leadership, was not to be informed until after the operation had got under way. The Soviet-German actress, Olga Chekhova and the Polish politician Prince

Janusz Radziwill were apparently appointed as emissaries. The former, experienced in foreign intelligence work, was to take soundings from close associates of Adenauer. Radziwill, who had agreed to work for Beria in exchange for his release from captivity, was instructed to use his extensive contacts in the United States to canvass support for the aid package. The Soviet interior minister allegedly foresaw Germany's reunification with a coalition government under Four Power auspices.[131] According to Sudoplatov, Beria wanted the GDR to become an autonomous province inside a unified German state.[132] In the absence of any corroborating archival evidence, however, there are doubts about the authenticity of this testimony.

Both these initiatives must be viewed in the context of the Kremlin's fear of instability following Stalin's death. At the latter's funeral in March, Molotov, Malenkov and Beria had all spoken in favour of peaceful coexistence. In the ensuing months the USSR renounced all territorial claims on Turkey, re-established diplomatic relations with Yugoslavia and Israel and ended the Korean War. On 11 May Winston Churchill proposed an international conference to resolve the German question. Despite American opposition, the British prime minister did not rule out the country's reunification as a neutral state.[133] According to one observer, Churchill's call for negotiations with the USSR was inspired by suggestions from Beria.[134]

On 27 May the Soviet presidium met to discuss the situation in the GDR. We do not know precisely what happened at this meeting because the transcript of its deliberations remains classified in the presidential archive in Moscow. Until it is made available, we are compelled to rely on the retrospective testimony of those who attended. While the majority claim to have favoured merely slackening the pace of socialist development, Beria is said to have proposed a united, 'bourgeois' and neutral Germany.[135] Apparently, the Soviet prime minister, Malenkov, was also initially sympathetic to this idea.[136] As Molotov later recalled, Beria kept insisting that 'it made no difference whether Germany was socialist or otherwise . . . the most important concern was that Germany be peaceful.'[137] According to Gromyko, who was also present, Beria exclaimed: 'What does it amount to, this GDR? It's not even a real state. It's only kept in being by Soviet troops, even if we do call it the "German Democratic Republic".'[138] Writing to Malenkov from his prison cell on 1 July 1953, however, Beria would only plead guilty to 'inadmissible rudeness and insolence' towards Nikita Khrushchev and Nikolai Bulganin 'during the discussion on the German question'.[139] Whatever the substance of the divisions, a decision could not be reached at this meeting and the matter was referred to a special committee. Beria was then forced to compromise,[140] although he is said to have secretly pushed ahead with his plan for Germany's reunification as a 'bourgeois-democratic' and neutral state.[141] Next day, he fretted to Soviet defence minister Bulganin about the danger Germany might pose if it were not neutralized and suggested that some presidium members be removed from the government to facilitate this.[142]

At the beginning of June, Ulbricht, Grotewohl and Oelßner were summoned to Moscow to be informed of the necessity for a New Course in their country. Perhaps it was a reflection of the continuing divisions in the CPSU presidium that the instructions handed to them by the Soviet leadership amounted to more than a rejection of the 'accelerated construction of socialism' in the GDR. Many of the measures introduced in the wake of the second party conference were either discontinued or reversed completely. The result was an unprecedented U-turn across the entire spectrum of policy. With regard to the economy, satisfaction of consumer needs replaced the emphasis on heavy industry, restrictions on private capital were lifted and the collectivization of agriculture abandoned. In the political sphere, measures were announced to guarantee civil rights, restore the position of the middle classes and intelligentsia, correct abuses by the Soviet occupation authorities, strengthen the role of the bloc parties and mass organisations and end the campaign against the Church. All propaganda about the necessity for socialism in the GDR was condemned as inappropriate. The creation of a 'united, democratic, peace-loving and independent Germany' was proclaimed as the *raison d'être* of the New Course. In the light of this it was deemed necessary to adopt a more conciliatory attitude towards the SPD and sign a peace treaty with the Allies.[143]

Grotewohl took handwritten notes of the talks in Moscow on 3 June. The beleaguered SED representatives were ordered to prepare a document based on a Soviet blueprint proclaiming the need for a change in direction. Their attempt was rejected by the Soviet presidium for being insufficiently radical in tone. Beria is said to have thrown it at Ulbricht across the table with the words: 'This is a bad rehash of our document!'[144] Kaganovich was milder in his criticism: 'Our document represents real change (*Wendung*), your's reform'. Molotov emphasized the all-German perspective: 'Correct all these errors so that the whole of Germany sees it.' The seriousness and urgency of Soviet intentions was summed up by Malenkov: 'if we fail to put things right now, there will be a catastrophe'.[145]

Meanwhile in Berlin, Hermann Axen, central committee secretary for agitation, received a coded telegram from Ulbricht and Grotewohl ordering the instant cessation of all propaganda pertaining to the construction of socialism in the GDR. Instead, the party was to begin working for the creation of a 'united, democratic and peace-loving Germany'. Axen, stunned by this sudden turn of events, vacillated before sending out the new instructions. Herrnstadt, however, is said to have unconditionally welcomed the change of policy.[146]

Ulbricht, Grotewohl and Oelßner returned to Berlin and reported to the politburo on 6 June. Although all its members formally declared their 'support' for the *volte-face* (it could hardly have been otherwise given Moscow's position), the old dichotomy between Ulbricht and his critics now became a battle between advocates and adversaries of the New Course. Ulbricht apportioned much of the blame for the crisis to Bonn.[147] Zaisser, by contrast, endorsed a radical break with the past: '*Total* change necessary, a change not seen since 1918.'[148] He expressed deep disappointment with the general secretary, blamed him for the East German debacle and lambasted his dictatorship over the party: 'Party democracy', he complained, 'only exists on paper.'[149] Fritz Ebert complained that he was being deliberately marginalized on account of his earlier membership of the SPD.[150] Herrnstadt condemned the loss of contact with the masses and railed against methods of 'naked administration' in the party apparatus.[151] The SED, he declared, had to become a 'party of the people'.[152] Grotewohl condemned the 'personality cult', 'agent psychosis', violations of intra-party democracy and the failure to respond to the needs of the population.[153] Semyonov, the new Soviet high commissioner in East Germany, stressed the radical nature of the New Course: 'Do away with the *old* measures and replace them with *new* ones!' The main task, he said, was to prepare the country for reunification. Only by becoming 'a magnetic field for West Germany, France and Italy'[154] could the GDR preserve some of its accomplishments in a reunited German state.

The politburo endorsed the New Course[155] in all its aspects except one. The Soviet instructions were strangely ambiguous on the issue of collective farms, hinting at the existence of conflict in the CPSU leadership.[156] On the one hand they seemed to support retaining viable collectives, or agricultural production co-operatives (LPGs), on the other to demand their wholesale destruction. Herrnstadt opposed the disbanding of those LPG's which were both 'viable' and 'voluntary'.[157] He succeeded in winning the rest of the politburo over to this position. This is significant because it casts doubt on the assumption that Herrnstadt was working in conjunction with Beria[158] to depose Ulbricht during the summer of 1953. It was Beria, after all, who is said to have pushed for the dissolution of the collective farms, causing the split in the CPSU presidium.[159] Herrnstadt was then delegated the task of drafting the politburo communiqué announcing the New Course. His plea to Semyonov for a two-week postponement to prepare the population for the drastic changes was rebuffed. 'In fourteen days', the Soviet high commissioner is reported as saying, 'you might not have a state any more.'[160]

Contemporaries underestimated just how seriously the SED took the New Course when it was announced on 11 June 1953. Heinz Brandt, secretary for agitation and propaganda in the district leadership of Berlin, later testified to the shell-shock of many comrades, especially those in Ulbricht's entourage. Others, however, rejoiced in the prospect of German reunification, believing that in the new 'democratic' state, a rejuvenated SPD would co-operate with a free and independent trade union movement to prevent a conservative restoration.[161] Hans Jendretzky, member of the politburo and head of the district SED leadership in Berlin, was overjoyed by the sudden turn of events and predicted an imminent agreement between the Allies: 'I have the best news in the world', he told Brandt, 'we are starting out afresh and with respect to the whole of Germany. It is the greatest turning point in the history of the party . . .'[162] Herrnstadt appealed to the two German states to emulate the Korean example and start negotiating.[163] His politburo communiqué proclaiming the New Course defined the priority as the 're-establishment of German unity' and called on both sides to take the necessary steps to facilitate rapprochement. Measures were announced to relax controls not only on the movement of people and goods within Berlin but between the two parts of Germany. Artists and scientists were permitted to attend conferences in the Federal Republic and their Western counterparts allowed to enter the GDR.[164] Responding to the new Soviet emphasis on German reunification, the SED drew up a detailed plan for the various parties and mass organizations in the event of all-German elections.[165] When President Pieck addressed the country in late June and early July, his main themes were national reunification, free elections and a peace treaty with the Allies.[166]

The perceptions of SED leaders were based on a plethora of statements from the Soviets themselves. On 13 June, *Tägliche Rundschau*, the newspaper of the Soviet occupation forces in Germany, published a leading article emphasizing the 'international significance of the New Course'. The intention, it declared, was to facilitate 'decisive progress in the struggle for the peaceful reunification of Germany' as a 'united, sovereign and economically powerful . . . democratic state'.[167] The position of the SED general secretary also began to look precarious, with Semyonov insisting that Ulbricht cancel grandiose plans to celebrate his sixtieth birthday. Instead, he was advised to follow Lenin's example by inviting 'a few guests in for the evening'.[168] If Sudoplatov is to be believed, Beria, Malenkov and Khrushchev favoured removing Ulbricht as party leader.[169]

Ulbricht became increasingly isolated in the politburo as he attempted to impede the introduction of the New Course. He was particularly sceptical about its central mission: the reunification of Germany. As Herrnstadt recalled three years later, Ulbricht and large parts of the party organization remained unconvinced 'that there was any real prospect of Germany being democratically united through the reduction of Cold War tensions'.[170] Fearing the consequences for his leadership and a reopening of the Dahlem affair, Ulbricht refused to call an extraordinary central committee plenum to discuss the dramatic reversal in policy.

The dichotomy between those members of the SED leadership who interpreted the New Course as a strategic departure and those who perceived it merely in terms of a temporary retreat became more obvious as the days went by. In a draft resolution for the fourteenth central committee plenum submitted to the politburo on 13 June, Herrnstadt allied himself firmly with the former. Describing the New Course as a long term strategy rather than as a tactical ruse, he lambasted the party's 'administrative methods' and 'disregard for the masses'. He also condemned its sectarianism and dismissive attitude towards the bloc parties. The cause of socialism, he declared, had been discredited by erroneous policies towards the farmers, intelligentsia and urban middle classes. It was time to start regarding the refugees from these social groups as a loss to the republic. He also called for the development of 'democracy' within the FDGB, including the election of officials not necessarily affiliated to any political party. Significantly, his plea for the re-election of the entire trade union leadership was deleted by Ulbricht. The intelligentsia, Herrnstadt argued, should be permitted to form their own, smaller organizations. The SED had to exercise its leading role in a manner which did not increase bureaucracy and duplicate decisions. This meant interfering less in the day-to-day affairs of other institutions. Many of the party's measures, he maintained, had harmed the very people it claimed to represent. Initiative from below and methods of persuasion had to replace dictatorship and intimidation from above.[171]

The ten per cent increase in factory work norms decreed on 14 May (a key factor in unleashing the uprising of 17 June) had been left untouched by the New Course. On 14 June, Herrnstadt sanctioned an article in *Neues Deutschland* attacking norm hikes imposed without the consent of the workers.[172] Two days later, as strikes got underway in Berlin, it was apparently Herrnstadt and Jendretzky who proposed rescinding the May resolution.[173] By the time the politburo granted its consent[174] it was too late.

The popular uprising of 17 June rocked East Germany to its foundations and, were it not for Soviet tanks, the Ulbricht regime would have collapsed, destroying the SED in its wake.[175] Over 500,000 people marched against the government and the demonstrations eventually engulfed more than 350 cities and villages in the GDR.[176] On 16 June, as reports began coming in of workers' unrest, the majority of the politburo united against Ulbricht. Even Honecker is said to have toyed with the idea of abandoning his mentor to save his political career.[177] Symptomatic of Ulbricht's plight is a resolution further restricting plans to celebrate his sixtieth birthday.[178] That evening Grotewohl and Ulbricht addressed a meeting of party activists in Berlin. Unlike the general secretary, the former put much of the blame for past mistakes on to the SED leadership.[179] Next day, as the East German uprising reached its climax, Semyonov personally took over the running of politburo affairs, incarcerating the SED leaders in Soviet headquarters where they were forced to witness events in helpless dismay.[180]

In a *Neues Deutschland* editorial of 18 June, Herrnstadt gave two reasons for the popular rebellion: the operations of western provocateurs and the 'serious failings' of the party.[181] By implication, he was contesting Ulbricht's version of 17 June as little more than a 'fascist putsch attempt'.[182] On 19 June, Herrnstadt described the events of the previous two days as a watershed. The activities of all sectors of public life since 1945 would now have to be subjected to rigorous criticism. In future, he wrote, the party would have to behave in a more just and sensitive way towards the people it claimed to represent. It was also necessary to adopt a more 'decisive' position in the struggle for peace and German unity. This meant continuing policies proclaimed on 11 June such as the opening of the border with the Federal Republic and the sectoral boundaries within Berlin. Unless these steps were followed through, Herrnstadt maintained, the two parts of Germany would never be reconciled.[183]

On 21 June, with the uprising still raging in some parts of the country, numbed SED functionaries convened for an extraordinary central committee plenum. The session, which had been summoned earlier that day,[184] was delayed while the politburo debated Herrnstadt's draft resolution.[185] Ulbricht wanted to concentrate on denouncing the 'imperialist coup attempt' (known as 'Day X') but Herrnstadt was more interested in defending the New Course. Ulbricht's critics seem to have prevailed on this occasion but, according to Jendretzky, Herrnstadt had to fight long and hard for inclusion of the sentence 'when masses of workers do not understand the party, then the party is guilty not the workers!'[186] In the end, the central committee meeting, which had been scheduled for 10pm, did not get under way until shortly before midnight.[187] Significantly, it was Grotewohl, not Ulbricht who chaired the proceedings. Apart from delivering the closing speech, he also presented the politburo's report which paid more attention to the SED's own failings than the machinations of foreign intelligence agencies. The re-establishment of German unity, he declared, remained the party's first objective. By alienating the population, however, the SED was jeopardizing its chances of fulfilment. He also warned against indulging in an orgy of retribution.'[188]

Former social democrat Otto Buchwitz gave the most vivid description of the atmosphere in the central committee: 'We are sitting here like the defeated! . . . What is the matter with the highest organ of our party? It is as if we have done something in our pants!'[189] The stenographic verbatim minutes reveal a difference of opinion between diehard advocates of the 'imperialist X-Day' theory and those who also blamed the party for the debacle. Criticizing the politburo for not convening a central committee meeting immediately after the proclamation of the New Course, Buchwitz deplored the failure to sanction a more detailed discussion of recent events – a protest Ulbricht tried to ignore.[190] Ackermann, however, broke ranks and seconded Buchwitz. The party, he said, had landed itself in a situation worse than anything inflicted on it in the past. The leadership would have to account for its mistakes. Questions needed to be asked about the unhealthy atmosphere in the central committee and the lack of collective leadership at all levels.[191]

Kurt Hager criticized the central committee resolution for understating the extent of popular disaffection: 'That is not simply ill-feeling, but a lack of confidence in us. We have not won over [the masses]. One cannot be blind to this fact.' In the party, he said, there was much to criticize, starting with the working methods of the central committee right down to the lowest factory organization. He also mocked the passage in the resolution accusing the West of exploiting the workers' demands to ensure a long-term decline in GDR living standards. In the eyes of the workers, he declared, things could hardly be worse than they already were.[192]

Willi Stoph, a member of Ulbricht's central committee secretariat, adopted a different tone, criticizing the lack of vigilance among party members. In a swipe at Zaisser's ministry for state security, he demanded to know how such a putsch could be organized without anybody noticing.[193] Oelßner, who had been one of Ulbricht's sharpest critics in the leadership, began to lean towards a hard line interpretation of events. There would be time later, he said, to discuss the party's shortcomings. The priority now was to defeat the enemy. Adamant that the uprising was a well-organized fascist provocation, he called for public trials of 'imperialist provocateurs'.[194]

After the fourteenth central committee plenum, members of the politburo were sent out to address the workers in the factories. Herrnstadt struck up a rapport with the strikers at Siemens, eventually bringing them around to a more conciliatory point of view. Avoiding the term 'fascist putsch', he merely referred to a network of western agents across the country.[195] Ackermann attributed the poor relationship between party and people to the SED's 'administrative' style of leadership.[196] Wilhelm Pieck, still in Moscow, enthusiastically endorsed the resolution of the fourteenth central committee plenum and condemned the rift between the trade unions and the workforce.[197] In a radio broadcast on 3 July, he admitted that some of the workers' demands were justified.[198] Ulbricht, by contrast, preferred to rail against subversive influences and received a hostile reception from factory employees. By comparing the New Course to Lenin's New Economic Policy (NEP) in the Soviet Union during the 1920s,[199] he also revealed his opposition to many of the policies announced in early June. A combination of economic liberalization and political repression, the NEP had been conceived as a temporary retreat from socialism. It was very different from the New Course which aimed to inaugurate a prolonged period of socio-economic, political and cultural liberalization to create the conditions for German reunification. The theme of inter-German rapprochement, neglected by Ulbricht, was addressed by Ebert and Grotewohl.[200]

The consensus has always been that Ulbricht was able to consolidate his position in the immediate aftermath of the revolt, claiming the need to close the Pandora's box of grievances opened by the New Course.[201] The uprising, so the conventional wisdom goes, persuaded Moscow to retain Ulbricht because to drop him would have been tantamount to surrender.[202] The evidence, however, does not wholly support this claim.

On 23 June, the Soviets wrote a letter to the SED leadership demanding the immediate implementation of measures to win the support of the masses.[203] A day later Vladimir Semyonov, Pavel Yudin[204] and Colonel General V. D. Sokolovskii[205], sent a report to the Kremlin assessing the recent disturbances and proposing remedies. Ulbricht was heavily criticized and his future as general secretary called into question. Described as 'the initiator' and 'primary author of the policy to increase output norms', he was blamed for ignoring the sporadic strikes and 'sloppily' implementing Soviet-inspired directives urging moderation.[206] Semyonov, Yudin and Sokolovskii recommended that Ulbricht be relieved of his duties as deputy prime minister and that the position of general secretary be abolished, to be replaced with several central committee secretariat posts.[207]

The report also advised that the New Course be carried out 'firmly and consistently' in accordance with the Soviet resolutions of 6 June. In view of the SED's monopoly on government and administration, it was considered necessary to separate the functions of the GDR government and SED central committee, giving the latter 'the power of oversight on solely the most important questions

of the state and its citizenry'. From now on, the attention of the central committee had to be focused on 'carrying out political campaigns among the populace
and on smoothening out intra-party operations by introducing broader intra-
party democracy, criticism, and self-criticism from top to bottom'.

It was also considered necessary to 'reorganize the government of the GDR
with the goal of strengthening and reducing the size of [the] government apparatus' and transforming the *Volkskammer* into 'an active parliament . . . that
would debate and legislate the laws of the Republic, establish commissions,
debate inquiries and demands voiced by its deputies, etc.' In future, any resolutions that were 'in effect laws' would be declared null and void unless they were
first approved by parliament. There was also a proposal to convene an extraordinary session of the *Volkskammer* so that the government could report on its
past mistakes and appoint 'more popular persons to ministerial positions,
drawing more widely from among representatives of other parties'.

Semyonov, Yudin and Sokolovskii proposed that the fourth party congress of
the SED be held in the next three to four months so as 'to seriously renew the
ranks of the central committee' with a view to including 'a greater number of
younger personnel' who had 'excelled in their work with the working classes,
working peasants, [and] the intelligentsia'. The politburo had to be purged of
members who did not demonstrate 'the necessary capabilities required of leaders
of the party and of the state in these times'. With regard to the trade unions, it
was considered necessary 'to make decisive changes in the ranks of the leaders
of the corresponding organs, as well as to introduce new regulations that would
radically [alter] the role of the professional unions in step with the requirements
of the new direction'. There were also proposals to create a national army similar
to the one in West Germany, transform the FDJ into a broad-based non-party
organization and restrict the functions of the central committee secretariat,
reducing the number of secretaries from eleven to five.[208] Molotov is said to have
welcomed the report, although he did comment that Semyonov had 'drifted off
to the right' with regard to Ulbricht's position.[209] The reactions of the other
Soviet leaders are unknown.

In the SED politburo, Ulbricht remained isolated in a minority of three until
mid-July. Only Honecker and Matern continued to back him, although even the
latter's support began to waver. On 2 July, Matern complained to executives of
the Soviet interior ministry in the GDR about 'the defective leadership methods'
of Ulbricht, whose motto was 'no one can do anything without me'.
Furthermore, he expressed a determination to criticize these methods at the
forthcoming central committee plenum.[210] Symptomatic of Ulbricht's precarious
position was the politburo's refusal to honour him with the freedom of Leipzig
at the end of June.[211] The only reference to his sixtieth birthday in *Neues
Deutschland* was a congratulation telegram from the central committee printed
on page five.[212] The Kremlin confined itself to a brief message in *Pravda*, which,
contrary to tradition, did not refer to Ulbricht as general secretary but merely as
one of the best known organizers and leaders of the SED.[213]

It was against this background that the SED leadership debated how best to implement the New Course. Grotewohl and Oelßner's handwritten notes from politburo meetings allow us to gauge the vicissitudes of the political struggle in the run-up to the fifteenth central committee plenum between 24 and 26 July. These sources broadly bear out Herrnstadt's own version of events.[214]

The proclamation of the New Course had been accompanied by the formation of a politburo commission (consisting of Ulbricht, Grotewohl, Oelßner, Zaisser, Herrnstadt and Jendretzky) charged with the task of preparing proposals for a structural reform of the politburo and central committee secretariat.[215] Its two meetings became the forum for conflicts that were to severely circumscribe the New Course and destroy the position of Ulbricht's critics in the SED leadership.

Zaisser and Herrnstadt feared that Ulbricht's dictatorial habits would strangle the New Course at birth. This is not to argue that they wished to purge Ulbricht from the leadership altogether, rather that they aimed to substantially diminish his power through personnel changes and the creation of new leadership structures. According to Ackermann, both expressed the opinion that 'the working style of comrade Ulbricht was incompatible with the party's New Course' (an opinion shared by the majority of politburo members). Still, neither of them gave any indication 'that they wished to expel comrade Ulbricht or anyone else from the leadership'.[216] As Herrnstadt himself put it on 6 June: 'Who is guilty? Of course, we are all guilty, and it would be ridiculous and provocative to concern ourselves now with the question of measuring guilt, instead of with the exact implementation of the change – that is to say with the achievement (*Herbeiführung*) of a decisive victory for our party.'[217]

At its first meeting on 25 or 26 June, the commission discussed ways of curbing Ulbricht's power and safeguarding the principle of collective leadership. To prevent the erosion of politburo authority by the central committee secretariat, Zaisser and Herrnstadt proposed the abolition of the latter and its replacement by a permanent commission within the politburo (renamed presidium) to oversee implementation of the New Course. The permanent commission would consist of the two party chairmen and four other presidium members. Herrnstadt's draft resolution to this effect also foresaw the scaling down of the central committee apparatus and the conversion of its departments into independent political units. Although the posts of party chairmen were retained, the function of general secretary was abolished,[218] effectively removing Ulbricht as party leader. In this way, Ulbricht's status was reduced to that of one politburo member among many.

The general secretary was to be replaced by a 'first secretary' whose task would be to co-ordinate the work of the presidium and permanent commission, thereby in effect supervising the party organisation. It is unclear exactly how this new post would have differed from its predecessor and, in his own account, Herrnstadt fails to provide a satisfactory answer to this question.[219] Zaisser and Herrnstadt both denied ever conceiving of the post as in any way related to that of SED leader.[220] Nonetheless, its occupant would apparently have enjoyed the status of first among equals within the presidium and therefore become leader almost by stealth. Control over the party organisation was, after all, the fountainhead of power and authority in the communist system. At the commission's second (and final) sitting held on about 2 July, Zaisser nominated Herrnstadt for the post of first secretary on the grounds that 'he was close to the masses and knew how to communicate with them.'[221] This was seized upon by Ulbricht as proof of a treacherous plot to depose him. Zaisser's proposal seems to have taken Herrnstadt totally by surprise and, on the basis of his poor relationship with the party apparatus, he expressed doubts about whether he possessed the right qualifications for the job.[222] Herrnstadt later complained to both Grotewohl and Ackermann about the unexpected proposal, which Zaisser himself later withdrew.[223]

It would therefore be fair to conclude that, while Zaisser and Herrnstadt were bent on removing Ulbricht as *de facto* SED leader, there was no co-ordinated plot to replace him with Herrnstadt. Their proposed structural and personnel changes would, if implemented, have amounted to much more than a check on Ulbricht's power – they would have constituted a disguised assault on his position as party leader. But both seemed willing to keep him in the presidium and even to offer him a place on its 'permanent commission' once he had been stripped of power. Ulbricht would later accuse them of wanting to preserve him 'as a living body for decoration'.[224] Even so, all proposals concerning leadership restructuring were presented to the commission (of which Ulbricht was a member) and there is no evidence of any conspiracy with the Soviets. This may, however, have been Zaisser and Herrnstadt's undoing. Without Soviet backing, any attempt to topple Ulbricht was doomed.

In marked contrast to Zaisser and Herrnstadt, the general secretary schemed with the headquarters of the Soviet Military Administration[225] to strengthen his position. While his critics never intended expelling anyone from the leadership, Ulbricht was bent on purging those not amenable to him. At the commission's second session in early July, Ulbricht went on the offensive, threatening to further undermine Grotewohl's position as one of only three former social democrats by proposing Ebert's expulsion from the politburo. This was rejected by all present, Herrnstadt even nominating Ebert for the new post of minister for all-German affairs.[226] Grotewohl retaliated by moving that Erich Honecker, Ulbricht's most reliable lackey, be dropped from the politburo.[227] But Ulbricht had come prepared for this indirect assault on his authority and announced that Honecker was being sent to Moscow on a party training course. In this way, he was able to save his young protégé as a future political ally and 'crown prince'. Herrnstadt moved that Ulbricht's other main disciple, Hermann Matern, be replaced as chairman of the central party control commission because of abuses committed under his stewardship. Herrnstadt did not, however, propose his expulsion from the leadership. A decision was postponed until an unspecified later date[228] and Matern was able to retain his post until 1971. By failing to seize the opportunities they were presented with, Zaisser and Herrnstadt gave Ulbricht time to consolidate his position and prepare a ruthless counter-attack.

At the next politburo meeting, Oelßner[229] joined forces with Ulbricht to accuse Zaisser and Herrnstadt of planning an intra-party coup. This version of events was, however, rejected by the politburo majority. Against this background, Herrnstadt had to compose part of a draft resolution[230] to be presented to the fifteenth central committee plenum later in the month. By so doing he played into the hands of Ulbricht who could now allege the existence of a 'manifesto' to go with the 'putsch'. That Zaisser had nothing to do with the draft (like his colleagues he saw it for the first time when it was presented to the politburo) did not prevent Ulbricht from alleging the existence of a 'Zaisser–Herrnstadt faction'.

In his draft resolution entitled 'the New Course and the renewal of the party', Herrnstadt defined the priority as 'the speedy establishment of a united, democratic, progressive Germany'.[231] The goal was realistic, he declared, because in all parts of the world the forces of peace were advancing, the forces of war and national division retreating. It was necessary for the two parts of Germany to take concrete steps to aid the process of reunification and to subordinate all other policies to this aim. The GDR had to become a model of freedom and social justice capable of attracting the support of all Germans.[232] In this way it could preserve its accomplishments in a reunited German state.

Reiterating the view that the New Course was a long-term strategy, he condemned abuses committed in the name of the 'accelerated construction of socialism', for example the numerous violations of the rule of law and restrictions on movement between the two parts of Germany. The party's greatest error had been to impose Soviet policies and organizational forms on to an alien national culture. This was a serious violation, not only of the interests of the German people but of Marxist–Leninist ideology which demanded that the conditions of individual countries be taken into account.[233] Bureaucracy, dictatorship, personality cult and disregard for the masses were defined as the four main evils from which the SED had to rid itself if it was to become both the 'party of the working class' and the 'party of the people'. This meant looking after the interests of other social groups such as the farmers, the intelligentsia and small businessmen. From now on, he declared, the state would encourage small-scale private enterprise and support independent farmers in the countryside. A mixed economy would improve the supply of consumer goods and improve living standards.[234]

The 'renewal' of the party was defined as the prerequisite for 'a broad democratization in all areas of life' – a process that would unleash the creativity and initiative of the workers, hitherto shackled by over-centralization and bureaucracy. The SED would have to adopt a new style of leadership, listening to the concerns of parliament and the bloc parties. The draft resolution ended with demands for the 'renewal' of the SED leadership and its central apparatus as well as of the trade unions and mass organizations. Herrnstadt also recognized that unless the party addressed these problems it would be rejected by the people.[235]

Some remarks scribbled by Grotewohl in the margin of Herrnstadt's draft resolution are of particular interest in this regard. Adjacent to Herrnstadt's contention that the aim of the New Course was to turn the GDR into a 'model democratic state' (by which he meant a state governed with the consent of the people), Grotewohl added: 'foster contact and strengthen understanding between Germans from all zones'.[236] These comments, three weeks *after* the East German uprising, reveal how central the goal of German reunification was to Grotewohl's political outlook and how he delayed casting in his lot with Ulbricht until it was politically inexpedient for him not to do so.

Herrnstadt's draft resolution was rejected by Ulbricht and his supporters at a politburo meeting on 3 July.[237] The term 'party of the people' was used to portray Herrnstadt as a closet social democrat bent on liquidating the party's proletarian character. Exception was also taken to the word 'renewal' in so far as it implied that the party had 'degenerated'.[238] By now the Ulbricht faction was on the attack and, by sowing fear and insecurity,[239] was successful in intimidating, although not neutralizing, the opposition which confronted it. Ackermann was assigned the task of drawing up a new draft resolution.

Herrnstadt had intensified his campaign against the party's weaknesses in the wake of the 17 June uprising. He even sent out his correspondents to uncover cases where the New Course was not being implemented.[240] On 7 July (almost two weeks after Beria's arrest) he published his most ferocious attack yet on the party bureaucracy and its disregard for the masses. Workers demanding that the SED redress grievances and start responding to their material needs, he complained, were being libelled as 'opportunists' and 'social democrats'. Too many functionaries were obsessed with production statistics rather than the welfare of factory employees. He appealed to the SED to put the interests of the population first: 'With the people and everything for the people – that must be the watchword of every party member.' He continued to believe that the New Course would facilitate the speedy and peaceful reunification of Germany.[241]

This article provoked the fury of Ulbricht's supporters who, given the party's parlous state in the summer of 1953, regarded Herrnstadt's critique as the ultimate stab in the back. Hanna Wolf, director of the party training college and one of Ulbricht's closest allies, wrote to Herrnstadt to protest that he was doing the bidding of the class enemy.

> If you read our press now, one cannot avoid but get the impression that *all* our party and economic functionaries . . . are cocooned (*verbonzt*), soulless (*entseelt*), bureaucratized and cut off from the masses. Nowhere has there been anything good and nowhere are the people provided for. I think ordinary folk (and not only them) must get the impression that RIAS[242] and others have been right all along.[243]

It was imperative, she insisted, in the light of the international situation and the relentless attacks of the enemy, to avoid creating the impression that the masses were being oppressed by a dehumanized party bureaucracy.[244] Her accusations reveal the depth of the split between protagonists and enemies of the New Course in the summer of 1953.

The anti-Ulbricht opposition reached its climax on the night of 8 July.[245] Grotewohl's notes from this politburo meeting support Herrnstadt's account and reveal that, were it not for the majority's indecisiveness, Ulbricht's position as party leader would have been untenable.[246] With the exception of Honecker and Matern (Oelßner[247] and Mückenberger declined to express a clear opinion) the politburo expressed its overwhelming lack of confidence in Ulbricht as general secretary. Zaisser, Schmidt and Ackermann[248] were especially outspoken in their criticism. The latter's remarks, as reported by Herrnstadt, were the highlight of the proceedings.

> I supported you for many years Walter. Despite everything I saw. I kept quiet for a long time – out of discipline, hope and fear. Today that is all behind me. The party is more important and I will speak the truth and only the truth. There are only two types of comrade in this politburo: those that dare to open their mouths and those that keep their mouths shut but think the same . . . It has been said, that the time for changes in the party leadership is unsuitable, because we have just had 17 June. No one is insisting on changes within twenty-four hours. But how can one trust this argument? At every point in time it can be said that precisely this moment is unsuitable and, if past experience is anything to go by, it always will be said.[249]

Once again, Zaisser proposed Herrnstadt for the post of first secretary, on the grounds that 'he had the ear of the masses'. To leave the apparatus in the hands of Ulbricht, he declared, would be 'a catastrophe for the New Course'. His methods of 'naked administration' were ruining the party.[250] Elli Schmidt was similarly scathing:

> The whole spirit that has got into our party, the sloppiness (*Schnellfertige*), the dishonesty, the turning of a blind eye (*Wegspringen*) to the people and their worries, the threatening and boasting – look where it has got us! You, my dear Walter, are the most guilty and this is something you don't want to concede, even though the 17 June would never have happened were it not for all these things.[251]

Ulbricht attempted to split the opposition by differentiating between Ackermann on the one hand and Zaisser and Herrnstadt on the other.[252]

There are four striking features about this politburo meeting. First, none of the members distinguished between the posts of general secretary and first secretary. The latter was perceived as a substitute for the former. Second, Herrnstadt unequivocally rejected his own nomination for this position.[253] Third, despite the politburo's agreement that Ulbricht should discontinue his activities as head of the party organization, no replacement candidate was considered. Fourth, the politburo failed to draw the logical conclusion from its own decision and immediately strip Ulbricht of power. Instead, it made the fatal error of permitting him to accompany Grotewohl to Moscow next morning. In this way, Ulbricht was able to rally support in the Kremlin before returning to avenge his opponents and consolidate his position at the helm of the party.

If there was a 'turning point at which GDR history failed to turn' it was the night of 8 July 1953. Ulbricht came within a hair's breadth of losing the SED leadership. Had the opposition been a genuine conspiracy, had there been even a hint of a strategic plan dominating its actions, East Germany might have been spared eighteen more years of Ulbricht's rule. The opposition lacked the courage to remove him without the Kremlin's prior approval. Fearing the accusation of factionalism, none of Ulbricht's critics seemed willing to take the initiative, instead waiting for the Soviets to do it for them. If they had presented Moscow with a *fait accompli* on this question, the Soviets would have found it difficult to reinstate a general secretary so unequivocally rejected by his colleagues.

Between 9 and 10 July, Ulbricht and Grotewohl were summoned to Moscow along with other East European leaders to be informed of Beria's arrest. Ulbricht used the occasion to consolidate his own position as general secretary, although he seems to have done so rather discreetly once the official briefing was over. In what appear to be Grotewohl's notes from a meeting with Soviet leaders on 9 July, the need for 'friendly co-operation between Pieck, Ulbricht and Grotewohl' was discussed – an indication of the Kremlin's intention to preserve the status quo.[254] Still more telling was Molotov's dark warning about the need to strengthen the SED politburo against 'waverers' in its ranks[255] – an oblique but unmistakable signal that the days of Ulbricht's opponents in the leadership were numbered.[256]

The highlight of the Moscow trip, however, was the sensational news of Beria's downfall. Sudoplatov claims that after 17 June the Soviet interior minister had continued to pursue his scheme for German reunification.[257] Apparently, he had vigorously advocated military intervention to quell the East German uprising[258] in the belief that this would bring the West to the negotiating table.[259] On 24 June, Zoya Rybkina was flown to Berlin where she joined forces with Olga Chekhova to canvass support for the plan. They allegedly succeeded in winning over Ernst Wollweber, soon to be given responsibility for GDR state security. But before Beria could be informed of these developments he was arrested at a meeting of the CPSU presidium on 26 June.[260] As can be discerned from the central committee resolution of 7 July, Beria's reunification initiative played a relatively minor role in his overthrow. More important were his alleged attempts to subjugate the party to the control of the secret police, to grant greater autonomy to the various nationalities in the USSR and to 'undermine' the collectivization of agriculture.[261] His efforts to facilitate rapprochement with Yugoslavia, although denounced in the resolution,[262] were allowed to continue.

Grotewohl reported back to the politburo on 10 July.[263] Herrnstadt and Ackermann (although not Zaisser) believed that the 'unmasking' of Beria spelled the end of Ulbricht's vendetta against his critics.[264] Within a few days, however, the balance of power in the SED politburo had been fundamentally altered. The lessons drawn from Beria's overthrow (the need for 'collective leadership' and 'empathy with the masses') should have been to Ulbricht's detriment. Instead Ulbricht went on the offensive and, with the support of Moscow, consolidated his position.

Ackermann presented his draft central committee resolution to a politburo meeting on 14 July. Stressing the importance of a 'united, democratic, peace-loving and independent Germany', he appealed for 'more democracy', both within the party and in its relations with the people. Greater emphasis, he declared, needed to be placed on the statutory rights of party members to criticize and dismiss their leaders. Members who persecuted their colleagues for making use of these rights deserved to be expelled from the SED. Arrogant, self-satisfied and bureaucratic functionaries had to be removed from their posts. He also condemned the party's 'administrative' interpretation of its leading role, its arbitrary interference in trade union affairs and its suppression of individual initiative. Like Herrnstadt, Ackermann used the word 'renewal' to describe the process the party would have to undergo if it was to justify its leading role in society.[265]

Without mentioning him by name, Ackermann also attacked Ulbricht's leadership of the party: 'However experienced a leading comrade may be, and whatever knowledge and capabilities he may possess, this does not put him in a position to replace the initiative, knowledge and experiences of the whole collective. That is why the renewal of internal party life must begin from above.'[266] Violations of collective leadership, he declared, gave rise to false and ill-conceived policies. Ackermann's call for self-criticism in the spirit of the resolution of 21 June was deleted from Grotewohl's copy – a sign of the latter's decision to side with Ulbricht.[267] The general secretary also seems to have succeeded in winning Jendretzky over to his side, thereby weakening the opposition still further.[268] Ackermann's draft (very similar in tone to Herrnstadt's) was rejected and the politburo intimidated into nominating Ulbricht, Grotewohl and Oelßner to draw up an alternative.[269]

The 14 July marks a turning point in the history of the Zaisser–Herrnstadt opposition. The politburo records reveal the true extent of the backlash. Adalbert Hengst, member of the central committee secretariat, was expelled from the party for his solidarity with the workers of Rostock during the June uprising. Former social democrat Otto Buchwitz (who had been the leadership's most vocal critic at the fourteenth central committee plenum) seemed poised for a similar fate.[270] Only twelve days earlier, Matern had told executives of the Soviet interior ministry in the GDR that Buchwitz was leader of a group of former social democrats who 'considered that if the former social democratic party still existed, the events of 17 June would never have happened'.[271] But most sensational of all was the expulsion and arrest of justice minister Max Fechner. The former social democrat and politburo member had defended the workers' constitutional right to strike in a interview in *Neues Deutschland*,[272] and for this he spent three years in prison. Herrnstadt denied any knowledge of the interview prior to its publication[273] and the whole affair remains shrouded in mystery. A deliberate provocation by Ulbricht to discredit Herrnstadt (who was later accused of being Fechner's accomplice) cannot be ruled out.[274] The campaign, after all, was conceived some two weeks *after* the interview's release. Ulbricht only took the initiative once he was assured of the Kremlin's support as SED leader.

According to Herrnstadt, Fechner was summoned before the politburo to account for his remarks. Instead of expressing regret, Fechner apparently caused consternation by defending the interview. Ulbricht in particular had difficulty controlling his rage. On Fechner's departure, Yudin apparently leapt to his feet in fury: 'In the Soviet Union one would get twelve years for something like this.' Following this outburst, Ulbricht allegedly whispered something inaudible to Zaisser who then left the room. Herrnstadt had the impression that he had gone to order Fechner's arrest.[275]

There is a marked discrepancy between the politburo record in its final form and the rough copy in its original form.[276] The original resolutions merely envisaged Fechner's resignation as justice minister, there is no mention of his expulsion from the SED or arrest for treason. These passages were then deleted and replaced with resolutions approving Fechner's imprisonment and expulsion[277] (which were then reproduced in the final version).[278] The typed-up record of this meeting was therefore drafted *after* the purge of Fechner and probably never presented to the politburo for approval. Honecker's claim that he knew nothing of Fechner's arrest until 1956[279] is therefore not as incredible as it sounds.

According to the reported testimony of Fechner, Zaisser believed that the strikers' demands were justified.[280] In a speech to the fifteenth central committee plenum later in the month, Zaisser said that the party had been faced with two 'alarm signals'. First, the tide of refugees fleeing to the West and second, the popular uprising of 17 June. The latter had affected him deeply because it revealed that certain sections of the working class no longer supported the SED. It was against this background that he had campaigned against methods of dictatorship and 'naked administration' in the party.[281]

Although Zaisser and Herrnstadt were themselves soon to be scapegoated, they demonstrated no solidarity with the hapless Fechner. By acting as accomplices to his arrest, they aided and abetted Ulbricht's consolidation of power. Divisions among Ulbricht's critics (who failed to draw up a common platform or establish contacts lower down in the party) and a willingness (albeit under great pressure) to sacrifice their principles on the altar of party discipline was one of the most grotesque spectacles of Stalinist politics and contributed decisively to their defeat at the fifteenth central committee plenum.

According to Oelßner's notes, only Ackermann, Rau and Ebert actively defended Zaisser and Herrnstadt against the attack launched by Ulbricht at the politburo meeting on 14 July. While Zaisser spurned the allegation that he had (like Beria) attempted to subjugate the party to MfS control, Herrnstadt tried to rebuff accusations that he had 'capitulated before the class enemy'. Rau worried that the failures of the leadership were being eclipsed by concentration on Zaisser's 'shortcomings' as minister for state security. Ebert tried to put Ulbricht's accusations in their proper perspective: 'Nobody wanted to remove comrade Ulbricht from the leadership – the question was about the position he should have.' Ackermann condemned the use of draft documents to discredit party leaders. Semyonov (who participated in the meeting to ensure the other members were in no doubt about the Soviet position) indirectly accused Zaisser and Herrnstadt of doing the enemy's bidding by proposing changes in the leadership after 17 June.[282]

The politburo convened again on 18 July to be confronted with the draft resolution (drawn up by Ulbricht, Grotewohl and Oelßner) for the fifteenth central committee plenum. The resolution played down the failures of the SED and concentrated on the 'fascist, counter-revolutionary coup attempt' of 17 June.[283] Zaisser was sacked as minister for state security and the MfS taken over by the ministry of the interior.[284]

Both Oelßner's notes and the politburo records testify to acrimonious conflict at this meeting. Zaisser voted against the section in the resolution[285] alleging membership of an 'anti-party' faction and 'capitulation before the class enemy.' Herrnstadt protested against the description of his draft resolution as 'an indictment of the party' and rejected the word 'defeatist' to describe his position. Ulbricht's attack on Herrnstadt's 'platform' revealed a deep-seated fear of its contents: 'The point is the spirit of the document – it must lead to the destruction of the party.'[286] For Grotewohl, the behaviour of Ulbricht was now of secondary importance compared with the need for a 'Zaisser–Herrnstadt affair'. Ackermann tried to focus attention on the general secretary and opposed turning the plenum into an inquisition of Zaisser and Herrnstadt: 'We must get to work on serious changes in the leadership . . . Critique of Walter Ulbricht . . . things must not be allowed to stay as they are.' Ebert went furthest in defending Zaisser and Herrnstadt: 'from my experience in the politburo, I did not have the impression that they wanted to seize the leadership for themselves. I am not convinced that the *intention* was there.' Herrnstadt could only express utter bewilderment at the dramatic turn of events: 'The picture gets gloomier from hour to hour . . . It never occured to me in my whole life to want to replace Ulbricht – what took place was a bitter struggle over collective leadership' (*die Kollektivität*). Matern revealed the true mentality of the hard-line Stalinists when he insisted: 'the period of penitence must be ended, it is dangerous for the party and its cadres. The workers are not conscious of *what* they have.' But it was Ulbricht who summed up their case best: 'in a situation in which the enemy is concentrating all its fire on us, only a madman would endanger [party] unity.'[287]

At a politburo meeting on 22 July, Zaisser and Herrnstadt finally capitulated and approved the aspersions levelled against them. Ulbricht attributed Herrnstadt's behaviour to his past as a 'bourgeois' journalist. Ackermann also engaged in self-criticism.[288] The politburo met one more time on 23 July to approve Ulbricht's central committee speech and discuss new additions to the politburo. The candidate members were excluded from voting, thereby ensuring that there could be no last minute rebellion. This measure proved unnecessary, however, because Herrnstadt, Ackermann, Schmidt and Jendretzky would have voted for the resolution anyway.[289] Interestingly, the names of both Schmidt and Jendretzky were cleared for re-election,[290] meaning that Ulbricht violated another politburo resolution when he demanded their expulsion at the plenum.[291]

Ulbricht's final victory was now assured and, celebrating in truly macabre fashion, the politburo ordered the publication of a brochure containing the central committee's reports on the Slansky trial and the condemnation of the 'western émigrés' in August 1950.[292] The Dahlem and Merker cases had facilitated Ulbricht's rise to supremacy as undisputed SED leader. The 'Zaisser–Herrnstadt affair' was conceived to re-establish his shattered authority.

As was to be expected, the central committee obediently rallied to Ulbricht, aided by Zaisser and Herrnstadt who failed to mount an effective counter-attack. In the end, a mixture of fear and party discipline took priority over the need to defeat the Ulbricht faction. Yet subservience does not fully explain the rout of the opposition at the fifteenth central committee plenum. When Herrnstadt protested that the aim had not been to carry out a counter-revolution, Ulbricht retorted that he was concerned with consequences not aims.[293] In this way, Ulbricht united those who genuinely believed in a dastardly plot to restore capitalism with those who remained unconvinced of Zaisser and Herrnstadt's treacherous intentions. Fears that reform might inevitably culminate in counter-revolution (defined as the collapse of SED rule) were not without foundation and Ulbricht exploited them to the full.

In adducing collaboration between Zaisser, Herrnstadt and Beria, Ulbricht violated the resolution adopted by the politburo the previous day which contained no such allegations. When confronted with this discrepancy by Zaisser, Ulbricht hinted that he had obtained Moscow's permission for the new charge.[294] One central committee member, Fritz Lange, reported an alleged conversation with the GDR minister for state security three or four days before the June uprising in which the latter is said to have predicted imminent reunification under 'bourgeois' auspices. The Soviets, he is alleged to have said, were about to sacrifice the GDR in the interests of world peace.[295] Zaisser strenuously denied that such a conversation ever took place[296] and Herrnstadt dismissed Lange's comments as an attempt to curry favour with Ulbricht and Matern (who suspected him of operating as a Gestapo agent during World War Two).[297] Given that Semyonov was an accomplice of Ulbricht, his claim that Zaisser spoke at one politburo meeting in favour of 'liquidating the GDR in the interests of the international communist movement'[298] lacks credibility. In his speech to the seventeenth central committee plenum in January 1954, Matern conceded that there was no evidence directly linking the three men.[299]

Zaisser and Herrnstadt were relieved of all their leadership functions and expelled from the central committee in July 1953. Although their 'crimes' were sufficiently grave to warrant immediate expulsion from the party, a compromise between Ulbricht, Semyonov and Grotewohl was probably instrumental in denying the former his final act of retribution until January 1954.[300] When one member of the central committee wrote to Matern complaining that the punishment was too lenient, he was told: 'The central committee could not decide otherwise, because several questions still need to be cleared up, some of them not by us.'[301]

The resolution passed at the fifteenth central committee plenum represented a toning down of the New Course. Its central aim was no longer defined as the reunification of Germany but the improvement of economic and political conditions in the GDR.[302] The party, it declared, had been right to begin laying the foundations of socialism and would continue to do so.[303] Although lip service was paid to the goal of national reunification, there was no mention of negotiations or of measures to facilitate rapprochement. Neither was there any condemnation of the party's blind emulation of the Soviet example. The June uprising was characterized almost exclusively as a 'fascist putsch attempt' organized by West German 'Junkers' and 'monopoly-capitalists' in the service of American imperialism.[304] Few members attempted to rescue anything of the New Course in its original form. Ackermann criticized the resolution for omitting the issue of a peace treaty and neglecting the 'struggle for German reunification'.[305] Buchwitz amplified the need to strengthen the central committee, grant a more active role to parliament and resuscitate the dormant bloc parties.[306]

After approving the expulsions of Zaisser, Herrnstadt, Ackermann, Schmidt and Jendretzky,[307] the central committee elected a new politburo.[308] Since it was customary for members to be elected unanimously, the dissenting votes cast in the cases of Hans Jendretzky, Heinrich Rau and Bruno Leuschner[309] should be noted. The SED's perverse concept of democracy was particularly evident in the case of Jendretzky, who was denied a place on the politburo despite being opposed by only eleven members.[310] The post of general secretary was abolished and Ulbricht elected to the new but identical position of first secretary.[311] The defeat of Zaisser and Herrnstadt provided the party with scapegoats for the June 1953 uprising and hastened the further consolidation of the Stalinist system.

The aftermath

In a document sent to the CPSU leadership in early August 1953, the third European department of the Soviet foreign ministry raised the possibility of an SPD victory in the West German elections on 6 September. This would mean the end of Adenauer's rule in the Federal Republic and the coming to power of a party which described itself as Marxist and had been willing to test earlier Soviet offers on German reunification.[312]

On 15 August 1953, the Soviet Union therefore sent a note to each of the Western Powers proposing a peace treaty and the formation of an all-German provisional government. The latter, to consist of the two German parliaments, would either replace or temporarily coexist with the governments of the GDR and Federal Republic. Apart from preparing the ground for all-German free elections, it would also participate in negotiations over a peace treaty; abstain from entering into military alliances against the victors of World War Two; guarantee freedom of activity for all democratic parties and organizations; ban 'fascist, military and other organizations opposed to peace and democracy'; expand economic and cultural ties between the two parts of Germany; run postal and telecommunications services; decide matters relating to German citizenship; regulate free travel and the exchange of goods independent of existing zonal frontiers. The country would also be released from its reparations and postwar debt obligations.[313]

The note affirmed the right of the German people to decide the nature of their socio-political system without foreign interference.[314] Free elections, however, would only be held *after* the formation of a provisional government, in which the Soviets would have insisted on equal representation. The SED would have claimed to speak for one half of the German nation, despite the fact that it had never been freely elected and the GDR only comprised one-third of Germany. The USSR would have demanded unanimity of decision as well, thereby allowing them to block every decision which did not serve its ends.[315]

Not only would this unelected government have been given substantial powers over the German people, it alone would have decided and safeguarded the conditions for free elections. Any electoral law would have had to guarantee the participation of all 'democratic' organizations (hence the GDR mass organizations) and prevent pressure being applied by the 'big monopolies'.[316] This was tantamount to demanding that capitalism be restricted and the communist vote inflated. The banning of 'fascist, military and other organizations opposed to peace and democracy' was also open to abuse, given the Soviet characterization of Adenauer's government as 'fascist'.

Between 20 and 23 August a delegation headed by Grotewohl, Ulbricht and Honecker held talks with the Soviet leadership in the Kremlin. After reiterating the details of the latest proposal Malenkov, the Soviet prime minister, said it was 'abnormal' that the Allies had still not signed a peace treaty with Germany eight years after the end of the war. For this reason it was necessary to convene a conference of the Great Powers within six months. Unlike Beria, however, he was unwilling to simply sell off the GDR, which he described as 'a state of the whole German people'. Instead, he announced a substantial aid package, including 430 million roubles of debt relief, additional supplies of foodstuffs and raw materials and a credit of 485 million roubles. Occupation fees were also slashed and reparation payments cancelled from January 1954. These measures were designed to strengthen the country in preparation for eventual reunification. According to Malenkov, the GDR was a temporary entity 'born to create a new, large, peace-loving Germany to guarantee peace and security in Europe and the world as a whole'.[317]

Grotewohl warmly welcomed the Soviet initiative. Until now, he said, hostile elements in the Federal Republic had demanded concrete evidence of Moscow's sincerity. 'We believe, here it is . . . What you have proposed today is so surprising and overwhelming . . . that we can hardly find the words to say what has to be said . . .' All 'peace-loving Germans', he declared, were hopeful about the prospects of being liberated from the impossible situation arising from the division of their country. A peaceful solution to the German question, he said, would reduce tensions and banish the threat of war from Europe.[318] The official

GDR–Soviet communiqué from these talks defined the aim as the creation of a 'united, democratic and peace-loving' Germany.[319]

News of the Soviet offer hit Berlin like a bombshell. According to Heinz Lippmann (a close aide of Erich Honecker), no one could understand why the Kremlin had delivered such a note so soon after the June uprising. Even functionaries who had never deviated from the party line or doubted the wisdom of the Soviet Union, now began to ask uneasily what would happen if the Western Powers accepted the proposal. Honecker, who had participated in the Moscow talks, was said to be as perplexed as everybody else: 'Then we'll just have to fight and, if it comes to the worst, die like heroes.'[320]

All the indications are that the SED leadership took the prospect of all-German elections extremely seriously. The politburo met more frequently than usual and there was an atmosphere of feverish activity. Hermann Axen ordered the top representatives of all the mass organizations to draft, within a few days, an election plan for their own organization. A special unit of the central committee was set up to prepare the SED to go underground. The prevailing mood in the party was summed up by Erich Glückauf, head of the division for all-German affairs: '[The West] would be complete fools not to accept that kind of offer at this time. They know what we're up against now, since 17 June. If they don't jump at the opportunity, they're really beyond hope.' Moscow sent a senior official to East Berlin to goad a reluctant FDJ into sending twenty to thirty thousand young people into the Federal Republic to distribute more than a million leaflets containing the text of the Soviet note.[321] In a radio broadcast on 17 August, Wilhelm Pieck appealed to the two parliaments to bury their ideological differences and put the interests of the country first. What the German people needed, he said, was a peace treaty and 'democratic unification without militarists and fascists'.[322] In Bonn, the KPD demanded that the *Bundestag* convene immediately to discuss ways of forming an all-German provisional government with the *Volkskammer*.[323]

The Western Powers' lack of interest and Adenauer's resounding victory in the Federal elections of 6 September 1953 prevented the Soviet offer from being put to the test and helped Ulbricht consolidate his position. It was clear that the West German population preferred the division of their country to national reunification on terms favourable to Moscow.

Zaisser and Herrnstadt were expelled from the SED in January 1954. Ackermann was 'severely reprimanded' and lost his place on the central committee (four members opposed his expulsion, a further seven abstained).[324] Schmidt and Jendretzky were also 'reprimanded' and dropped from the central committee at the fourth party congress in April. All three were formally rehabilitated (although not restored to any position of influence) in 1956. One third of the central committee's eighty members were purged in the wake of the Zaisser–Herrnstadt affair.[325]

That Zaisser and Herrnstadt were spared the fate of Beria in the USSR (executed in December 1953) was probably not due to any altruism on Ulbricht's part. In the light of the unprecedented campaign of defamation during the autumn of that year, Herrnstadt himself was prepared for the worst.[326] Rather it was the result of a sea change in Soviet politics. First, the Zaisser–Herrnstadt affair was conceived four months after the death of Stalin. Second, the Soviets had begun to tackle his legacy at a central committee plenum in September 1953. Third, Moscow may have wanted to keep the two men in reserve, should Ulbricht fall back into disfavour.[327] After the persecution mania of the early 1950s, the Kremlin had lost interest in staging any show trials and Ulbricht therefore let the Zaisser–Herrnstadt case languish.

Zaisser was made a pensioner, the consequences of his ostracism exacerbating an already ailing health condition. He died a broken man in early 1958.[328] Matern forbade him from petitioning the fourth party congress in 1954[329] and deflected interventions on his behalf by members of the central committee three years later.[330] When Zaisser's widow appealed to the Soviet leader, Nikita Khrushchev, for redress, the Kremlin's official response was that it was an internal matter for the SED.[331] Her plea to Pieck in September 1959 was intercepted and passed to Ulbricht without the president's knowledge.[332] Some members of the politburo clearly feared another of his interventions on behalf of a persecuted comrade.

Herrnstadt was given employment at an archive in Merseburg – an industrial town near Halle. In such a polluted environment, his tuberculosis could only get worse. When he died in 1966, it was of lung cancer. His unremitting pleas for rehabilitation were summarily rejected or went unanswered.[333] Those responsible for the Zaisser–Herrnstadt affair obviously had a vested interest in denying their victims rehabilitation. As Matern wrote to Ulbricht in 1962: 'It seems to me that so long as Herrnstadt fails to show the slightest inclination to comment seriously and critically on his errors . . . there is no reason to investigate anything.'[334]

After the fifteenth central committee plenum, the SED was gripped by a wave of purges. Between 17 June and 21 July 1953, 1,266 members resigned because of policy disagreements or because they rejected the characterization of the June uprising as a 'fascist provocation'.[335] Between January and September of that year, the central committee department responsible for the 'leading organs of the party and mass organizations' was inundated with reports describing the mood of discontent in the lower echelons of the SED. Typical demands were for the release of prisoners, freedom of expression, a 'special German way to socialism', authorization of a social democratic faction, the refounding of the SPD and new approaches to German reunification after Stalin's death.[336] By 1954, 62.2 per cent of the members of the fifteen SED *Bezirk* committees elected in 1952 had been replaced. The purge at local authority level was even more draconian, with 71 per cent of all the first and second secretaries of the SED *Kreis* committees in office at the time of the uprising losing their positions.[337]

In what is either an anti-communist forgery or a statement from disaffected party members in Thuringia, Zaisser and Herrnstadt were portrayed as spokemen for the opposition inside the SED. Resentment towards bureaucracy and dictatorship, it was argued, was widespread. Numerous functionaries at local and district level were being removed from their posts for sympathizing with the workers on 17 June. The authors of the statement branded Ulbricht and his supporters 'enemies of the working class' for disrupting the New Course. They also accused him of denying party members their statutory right of access to the minutes of the fifteenth central committee plenum. This, they declared, was proof enough of his wanton disregard for intra-party democracy. The policy of linking German reunification to socialization in the Federal Republic was also ridiculed and the KPD's humiliating defeat at the polls cited as evidence of a discredited *Deutschlandpolitik*. A 'bourgeois-democratic republic' was, in their view, the only realistic alternative. Zaisser, Herrnstadt and Ackermann were credited with recognizing this fact and giving priority to the reunification issue.[338]

In Erfurt, the town council had to rebuke one of its members for demanding a debate in the party on the much-maligned 'Herrnstadt platform'.[339] In September 1954, Zaisser was reported as saying that the party was too weak to discuss the uprising in an atmosphere of openness and that this would only be possible in ten or fifteen years time.[340] He could not know that the SED would never come to terms with the events of 17 June and that Herrnstadt's draft resolution would be withheld from the party until 1990.

The New Course was the biggest casualty of Ulbricht's victory. In August 1953, the greater room for manoeuvre granted to the bloc parties[341] was rescinded[342] and at the start of 1954 the collectivization of agriculture began again in earnest.[343] At the fourth party congress in April, Ulbricht said it was time to resume laying the foundations of socialism in the GDR.[344] Shortly thereafter, the party began restructuring the education system along Soviet lines.[345] Socialization in other areas started again in 1955[346] and, at the twenty-fourth central committee plenum in June of that year, Ulbricht officially buried the New Course.[347]

Herrnstadt became increasingly critical of the system in which he had once invested so much hope. In 1956 he allegedly supported the rise of Gomulka in Poland, believing that the SED should instigate its own process of liberalization and expedite German reunification.[348] It is significant that he cited the disgraced Hungarian reformer Georg Lukacs in his book *The First Conspiracy Against the International Proletariat* in 1958.[349] His support for the dissident East German communist, Robert Havemann, was more clearly enunciated: 'What he wanted to say in the end, absolutely right. Namely, that the dogmatic interpretation of Marxist–Leninism is malicious (*unselig*), the language of the dogmatists never new, incorrigible . . . He who dares, while fighting for socialism, to laugh contemptuously over the struggle for democracy, also proves his "fight" for socialism to be bogus (*unecht*).'[350]

In his book *The origin of classes*, published one year before his death, Herrnstadt launched a thinly veiled attack on the 'dogmatists' inside the SED. Like the Jesuits, he claimed, they believed that 'the end justified the means' and were ruthless and dishonest in defending their interests. Men with character, he said, had no choice but to rebel against their 'insolence' and 'malice'.[351]

In 1963, he recorded his reaction to the posthumous acquittal of the 'Slansky conspirators' in Czechoslovakia and was shattered to discover that almost all his close associates from the period 1930 and 1953 had been murdered – either by fascists or by communist supporters of the personality cult.[352] A few words he scribbled on a small card during this period reveal the depth of his disillusionment: '*Such* sacrifice – and then this comes out; if I had the chance to do it all again – and knew this, the result – then no.'[353]

He also lamented the distortion of 'democratic centralism' and the deficit in democratic accountability.[354] From the costs of the personality cult in Germany, he wrote, 'one could build an entire small state.'[355] He was especially perturbed by the widespread corruption in public life. As for the tide of refugees who had fled to the West, 80 per cent of them had been 'literally chased out of the GDR'.[356] In Eurocommunism he saw perhaps the Soviet bloc's last chance to save itself from infamy.[357] Shortly before his death in 1966, he pronounced his final verdict on the system: 'We are rotting in socialism.'[358]

The myth of a 'Zaisser–Herrnstadt conspiracy' in the GDR dies hard among members of the former SED elite. According to Karl Schirdewan, Herrnstadt as first secretary would have been 'a disaster' for the party, opening the floodgates to Beria-inspired pogroms and purges. Herrnstadt was therefore a disguised enemy of renewal set on using the New Course as a locomotive for his own personal ambitions.[359] At the same time, however, Schirdewan claimed that he alone in the politburo opposed their expulsion from the SED. This was inconsistent with his vociferous stance in 1953. In 1992, however, he accepted Herrnstadt's rehabilitation.[360] Paul Wandel also claimed that he opposed their expulsion from the party. Zaisser and Herrnstadt were not 'controlled' by Beria, he said, but they did co-operate closely with him.[361]

As SED ideology chief, Kurt Hager must bear much of the responsibility for turning the calumnies of 1953 into official history. He was as convinced in 1992 as he was then of their guilt. For Hager, their crime lay in opposing Ulbricht at a time when the party was reeling from the June uprising. The author's observation that Ulbricht was as much responsible for the conflict as Zaisser and Herrnstadt was dismissed with the standard refrain that it was the duty of all party members to rally around their leader in times of crisis. As for Herrnstadt's 'platform', Hager remained adamant: At no time did the SED require 'renewal'. After reading Herrnstadt's own version of events, Hager remained convinced that his expulsion from the party was justified, although he did admit that Matern's methods as chairman of the central party control commission were too harsh.[362]

On 29 March 1982, SED leader Erich Honecker met with the first secretary of the Polish United Workers' Party (PUWP), General Wojciech Jaruzelski, in East Berlin to discuss the Solidarity crisis. Honecker lectured his guest on the need to 'restore unity' to the ranks of the Polish Communist Party and cited the SED's own successes in this regard. The crushing of the 'Zaisser–Herrnstadt opposition' was held up to Jaruzelski as an example worthy of emulation. Almost thirty years later, Erich Honecker was still celebrating the 'victory' of 1953 as one of the secrets of East German success.[363] In 1987, three years before the collapse of the GDR and with glasnost in full swing in the Soviet Union, a request by Herrnstadt's widow to reopen the Zaisser–Herrnstadt case was rebuffed for the last time.[364] Only when communism itself was swept away in 1989–90 could Zaisser and Herrnstadt be rehabilitated.[365]

Notes

1 W. S. Semjonow, *Von Stalin bis Gorbatschow. Ein halbes Jahrhundert in diplomatischer Mission 1939–1991* (Berlin, 1995), p. 246.

2 SAPMO-BArch, ZPA, IV 2/1/84. 1 CC plenum, 25.7.50.

3 See A. Mitter, S. Wolle, *Untergang auf Raten. Unbekannte Kapitel der DDR-Geschichte* (München, 1993), pp. 59–60, 142–3; T. Neumann, *Die Maßnahme: Eine Herrschaftsgeschichte der SED* (Reinbek bei Hamburg, 1991), p. 85. See also Mitter's lecture to a conference of Berlin's historical commission, 18 September 1992: 'it was a question of pure power struggle. The two men did not favour any reforms.'

4 A. Kantorowicz, *Deutsches Tagebuch*, II (Munich, 1962), pp. 251–2. See also A. Kantorowicz, *Deutsches Tagebuch* (Munich, 1959), p. 54.

5 O. Pfefferkorn, 'Wilhelm Zaisser. Pankows Berija', *SBZ-Archiv*, 8 (20.4.53), 123–4; p. 123.

6 SAPMO-BArch, ZPA, IV 2/4/392. Premier of Saxony's tribute to Zaisser in the state parliament on the occasion of the latter's departure as interior minister, 1.7.49. Cited in Else Zaisser's letter to 5 party congress of the SED, July 1958.

7 Interview with W. A. on 24.7.73 in B. W. Bouvrier, H. P. Schultz, '. . . *die SPD aber aufgehört hat zu existieren*'. *Sozialdemokraten unter sowjetischer Besatzung* (Bonn, 1991), pp. 171–81; p. 173.

8 As a member of the intelligentsia, Herrnstadt was regarded suspiciously by some of his working class comrades. Writing to Ulbricht and Matern on 10 August 1953, Hanna Wolf (Moscow émigré, diehard Ulbricht supporter and director of the party training college) dismissed him as an 'an arrogant intellectual' (BStU, 10993 – *Stasi* archive). At the 15 CC plenum in July 1953, Paul Wandel accused him of trying to subject the party to the control of the intellectuals. SAPMO-BArch, ZPA, IV 2/1/120.

9 A. Fischer, *Sowjetische Deutschlandpolitik im zweiten Weltkrieg 1941–1945* (Stuttgart, 1975), p. 89.

10 SAPMO-BArch, ZPA, IV 2/1.01/104. Stenographic record of a conference of east German newspaper editors, 1 December 1948. As Lex Ende (Herrnstadt's predecessor as chief editor of *ND*) put it: 'I know you want to prevent us from becoming an appendage of the Bolshevik party.'

11 *Ibid.* In 1950 Herrnstadt apparently disapproved of an attack on a former social democrat who had published an article defending Lassalle as a model socialist leader. SAPMO-BArch, ZPA, IV 2/4/390, letter from Klara Einhorn (foreign affairs section of *ND*) to CPCC, 17.2.54. Following his purge from the leadership, Herrnstadt justified his struggle against violations of intra-party norms by declaring the need to retain the support of the former social democrats. See BStU, 10993, Herrnstadt's letter to Matern, 31.8.53.

12 L. Kühn, ' "Neues Deutschland" unterstützt ungenügend die Anleitung der Parteiorganisation', *NW*, 10 (May 1950), 16–18.

13 SAPMO-BArch, ZPA, IV 2/4/114. Bauer's report to leadership, 12.7.50.

14 L. Bauer, ' "Die Partei hat immer Recht". Bemerkungen zum geplanten deutschen Rajkprozeß (1950)', *APZ*, B27 (4.7.56), 405–19; p. 410.

15 BStU, 10993. Letter from Hanna Wolf to Ulbricht and Matern, 10.8.53.

16 SAPMO-BArch, ZPA, IV 2/1/120. Heinz Hoffmann's speech to 15 CC plenum, 24.–26.7.53.

17 Ulbricht was as dictatorial in the CC secretariat as he was in the PB. In 1992, Karl Schirdewan recalled how Ulbricht intimidated and demoralized its members. Interview with Karl Schirdewan, 12.9.92.

18 C. Stern, *Ulbricht. A political biography* (London, 1965), p. 125.

19 SAPMO-BArch, ZPA, NL 62/146. Rau's letter to Pieck, 28.11.51.

20 Semjonow, *Von Stalin bis Gorbatschow*, pp. 270–1, 274.

21 BStU, 10993. Wolf's letter to Ulbricht and Matern, 10.8.53.

22 H. Lippmann, *Honecker and the new politics of Europe* (London, 1973), pp. 147–8.

23 SAPMO-BArch, ZPA, IV 2/2/172.

24 SAPMO-BArch, ZPA, IV 2/2/191. PB meeting, 5.2.52.

25 'Bericht des Genossen Willi Zaisser vor dem Politbüro der SED im März 1952 über die Rolle des Politbüros und das Verhältnis von Politbüro und Sekretariat' in W. Otto, 'Dokumente zur Auseinandersetzungen in der SED 1953', *BzG*, 5 (1990), 655–72; pp. 669–70.

26 SAPMO-BArch, ZPA, IV 2/1/119. Zaisser's speech to 15 CC plenum, 24.–26.7.53.

27 SAPMO-BArch, ZPA, IV 2/4/391. Herrnstadt's statement to CPCC, dated 1.12.53.

28 SAPMO-BArch, ZPA, IV 2/4/392. Letter from Else Zaisser to 5 party congress of SED, July 1958.

29 See Chapter 1: The purge of Merker and Dahlem.

30 SAPMO-BArch, ZPA, IV 2/1/120. Ulbricht's concluding speech to 15 CC plenum, July 1953.

31 BStU, 10993. Hanna Wolf's letter to Ulbricht and Matern, 10.8.53. Wolf was reporting a conversation with Zaisser at the party training college five months previously. The denunciatory nature of her account renders it unreliable.

32 SAPMO-BArch, ZPA, IV 2/1/120. Elli Schmidt's speech to 15 CC plenum, July 1953.

33 See the testimony of Grotewohl's personal aide F. Stempel in: F. Stempel, 'Erinnerung an Otto Grotewohl. Zu dessen 100. Geburtstag am 11. März 1994', *Utopie Kreativ* (März–April 1994), 154–65; p. 157.

34 H. Brandt, *Ein Traum, der nicht entführbar ist. Mein Weg zwischen Ost und West* (München, 1967), pp. 200–1, 204. Brandt worked closely with Jendretzky in the Berlin district leadership of the SED.

35 Alluded to in Herrnstadt's letter to W. S. Semyonov, 28.11.62, published in N. Stulz-Herrnstadt (ed.), *R. Herrnstadt, Das Herrnstadt-Dokument. Das Politbüro der SED und die Geschichte des 17. Juni 1953* (Reinbek bei Hamburg, 1990), p. 181.

36 The PB gave express instructions to intercept Dahlem's letters at a meeting on 9.6.53. See SAPMO-BArch, ZPA, J IV 2/2/288.

37 SAPMO-BArch, ZPA, IV 2/4/390. Letter from Rudi Wettengel (editorial team at *ND*) to CPCC, 10.2.53.

38 'Herrnstadt an der Reihe', *Neue Zeitung* (12.2.53), cited in H. Müller-Enbergs, *Der Fall Rudolf Herrnstadt. Tauwetterpolitik vor dem 17. Juni* (Berlin, 1991), pp. 164–5.

39 'Heraus mit der Sprache!', *ND* (25.1.52), 1. In a statement to the party leadership in December 1953, Herrnstadt wrote: 'If it had only been a question of comrade Ulbricht the danger would only have been half as great.' The general secretary, he said, was typical of 'a certain type of leading functionary . . . uncreative but quick, energetic, cunning and averse to any serious debate.' SAPMO-BArch, ZPA, IV 2/4/391. Herrnstadt's written statement to CPCC, 1.12.53.

40 'Bericht des Genossen Willi Zaisser'; p. 670.

41 SAPMO-BArch, ZPA, IV 2/4/389. Herrnstadt's handwritten notes from a PB meeting, 28.10.50.

42 'Kollege Zschau und Kollege Brumme', *ND* (14.10.51), 3–4. In a statement to the CPCC a month after being expelled from the SED, Herrnstadt recalled how reluctant Ulbricht had been to endorse this article. SAPMO-BArch, ZPA, IV 2/4/391. Herrnstadt's statement to CPCC, 1.12.53.

43 SAPMO-BArch, ZPA, IV 2/2/195. PB meeting, ?? 2.52.

44 'Heraus mit der Sprache!'

45 SAPMO-BArch, ZPA, IV 2/1/102. Herrnstadt's speech to 8 CC plenum, 21.–23.2.52.

46 SAPMO-BArch, ZPA, IV 2/1/102. Ulbricht's closing speech to 8 CC plenum.

47 SAPMO-BArch, IV 2/4/389. Typed record of a conversation between Herrnstadt and Ulbricht to evaluate the 8 CC plenum, 28.2.52.

48 Many years later, Herrnstadt took Semyonov to task for refusing to ensure that the resolution was implemented. See Herrnstadt's letter to Semyonov, 28.11.62, published in *Das Herrnstadt-Dokument*, p. 271.

49 SAPMO-BArch, ZPA, IV 2/1/107. Herrnstadt's speech to 10 CC plenum, 20.–22.10.52.

50 SAPMO-BArch, ZPA, IV 2/1/107. See Oelßner's speech to 10 CC plenum. Forty years later, Hager was still accusing Herrnstadt of damaging party morale by overemphasizing 'negative aspects' of its work. Interview with Kurt Hager, 1.12.92.

51 SAPMO-BArch, ZPA, IV 2/1/59. Ackermann's speech to 16 PE meeting, 24.1.49.

52 SAPMO-BArch, ZPA, IV 2/4/389. Herrnstadt's handwritten notes from a PB meeting, 23.1.50.

53 SAPMO-BArch, ZPA, IV 2/1/95. Herrnstadt's speech to 6 CC plenum, 13–15 June 1951.

54 SAPMO-BArch, ZPA, IV 2/1/95. Jendretzky's speech to 6 CC plenum.

55 BStU, 10993. Letter from Hanna Wolf to Ulbricht and Matern, 10.8.53.

56 M. Fulbrook, *Anatomy of a dictatorship. Inside the GDR, 1949–1989* (Oxford, 1995), p. 47.

57 SAPMO-BArch, ZPA, IV 2/2/202. PB meeting, 18.3.52. PB resolution encapsulating Zaisser's proposals to improve the work of the MfS. See also SAPMO-BArch, ZPA, IV 2/2/198, PB meeting 4.3.52.

58 BStU, 10993. Herrnstadt's letter to Matern, 31.8.53.

59 SAPMO-BArch, ZPA, IV 2/4/391. Herrnstadt's verbatim testimony during his interrogation by the CPCC, 11.9.53.

60 SAPMO-BArch, ZPA, IV 2/2/203. PB meeting, 18.3.52.

61 SAPMO-BArch, ZPA, IV 2/2/218. PB meeting, 1.7.52. Letter to Stalin of 2.7.52 concerning preparations for 2 party conference of SED, 9.–12.7.52.

62 Resolution of CPSU PB, 8.7.52. Cited in R. Stöckigt, 'Ein Dokument von großer historischer Bedeutung vom Mai 1953: "Über die Maßnahmen zur Gesundung der

politischen Lage in der Deutschen Demokratischen Republik" ', *BzG*, 5 (1990), pp. 648–54; p. 652.

63 *Protokoll der Verhandlungen der II. Parteikonferenz der Sozialistischen Einheitspartei Deutschlands 9.–12. Juli 1952* (Berlin, 1952), p. 58.

64 D. Staritz, *Die Gründung der DDR. Von der sowjetischen Besatzungszone zum sozialistichen Staat* II, (Munich, 1987), pp. 183–4.

65 Semjonow, *Von Stalin bis Gorbatschow*, p. 274.

66 *Ibid.*, p. 279.

67 SAPMO-BArch, ZPA, NL 90/699. Confirmed by Herrnstadt himself shortly after the proclamation of the New Course eleven months later. See signed record of Herrnstadt's remarks in a PB meeting, 6.6.53.

68 SAPMO-BArch, ZPA, IV 2/4/391. Herrnstadt's written statement to CPCC, 1.12.53.

69 Based on Herrnstadt's smaller 'plan for Zwickau' – the largest coal-mining area in the GDR. For more detail, see A. Baumann's speech to 2 party conference of SED in: *Protokoll der Verhandlungen der II. Parteikonferenz der Sozialistischen Einheitspartei Deutschlands 9.–12. Juli 1952* (Berlin-Ost, 1952), 220–33. See also R. Herrnstadt, 'Millionen vereinte Patrioten sind eine unüberwindliche Kraft', *ND* (24.5.53), 1.

70 SAPMO-BArch, ZPA, IV 2/4/391. Herrnstadt's verbatim testimony to CPCC, 11.9.53 and Herrnstadt's written statement to CPCC, 1.12.53. See also BStU, 10993: Herrnstadt's statement to CPCC, 31.8.53.

71 SAPMO-BArch, ZPA, IV 2/4/391. Herrnstadt's written statement to CPCC, 1.12.53.

72 SAPMO-BArch, ZPA, IV 2/1/119. Zaisser's speech to 15 CC plenum, July 1953.

73 SAPMO-BArch, ZPA, IV 2/4/391. Herrnstadt's written statement to CPCC, 1.12.53.

74 SAPMO-BArch, ZPA NL 36/696. Stalin had instructed the SED not to force farmers into the new collectives. See also SAPMO-BArch, ZPA, IV 2/4/391, Herrnstadt's verbatim testimony to CPCC, 11.9.53.

75 SAPMO-BArch, ZPA, IV 2/4/391. Herrnstadt's verbatim testimony to CPCC, 11.9.53. Ackermann also criticized Ulbricht's policy of all-out collectivization. BStU, 10993, Ackermann's letter to Matern, 14.9.53. According to Oelßner there was considerable disagreement in the PB over the party's agrarian policy (see SAPMO-BArch, ZPA, IV 2/1/119. Oelßner's speech to 15 CC plenum, 24.–26.7.53).

76 SAPMO-BArch, ZPA, IV 2/4/391. Herrnstadt's written statement to CPCC, 1.12.53.

77 Cited in W. Loth, *Stalins ungeliebtes Kind. Warum Moskau die DDR nicht wollte* (Berlin, 1994), p. 196; R. Stöckigt, 'Eine historische Chance wurde vertan . . .', *ND* (16.–17.6.90), 13.

78 SAPMO-BArch, ZPA, IV 2/4/392. Else Zaisser's letter to 6 party congress of SED, 5.1.63.

79 O. Grotewohl, 'Die gegenwärtige Lage und der neue Kurs der Partei', *Der Neue Kurs und die Aufgaben der Partei* (Berlin-Ost, 1953), p. 9. See also A. Baring, *Uprising in East Germany: June 17, 1953* (London, 1972), p. 20.

80 F. Schenk, *Mein doppeltes Vaterland* (Würzburg, 1989), p. 99.

81 Resolution of council of ministers, 9.4.53. Cited in Loth, *Stalins ungeliebtes Kind*, p. 197.

82 For more detail, see: K. Larres, 'Neutralisierung oder Westintegration? Churchill, Adenauer, die USA und der 17. Juni 1953', *DA*, 6 (1994), 568–85; J. Richter, 'Reexamining Soviet policy towards Germany in 1953', *Europe–Asia Studies*, 4 (1993), 671–91.

83 Brandt, *Ein Traum,* p. 201.
84 SAPMO-BArch, ZPA, IV 2/1/115–116. Resolution of 13 CC plenum, 14.–15.5.53.
85 SAPMO-BArch, ZPA, IV 2/1.01/104. Stenographic record of conference of east German newspaper editors, 1.12.48.
86 R. Herrnstadt, 'Kollege Zschau und Kollege Brumme', *ND* (14.10.51), 1.
87 SAPMO-BArch, ZPA, IV 2/1/89. Herrnstadt's speech to 3 CC plenum, 26.–27.10.50.
88 SAPMO-BArch, ZPA, IV 2/1/89. Ackermann's speech to 3 CC plenum. See also 'Prager Vorschläge sachlich und nüchtern prüfen!', *ND* (25.10.50), 1.
89 SAPMO-BArch, ZPA, IV 2/1/89.
90 According to one of Ulbricht's aides, Wolfgang Berger, SED leaders were also nervous and fearful about West Germany's rearmament programme. Interview with Wolfgang Berger, 14.12.92.
91 George Kennan's report of a conversation with Mario di Steffano (the Italian ambassador to Moscow), 25.7.52. Nenni had informed Di Steffano of Pieck and Grotewohl's comments. Kennan was US ambassador to the Soviet Union at the time. See Hermann-Josef Rupieper, 'Zu den sowjetischen Deutschlandnoten 1952. Das Gespräch Nenni–Stalin', *VfZ,* 3 (July, 1985), pp. 547–57; p. 554. Confirmed by Nenni himself in an interview to the New York Times, 16.3.63.
92 SAPMO-BArch, ZPA, IV 2/1/93. Herrnstadt's speech to 5 CC plenum, 15.–17.3.51.
93 The question asked was: 'Do you oppose remilitarization and favour a peace treaty with Germany in 1951?' The referendum took place between 3 and 6 June 1951. Attempts to include the West German population were only partially successful.
94 SAPMO-BArch, ZPA, IV 2/1/93. See Ulbricht and Grotewohl's speeches to 5 CC plenum.
95 SAPMO-BArch, ZPA, IV 2/1/95. Herrnstadt's speech to 6 CC plenum, 13.–14.6.51.
96 R. Herrnstadt, 'Kollege Zschau und Kollege Brumme', *ND* (14.10.51), 3–4.
97 See Chapter 1: The defeat of Ackerman and the 'special German way to socialism'.
98 SAPMO-BArch, ZPA, IV 2/2/218. Letter to Stalin, 2.7.52.
99 SAPMO-BArch, ZPA, NL 90/699. Signed record of Herrnstadt's remarks to a PB meeting, 6.6.53.
100 *ND* editorial, 'Millionen vereinte Patrioten sind eine unüberwindliche Kraft'.
101 G. Wettig, 'Die Deutschland-Note vom 10. März 1952 auf der Basis diplomatischer Akten des russischen Außenministeriums. Die Hypothese des Wiedervereinigungsangebots', *DA,* 7 (1993), 786–805; pp. 794–5.
102 An extract of the note is published in W. Erfurt, *Moscow's policy in Germany. A study in contemporary history* (Esslingen, 1959).
103 Cited in J. Gaddis, *We now know. Rethinking Cold War history* (Oxford, 1997), p. 127.
104 Cited in Loth, *Stalins ungeliebtes kind,* p. 181.
105 *Tagesspiegel* (23.4.52), cited in M. Jänicke, *Der dritte Weg. Die antistalinistischer Opposition gegen Ulbricht seit 1953* (Köln, 1964), p. 228.
106 Erfurt, *Moscow's policy in Germany,* p. 37.
107 Cited in A. Baring 'Volksarmee schaffen – ohne Geschrei', *FAZ* (25.9.91), 35.
108 Soviet minutes of Stalin's meeting with East German leaders. Published in 'Stalin and the SED leadership, 7 April 1952: "You must organize your own state"', *CWIHP Bulletin* (Fall, 1994), pp. 35, 48. The account is corroborated in Pieck's notes from his conversations with Stalin, 1 to 7 April 1952, in D. Staritz, 'Die SED, Stalin und der "Aufbau des Sozialismus" in der DDR', *DA,* 7 (July, 1991), 686–700; pp. 696–7.

109 Erfurt, *Moscow's policy in Germany*, p. 40.

110 Extract published in *ibid.*, p. 112.

111 'Rechenschaftsbericht des Zentralkomitees der KPdSU (B) an den XIX. Parteitag', *Bericht des Sekretärs des ZK der KPdSU (B)* (Berlin-Ost, 1952), p. 32.

112 'Das demokratische Deutschland feiert den 3. Jahrestag der DDR', *TR* (7.10.52), 1.

113 V. Mastny, *The Cold War and Soviet insecurity. The Stalin years* (Oxford, 1996), p. 135.

114 SAPMO-BArch, ZPA, IV 2/2/204. PB meeting, 25.3.52.

115 SAPMO-BArch, ZPA, IV 2/2/204. 'Brief an den Landesvorstand und Landesausschuß der SPD Groß-Berlin'.

116 Müller-Enbergs, *Der Fall,* p. 139. See also V. Falin, *Politische Erinnerungen* (München, 1993), p. 307.

117 See, for example, 'Vorwärts zum Abschluß eines Friedensvertrages!', *ND* (15.3.52), cited in Müller-Enbergs, *Der Fall,* p. 372.

118 Müller-Enbergs, *Der Fall,* p. 139.

119 Interview with Hager, 1.12.92.

120 F. Oelßner, 'Antwort auf Diskussionen über den Vorschlag der Sowjetunion für einen Friedensvertrag mit Deutschland', *NW*, 8 (1952), 1–4; p. 4.

121 SAPMO-BArch, ZPA, IV 2/1/119.

122 BStU, 10993. O. Last to CPCC, 5.8.53. The testimonies are also in SAPMO-BArch, ZPA, IV 2/4/391.

123 SAPMO-BArch, ZPA, IV 2/4/391. Matern's remarks to Zaisser during interrogation of CPCC, 11.9.53.

124 Herrnstadt underlined the severity of the conflicts inside the SED PB in a statement to Matern on 31 August 1953: 'there were situations when the behaviour of comrade Ulbricht acutely endangered the unity of the leadership.' BStU, 10993.

125 H. Harrison, 'The Bargaining Power of Weaker Allies in Bipolarity and Crisis: Soviet–East German Relations 1953–1961', PhD dissertation (University of Columbia, 1993), pp. 43–4.

126 Statement to Molotov from the head of the diplomatic mission in Berlin, G. Pushkin and the deputy Soviet foreign minister, J. Malik, 24.4.53. Cited in G. Wettig, 'Die beginnende Umorientierung der sowjetischen Deutschland-Politik im Frühjahr und Sommer 1953', *DA*, 5 (1995), 495–507; p. 499.

127 Cited in *ibid.*, p. 496.

128 See Khrushchev's speech of 8 March 1963, quoted in *ND*, 14.3.63. Cited in W. Loth, *The division of the world 1941–1955* (London, 1988), p. 269. Also see Semjonow, *Von Stalin bis Gorbatschow,* p. 290.

129 L. Besymenski, '1953 – Berija will die DDR beseitigen', *Die Zeit*, 42 (15.10.93), 81–3. See also P. Sudoplatov, A. Sudoplatov, J. L. Schecter, L. P. Schecter, *Special tasks. The memoirs of an unwanted witness – a Soviet spymaster* (London, 1995), pp. 363–6.

130 Falin, *Politische Erinnerungen*, pp. 314–15.

131 Besymenski, '1953 – Berija will die DDR beseitigen', pp. 82–3. Sudoplatov, *Special tasks,* p. 363–4.

132 Sudoplatov, *Special tasks,* p. 364.

133 Larres, 'Neutralisierung oder Westintegration?', p. 572. His proposal was strongly opposed by the Americans. Churchill wanted to negotiate with the Soviets on a whole range of issues, holding out the possibility of a 'generation of peace'.

134 B. Nicolaevsky, 'Sovetsyaiya diktatura i germanskaia problema', *Sotsialisticheskii*

vestnik (November 1955), pp. 209–10. Cited in A. D'Agnostino, *Soviet succession struggles. Kremlinology and the Russian question from Lenin to Gorbachev* (Massachusetts, 1988), p. 183.

135 See resolution of CPSU CC, 7.7.53: 'Über die verbrecherische partei- und staatsfeind-liche Tatigkeit Berijas'. Published in V. Knoll, L. Kölm, *Der Fall Berija. Protokoll einer Abrechnung. Das Plenum des ZK der KPdSU Juli 1953. Stenographischer Bericht* (Berlin, 1993), pp. 327–41; p. 335. See also *ibid.*, speeches of Malenkov (p. 35), Khrushchev (p. 66), Molotov (pp. 78–9) and Bulganin (p. 101).

136 Richter, 'Reexamining Soviet Policy', p. 686.

137 A. Resis (ed.), *Molotov remembers. Inside Kremlin politics. Conversations with Felix Chuyev* (Chicago, 1993), pp. 334–5.

138 A. Gromyko, *Memories* (London, 1989), p. 316.

139 Beria's letter to Malenkov, 1.7.53. Published in C. F. Ostermann, ' "This is not a polit-buro, but a madhouse". The post-Stalin succession struggle, Soviet *Deutschland-politik* and the SED: New evidence from Russian, German and Hungarian archives', *CWIHP Bulletin*, 10 (March 1998), 61–110; p. 99.

140 See speeches of Molotov and Bulganin to CPSU CC, July 7 1953 in Knoll, Kölm, *Der Fall Berija*, pp. 78–9, 101.

141 Besymenski, '1953 – Berija will die DDR beseitigen', p. 83.

142 Mastny, *The Cold War*, p. 180.

143 'Über die Maßnahmen', 648–54.

144 Stulz-Herrnstadt, *Das Herrnstadt-Dokument*, p. 59

145 SAPMO-BArch, ZPA, NL 90/699. Grotewohl's handwritten notes of meeting with Soviet leaders in Moscow, 3.6.53.

146 'Der Berija-Plan und ein chiffriertes Telegramm. Hermann Axen über die deutsch-landpolitische Problematik im Jahre 1953 – Auszüge aus einem Gespräch mit Prof. Dr. Harald Neubert', *ND* (25.6.93), 3.

147 SAPMO-BArch, ZPA, NL 62/145. Rau's handwritten notes from PB meeting, 6.6.53.

148 SAPMO-BArch, ZPA, NL 90/699. Grotewohl's handwritten notes from PB meeting, 6.6.53.

149 SAPMO-BArch, ZPA, NL 62/145, Rau's handwritten notes from PB meeting, 6.6.53. See also SAPMO-BArch, ZPA, NL 90/699, Grotewohl's handwritten notes from PB meeting, 6.6.53.

150 SAPMO-BArch, ZPA, NL 90/699. See also *ibid.*, Ebert's account of his remarks in PB meeting, 6.6.53.

151 SAPMO-BArch, ZPA, NL 90/699. Herrnstadt's record of his remarks in PB meeting, 6.6.53. See also SAPMO-BArch, ZPA, J IV 2/2/287, Ulbricht's handwritten notes from PB meeting, 6.6.53.

152 SAPMO-BArch, ZPA, NL 90/699. Grotewohl's handwritten notes from PB meeting, 6.6.53. This expression was later used by Herrnstadt in a draft resolution for the 15 CC plenum. It was cited by Ulbricht as proof of Herrnstadt's 'counter-revolutionary' intentions. That Herrnstadt already used the term on 6 June is significant, implying it was more than a slip of the pen.

153 SAPMO-BArch, ZPA, NL 62/145. Rau's handwritten notes from PB meeting, 6.6.53.

154 SAPMO-BArch, ZPA, NL 90/699. Grotewohl's handwritten notes from PB meeting, 6.6.53. The PB records note the regular presence of Semyonov and other Soviet rep-resentatives at PB meetings in June and July 1953.

155 Immediate measures were agreed to dissolve quarantine camps for refugees return-

ing from the West and to restore confiscated church properties to their rightful owners. SAPMO-BArch, ZPA, J IV 2/2/287, PB meeting, 6.6.53.

156 See 'Über die Maßnahmen', p. 652.

157 SAPMO-BArch, ZPA, NL 90/699. Herrnstadt's typed-up notes of his remarks to PB meeting, 6.6.53. Collectivization raised social tensions in the countryside to unprecedented levels and swelled the numbers fleeing the GDR in 1952–53.

158 The accusation that Zaisser and Herrnstadt were accomplices of Beria was first made by Ulbricht at the 15 CC plenum. Ulbricht could not provide any evidence to substantiate the charge which was not included in the original speech approved by the PB (see SAPMO-BArch, ZPA, IV 2/1/120, Ulbricht's closing speech to 15 CC plenum, 24.–26.7.53). Western historians have based their accounts on Ulbricht's version of events, pointing out that he was only able to consolidate his position as general secretary after Beria's arrest. See Stern, *Ulbricht*, p. 148; M. Fulbrook, *The Fontana history of Germany 1918–1990. The divided nation* (London, 1991), p. 190; H. Krisch, *The German Democratic Republic. The search for identity* (Colorado, 1985), p. 16; Richter, 'Reexamining Soviet policy', p. 686.

159 Resolution of CPSU CC, 7.7.53, published in Knoll, Kölm, *Der Fall Berija*, pp. 335–6. See also Grotewohl's handwritten notes of talks in the Kremlin, 9.7.53, SAPMO-BArch, ZPA, NL 90/699.

160 Stulz-Herrnstadt, *Das Herrnstadt-Dokument*, p. 74.

161 H. Brandt, 'Die sowjetische Deutschlandpolitik im Frühjahr 1953 aus der Sicht fortschrittlicher Kräfte in der SED', *Osteuropa*, 6 (June 1965), 369–77.

162 *Ibid.*, p. 369. See also Brandt, *Ein Traum*, p. 209.

163 Editorials: 'Der Weg der Verhandlungen ist der erfolgreiche Weg!', *ND* (10.6.53), 1; 'Über die Patriotismus unseres Volkes', *ND* (11.6.53), 1.

164 'Kommunique des Politbüros des Zentralkomitees der SED vom 9. Juni 1953', *ND* (11.6.53), 1.

165 'Ein Generalplan der SED. Wie gesamtdeutsche Wahlen vorbereitet werden sollen', *SBZ-Archiv*, 10 (25.5.55), 147–9. The author claims to have been directly involved in the plan's conception. See also E. Richert, *Macht ohne Mandat* (Köln, Opladen, 1958), p. 14. The plan even outlined a strategy for the SED and KPD should they become opposition parties in an all-German parliament.

166 See 'Präsident Wilhelm Pieck an die Bevölkerung der Deutschen Demokratischen Republik', *ND* (28.6.53), 1; W. Pieck, 'Vorwärts auf dem Neuen Kurs', *ND* (2.7.53), 1; 'Rundfunkansprache des Präsidenten Wilhelm Pieck an die Bevölkerung der Deutschen Demokratischen Republik', *ND* (3.7.53), 1. Pieck spent the spring and summer of 1953 convalescing in the Soviet Union.

167 'Wichtige Beschlüsse', *TR* (13.6.53), 1–2. The same message was conveyed in other articles during this period. See, for example: 'Prof. Dr. Friedrich zum Abkommen von Panmunjoon: "Verhandlungen zur Deutschlandfrage jetzt nötiger denn je"', *TR* (10.6.53), 1; 'Echo auf die Beschlüsse des Ministerrats der DDR: Im Interesse aller Deutschen', *TR* (14.6.53), 1; 'Die westdeutsche Presse zu den Ministerratsbeschlüssen', *ibid.*

168 Stern, *Ulbricht*, p. 137. The PB approved the necessary changes at a meeting on 9 June. It also prohibited the naming of factories, institutions and roads after members of the SED leadership. SAPMO-BArch, ZPA, J IV 2/2/288.

169 Sudoplatov, *Special tasks*, p. 365.

170 Stulz-Herrnstadt, *Das Herrnstadt-Dokument*, p. 109.

171 SAPMO-BArch, ZPA, J IV 2/2/289. Rudolf Herrnstadt, 'Notizen für eine Entschließung des ZK auf dem 14. Plenum' (with Ulbricht's handwritten comments), 13.6.53.

172 S. Kühn, K. Stern, 'Es wird Zeit, den Holzhammer beiseite zu legen', *ND* (14.6.53), 6.

173 Brandt, *Ein Traum*, p. 231.

174 SAPMO-BArch, ZPA, J IV 2/2/290. PB meeting 16.–17.6.53.

175 The best and most recent account of the uprising is Mitter, Wolle, *Untergang auf Raten*, pp. 27–162. See also M. Hagen, *DDR – Juni 1953. Die erste Volkserhebung im Stalinismus* (Stuttgart, 1992).

176 Ostermann, ' "This is not a politburo" ', p. 67.

177 Lippmann, *Honecker*, p. 158. Lippmann was one of Honecker's officials in the FDJ. He talked to Honecker during a break in the PB proceedings. Interestingly, Herrnstadt does not mention the meeting of 16 June in his account.

178 SAPMO-BArch, ZPA, J IV 2/2/290. PB meeting, 16.–17.6.53.

179 Cited in Hagen, *DDR – Juni 1953*, pp. 54–5, 182. See also 'Von der Tagung des Berliner Parteiaktivs', *ND* (18.6.53), 3.

180 Stulz-Herrnstadt, *Das Herrnstadt-Dokument*, pp. 82–3.

181 'Was ist in Berlin geschehen?', *ND* (18.6.53), 1.

182 Ulbricht's version of the uprising as a coup planned by Western intelligence (code-named 'Tag X') is still accepted today by members of the former SED elite. Alfred Neumann, deputy leader of the Berlin SED (promoted to the PB at the 15 CC plenum) is adamant that the uprising was a Western-inspired coup attempt. Neumann claims the Dulles brothers had arrived in West Berlin the week before to lead the action. He recalls how those marching in the processions wore Western clothes and how Potsdamer Platz suddenly emptied of demonstrators following his decree shutting down the U-Bahn (underground railway) link with West Berlin. Suggestions that the norm increases may have been instrumental in provoking the workers' wrath are dismissed with the remark that the factories were full of purged Nazis and a provocation was therefore to be expected at any time. Besides, he protested, the norm increases were rescinded on 16 June whereas the uprising spread from the capital to other areas of the country twenty-four hours later. The argument that the revocation of the norm hikes was 'too little, too late' and simply fuelled a rebellion already underway made no impression on Neumann. Interview with Alfred Neumann, 16.10.92. Ulbricht's private aide, Wolfgang Berger, blames the uprising on the 'West German bourgeoisie' and 'fascist workers' in the GDR, although he does concede that the SED made 'certain political and psychological mistakes' in 1952–53. Interview with Berger, 14.12.92.

183 Editorial: 'Der Zusammenbruch des faschistischen Abenteurs', *ND* (19.6.53), 1. On 4 July, two weeks after the uprising, the PB decided to open the sector borders in Berlin. SAPMO-BArch, ZPA, J IV 2/2/300.

184 SAPMO-BArch, ZPA, J IV 2/2/293. First PB meeting, 21.6.53.

185 SAPMO-BArch, ZPA, J IV 2/2/294. Second PB meeting, 21.6.53 convened for the sole purpose of discussing the proposed 'statement of the SED central committee regarding the situation and the immediate tasks of the party'.

186 Jendretzky, cited in Brandt, *Ein Traum*, pp. 250–2.

187 SAPMO-BArch, ZPA, IV 2/1/117.

188 SAPMO-BArch, ZPA, IV 2/1/117. Grotewohl's report to 14 CC plenum, 21.6.53.

189 SAPMO-BArch, ZPA, IV 2/1/117.

190 SAPMO-BArch, ZPA, IV 2/1/117.
191 SAPMO-BArch, ZPA, IV 2/1/117. Ackermann's speech to 14 CC plenum.
192 SAPMO-BArch, ZPA, IV 2/1/117. Hager's speech to 14 CC plenum.
193 SAPMO-BArch, ZPA, IV 2/1/117. Stoph's speech to 14 CC plenum.
194 SAPMO-BArch, ZPA, IV 2/1/117. Oelßner's speech to 14 CC plenum.
195 Müller-Enbergs, *Der Fall*, pp. 215–16.
196 F. Stößel, *Positionen und Strömungen in der KPD/SED 1945–54* (Köln, 1985), p. 582.
197 W. Pieck, 'Vorwärts auf dem Neuen Kurs', *ND* (2.7.53), 1.
198 'Rundfunkansprache des Präsidenten Wilhelm Pieck an die Bevölkerung der Deutschen Demokratischen Republik', *ND* (3.7.53), 1.
199 Cited in Müller-Enbergs, *Der Fall*, p. 215.
200 *Ibid.*, pp. 214–15.
201 H. Lippmann, 'Der 17. Juni im Zentralkomitee der SED; Vorgeschichte, Ablauf und Folgen' *APZ*, B24 (13.6.56), 369–76; pp. 375–6.
202 Baring, *Uprising in East Germany*, p. 110; Stern, *Ulbricht*, pp. 149–150.
203 Cited in Hagen, *DDR – Juni 1953*, p. 186.
204 On 21 April 1953, Pavel A. Yudin had replaced Semyonov as chairman of the Soviet control commission. In June he became deputy Soviet high commissioner.
205 Deputy defence minister of the USSR. He had arrived in Berlin at the height of the uprising.
206 Report to Soviet foreign minister Molotov and defence minister Bulganin, 24.6.53. Recently discovered in foreign ministry archive of the Russian Federation. Published in C. F. Ostermann, 'New documents on the East German uprising of 1953', *CWIHP Bulletin*, 5 (Spring 1995), 10–21, 57; p. 17.
207 *Ibid.*, p. 20.
208 *Ibid.*
209 Semjonow, *Von Stalin bis Gorbatschow*, pp. 297–8
210 Note from Soviet minister for internal affairs, S. Kruglov, to Malenkov with accompanying communication from interior ministry executives P. Fedotov and I. Fadeikin, 9.7.53. Published in Ostermann, ' "This is not a politburo" ', 101–3; p. 103.
211 SAPMO-BArch, ZPA, J IV 2/2/296. PB meeting, 27.6.53.
212 Stern, *Ulbricht*, p. 137.
213 W. Leonhard, *Kreml ohne Stalin* (Frankfurt, 1959), p. 59.
214 Herrnstadt's account was confirmed in all its aspects by Wilhelm Zaisser. See Stulz-Herrnstadt, *Das Herrnstadt-Dokument*, p. 11.
215 SAPMO-BArch, ZPA, J IV 2/2/287. PB meeting, 6.6.53. The commission was presided over by a Soviet official (either Semyonov or one of his subordinates). Jendretzky was prevented from attending due to illness.
216 BStU, 10993. Ackermann's letter to Matern, 14.9.53.
217 SAPMO-BArch, ZPA, NL 90/699. Herrnstadt's record of his remarks to PB meeting, 6.6.53.
218 W. Otto, 'Dokumente zur Auseinandersetzung in der SED 1953. "Entwurf. Beschluß der Kommission" ', pp. 655, 658.
219 Stulz-Herrnstadt, *Das Herrnstadt-Dokument*, p. 118.
220 SAPMO-BArch, ZPA, IV 2/1/119. Zaisser's speech to 15 CC plenum, 24.–26.7.53.
221 SAPMO-BArch, ZPA, IV 2/1/119–120. Zaisser's speeches to 15 CC plenum. See also Stulz-Herrnstadt, *Das Herrnstadt-Dokument*, p. 118.
222 According to Schirdewan, Herrnstadt was a 'power-hungry' politician. Both men

suffered from tuberculosis and became acquainted in a sanatorium in Sülzhayn in 1946. Schirdewan recalls that during their stay the latter revealed his ambition to scale the heights of SED politics (interview with Schirdewan, 12.10.92). He gave the same testimony to the CPCC two weeks before Herrnstadt's expulsion from the leadership in 1953 (SAPMO-BArch, ZPA, IV 2/4/391, stenographic record, 11.7.53). When questioned about the source of the conflict between them, Schirdewan traced it back to his attempt to dissuade Herrnstadt from pursuing his leadership ambitions ('you are not the type to be a worker's leader – you have no contact with the masses'). He also claims to have resisted an attempt by Herrnstadt to recruit him as a Soviet secret agent after the war. Both factors were apparently instrumental in permanently souring relations between them (interview with Schirdewan, 12.10.92). In late June 1953, Herrnstadt described Schirdewan as a 'dangerous intriguer and a careerist' and spoke out against his appointment to the PB (Stulz-Herrnstadt, *Das Herrnstadt-Dokument*, p. 112). Schirdewan's attacks on Herrnstadt became particularly vituperative after the latter's expulsion from the leadership in 1953. Given the personal antagonism between the two men, Schirdewan's remarks cannot be taken as a reliable assessment of Herrnstadt's character.

223 BStU, 10993. Ackermann's letter to Matern, 14.9.53. See also Herrnstadt's statement to CPCC, 31.8.53; BStU, 10993; and Stulz-Herrnstadt, *Das Herrnstadt-Dokument*, pp. 118–19.

224 SAPMO-BArch, ZPA, IV 2/1/120. Ulbricht's interjection during Zaisser's second speech to 15 CC plenum.

225 Ulbricht seems to have persuaded Semyonov that his interests lay in helping to fabricate a case against Zaisser and Herrnstadt. After 17 June, the Soviet high commissioner was probably instrumental in persuading the Kremlin to support Ulbricht. At the second meeting of the PB commission, Herrnstadt gained the impression 'that things had been going on behind the scenes of which [he] had no knowledge'. Stulz-Herrnstadt, *Das Herrnstadt-Dokument*, p. 113.

226 *Ibid.*, p. 114. Confirmed in Grotewohl's notes from this meeting. SAPMO-BArch, ZPA, NL 90/699. Ebert had originally been proposed by Ackermann.

227 Stulz-Herrnstadt, *Das Herrnstadt-Dokument*, p. 115. Grotewohl's notes from this meeting confirm Herrnstadt's account. Next to Honecker's name, Grotewohl placed a question mark, showing the precarious position of the future East German leader. SAPMO-BArch, ZPA, NL 90/699.

228 Stulz-Herrnstadt, *Das Herrnstadt-Dokument*, pp. 116–17.

229 Oelßner's defection to Ulbricht might partially have been due to personal tension with Zaisser and Herrnstadt. In the PB commission, Zaisser had accused Oelßner of cowardice, threatening that the day might come when he would propose his expulsion from the PB. An alliance with Ulbricht also presented Oelßner with the opportunity to avenge Herrnstadt's veiled attack on him at the 10 CC plenum.

230 Those sections dealing with the party and the political situation were drafted by Herrnstadt. Rau composed the part dealing with the economy.

231 SAPMO-BArch, ZPA, IV 2/4/391. Draft resolution of SED CC: 'The New Course and the renewal of the party'. Also published in Otto, 'Dokumente zur Auseinandersetzung in der SED 1953', pp. 659–67. Herrnstadt emphasized the importance of this aim by putting it in capital letters.

232 SAPMO-BArch, ZPA, IV 2/4/391. 'The New Course and the renewal of the party'. There is no evidence, however, to support Jänicke's contention that Zaisser and

Herrnstadt might have been willing to accept the West German political system as the price of reunification. See Jänicke, *Der dritte Weg*, p. 34.

233 SAPMO-BArch, ZPA, IV 2/4/391: 'The New Course and the renewal of the party'. Herrnstadt was therefore reiterating his warning of 1948–49 that the 'party of the new type' reflect German rather than Soviet traditions.

234 SAPMO-BArch, ZPA, IV 2/4/391: 'The New Course and the renewal of the party'.

235 *Ibid.*

236 SAPMO-BArch, ZPA, NL 90/290. Grotewohl's copy of Herrnstadt's draft resolution for the 15 CC plenum.

237 SAPMO-BArch, ZPA, J IV 2/2/299.

238 Stulz-Herrnstadt, *Das Herrnstadt-Dokument*, pp. 124–5. See also Ulbricht's speech to 15 CC plenum, SAPMO-BArch, ZPA, IV 2/1/119; party news service report, 21.8.53, 'Über die sozialdemokratische Ideologie der Gruppe Zaisser–Herrnstadt', BStU, 10993. There is no evidence to support one historian's claim that Zaisser and Herrnstadt favoured converting the SED into some kind of social democratic party. See P. Garabiol, 'Berlin, 17 juin 1953. Une premiére tentative de réunification de l'Allemagne', *Revue d'histoire diplomatique*, 104 (1990), 57–75; p. 71.

239 According to Herrnstadt, everyone had the feeling that another purge was imminent. He also recalls the widespread unease that something was being agreed behind the scenes 'against which it was better not to fight'. Stulz-Herrnstadt, *Das Herrnstadt-Dokument*, p. 126.

240 H. Annas, H. Stadler, W. Müller, 'Herzlose Bürokraten und ein erfrischendes Gewitter. Warum im Dorf Letschin noch nichts vom neuen Kurs zu spüren war', *ND* (7.7.53), 3.

241 Editorial: 'Unsere ganze Sorge muß den Menschen gelten', *ND* (7.7.53), 1.

242 RIAS was a West Berlin radio station renowned for its virulent anticommunist stance in the 1950s. For new archival evidence on US policy towards East Germany in summer 1953, see C. F. Ostermann, 'The United States, the East German uprising of 1953, and the limits of roll-back', *CWIHP* Working Paper no. 11 (December 1994).

243 BStU, 10993. Wolf's letter to Herrnstadt, 7.7.53.

244 *Ibid.*

245 Not 7 July as recalled by Herrnstadt (*Das Herrnstadt-Dokument*, p. 126). See SAPMO-BArch, ZPA, IV 2/2/302–303, PB meetings, 8.7.53 (there is no record of any meeting held on 7 July).

246 SAPMO-BArch, ZPA, NL 90/699. Grotewohl's handwritten notes from PB meeting, 8.7.53.

247 *Ibid.* In Oelßner's view, Zaisser and Herrnstadt were engaging in factional activity. Ulbricht, however, had 'learnt nothing' and continued to treat his colleagues like 'thick-heads'. There was no need for a first secretary, just collective leadership.

248 SAPMO-BArch, ZPA, NL 90/699.

249 Stulz-Herrnstadt, *Das Herrnstadt-Dokument*, pp. 128–9.

250 SAPMO-BArch, ZPA, NL 90/699. Grotewohl's handwritten notes from PB meeting, 8.7.53.

251 Stulz-Herrnstadt, *Das Herrnstadt-Dokument*, p. 127.

252 *Ibid.*, p. 129. SAPMO-BArch, ZPA, NL 90/699. Grotewohl's handwritten notes from PB meeting, 8.7.53.

253 SAPMO-BArch, ZPA, NL 90/699. Herrnstadt quoted in Grotewohl's handwritten notes from PB meeting, 8.7.53.

254 SAPMO-BArch, ZPA, NL 90/699. Grotewohl's handwritten notes of meeting with Soviet leaders in the Kremlin. Malenkov is cited as saying: 'Grotewohl and Ulbricht must work together . . . and form a collective.' The Kremlin's perception of Ulbricht and Grotewohl as the core of the SED leadership persuaded the latter that it was in his interests to support the general secretary.

255 *Ibid.*

256 Loth's claim that the Soviets were indifferent to Ulbricht's fate is not supported by the evidence. See Loth, *Stalins ungeliebtes Kind*, pp. 215–16.

257 Besymenski, '1953 – Berija will die DDR beseitigen', p. 83. See also Falin, *Politische Erinnerungen*, p. 316.

258 Semyonov, *Von Stalin bis Gorbatschow*, p. 295.

259 Besymenski, '1953 – Berija will die DDR beseitigen', p. 83. See also Sudoplatov, *Special tasks*, p. 366.

260 *Ibid.* Sudoplatov himself was arrested on 21 August. He was not released until 21 August 1968. Sudoplatov, *Special tasks*, pp. 381–2, 419. For more detail of Beria's relations with his presidium colleagues, see V. Nekrassov [translated from the Russian by Barbara and Lothar Lehnhardt], *Berija. Henker in Stalins Diensten. Ende einer Karriere* (Berlin, 1992), pp. 323–51. Following his conviction by a military tribunal, Beria was executed by firing squad in December 1953.

261 Resolution of CPSU CC 'concerning the criminal anti-party and anti-state activities of Beria', 7.7.53. Published in: Knoll, Kölm, *Der Fall Berija*, 327–41; pp. 333–6.

262 *Ibid.*, p. 336. See also SAPMO-BArch, ZPA, NL 90/699 (Grotewohl's handwritten notes of meeting with Soviet leaders in the Kremlin) and Besymenski, '1953 – Berija will die DDR beseitigen', pp. 81–3. For more detail on Beria's policies, see A. Knight, *Beria. Stalin's first lieutenant* (Princeton, 1993).

263 SAPMO-BArch, ZPA, IV 2/2/304. PB meeting, 10.7.53.

264 Stulz-Herrnstadt, *Das Herrnstadt-Dokument*, p. 131.

265 SAPMO-BArch, ZPA, NL 90/290.

266 *Ibid.*

267 *Ibid.*

268 Stulz-Herrnstadt, *Das Herrnstadt-Dokument*, p. 133.

269 *Ibid.*, pp. 134–6. See also SAPMO-BArch, ZPA, IV 2/2/305, PB meeting, 14.7.53.

270 SAPMO-BArch, ZPA, J IV 2/2/305. PB meeting, 14.7.53. In the end Buchwitz narrowly escaped the persecution visited on other former social democrats after the June uprising.

271 Note from Soviet minister for internal affairs, S. Kruglov, to Malenkov with accompanying communication from interior ministry executives P. Fedotov and I. Fadeikin, 9.7.53. Published in Ostermann, ' "This is not a politburo" ', 101–3; p. 103.

272 Fechner's assurance that only those who had committed violent crimes on 17 June would be liable to prosecution was published in *ND* on 30 June. In an 'amendment' of 2 July, the same newspaper published his defence of the constitutional 'right to strike'.

273 Stulz-Herrnstadt, *Das Herrnstadt-Dokument*, pp. 144–5.

274 Ulbricht later used Fechner's remarks to accuse Herrnstadt of practising 'social democracy'. The 'agitation department' which cleared the interview was ultimately responsible to Ulbricht. The former social democrat was immediately replaced as justice minister by Hilda Benjamin who administered a new wave of purges.

275 Stulz-Herrnstadt, *Das Herrnstadt-Dokument*, pp. 145–7.

276 Stulz-Herrnstadt (*ibid.*, pp. 145–7) and Müller-Enbergs (*Der Fall*, pp. 258–61) both confuse the chronology of the events culminating in Fechner's arrest. According to Herrnstadt, the above PB meeting was held between 20 and 30 June. The records (which note the presence of both Fechner and Yudin) are, however, dated 14.7.53. The rough copy – also dated 14.7.53 – carries the reference SAPMO-BArch, ZPA, J IV 2/2 A/289.

277 SAPMO-BArch, ZPA, J IV 2/2A/289. Rough copy of resolution for PB meeting, 14.7.53.

278 SAPMO-BArch, ZPA, J IV 2/2/305. PB meeting, 14.7.53. Oelßner drew up the resolutions for this PB meeting. It is therefore conceivable that only Ulbricht, Oelßner and Zaisser knew of the decision to arrest Fechner.

279 R. Andert, W. Herzberg, *Der Sturz. Erich Honecker im Kreuzverhör* (Berlin – Weimar, 1991), pp. 228–9. Shortly after the 15 CC plenum, Honecker matriculated at the party training school in Moscow. He did not return to Berlin until 1956.

280 SAPMO-BArch, ZPA, IV 2/4/391. Typed document (anonymous and undated) containing Fechner's reported testimony. Zaisser allegedly made his remarks at a meeting of the council of ministers.

281 SAPMO-BArch, ZPA, IV 2/1/120. Zaisser's second speech to 15 CC plenum, 24.–26.7.53.

282 SAPMO-BArch, ZPA, NL 215/111. Oelßner's handwritten notes from PB meeting, 14.7.53.

283 SAPMO-BArch, ZPA, NL 90/390.

284 SAPMO-BArch, ZPA, J IV 2/2/307.

285 *Ibid.*

286 SAPMO-BArch, ZPA, NL 215/111. Oelßner's handwritten notes from PB meeting, 18.7.53.

287 *Ibid.* Oelßner's account is supported by Grotewohl's notes from what appears to be the same meeting (SAPMO-BArch, ZPA, NL 90/699).

288 SAPMO-BArch, ZPA, NL 215/111. Oelßner's handwritten notes from PB meeting, 22.7.53.

289 Stulz-Herrnstadt, *Das Herrnstadt-Dokument*, p. 157. According to Herrnstadt, issues were rarely decided by vote in the PB. On those occasions when votes were held, they were as a rule unanimous, no distinction being made between PB members and candidates.

290 SAPMO-BArch, ZPA, IV 2/2/309. PB meeting, 23.7.53.

291 SAPMO-BArch, ZPA, IV 2/1/120. Ulbricht's closing speech to 15 CC plenum, 24.–26.7.53.

292 SAPMO-BArch, ZPA, J IV 2/2A/293. PB meeting, 23.7.53.

293 SAPMO-BArch, ZPA, IV 2/1/120.

294 SAPMO-BArch, ZPA, IV 2/1/120. Ulbricht's closing speech to 15 CC plenum.

295 SAPMO-BArch, ZPA, IV 2/1/120. Lange's speech to 15 CC plenum.

296 SAPMO-BArch, ZPA, IV 2/1/120. Zaisser's interjection during Lange's speech.

297 Stulz-Herrnstadt, *Das Herrnstadt-Dokument*, pp. 175–6. In a letter to Khrushchev six years later, Herrnstadt reported a coincidental encounter with Lange in May 1959, during which the latter provided the background against which he had made the allegations. According to Herrnstadt, Lange maintained that he had been acting on the instructions of a third party, leading inexorably to the conclusion that this was 'a cold-blooded, meticulously calculated provocation'. SAPMO-BArch, ZPA, IV 2/4/392, Herrnstadt's letter to Khrushchev, November 1959.

298 Semjonow, *Von Stalin bis Gorbatschow*, p. 292.

299 SAPMO-BArch, ZPA, IV 2/1/125.

300 Stulz-Herrnstadt, *Das Herrnstadt-Dokument*, p. 172.

301 SAPMO-BArch, ZPA, IV 2/11/v519. Matern's reply to Richard Bauerschäfer, 2.9.53.

302 'Der neue Kurs und die Aufgaben der Partei', *Entschließung der 15. Tagung des Zentralkomitees der Sozialistischen Einheitspartei Deutschlands vom 24. bis 26. Juli 1953* (Berlin-Ost, 1953), 103–38; p. 105.

303 *Ibid.*, p. 126.

304 *Ibid.*, pp. 107–15.

305 SAPMO-BArch, ZPA, IV 2/1/120. Ackermann's speech to 15 CC plenum, 24.–26.7.53.

306 SAPMO-BArch, ZPA, IV 2/1/119. Buchwitz's speech to 15 CC plenum.

307 Ackermann, Schmidt and Jendretzky were allowed to retain their seats on the CC until January 1954.

308 Schirdewan, Stoph, Neumann, Warnke and Leuschner were the new members.

309 Leuschner's election was secured with three abstentions. Rau was re-elected with four abstentions.

310 SAPMO-BArch, ZPA, IV 2/1/121. Thirteen votes were cast in his favour. There were eleven abstentions.

311 SAPMO-BArch, ZPA, IV 2/1/120.

312 Wettig, 'Die beginnende Umorientierung', pp. 503–4.

313 SAPMO-BArch, ZPA, NL 90/471. 'Note der Sowjetregierung an die Regierungen Frankreichs, Großbritanniens und der USA zur Deutschlandfrage', *Rundschau am Montag* (17.8.53), 1.

314 *Ibid.*

315 Erfurt, *Moscow's policy in Germany*, p. 42.

316 SAPMO-BArch, ZPA, NL 90/471. 'Note der Sowjetregierung an die Regierungen Frankreichs, Großbritanniens und der USA zur Deutschlandfrage'.

317 SAPMO-BArch, ZPA, NL 90/471. Stenographic minutes of meeting with Soviet leaders in the Kremlin, 20.8.53.

318 *Ibid.*

319 SAPMO-BArch, ZPA, NL 90/471.

320 Lippmann, *Honecker*, p. 160.

321 *Ibid.*, pp. 160–1.

322 'Friedensvertrag und demokratische Einheit – die tiefste Sehnsucht des deutschen Volkes. Rundfunkansprache des Präsidenten der Deutschen Demokratischen Republik, Wilhelm Pieck, vom 17. August 1953', *TR* (18.8.53), 1.

323 'Max Reimann fordert sofortige Einberufung des Bundestages', *TR* (20.8.53), 1; 'Unterstützt die Forderung den Bundestag einzuberufen!', *TR* (22.8.53), 1.

324 SAPMO-BArch, ZPA, IV 2/1/126.

325 Jänicke, *Der dritte Weg*, p. 39.

326 Stulz-Herrnstadt, *Das Herrnstadt-Dokument*, p. 241.

327 This view was put forward by the office of the US high commissioner for Germany in 1954. ' "Ehemaliger führender Kommunist büßt in einem kleineren Archiv der Soviet-Zone". In: Office of the US High Commissioner for Germany Berlin Element. Office of Public Affairs – Information Branch, 7.5.1954.' Cited in Müller-Enbergs, *Der Fall*, pp. 325–6.

328 SAPMO-BArch, ZPA, IV 2/4/392, Else Zaisser's letter to delegates of 5 party congress of the SED, 10.6.58. Zaisser apparently suffered a fatal stroke after reading Matern's speech to the 35 CC plenum in February 1958 in which he reduced the Zaisser–Herrnstadt opposition to personal animosity against Ulbricht.

329 SAPMO-BArch, ZPA, IV 2/11/v519. Zaisser's note to 4 party congress of SED with Matern's response.

330 SAPMO-BArch, ZPA, IV 2/4/392. Else Zaisser's letter to 6 party congress of the SED, 5.1.63.

331 SAPMO-BArch, ZPA, IV 2/4/392. Letter from PB secretary Otto Schön to Ulbricht, 25.7.58.

332 SAPMO-BArch, ZPA, IV 2/11/v519. See letter from Max Opitz (Pieck's secretary) to Ulbricht, 15.9.59.

333 See Herrnstadt's letters to party leadership, SAPMO-BArch, ZPA, NL 90/303.

334 SAPMO-BArch, ZPA, IV 2/4/392. Matern's letter to Ulbricht, 27.6.62.

335 Cited in W. Otto, 'Expertise im Auftrag der Enquete-Kommission des Bundestages "Ausarbeitung von Geschichte und Folgen der SED-Diktatur in Deutschland". Thema: "Widerspruch und abweichendes Verhalten in der SED" ' (manuscript), p. 9.

336 Cited in *ibid*. An MfS report from 1 July discerned 'a hostile attitude towards the party' among many of its members. See SAPMO-BArch, ZPA, IV 2/5/560 (cited in Mitter, Wolle, *Untergang auf Raten*, p. 142).

337 M. McCauley, *The German Democratic Republic since 1945* (London, 1983), p. 70.

338 SAPMO-BArch, ZPA, IV 2/11/v519. Otto Schön to Matern, 14.1.54. 'Feindmaterial gegen die Partei aus Thüringen' (undated, but distributed to PB members in January 1954).

339 Schirdewan's report to 4 party congress of the SED, 'Über die Abänderungen am Statut der Sozialistischen Einheitspartei Deutschlands', *Protokoll der Verhandlungen des IV. Parteitages der Sozialistischen Einheitspartei Deutschlands*, II (Berlin-Ost, 1954), pp. 904–71; p. 915.

340 SAPMO-BArch, ZPA, IV 2/4/391. Letter from Dr Med. Rud. Baumann to Matern, 30.10.54.

341 After the proclamation of the New Course, the CDU and LPD had attempted to reclaim their former status under the political system of 1946. See Müller-Enbergs, *Der Fall*, p. 316. Some of their branches at district level went further, demanding the resignations of Ulbricht and Grotewohl and all-German free elections. The Rostock CDU issued the following declaration on 19 June: 'We call on the entire work force to pursue their demands further. As members of the CDU we demand the resignation of Otto Grotewohl and Walter Ulbricht. We wish the workers much success and ask them to vote for the CDU in all-German elections.' MfS situation report, cited in 'Der mit dem Bart muß weg', *Der Spiegel* (14.6.93), 65–9; p. 68.

342 In a circular to all its members and district 1 secretaries on 25 August, the CC emphasized the importance of recruiting 'reliable and progressive forces' to the other political parties. SAPMO-BArch, ZPA, NL 90/504.

343 Jänicke, *Der dritte Weg*, p. 40.

344 Cited in Loth, *Stalins ungeliebtes Kind*, p. 219.

345 Jänicke, *Der dritte Weg*, p. 40.

346 *Ibid*.

347 Stern, *Ulbricht*, p. 151.

348 SAPMO-BArch, ZPA, IV 2/4/391. Memo from academic department of CC to

Matern dated 6.2.59, containing Felix Heinrich Gentzen's account of his conversations with Herrnstadt in 1956–57.

349 Cited in Müller-Enbergs, *Der Fall*, p. 331.

350 Herrnstadt's notes, April 1964. N. Stulz-Herrnstadt in *Das Herrnstadt-Dokument*, p. 41.

351 R. Herrnstadt, *Die Entstehung der Klassen* (Berlin-Ost, 1965), pp. 98–9.

352 Excerpt from a Herrnstadt's papers, 1963. Cited in Stulz-Herrnstadt, *Das Herrnstadt-Dokument*, p. 282.

353 Cited by Stulz-Herrnstadt in *Das Herrnstadt-Dokument*, p. 44.

354 Herrnstadt's notes written in about 1964, 'Welches sind die untrüglichen Zeichen des Personenkults?', Stulz-Herrnstadt in *Das Herrnstadt-Dokument*, pp. 45–6.

355 Herrnstadt's notes from 7.5.64. Stulz-Herrnstadt in *Das Herrnstadt-Dokument*, p. 45. See also Herrnstadt's letter to Semyonov dated 28 November 1962, published in *Das Herrnstadt-Dokument*, pp. 264–78; p. 276: Despite the 22 party congress of the CPSU in 1962, the SED continued to argue that there was no personality cult in the GDR. Herrnstadt was appalled: 'This assessment is dreadful for many reasons: It contradicts all the experiences accumulated by the masses themselves, it turns party functionaries (and hundreds of other people who represent the party line in public, for example the teachers) into liars and undermines their authority . . . Such behaviour must inevitably lead to new tensions and untruths.'

356 Herrnstadt's notes from 7.5.64. Stulz-Herrnstadt in *Das Herrnstadt-Dokument*, p. 45.

357 Stulz-Herrnstadt in *Das Herrnstadt-Dokument*, p. 44.

358 Cited in Müller-Enbergs, *Der Fall*, p. 342. The remarks, allegedly made shortly before his death, were recalled in 1990 by Margot Pfannstiel, one of Herrnstadt's erstwhile colleagues on *ND*.

359 Schirdewan cites Herrnstadt's silence on the PB opposition of 1956–58 (see Chapter 3) as evidence of Herrnstadt's false pretences. In claiming that he wanted the New Course without Beria, Schirdewan places himself between Ulbricht and Herrnstadt. Taped interview with Schirdewan, 12.9.92.

360 Taped interview with Schirdewan, 12.10.92.

361 Interview with Paul Wandel, 30.11.92.

362 Interview with Hager, 1.12.92.

363 SAPMO-BArch, ZPA, IV 2/2.035/46. Record of a personal conversation between Honecker and Jaruzelski after the completion of official talks in East Berlin, 29.3.82.

364 V. Herrnstadt, 'Parteidisziplin hat Menschen kaputt gemacht', *Mitteldeutsche Zeitung* (27.4.90), 12.

365 Herrnstadt was rehabilitated by the SED on 29 November 1989. On 25 April 1993, the PDS annulled Zaisser's expulsion from the party while reserving judgement on his record as minister for state security. See W. Otto, G. Lauter, 'Wilhelm Zaisser: Zwischen Parteibefehl und Bannbulle', *Disput*, 12 (1993), 12–15; p. 15.

3

The anti-Ulbricht opposition 1956–58

The twentieth party congress of the CPSU held between 14 and 25 February 1956 opened a Pandora's box of grievances in the satellite countries of East-Central Europe. Not only did the Soviet leader Nikita Khrushchev condemn Joseph Stalin's personality cult, he debunked his other doctrines too, for example the inevitability of war and the intensification of class struggle during the period of socialist development. The necessity for 'collective leadership' and policies attuned to the special needs of indigenous populations were also proclaimed. 'Coexistence' with the West became the guiding principle of Soviet foreign policy.

In October 1956, the Polish communist Wladyslaw Gomulka[1] was swept to power on a wave of popular revulsion against Stalinist excesses perpetrated during the Bierut era. In Hungary the Gero regime was overthrown in a violent revolution leading to the disintegration of the Communist Party, the proclamation of a multi-party system and an attempt to withdraw Hungary from the Warsaw Pact. Only Soviet tanks could liquidate the revolution and restore communist rule.

Ulbricht's greatest fear was that the ferment would spread to East Germany and that a 'German Gomulka' would emerge to channel popular demands for renewal and obtain Soviet support for a change of leadership.[2] Symptomatic of Ulbricht's insecurity in this regard was his condemnation of the Polish state security service for failing to prevent Gomulka's meteoric rise to power.[3] A report compiled for the twenty-eighth central committee plenum in July 1956 must have been deeply unsettling for the SED leadership. Not only had Ulbricht alienated the East German people, he had also lost the confidence of many comrades. Some at grass-roots level even praised the SPD as an example worthy of emulation. In Halle there were calls for Ulbricht's resignation and radical restructuring to guarantee ordinary party members a say in the election of a new politburo. In the population as a whole discord was rife. At a gathering in Erfurt there was praise for democracy in Bonn and criticism of one-party dictatorship in the GDR. Discontent was especially prevalent among the young who vociferously demanded the rights and freedoms accorded to their brothers and sisters in the Federal Republic. Sections of the intelligentsia called for free and secret elections, condemning those of 1954 as a fraud. The poor economic situation relative to West Germany was a central issue for all social strata and the GDR's 'socialist' transformation was widely regarded as the main impediment to German reunification.[4]

It was against this background that SED high politics were conducted in the years 1956 to 1958. We can divide the anti-Ulbricht opposition into three sections, each to be examined in turn. First, the potential threat presented by Merker and Dahlem – Ulbricht's partly rehabilitated purge victims. Second, the Schirdewan–Oelßner opposition in the politburo. Third, the opposition in the central committee.

Merker or Dahlem: A 'German Gomulka' in waiting?

If the 'Polish October' was to be replicated in the GDR there were two candidates for the role of 'German Gomulka': Paul Merker and Franz Dahlem. The former had been a member of the SED leadership from 1947 to 1950 before being excommunicated and imprisoned after the Rajk trial in Hungary. The latter was purged as a result of the Slansky trial in Czechoslovakia, but spared imprisonment and expulsion from the party.

Unlike Gomulka in Poland, Merker had not played an important role in the SED leadership during the late 1940s. Despite misgivings, Merker had collaborated with the Stalinization process and, since he was not widely known in the party, it is unlikely that he would have been able to establish a solid base of support within its ranks. Still, Ulbricht viewed the prospect of his rehabilitation with trepidation. If Pieck used his influence to secure Merker's release from prison,[5] Ulbricht did everything to obstruct his readmission to the party.[6]

Merker was first and foremost an intellectual and it was to him that some intellectuals turned in their search for a 'third way'. Merker, however, showed no sign of harbouring any political ambitions. In a draft statement of 8 December 1956, he set out his plans for the future: 'My health no longer permits me to work . . . I therefore intend to write and – in so far as the opportunity exists – to participate in the activities of temporary commissions and perhaps to teach part-time at the FDGB school.'[7] Released from prison in January 1956 he was ill, weary and disorientated after three years solitary confinement. Deprived of both public rehabilitation and material redress, Merker was supported by his old friend Walter Janka. Merker's years in isolation had taken their toll. Unaware of such elementary facts of political life as Stalin's death and the popular uprising of 17 June 1953, it was Janka who brought him up to date with political reality. Hoping to mobilize him as an alternative to Ulbricht,[8] Janka invited Merker to a meeting of intellectuals at his home in Kleinmachnow, East Berlin on 21 November 1956.[9]

Some of the ideas discussed at this meeting were subsequently put to paper by Wolfgang Harich in the form of a fifty-page manifesto. This document is remarkable both for its detailed analysis and concrete proposals. Harich wanted to combine the 'socio-economic achievements' of the East German regime (land reform, nationalization of industry, the 'right' to employment, education and medical treatment) with the democratic traditions of a 'bourgeois' state (parliamentary democracy, the rule of law, freedom of the press). Stalinism – defined as 'counter-revolutionary' – was perceived as the main obstacle to democratization. Before it could be presented to the central committee, the programme was confiscated and Harich arrested.

The highlight of the manifesto is a nine-stage programme for Germany's reunification as a democratic and neutral state under SPD/SED auspices. To promote a 'special German way to socialism', a plethora of de-Stalinization measures were proposed: democratization of SED party structures; the election of a new politburo; a purge of 'extreme Stalinists' from the party apparatus; abolition of the East German army and ministry for state security; expulsion and prosecution of party and MfS officials guilty of violating the law; restoration of the old German Länder; maximum decentralization of decision-making; abolition of censorship; guarantees of religious freedom and the right to strike; approval for limited capitalist activity in the economy; election of workers' councils in industry; dismantling of the economic apparatus; factory independence within the framework of a new 'perspective plan'; clearer delimitation of powers between party and state; reduction in the remit of the party apparatus; increased room for manoeuvre for the bloc parties and mass organizations; immunity for elected representatives; denunciation of the undemocratic means by which the SPD and the KPD were united in 1946; SED independence from the CPSU; KPD autonomy from the SED; critical reappraisal of the ideas of Bukharin, Trotsky, Luxemburg, Gramsci, Herrnstadt and other alleged 'traitors' in the formulation of party policy. The reforms were supposed to culminate in victory for the SPD and the SED in free multi-party elections to an all-German national assembly.[10] Harich even seemed prepared to risk the hijack of this process by the conservative right: 'that was for me . . . the lesser evil compared to the maintenance of division and membership of opposing military blocs . . . On balance, I would have preferred a reactionary-conservative Germany to a divided one. That would have been a sour apple into which one would have had to bite.'[11] Better 'capitalism in one country' than 'communism in half a country.'

Janka did not inform Merker who would be attending the meeting or what would be discussed. Neither was he aware that Ulbricht had issued a warning and that the Soviet ambassador had already rejected Harich's ideas. Merker only learned these facts at the meeting itself and said very little throughout. Presented with Harich's proposals Merker was 'sympathetically disposed, friendly and interested but cautious and reserved.'[12] According to Harich, Merker emphasized both the importance of party unity and the need for a change of leadership once the situation in Poland and Hungary had stabilized.[13] He welcomed the twentieth party congress of the CPSU as an historic opportunity and criticized Stalin's 'inflexible' foreign policy for bringing the world to the brink of World War Three.[14]

Apparently sympathetic to the general tenor of Harich's concept,[15] Merker agreed that certain reforms were necessary to make the GDR more attractive as an alternative to West German capitalism. Special emphasis was placed on the need to increase the participation and well-being of the working class through pension increases, wage bonuses and workers' committees in industry.[16] In other areas he advised caution. Harich, for example, favoured the wholesale decollectivization of agriculture; Merker only the dissolution of those farms which had proved themselves 'unviable.'[17] Janka advocated lifting censorship on all famous authors regardless of nationality; Merker believed censorship might still be necessary in certain cases.[18]

On the issue of German unity, Merker endorsed the need for co-operation with the SPD but criticized Harich for disregarding the geopolitical situation. As Harich testified in 1992: 'A few questions were controversial. Merker, for example, was of the opinion that I only saw the two German states, that I did not see the larger context and that such reforms . . . could only be implemented with the agreement of the Soviet Union and USA.'[19] Still, Merker was cautiously optimistic in this respect, interpreting superpower co-operation against the Israeli–British–French expedition in the Suez Canal as a sign of US–Soviet rapprochement. If the trend continued 'there could certainly be new and positive aspects for the German question.'[20] Returning home from the meeting, Merker reportedly told Janka that it was good for the party that there were such 'lively thinkers' in its ranks.[21]

After Janka's arrest, Merker felt obliged to clear his name by reporting the meeting to the party.[22] Ulbricht then demanded his full co-operation in unmasking the 'counter-revolutionary conspiracy.' The man seen by many in the West as a 'German Gomulka' was too weak to resist the threats of a leader determined to crush all hope of reform.

Franz Dahlem represents something of a contrast to Paul Merker. Although no popular hero, he had a potential reservoir of support among Spanish Civil War veterans and communists who had spent the war in Western Europe. He was liked by the party rank and file and bore the distinction of having been Ulbricht's main rival in the SED leadership between 1946 and 1953. Unlike Merker, he had not spent three years in solitary confinement and was therefore in touch with both political events and erstwhile comrades. As always, Ulbricht was taking no chances. Dahlem's formal 'rehabilitation' at the twenty-eighth central committee plenum in July 1956 was not even publicized.[23]

Widely regarded as a spent force by 1957,[24] new archive material reveals that Dahlem cherished high political ambitions. In a letter to Ulbricht in February of that year, he stated his desire to scale the heights of SED politics once again: 'I will try, through successful work as a member of the central committee, to gain its confidence so that I can be re-elected to the politburo. I regard that as the keystone of my full rehabilitation.'[25] Moreover, he expressed a determination to participate fully in public life through the press and media, to regain his place on the 'German committee of antifascist resistance fighters'[26] and to use his rehabilitation to help other members of the party purged in the early 1950s.[27] It remains an open question whether he wanted to see Ulbricht deposed as first secretary or whether he wanted the top job himself.[28]

A salient theme in Dahlem's letters to the leadership between 1955 and 1957 is his disagreement with SED policy on the issue of German unity. His greatest wish was to be re-elected to the international and all-German committees 'for the peaceful resolution of the German question.' Instead, he was assigned the relatively insignificant post of first deputy in the state secretariat for higher education.

In a letter to Pieck and Ulbricht in January 1955, Dahlem set out his views on the need for a more active *Deutschlandpolitik*:

> in view of the great possibilities now of drawing new, broad sections of French, English and Italian politicians and public figures into a fighting alliance (*Kampfverbindung*) with the patriotic peace forces in Germany and the People's Republics, I think it expedient and promising to organize a new international conference for the peaceful resolution of the German question.[29]

He supplemented a proposal for reactivation of the defunct, SED-sponsored 'all-German committee for peaceful resolution of the German question' with a call for extensive links with social democrat and trade union functionaries, church representatives and 'bourgeois' parties in the Federal Republic.[30] Such ideas were, of course, anathema to Ulbricht. In subsequent letters Dahlem drew attention to the many international contacts he had established during the war and as SED functionary responsible for inter-German relations. Such links needed to be strengthened, he insisted, if 'remilitarization' in West Germany was to be halted. His call for closer ties with the Polish Communist Party is particularly striking, given the rift between Ulbricht and Gomulka at this time.[31]

With regard to domestic policy, Dahlem declared that the party could only win popular support if it respected 'legality' and corrected mistakes resulting from its emulation of Stalin's course in the USSR.[32] The third party conference between 24 and 30 March 1956, he believed, was an opportunity to demonstrate that the party was trustworthy, that it was an ally of 'truth and legality.' Only then, he insisted, could the SED appeal to 'passive workers' in the GDR and social democrats in the Federal Republic.[33]

As first deputy in the state secretariat for higher education, Dahlem was suddenly presented with a crisis which, unless dealt with quickly, threatened to rock the SED to its foundations. Inspired by the Polish example, students at East Berlin's Humboldt University staged a rebellion. At first their grievances were limited to the academic syllabus, for example compulsory lessons in Russian and Marxist–Leninist theory. But when the students began agitating for political reform, Ulbricht sent in the workers' militia to quell what he believed was counter-revolutionary agitation directed from West Berlin.

Dahlem refused to condemn the students unequivocally: 'Now it is nothing unusual that young students hold vigorous (*scharf*) discussions. After all, we are dealing here with young people who think.'[34] Instead of putting all the blame on Western secret intelligence, Dahlem pointed the finger at Honecker's FDJ.[35] Although he did not defend the 'Harich–Janka Group',[36] he did sympathize with student demands on mandatory lessons in Russian and Marxist–Leninist ideology.[37] He adopted a pragmatic stance in commending certain aspects of the revolt while attempting to disassociate himself from others.[38] Dahlem also endorsed Gomulka as the new leader of Poland.[39] This was in stark contrast to Ulbricht who blocked publication of Gomulka's speech to the Polish central committee.[40] According to the GDR minister for state security, Ernst Wollweber, 'Gomulka was to Ulbricht what a red rag is to a bull.'[41]

Dissatisfied with being sidelined to the state secretariat for higher education, Dahlem incessantly appealed for a higher ranking post to match his experience in international affairs.[42] It is obvious from Dahlem's letters to the party leadership that Ulbricht was waging a campaign against him. *Neues Deutschland* refused to publish his article on the tasks facing higher education in the wake of the third party conference. He was prevented from taking part in senate deliberations at the Humboldt University, despite being officially responsible for that institution.[43] The purge of Dahlem had so soured relations with former politburo comrades that they could neither abide his articles in the press nor his presence at public meetings.

If Dahlem was unhappy with the incomplete nature of his rehabilitation, he also enjoyed some support on the central committee commission[44] set up in March 1956 to review the cases of purge victims. That one of its members should emphasize the need to respect grass-roots feeling on this issue[45] suggests a groundswell of support for Dahlem in the lower echelons of the party. Following his rehabilitation, the latter was inundated with congratulation telegrams and messages of support.[46]

When the student revolt was reaching its climax in November 1956, Ulbricht moved decisively to outmanoeuvre his rival. On 10 November, the politburo passed a resolution inviting Dahlem to express full support for the policies of the party and government.[47] Exploiting the latter's desire for political recognition, Ulbricht made full rehabilitation conditional on good behaviour. In summoning both Harich and Dahlem to his office on the same morning (the two briefly met in the doorway as Dahlem was leaving) Ulbricht seemed to be issuing the latter a warning.[48] Two weeks later Dahlem learned that the young intellectual had been arrested.

Ulbricht seized the political initiative at the thirtieth central committee plenum between 30 January and 1 February 1957, declaring war on 'revisionism' and accelerating the tempo of 'socialist development.' In this way he was able to strengthen his position and end hopes for reform. Craving full rehabilitation, Dahlem capitulated and endorsed the Ulbricht course. No doubt seduced by the promise of high office (a promise never fulfilled), Dahlem denounced the 'Schirdewan group' in February 1958.[49] If Schirdewan had helped Ulbricht destroy Dahlem in 1953,[50] it was now Dahlem's turn to return the favour. Yet again Ulbricht succeeded in playing rivals off against each other. At the thirty-fifth central committee plenum in February 1958, Dahlem provided some of the background to his 'conversion.' After returning from Poland in October 1956, he had apparently sought an audience with Ulbricht to emphasize the need to rectify past mistakes. Ulbricht, however, succeeded in persuading him that the party line was correct.[51]

Neither Merker nor Dahlem enjoyed mass popular support and both were somewhat discredited by their role in the Stalinization process. Ultimately, it was Ulbricht's success in preventing an 'East German October' which sealed the fate of any would-be pretender. There is no evidence of any contact between Dahlem and Merker in 1956–57 – perhaps due to the former's complicity in the downfall of the latter in 1950.[52] According to Harich: 'Janka said . . . Merker was all too cautious and reserved, he did not, for example, think about . . . making contact with Franz Dahlem, because he wanted to avoid all suspicion of factional activity against Walter Ulbricht.'[53]

The willingness of both men to endorse the status quo in 1957 did not spare them further humiliation. Merker died in 1969, leaving his widow to bear the legacy of an incomplete rehabilitation. In 1958 Dahlem was struck off the list of candidates for the parliamentary elections, excluded from official Soviet functions and prevented from participating in the work of the 'committee of antifascist resistance fighters.' His name continued to be airbrushed out of books, documents, photographs and other party records.[54] In 1965 he was the only member of the old KPD leadership not invited to commemorate the twentieth anniversary of the 'antifascist-democratic bloc.'[55] Ten years later his call for an investigation into Matern's responsibility for the purges of the early 1950s was rejected out of hand.[56] In one of his last letters, Dahlem confessed: 'I cannot and will not forget the years 1950 to 1953.'[57] Franz Dahlem, like Paul Merker before him, died a bitter and disillusioned man.

The Schirdewan–Oelßner opposition in the politburo[58]

Karl Schirdewan was born illegitimate in 1907 and adopted by devout catholic parents. Despite a proletarian upbringing, the young Schirdewan aspired to a career in the book trade. Initially employed as an office boy, he joined a trade union at fifteen, the Communist Youth Association a year later. At the age of eighteen he joined the KPD and in 1927 was deployed as youth secretary for East Prussia. Arrested by the Gestapo in 1934, he spent the next eleven years as an inmate of the Sachsenhausen and Flossenbürg concentration camps. After the war, Schirdewan was responsible for researching the activities of party members during the Nazi era. In 1947 he was appointed head of the SED's western commission, charged with the task of overseeing communist activity in West Germany. He then served as first secretary in *Land* Saxony and *Bezirk* Leipzig, before being appointed to the central committee staff responsible for controlling the 'leading organs of the party and mass organizations.' Co-opted as a member of the central committee and its secretariat in late 1952, Schirdewan's swift climb to the summit of SED politics was consummated in July 1953 when he joined the politburo after the purge of the 'Zaisser–Herrnstadt opposition.' As cadre-chief he was especially well placed to gauge the political mood in both the party and population. Perceived by some sections of the SED as Ulbricht's 'crown prince', he was the latter's main rival for the leading position.

Fred Oelßner was born in 1903. He joined the KPD at the age of seventeen and in the 1920s edited a communist newspaper. A student in Moscow between 1926 and 1932, he briefly returned to Germany before fleeing to Czechoslovakia and then France to escape Nazi persecution. In 1935 he returned to the Soviet Union where he headed the German department of Radio Moscow during World War Two. After the war the SED made use of Oelßner's considerable intellectual talents, appointing him head of 'party instruction' in 1946. Already a member of the party executive in 1947, he joined the politburo in 1950. Regarded as the SED's leading theoretician until 1958, he was central committee secretary for propaganda from 1950 to 1955 and chief editor of the journal *Einheit* until 1956. Between 1955 and 1958 he was deputy chairman of the council of ministers, until 1957 chairman of its commission for 'consumer production and provision of the population.'

In February 1956, Ulbricht, Grotewohl, Schirdewan and Neumann visited Moscow for the twentieth party congress of the CPSU. The night before Khrushchev made his sensational 'secret speech' denouncing Stalin, he sent the SED leaders a personal envoy informing them of its contents.[59] After returning to Berlin, Ulbricht (fearing the consequences for his own leadership) set out to suppress debate over the lessons the SED might learn from the revelations. On 4 March, he flatly declared that Stalin was no longer a classic exponent of Marxist theory.[60] For Schirdewan and Oelßner, however, the dramatic sea change sanctioned in Moscow warranted more than a dismissive article in *Neues Deutschland*.[61] Their opposition to the Ulbricht course remained hidden from the general public until it was officially denounced at the thirty-fifth central committee plenum in early February 1958.

The SED convened the third party conference between 24 and 30 March 1956 to take stock of the momentous CPSU proceedings. Given that Ulbricht regarded any critical discussion of the Stalin issue as anathema, it is hardly surprising that the agenda concentrated on economic policy instead. The first secretary allegedly directed Schirdewan to read extracts of Khrushchev's 'secret speech' to delegates in a closed session and to speak quickly so as to prevent the stenographers from recording the details. Schirdewan apparently refused to carry out the second of these instructions.[62]

On 29 April 1956, *Neues Deutschland* published an anonymous article[63] assessing the lessons to be learned from the twentieth party congress of the CPSU. Interviewed in 1994, Schirdewan claimed to be its author.[64] The article rejected 'all dictatorial behaviour' and called for, among other things, collective leadership, 'an open exchange of opinions', 'the safeguarding of democratic legality' and 'complete protection of the rights of party members.'[65] These demands must be seen in the context of Schirdewan's desire to encourage greater transparency at all levels of the SED. Already in 1953–54, Honecker was making disparaging comments to FDJ colleague Heinz Lippmann about the 'debating society' in Schirdewan's division.[66]

Schirdewan's call for more open discussion was designed to improve the atmosphere in the party, poisoned as it was by Ulbricht's personality cult. In 1992, Schirdewan's wife testified to the reality of party life for thousands of its members: 'It was an almost unbearable atmosphere. One only talked openly in the company of family or close friends. When one said something in the party, one never knew where it would be reported and what the consequences would be.'[67] In the politburo, Oelßner spoke in a similar vein, blaming the 'unhealthy atmosphere' of 'fear, hypocrity, deceitfulness and resignation' for 'the emigration of many comrades in responsible positions'.[68] To revitalize party life, Schirdewan allegedly favoured summoning an extraordinary party congress to elect a new central committee charged with carrying through a programme of 'controlled democratization.'[69] His draft report for the twenty-ninth central committee plenum in November 1956 (which called for more intra-party consultation and discussion)[70] was rejected by the politburo on the grounds that it emphasized 'democratization' at the expense of state security.[71] Schirdewan also claims to have favoured easing media censorship to stimulate a constructive and wide-ranging debate over the future direction of policy.[72]

According to Schirdewan, policy was seldom subject to open or objective consideration in the politburo and issues rarely put to the vote. Instead, he claims, members spent most of their time rubber-stamping policy statements prepared in advance.[73] At a politburo meeting on 29 December 1956, Schirdewan protested against the atmosphere of 'vindictiveness, anxiety and fear' spawned by Ulbricht's dictatorship: 'One must be able to speak out critically in the politburo, without having to fear disadvantages as a result . . . From my experience I can say that I don't have this conviction, despite the [party] statutes.' At this meeting Schirdewan also compared Ulbricht with the disgraced Hungarian leader, Matyas Rakosi.[74] Oelßner gave the following character assessment of the SED leader: 'Ulbricht is arrogant, egoistic . . . [has] great need for admiration, cannot take criticism – is at the same time vindictive. Replaces collective through personal decisions.'[75] On another occasion, he even went so far as to accuse Ulbricht of 'pathological persecution mania.'[76]

There are plenty of examples of Ulbricht's dictatorial behaviour. His condemnation of the New Course in 1955, for example, was made without prior consultation. Neither was his speech to the third party conference submitted to the politburo for approval.[77] In 1992, Neumann insisted that Ulbricht 'relished debate',[78] but this is merely a euphemistic way of saying that the first secretary frequently abused his colleagues. After Khrushchev's defeat of the Molotov–Kaganovich–Bulganin 'anti-party group' in June 1957, Ulbricht is said to have rounded on his own critics, threatening to throw them all in prison.[79] It was this fearful atmosphere in the party leadership that allegedly moved Schirdewan to favour granting immunity from prosecution to all members of the politburo and central committee.[80]

Schirdewan also claims to have been instrumental in speeding up the rehabilitation of persecuted party members, canvassing heavily on behalf of Paul Merker and other 'western émigrés.' Apparently, he was also responsible for the decision to award five to six thousand marks to rehabilitated purge victims returning from the USSR.[81] In the unsigned *Neues Deutschland* article of 29 April 1956, Schirdewan advocated full redress for all members of the SED whose rights had been violated.[82]

In a written statement to the politburo on 3 July 1956, Oelßner addressed the 'Ulbricht question' directly:

> One must take the twentieth party congress as a whole, and not leave out what is uncomfortable . . . For us the important question in this regard is: Is there a personality cult in the SED? Yes indeed, there is one, and in connection with it a personal regime that is practised in the main by comrade Ulbricht. After the twentieth party congress it has . . . in fact become stronger. Any public criticism of comrade Ulbricht is declared inadmissible.[83]

At a meeting of party activists at Berlin's Humboldt University on 13 June 1956, Ulbricht uttered a few words of self-criticism. The politburo decided to publish his remarks in *Neues Deutschland*. Ulbricht, however, acted to block this. The protests of Oelßner and Schirdewan were ignored.[84] Oelßner demanded that the politburo sanction discussion of the personality cult at the twenty-eighth central committee plenum in July,[85] deriding the standard Stalinist refrain that deflection of enemy attack required the suppression of free debate.[86] Infuriated, Ulbricht refused to discuss the statement in the politburo, preferring to gloss over the objections in a written reply to Oelßner personally.[87] In this way he was able to isolate his critics and suppress debate over his style of leadership. In conversation with the Soviet ambassador Georgi Pushkin, Ulbricht apparently attempted to deflect criticism from himself by condemning the 'personality cult' around Wilhelm Pieck.[88]

In the debate over Ulbricht's style of leadership, Schirdewan and Oelßner were occasionally supported by Herbert Warnke and Otto Grotewohl. At a politburo meeting on the eve of the twenty-eighth central committee plenum, for example, Warnke complained: 'Working methods make comrades feel insecure . . . often I did not state my point of view, because I would have been attacked (*weil ein Überfall kommt*).'[89] Grotewohl, although rejecting extensive discussion of the first secretary, felt it necessary to caution him: 'Walter Ulbricht must show that the situation is changing!'[90] For Matern, however, Ulbricht's tendency to take decisions without first consulting his colleagues was a sign of strong leadership: 'I understand collective leadership (*Kollektivität*) to mean that all comrades display initiative . . . comrade Ulbricht [therefore] displays the most . . . Fear of collective leadership means that we have to look through mountains of material that actually should be dealt with by the [party] apparatus.'[91] According to Ulbricht himself: 'Comrade Oelßner wants to bind the hands and also the head of the first secretary so that he plays the role of a secretary in the office of the politburo.'[92]

Sanctioning a more open discussion in the party and ridding it of Ulbricht's personality cult were issues in their own right, but they were also the prerequisites for policy changes in a number of other areas. Harich believed Schirdewan and Oelßner were interested in little more than the restoration of collective leadership.[93] In the politburo on 1 January 1958, however, Mückenberger is recorded as saying: 'The issue is not the style of working but principal questions of policy.'[94] His remarks were echoed on another occasion by Willi Stoph ('there are disagreements on the question of the workers' and farmers' state')[95] and Ulbricht himself ('the attempt to alter policy by criticizing the style of working will not succeed').[96]

Schirdewan and Oelßner were deeply concerned by the ever increasing numbers of people leaving the GDR for the Federal Republic. Their attempts to stimulate a debate on the issue were to no avail.[97] According to statistics Oelßner presented to the politburo in December 1956, the numbers of refugees rose from 173,000 in 1954 to 210,000 in 1955 (rising still further in 1956). More than half were members of the working class, the majority young people aged between eighteen and twenty-five.[98]

In the politburo a difference may be discerned between those who simply saw the mass exodus as a manifestation of Western destabilization attempts and those who also blamed inappropriate domestic policies for the phenomenon. According to Wollweber, Schirdewan planned to broach the issue at the thirty-fifth central committee plenum in February 1958.

> He informed me that we could no longer put a taboo around the refugee problem. The question arose, why so many workers and farmers were leaving the workers' and farmers' state. He would show that, besides the main reason of enemy activity, there was another reason rooted in our policies. He would prove that the refugee numbers rose and fell depending on our resolutions. With that he would pose the question of whether our policies were correct in all areas. And on this question there would be conflict.[99]

In his statement to the politburo of 1 January 1958,[100] Schirdewan rejected central committee member Hanna Wolf's characterization of the refugees as 'traitors' and 'deserters.'[101] Instead, he held the FDJ partly responsible for the growing flight of young people and blamed 'sectarianism', 'arrogance towards criticism' and 'blindness to good advice . . . from patriots in our Republic' for unsatisfactory relations between party and population.[102] Oelßner chided Ulbricht for aggravating the crisis, complaining 'that we are playing with the trust of the masses', that 'we ourselves are creating difficulties'.[103] He even accused Ulbricht of lying to the working class. Nobody, Oelßner protested, had believed his claim at the fourth party congress in April 1954 that the 'situation in the GDR' was 'better than in West Germany.'[104] Willi Stoph, however, absolved the first secretary of any blame: 'Flight from the Republic has nothing to do with personal regime.'[105] Matern took the East German authorities to task for their laxness: 'Every month, four thousand leave legally, that is to say some of our officials (*Organe*) have gone soft (*aufgeweicht*)'.[106] Ulbricht emphasized the importance of class enemy machinations[107] and former social democrat Erich Mückenberger hinted that it might soon be necessary to seal the border with West Berlin: 'Flight from the Republic is due, not to our policies, but to the fact that one can travel from Germany to Germany.'[108]

But Oelßner and Schirdewan did not confine their criticism to politburo meetings. The former tackled the issue at the twenty-eighth central committee plenum in July 1956, arguing that the large numbers of workers leaving for a new life in the West were 'voting with their feet.'[109] Schirdewan even tried to communicate his dissent to the party rank and file. Addressing a meeting of party activists in Karl-Marx-Stadt (now Chemnitz) in 1957, Ulbricht, Grotewohl and Matern insisted 'Whoever leaves the Republic commits treason against the working class.' Given the unique connotations of the word 'treason' (*Verrat*) in East Germany during the Cold War, Schirdewan's language was rather less emotive: 'Whoever leaves the Republic is insulting the working class.'[110]

If the tide of refugees was to be stemmed, new policies were required to win the confidence of a disillusioned working class. Schirdewan was in no doubt about the severity of the crisis: 'Many comrades fear the working class – we have not yet properly considered the lessons of 1953 – the views of the masses are being suppressed.'[111] As Oelßner pointed out in the politburo on 30 December 1956: 'No Petöfi-club can inflict great damage when the workers and farmers stand solidly behind the government!'[112]

In 1956 East German workers (no doubt influenced by events in Poland) began setting up 'factory councils' on the pre-1948 model.[113] Infuriated by this spontaneity, Ulbricht decided to seize the initiative at the twenty-ninth central committee plenum with a tentative proposal to establish workers' committees in industry. However, it is clear from corrections he made to an article drafted by Heinrich Rau on the issue that they were never intended as more than window-dressing for increased SED control. All references to 'self-administration' in the draft were deleted and replaced with the words 'state power.'[114] Presumably to ensure a degree of co-determination on the factory floor, Schirdewan instead proposed that workers elect 'factory councils'[115] to oversee the work of the trade unions.[116] He was apparently supported for a time by Heinrich Rau, Herbert Warnke,[117] Max Reimann and Bruno Leuschner,[118] until Ulbricht dashed all hopes of increasing worker participation by rejecting both proposals in early 1957.

As head of the central committee department 'leading organs of the party and mass organizations', Schirdewan supervised the activities of the FDJ. Given his frequent criticisms of this organization, it is hardly surprising that he is said to have welcomed Honecker's replacement as chairman in 1955.[119] In 1953, he had re-established the central committee youth secretariat to keep a closer check on his activities.[120] After Honecker's return from Moscow three years later, Schirdewan allegedly tried to prevent his appointment to the central committee secretariat.[121]

Even before the twentieth party congress of the CPSU, Schirdewan was advocating an alternative youth policy to that of Ulbricht and the rest of the politburo. In January 1956 he oversaw the drafting of new FDJ proclamations and resolutions which differed markedly from those drawn up under Honecker. The organization was criticized for being excessively bureaucratic and out of touch with the needs of young people. There was no mention of the 'leading role' of the SED or of the need to inculcate Marxist–Leninist ideology into the country's youth. Instead, the organization was to concentrate on fulfilling the needs and aspirations of its members. This meant listening to their views and organizing a more varied and interesting range of activities. To stimulate dialogue, discussion forums were set up so that young people could air their grievances and question leading functionaries. It was even proposed that the FDJ relinquish its monopoly of control and set up independent 'youth committees' in residential areas, big factories, large construction sites, allotments, angling clubs and stockbreeding associations. This is not to suggest that Schirdewan favoured 'depoliticizing' the FDJ or turning it into an 'independent' youth organization – after all, he called on it to prove itself 'the best helper of the SED.' Rather, he regarded ideological tasks as secondary to addressing the everyday needs and concerns of young people. His aim, of course, was to increase the credibility of the party and stem the flood of young people leaving the GDR.

Ulbricht, however, disagreed with this approach. While Schirdewan was drawing up his more flexible policy, the politburo was emphasizing the importance of educating the country's youth in socialist ideology. In April 1957, while Schirdewan was vacationing in the Soviet Union, Ulbricht seized the initiative and set about imposing his own agenda. On 25 April, the sixteenth session of the FDJ central council passed a resolution declaring the FDJ a 'socialist' youth organization. Rather than listening to the concerns of young people, the organization was now expected to indoctrinate them with communist values.[122]

Schirdewan, however, was not won over to the new line. Instead, he claims to have wanted the FDJ to remain a broadly based 'antifascist democratic' organization, catering for the interests of all political groups.[123] On 3 September 1957, the politburo expressed reservations about a report he had presented on behalf of the central committee youth commission. Significantly, it demanded that a section be inserted on the ideological education of young people.[124] At the thirty-fifth central committee plenum in February 1958, Karl Mewis, first secretary of the SED district leadership in Rostock, accused Schirdewan of trying to prevent his local branch of the FDJ from propagating communist ideology.[125]

Schirdewan also opposed Ulbricht's decision to deploy the workers' militia against student rebels in November 1956.[126] At a meeting of the central committee youth commission in December, he appealed for dialogue and conciliation.[127]

While Honecker railed against 'subversive' influences imported from Hungary and Poland,[128] Schirdewan interpreted the student disturbances as a vote of no confidence in the FDJ. It was time, he said, for the youth organization to eradicate mistakes from its work and begin representing the real interests of students.[129] While the rebellion was being quelled, Schirdewan apparently telephoned Alfred Neumann, first secretary of the district SED in East Berlin, to protest about the use of draconian measures, only to be curtly reminded that the maintenance of security in the capital was not his responsibility.[130] In his draft report for the twenty-ninth central committee plenum, Schirdewan blamed party dogmatists for the student debacle: 'The dogmatic attitude and the inability to convey the doctrine of Marxist–Leninism in a lively way, has given the enemy the possibility of turning students against the Russian and social-science courses.'[131] Significantly, Schirdewan did not attend the politburo meeting on 20 November which passed a resolution terminating the studies of students deemed responsible for inciting the unrest.[132] He was also accused by Ulbricht of attempting to defend a modicum of free discussion in the country's educational institutions.[133]

In 1956 Schirdewan apparently agreed with Bruno Haid,[134] the GDR's deputy state prosecutor, that there were insufficient grounds for keeping certain members of the 'Harich Group' in prison.[135] In this regard he seems to have been particularly concerned to secure the release of Walter Janka.[136] Oelßner, Rau and Grotewohl allegedly supported a proposal by Schirdewan to invite Harich to discuss his ideas with the politburo before any arrests were made but, in a rare vote to decide the issue, were defeated.[137] Uneasy at his colleagues' demands for increased repression against an ill-defined 'enemy within',[138] Schirdewan is said to have condemned the arbitrary crushing of dissent as 'a return to the old days.'[139] Ulbricht and his supporters feared the consequences of relaxing their control over the population. Addressing district party activists in February 1958, Matern declared: 'In Hungary, they also created a "safety-valve" which then had to be closed by Soviet tanks.'[140]

The collectivization of agriculture had been proceeding apace since the jettisoning of the New Course. This swelled the numbers of those fleeing to the West and, by disrupting food deliveries, encouraged still more people to leave in a seemingly endless vicious circle. With these realities in mind Oelßner and Schirdewan[141] opposed Ulbricht's policy of forced collectivization. Oelßner even went so far as to demand that the party stop subsidizing agricultural production co-operatives (LPGs) which proved themselves incapable of gaining the confidence of the rural population.[142]

Oelßner called for a more flexible agrarian policy which eschewed the one-sided promotion of collectives and took account of other organizational forms.[143] At a politburo meeting on 30 December 1956, Oelßner expressed his dismay at the dislocating effects of forced collectivization on the food distribution network ('the more collectives, the fewer deliveries!') and painted a bleak picture of life on a collective farm.[144] To ease the rural recession, Oelßner proposed selling tractors and other surplus equipment to private farmers who were still the largest rural constituency at this time, owning 70 per cent of the land.[145] Such pragmatism was anathema to Ulbricht, who accused Oelßner of proposing the restoration of capitalism in the countryside.[146] Addressing a conference of district party activists in Berlin after Oelßner's expulsion from the politburo in February 1958, Ulbricht was adamant: 'A road which begins like that will lead one year later to the return of capitalism.'[147] According to Hanna Wolf, member of the central committee and a diehard Ulbricht supporter, any attempt to slacken the tempo of collectivization was an attack on the unity of the 'workers' and peasants' state' because it drove a wedge between town and country.[148] As for the other members of the politburo, they too seemed unsympathetic to the proposals.

By the end of 1959, independent farmers in East Germany were still working 50 per cent of the tilled soil. At an agricultural conference of Soviet bloc countries held in Moscow on 2 February 1960, there was general agreement that something had to be done about the agricultural crisis. There were differences, however, over how best to proceed. Khrushchev allowed the leaders of each country to decide for themselves. While in Poland Gomulka continued his policy of relying on the private peasant economy, Ulbricht opted for forced collectivization.[149] By the middle of 1960 there were virtually no private farmers in the GDR and collective farms accounted for 85 per cent of the productive land.[150]

The second five-year plan ratified by the third party conference in March 1956 aimed to 'overtake' West Germany by increasing gross industrial output by 55 per cent. The propagation of this target reflected Ulbricht's utopian assessment of the GDR's potential and was a primary cause of severe economic dislocation in the late 1950s. Urged by the Soviets to reduce targets in January 1957, Ulbricht unilaterally raised them again later in the year.[151]

Ulbricht's economic policy was dictated above all by political considerations – the need to turn the GDR (and particularly East Berlin) into an economic magnet, a 'display window' to convince West Germans of socialist superiority. This, he believed, would further the interests of both the GDR and the international communist movement.[152] Schirdewan and Oelßner became increasingly worried about the adverse effects of these policies on both the party's credibility and economic stability. In a statement to the politburo in late 1957, Oelßner complained about insufficient supplies of goods to the population.[153] In January 1958, he criticized 'imbalances' in the new five-year plan and said it was about time the party put its economic house in order. It was no longer acceptable, he declared, to create problems and then expect Moscow to solve them.[154] Dismayed by Ulbricht's demands for additional money, food supplies and raw materials from an already overstretched Soviet economy, Schirdewan took a similar position to Oelßner.[155] They were supported for a time by the head of the state planning commission Bruno Leuschner.[156] According to Schirdewan, Khrushchev and Molotov did not hide their displeasure at Ulbricht's demands.[157] In February 1958, Oelßner recalled Khrushchev giving Ulbricht 'a very stern lesson in economics.'[158]

At the thirty-third central committee plenum between 16 and 19 October 1957, Ulbricht unilaterally jettisoned the sugar programme approved in February. According to Oelßner 'neither the plan commission, nor the food industry, nor the agriculture ministry knew anything about it',[159] Ulbricht's new plan undertook a massive extension of the plantation programme and foresaw a yield of one million tonnes of white sugar per year – this despite the failure to meet existing targets in 1957. Oelßner was so disgusted by these arbitrary methods that he took his objections to the central committee. The new sugar programme, he complained, was beyond the country's means.[160] The episode confirms the picture of a first secretary bent on enforcing the primacy of politics over all other considerations.

Emulating Khrushchev's reforms in the USSR, Ulbricht set about restructuring the GDR state apparatus to facilitate the transfer of certain economic responsibilities to local and district organs. The 'decentralization' project was strongly opposed by Oelßner on the grounds that it was ill thought out, failed to take account of special East German conditions and threatened to increase rather than diminish bureaucracy at all levels. Oelßner wanted more consultation of the factory workforce and not delegation of responsibility to local bureaucrats.[161] In the light of this evidence it is necessary to revise previous assumptions that Oelßner favoured maximum centralization of economic decision-making. The conclusion of one historian that, on this issue, Oelßner 'criticized Ulbricht from a more Stalinist viewpoint'[162] requires qualification.

On 18 December 1957, the politburo met to consider policy towards the Church. Ulbricht was determined to suppress the activities of bishops and provosts he regarded as subversive. The memorandum prepared by a working group and discussed at this meeting was decidedly threatening in tone. Top religious leaders were accused of supporting the aggressive policies of NATO. The governing bodies of the Church were warned that they had no right to interfere in the internal matters of the state or to adopt a hostile stance towards the GDR.[163] In the end, the politburo decided to publish a policy statement based on proposals put forward by Grotewohl, but eliminating his reference to the 'separation of Church and state.'[164]

At a politburo meeting on 11 January 1958, Oelßner recorded Ulbricht as saying: 'The SED has departed from the social democratic position that religion is a private matter. We now make scientific-atheistic propaganda.'[165] According to Schirdewan, Ulbricht wanted to 'nationalize' totally the protestant church. But the proposal apparently met with little sympathy among politburo colleagues and was subsequently dropped. Schirdewan, Grotewohl and Rau were said to have been especially vocal in their criticism and even the usually compliant Mückenberger expressed misgivings.[166] In his speech to the thirty-fifth central committee plenum in February 1958, Schirdewan hinted that he had doubts about party policy on this issue.[167]

While Ulbricht crassly intimidated Church officialdom, Schirdewan showed an ability to work with people of different backgrounds and persuasions. The

protestant provost Heinrich Grüber, a leading figure in the GDR Church hierarchy during the 1950s, testifies to a close personal friendship with Schirdewan – a
friendship which began in the Sachsenhausen concentration camp and survived
the vicissitudes of the postwar period.[168] Perhaps Schirdewan's catholic upbringing was a factor in his less than wholehearted support for Ulbricht's persecution
of the Church.

The conclusions Schirdewan drew from the twentieth party congress of the
CPSU may have been more radical than some historians have assumed. Manfred
Gerlach, leader of the Liberal Democratic Pary of Germany (LDPD), recalls a
private conversation with Schirdewan in early 1956 during which the latter
expressed support for granting an opposition role to the bloc parties and invest-
ing parliament with new powers:

> Suddenly he asked me whether I was satisfied with the multiparty system in the
> GDR. He, at any rate, believed that it would be good for the country if there was
> a real opposition in the *Volkskammer*. The LDPD should be such an opposition
> party. Parliament anyway had to play a greater role. He then showed me his
> *Volkskammer* pass . . . he only carried this with him; it was the most important and
> not the party card.[169]

Gerlach was convinced of Schirdewan's sincerity: 'I was speechless. It could not
have been a provocation – we knew each other too well for that.'[170] In his draft
report to the twenty-ninth central committee plenum, Schirdewan also proposed
granting a degree of autonomy to the mass organizations.[171]

Such ideas were abhorrent to Ulbricht and his supporters. Neumann remains
convinced that permitting the bloc parties an 'opposition' role would have
opened the floodgates to counter-revolution. With the SPD existing as an underground organization in East Berlin until 1961 there was more than enough opposition in the GDR already.[172] According to one of Ulbricht's close advisers,
Wolfgang Berger, the bloc parties enjoyed more influence in the GDR than the
non-governmental parties in the Federal Republic.[173]

On 15 May 1955, the Soviet Union and the Western Powers signed the
Austrian State Treaty, sanctioning the country's right to exist as an independent,
democratic, capitalist and neutral state in the heart of Europe. This raised hopes
that Moscow might permit a similar solution for Germany. There were, however,
important differences between the two nations. Austria, unlike her divided
neighbour, had always had only one government. As a country of just eight
million inhabitants, she was not regarded with the same suspicion as Germany,
whose population would have been sixty-five millions. From the Soviet point of
view, Germany's size, history and strategic position made reunification unthinkable unless she eliminated the 'capitalist' roots of militarism and Nazism. In
1956, the French prime minister, Guy Mollet, recalled Khrushchev telling him:
'We prefer seventeen million Germans under our influence to seventy million in
a reunited Germany, even though they may be neutralized.'[174]

Following the French national assembly's rejection of the European Defence

Community in 1954, the Federal Republic was accepted as a member of NATO on 9 May 1955. In response to this, the Warsaw Pact was founded on 14 May with the GDR as a full member. At the Geneva conference of the Great Powers between 18 and 23 July 1955, the United States and the Soviet Union seemed resigned to the existence of two German states, even if the USSR did commit itself to the principle of 'free elections'.[175] Afterwards, Khrushchev and Bulganin stopped off for a four-day visit in the GDR. On 26 July, Khrushchev declared reunification 'a matter for the Germans themselves.' He also stated that there could be no 'mechanical reunification of the two parts of Germany' and excluded the possibility of sacrificing the GDR's 'social achievements.'[176] In September 1955, the Soviet Union confirmed the GDR's 'full sovereignty', signed a mutual assistance pact with her and abolished the office of Soviet high commissioner.[177] Even so, it was not until the building of the Berlin Wall in 1961 that the division of Germany was set in concrete.

When members of the Soviet leadership revisited the GDR in November 1955, foreign minister Molotov allegedly held a conversation with Schirdewan during which the question of all-German free elections was discussed. At a farewell banquet for the Soviet visitors, Molotov took Schirdewan aside to emphasize the need for links with the SPD to prepare for this eventuality. Schirdewan welcomed Molotov's remarks, but was concerned that his own party first adopt a long-term programme of reform. His account of the conversation, as he recalled it in 1992, is so remarkable that it warrants quotation in full.

> *Molotov*: Tell me, comrade Schirdewan, when can we hold free and secret elections?
>
> *Schirdewan*: Certainly not now.
>
> *Molotov*: Why? Perhaps in two years?
>
> *Schirdewan*: No, not then either. We must make careful preparations for that over a period of years. First we must properly develop our internal party democracy because the party cannot be strong without it. Second, we must abolish democratic centralism in the state apparatus, find new economic forms and grant factory councils influence against the absolutism of the trade unions. And third, we must give the bloc parties more room for independence. We must be able to show certain democratic principles . . . We must have preparations . . . so that we can count on winning 50 or 60 per cent [of the vote].[178]

The SED cadre-chief had the distinct impression that the Soviet foreign minister wanted to hear a positive response about the possibility of all-German elections. Even so, Molotov apparently accepted Schirdewan's analysis that they could not be held in the forseeable future.[179]

This testimony must obviously be treated with the utmost caution because Schirdewan was recalling an event which occurred thirty-seven years previously. It should also be borne in mind that the conversation took place immediately after the Allied foreign ministers' conference in Geneva between 27 October and 16 November 1955 at which Molotov had, to all intents and purposes, ruled out the idea of free elections.[180] On 5 November, a delegation of observers from the

GDR declared that all-German elections would only be possible once the Federal Republic had completed a process of 'democratization' and 'demilitarization.'[181]

Nonetheless, Schirdewan's account warrants closer examination. Perhaps Molotov's reported remarks should be interpreted in the context of his initial objection to the GDR becoming a member of the Warsaw Pact in May 1955. According to Khrushchev, Molotov had argued: 'Why should we fight with the West over the GDR?'[182] In 1992, Schirdewan was convinced that 'democratization' need not necessarily have ended in counter-revolution, and cited two reasons why he believed the SED could eventually have won a majority in all-German free elections. First, the Federal Republic in the 1950s was not the economic and political magnet it later became. Second, the Soviet Union was strong enough to prevent the kind of 'Western interference' which culminated in the debacle of 1990. An SED election victory, he declared, 'would have been possible under certain conditions . . . but time was needed to prepare for it'.[183] Ulbricht, by contrast, opposed the reunification of Germany through free elections under any circumstances. In December 1956, he declared: 'I say quite clearly: the way will never lie over free elections throughout Germany. There is only one way . . . the winning of the West German working class for our policy and revolution of the West German working class against existing West German conditions. We must resist all illusions about reunification by way of elections.'[184]

In 1958, Honecker claimed that Schirdewan was willing to pay any price to achieve German reunification.[185] The evidence, however, does not support this assertion. What can be established is that the latter adopted a more flexible stance on the 'national question.' Addressing the third party conference in March 1956, Schirdewan placed special emphasis on the need for rapprochement with the SPD.[186] In the unsigned *Neues Deutschland* article of 29 April, he reiterated this theme and called for talks with the West German government.[187] Seven months later he reaffirmed these positions again in his draft report to the twenty-ninth central committee plenum. Against the background of attempts by some West German politicans to establish high-level contacts in the GDR (on 20 October 1956 Bonn's finance minister Fritz Schäffer travelled to East Berlin to meet deputy defence minister Vincenz Müller and Soviet ambassador Pushkin[188]), Schirdewan advocated putting the struggle for German reunification at the top of the SED's agenda.[189] He would later be accused of underestimating the imperialist threat[190] and believing that the Cold War was over.[191]

At the thirtieth central committee plenum in early 1957, Ulbricht proposed a confederation of the two German states. Both the GDR and the Federal Republic would, in accordance with their respective electoral systems, elect equal numbers of representatives to an all-German council charged with the task of drafting proposals for customs and currency union, common administration of the media and transport services and free elections for the country as a whole.[192] Other all-German bodies would not initially have been granted executive powers, only advisory functions.[193] Had they been implemented, these proposals would have given the SED a veto over every decision which did not suit its agenda.

The proposal would also have meant the Federal Republic scrapping the Hallstein Doctrine[194] and recognizing the GDR. This, together with other preconditions, such as the abolition of 'militarism' and 'monopoly capitalism' in West Germany, ensured instant rejection of the offer by all political parties in Bonn.[195]

Ulbricht believed that the 'accelerated construction of socialism' in the GDR increased the probability of German reunification by forcing the West to make concessions. In a speech to party activists in February 1958, he chided those in the party willing to compromise to achieve inter-German dialogue. Negotiations were only possible, he insisted, once the enemy had understood that the GDR could not be undermined.[196] This approach exacerbated the division of the country even if Ulbricht believed the opposite to be true.

Like Ulbricht, Matern regarded the speedy construction of socialism in the GDR as the indispensable corollary to German reunification. Given its geopolitical status as an industrially advanced country sharing a common border with the West, Matern believed the GDR had a special responsibility to set an example for communism. Addressing a conference of district party activists in Dresden in February 1958, he declared: 'If we . . . hurry things along a bit here . . . if we decide socialism for the whole of Germany. . . then it is decided for the whole of Europe.' The idea of reaching a negotiated settlement with the 'class enemy' was repugnant to him: 'We understand by the road to a united Germany, not horse-trading at a round table, but . . . class struggle and the national struggle.'[197]

Schirdewan, however, pursued a different logic. He believed a confederation between the two German states was only possible if both sides were prepared to make concessions[198] and this meant slowing the tempo of socialist development in the GDR. Domestic policy had to be predicated on the need for German–German rapprochement. As Matern put it, Schirdewan wanted to proceed at a slower pace 'so as not to annoy (*verschnupfen*) the capitalists over there [and] to remove tensions in order to find a way of reaching an amicable agreement.'[199] Like Ulbricht, however, Schirdewan insisted that the Federal Republic recognize the sovereignty of the GDR and conduct negotiations with her as an equal partner.[200] Speculation that Schirdewan wholeheartedly endorsed the Schäffer concept (designed to eschew formal recognition) is therefore misplaced.[201] In 1992, Schirdewan confessed that, although he pursued confederation as a political goal, he did not believe it would be realized in the 1950s.[202]

In August 1957 Khrushchev apparently invited Schirdewan for a holiday in the Crimea to discuss new approaches to the West German SPD. Schirdewan, anticipating Ulbricht's response, reluctantly turned down the offer.[203] If Ulbricht was forced to adopt a slightly softer line towards the SPD in early 1956,[204] he had returned to an unashamedly confrontational stance by the autumn. Grotewohl's attitude, however, was more flexible. In a letter dated 22 February 1957, he advised the continuation of efforts to engage the leading West German social democrat, Herbert Wehner, in dialogue.[205]

Schirdewan seems to have found a close friend and political ally in Grotewohl.

Vacationing in the Soviet Union in 1954, he was apparently approached by Khrushchev's friend and ally, Anastas Mikoyan, who inquired whether he would mind spending the rest of his holiday with the East German prime minister. Schirdewan accepted and there followed 'a political holiday' during which he discovered that for Grotewohl too 'the most important problem was German reunification.'[206]

If the German question provoked conflict in the SED politburo, it also strained relations with the KPD – its sister party in the Federal Republic. On 15 January 1956, the latter submitted a policy declaration containing a number of heretical ideas. Most striking of all was the KPD's sudden insistence on pursuing its own path to the 'peaceful and democratic reunification of Germany.'[207] Annoyed by this disobedience, Matern and Verner immediately dispatched a rebuttal accusing the KPD leadership of neglecting the class struggle and denying the 'leading role' of the SED. In a thinly disguised warning, Matern demanded that the KPD insert a passage pledging to fight the twin evils of factionalism and revisionism.[208] It is not known who drafted the rogue policy declaration. But on 11 January 1958, KPD leader Max Reimann informed his SED colleagues that a member of his party's secretariat, Walter Fisch,[209] favoured 'making the party more receptive to the opinions of the Italian comrades'.[210] Apparently, Fisch had also predicted imminent changes in the GDR leadership.[211]

It would seem that Ulbricht's differences with Schirdewan and Oelßner predated the twentieth party congress. According to Schirdewan, the fact that he had spent the war in Nazi concentration camps rather than in Soviet emigration sufficed to make him unreliable in Ulbricht's eyes.[212] Heavily criticized by the latter while head of the western commission, Schirdewan is certain that, were it not for Soviet insistence, he would never have entered the politburo. His support for a more radical version of the New Course was apparently a source of considerable tension with Ulbricht between 1953 and 1955.[213]

Oelßner had been one of Ulbricht's strongest critics in the early 1950s and resented his gradual isolation after 1953. Ulbricht despised Oelßner's 'intellectualism' and was bent on reducing his considerable influence as SED ideology chief. Relieved of responsibility for propaganda in July 1954, he suffered further humiliation in April 1955 when he was sacked as central committee secretary for agitation. In his statement to the politburo in January 1958, he wrote: 'I have had the impression for a long time, that the intention exists to remove me from the leadership. I will not allow myself to be shunted off (*abschieben*) in a cold-blooded way.'[214]

As we have seen, it was primarily political considerations which brought Schirdewan into conflict with Ulbricht between 1956 and 1958. His unhappiness with the party line is perhaps reflected in the fact that he did not address the central committee a single time between February 1957 and February 1958. That he continued to oppose the SED leader in the politburo, despite being in a minority of two, refutes Wolfgang Berger's claim that he was motivated by 'naked ambition.'[215] This is not to argue that Schirdewan did not *also* aspire to the job of first secretary. In 1992, he averred that the logic of reform meant electing somebody new to this post – a post he had been willing to accept.[216] When Khrushchev and Bulganin[217] visited the GDR in 1955, Schirdewan had apparently ordered factories to display huge placards welcoming 'Bulganin – Grotewohl – Khrushchev – Schirdewan' – much to the chagrin of Ulbricht who was away on vacation at the time.[218] In a speech to local SED functionaries in November 1956, Schirdewan is said to have launched another indirect assault on Ulbricht's authority by asserting that all attempts to 'concentrate power' had been thwarted.[219] His campaign was discreet but unmistakable. Rehabilitated 'western émigrés' were apparently sent warm letters of congratulation commending Schirdewan for their change of fortune.[220] By December 1956 Rau was observing 'two poles in the party apparatus – Walter and Karl'.[221] A year later the dyarchy had developed into a full-blooded power struggle: 'In the press, popularity races between Walter and Karl. The first secretary is comrade Walter Ulbricht – there are not two first secretaries.'[222] According to Wollweber, Grotewohl had promised Schirdewan that, 'if things turned out favourably', he would support his election to this position.[223]

Schirdewan was supported, even encouraged in his endeavours by leading Soviet officials. Already in 1954 he felt that he was being groomed as a counterweight to Ulbricht. During his trip to the USSR in April of that year, Schirdewan recalled Mikoyan asking him to mediate between Ulbricht and Grotewohl.[224] As Rau put it in his speech to the thirty-fifth central committee plenum: 'He was therefore . . . the big man, who had to smooth everything over in the politburo . . . That is to say, he tried to play politics in the politburo with the help of Soviet comrades. He also attempted to play Grotewohl and Ulbricht off against each other.'[225]

It became clear to Schirdewan while on a trip to Moscow in early 1956 that the Soviet leadership no longer regarded Ulbricht as indispensable.[226] He also claimed to have received a degree of moral support from senior Soviet diplomats such as Tiul'panov and Semyonov.[227] Certainly Pushkin made no secret of his wish to see Ulbricht deposed.[228] According to Valentin Falin, the Soviet ambassador expressed displeasure at Ulbricht's 'persecution of the old guard' and it was only to avoid a confrontation with the SED leader that the Kremlin agreed to Pushkin's replacement.[229] At the end of 1957 the GDR's ambassador in Moscow, Johannes König, apparently believed the Soviets favoured a change of leadership before the fifth party congress in 1958.[230]

Khrushchev's role has been a matter for speculation. Certainly, his relations with Ulbricht were strained. His ire was particularly aroused by Ulbricht's stance on the Stalin question and, at Bierut's funeral in October 1956, he allegedly communicated his displeasure to Schirdewan.[231] There were conflicts over other issues too. Recalling a visit by Khrushchev to the GDR in the late 1950s, Ulbricht complained that the Soviet leader had 'scolded him the whole way to Magdeburg' because of his lack of enthusiasm for maize plantation.[232]

According to another party reformer, Heinz Brandt,[233] Schirdewan received

Khrushchev's blessing to oust Ulbricht while visiting Moscow in 1956.[234] In 1992, Schirdewan refuted this account as simplistic and denied having received any unequivocal pledge of support.[235] Buffeted by his own internal problems and concerned to preserve the greater room for manoeuvre afforded to the East European leaderships after the twentieth party congress, the Soviet leader seems to have adopted a stance of 'benevolent neutrality.' Ulbricht was therefore able to use the 'fight against revisionism' (proclaimed at the conference of twelve Communist and Workers' Parties in Moscow between 14 and 16 November 1957) to consolidate his position.

In January 1958 Ulbricht, Grotewohl, Matern, Stoph, Ebert and Neumann travelled to Moscow to obtain Khrushchev's permission to purge Schirdewan and Oelßner from the leadership. Yet Khrushchev was loathe to oblige and even went so far as to defend Schirdewan: 'You must resolve internal questions by yourselves . . . We value Schirdewan as a good communist . . . Ulbricht mistrusts Schirdewan. Grotewohl also finds himself in a desperate situation . . . Ulbricht cannot accustom himself to others. [His] character is too harsh – he cuts himself off.' Grotewohl concluded from this meeting: 'We must decide by ourselves.'[236] In 1953 the Soviet leadership had helped rescue Ulbricht from his own politburo. In 1958, however, the majority of his comrades stood by him while Khrushchev attempted to save Schirdewan from their clutches. According to most observers, Ulbricht's success in averting a 'second Hungary' in the GDR was the decisive factor in persuading Khrushchev to back him.[237] Whether or not this is true, his support for the SED first secretary could hardly have been more equivocal.

On 11 January 1958 the politburo met to consider defiant declarations sub-mitted by Schirdewan and Oelßner.[238] With nine colleagues firmly behind him,[239] Ulbricht felt strong enough to obtain Schirdewan's expulsion from the central committee secretariat. This move was opposed by Oelßner, Schirdewan himself and also Grotewohl. The latter mounted a careful defence of the embattled cadre-chief. According to records of this meeting held at the *Stasi* archive, 'comrade Grotewohl stated . . . that the twentieth party congress had called a halt to the application of certain methods . . . the discussion in the politburo was too petty. One must not anticipate the decision before the trip to Moscow.'[240] The East German prime minister was obviously banking on the Soviet leadership taking action to thwart Ulbricht's plans. Oelßner's notes from this meeting cor-roborate the *Stasi* account and record Grotewohl's essential unhappiness with the Ulbricht regime: 'Collective co-operation is not as good as it could be . . . Resolutions do not always mean the right solutions.'[241] Ulbricht then moved that Schirdewan and Oelßner be excluded from the delegation sent to consult with Khrushchev. Again, Schirdewan and Oelßner voted against. To ensure that the two be given an opportunity to present their case, Grotewohl suggested inviting a Soviet delegation to Berlin. This proposal – accepted by the politburo – came to nothing.[242] Whether this was due to Ulbricht (who knew such a visit was not in his interests) or to a negative Soviet response is uncertain.

On 31 January, with the SED delegation back in Berlin, a resolution was passed suspending Schirdewan and Oelßner from the politburo. The former was also barred from the central committee secretariat. Schirdewan broke with tradition and abstained.[243] After a delay to enable Ulbricht to settle scores with his opposition, the thirty-fifth central committee plenum was finally convened between 3 and 6 February 1958.[244] It would seem that Khrushchev wished to retain Schirdewan as member of the central committee[245] because the original resolutions only proposed his expulsion from the politburo and central committee secretariat. Unlike Oelßner, however, Schirdewan was also to be 'severely reprimanded.'[246] There were probably three reasons for this. First, Oelßner's opposition had not gone as far as Schirdewan's on some issues. Second, Ulbricht probably wanted to split the opposition levelled against him. Third, Oelßner's status as a former émigré of the Soviet Union made him difficult to handle. Schirdewan's assessment – 'Oelßner was a dangerous man for Ulbricht'[247] – is confirmed by the latter's refusal to engage in self-criticism at the thirty-fifth central committee plenum.[248] On the evening of 5 February, the politburo met in emergency session to increase the severity of the punishments. With Schirdewan and Oelßner barred from attending by the resolution of 31 January, it was decided to expel the former from the central committee.[249] Once again Ulbricht seems to have disregarded Khrushchev's wishes.

Schirdewan's capitulation before the central committee can be attributed to two factors. First, despite his disagreements with Ulbricht, Schirdewan remained a diehard communist and therefore felt compelled to sacrifice his principles on the altar of party discipline. A last-ditch stand would merely have ensured his expulsion from the SED, or 'political and existential death' as Matern once put it.[250] Second, since Schirdewan could only count on the support of about thirty-four central committee members (out of a total membership of 133) his cause was all but lost.[251] Apparently under constant surveillance by Honecker's central committee security section,[252] Schirdewan would have found it difficult to appeal directly to the party or population even had he wanted to. Perhaps his last hope lay with Otto Grotewohl: 'If [he] had said at the decisive thirty-fifth central committee plenum: "this far and no further", then a big crisis would have broken out . . . nobody could could have climbed over Grotewohl.' But the East German prime minister 'was too weak and always underestimated his influence'. During a break in the plenum proceedings, Grotewohl urged his friend to concede.[253]

Relieved of all party functions, Oelßner lost his seat on the central committee at the fifth party congress in July 1958. He was then made director of the economics institute at the GDR's Academy of Sciences. Schirdewan became head of the GDR state archive administration in Potsdam – a post he retained until 1965. In early 1959, the latter was summoned to Matern and apparently threatened with imprisonment, perhaps even execution if he did not engage in self-criticism.[254] Schirdewan suspected Ulbricht of preparing a show trial.[255] Had it come to this, he later insisted, he would have defended himself.[256] That it did not was probably due to the twentieth party congress of the CPSU, Khrushchev's opposition and Schirdewan's eventual willingness to obey Matern's instructions.

Later in the year, the journal *Neuer Weg* published a statement of self-criticism in which Schirdewan pleaded guilty to favouring a slower tempo of socialist development and drawing 'opportunist conclusions with regard to the further strengthening of socialist democracy'. He also expressed regret for supporting 'a mechanical ... application of resolutions from the twentieth party congress' and swore allegiance to Ulbricht as party leader.[257] In September 1959 Oelßner too donned sackcloth and ashes. Distancing himself from the 'anti-party Schirdewan-group' he surrendered on what had been, for him, one of the key issues: 'I underestimated the strength and superiority of socialist methods of production in agriculture.'[258]

Schirdewan only began to perceive Stalinism as a socio-political system many years later.[259] Between 1956 and 1958, however, he advocated an alternative political course based on the conclusions of the twentieth party congress of the CPSU.[260] His defeat at the thirty-fifth central committee plenum accelerated the final consolidation of the Stalinist system and allowed Ulbricht to continue as first secretary until 1971. It is worth noting that the policies adopted at the fifth party congress in July 1958 led inexorably to the building of the Berlin Wall.

During his years in the political wilderness, Schirdewan apparently found solace in the transmissions of the BBC World Service.[261] He was rehabilitated by the Party of Democratic Socialism (PDS), the SED's successor party, on 21 January 1990.[262] In 1992, he was deeply worried by the social consequences of German reunification and opposed the Maastricht Treaty as the harbinger of a new bureaucratic centralism. A supporter of the Prague Spring in 1968, he saw a 'third way' between communism and capitalism as the solution to the conflicts of the twenty-first century.[263]

The opposition in the central committee

Three other senior SED functionaries were condemned with Schirdewan and Oelßner at the thirty-fifth central committee plenum: the minister for state security Ernst Wollweber; the central committee economics secretary Gerhart Ziller; the industry specialist and deputy prime minister Fritz Selbmann.

Ernst Wollweber was born in Hannover in 1898. A sailor by profession (he took part in the 1918 sailors' mutiny in Kiel), he joined the KPD in 1919 before becoming head of the German section of the Seamen's International. He was elected to the *Reichstag* in 1932 after serving as a member of the Prussian parliament. Following Hitler's seizure of power, Wollweber worked underground for the KPD in Germany before emigrating to Scandanavia. In Denmark he headed the Comintern's Western European office, specializing in weapons smuggling. Arrested and condemned to three years' imprisonment in Sweden in 1940, he was deported to the USSR at the Soviet government's own request. Following his return to Germany in 1945, he headed the directorate of shipping before being appointed state secretary in the ministry of transport in 1949. After a brief spell as state secretary for shipping, Wollweber became first deputy minister of the interior and state secretary for national security in July 1953. He joined the central committee in 1954 but, unlike Zaisser, was denied politburo status. According to Wollweber, he was foisted on Ulbricht by the Soviets.[264] When the state secretariat became the ministry for state security (MfS) in November 1955, Wollweber was appointed minister for state security.

Ulbricht's determination to crush immediately all manifestations of dissent clashed with Wollweber's preference for a more cautious policy. At the thirty-fifth central committee plenum, Wollweber was accused of neglecting internal security and proposing a cut in *Stasi* personnel of 15 to 20 per cent.[265] The final two years of Wollweber's tenure were the only times in the history of the GDR when the MfS apparatus was actually reduced.[266] In conversation with one of his deputies in February 1957, Wollweber allegedly avowed his determination to prevent any recurrence of the state security outrages of the early 1950s.[267] Already in 1954 he had persuaded the central committee to review cases where former members of the party and state police had been given unusually long prison sentences for relatively minor offences.[268] One factor determining his overall approach may have been the experiences of his long-time companion, Clara Vater, who had been a victim of the purges in the Soviet Union during the 1930s.[269]

Addressing the third party conference in March 1956, Wollweber emphasized the importance of political as opposed to police methods when neutralizing opposition.[270] Convinced that Ulbricht had exaggerated the counter-revolutionary threat posed by the students,[271] he called on the party to adopt a more nuanced approach when dealing with dissent.[272] With regard to the trial of the 'Harich group', Wollweber allegedly rejected Ulbricht's attempts to fix the verdict in advance[273] and, in a speech to the thirtieth central committee plenum, appeared to suggest that some of its members had been wrongly arrested.[274] He also contested claims that the eastern bureau's campaign against the GDR was being orchestrated by social democrats.[275]

In August 1955 Wollweber had ordered his district administrators to concentrate 'more than half their efforts' on penetrating the enemy in the West.[276] Two years later he was criticized for giving priority to Western intelligence work at the expense of domestic security in the GDR.[277] On this issue, Wollweber claims to have been supported by his Soviet advisers.[278] Obviously, given the international situation, the perceived threat from the Federal Republic and West Berlin was of more concern to the CPSU than the activities of 'revisionist' intellectuals in the GDR.

To some extent, Soviet officials attached to the MfS seem to have regarded Wollweber as a guarantee of their influence. As the conflict with Ulbricht intensified, Wollweber considered resigning on grounds of ill health. His chief adviser, however, allegedly persuaded him to stay.[279] On 9 February 1957, the SED politburo passed a resolution tightening the party's grip over the MfS.[280] Three days later, Wollweber told his officials that the number of Soviet advisers was being reduced. Previously, he said, they had been the 'driving force' of the MfS. Now, however, the ministry had to be more independent in its activities.[281]

Addressing the twenty-ninth central committee plenum in November 1956, Ulbricht criticized Wollweber's 'liberal' regime and accused him of misinterpreting the resolutions of the twentieth party congress.[282] After consultations on the 18, 19 and 20 December, the politburo instructed Wollweber to improve MfS efficiency in tracking down subversives.[283] At the thirtieth central committee plenum in February 1957, Ulbricht expressed nostalgia for the early 1950s when 'enemy agents' had been imprisoned in their thousands. He then took the unprecedented step of warning Wollweber that his days as minister for state security were numbered: 'For a long time the state security service has arrested absolutely nobody . . . In the past, one was not only responsible for finding the enemy, but also held responsible if one worked so negligently, that the person concerned fled (*abhaut*) to the West.'[284] Of course, one must not put too much store by Ulbricht's account. Under Wollweber's tutelage, the MfS continued to oppress the East German population,[285] even if it failed to live up to the first secretary's aspirations.

As minister for state security, Wollweber was particularly well placed to gauge the political mood in the country. On the basis of information gathered from his network of informers, he concluded that unless the SED adopted a less sectarian approach, an embittered population would be alienated still further. In an article in *Neues Deutschland* at the end of 1956, Wollweber argued that the best guarantee of internal security was a closer relationship between the party and people.[286] Wollweber was apparently concerned that Ulbricht's policies might provoke another popular uprising.[287] To reduce tension in the country, he claims to have advocated limiting the scope of the party apparatus; ending Ulbricht's personality cult;[288] moderating the campaign against the Church; formulating a more realistic economic plan[289] and allowing workers to elect factory committees in free and secret elections.[290] He also criticized the decision to collectivize the whole of East German agriculture in the months before the building of the Berlin Wall.[291] Although there is no evidence to support allegations that he championed German reunification 'at any price',[292] his promotion of a less sectarian brand of politics by the SED and KPD was intended to increase communist appeal in the Federal Republic.[293] He apparently favoured granting immunity from prosecution to all members of the central committee so that they could engage in debate over policy.[294]

Ulbricht used Wollweber's deputy, Erich Mielke, to obtain unauthorized information about MfS activities, thereby undermining Wollweber's position.[295] The latter responded with a directive ordering MfS staff to inform him of all reports concerning state security passed to members of the party and state leaderships.[296] Ulbricht seized on this to accuse Wollweber of attempting to subjugate the party to MfS control.[297] Yet when the latter offered to resign in June 1957, his request was refused[298] – an indication that the minister had allies in both East Berlin and Moscow. Instead, Ulbricht launched an attack on him at the thirty-second central committee plenum. Accusations that Wollweber had 'underestimated' the activities of western agents in the GDR[299] were subsequently removed from the official minutes.[300]

On 8 October 1957, Ulbricht felt strong enough to replace Wollweber as minister for state security.[301] Although ill health was given as the official reason, there can be little doubt that he was forced out. According to one witness, this was done with Khrushchev's blessing.[302] He was succeeded by Erich Mielke, who headed the ministry until its dissolution in 1989. His views on internal security were more hard line than those of Wollweber. At the twenty-sixth central committee plenum in March 1956, Mielke had called for 'increased vigilance' in tracking down 'the enemy within.'[303] Two months after his promotion, he was decorated with the 'Karl Marx medal' in recognition of his services in securing the 'workers' and peasants' state.'[304] From the late 1950s onwards, the ministry was charged with the task of countering what were seen as 'new enemy tactics' of 'political and ideological subversion.' In 1957, the MfS apparatus comprised 14,442 full-time employees. Within a year, this figure had risen by 9 per cent. The number of personnel had tripled by the time Ulbricht left office in 1971.[305]

In sessions of the central party control commission, former colleagues testified to Wollweber's support for Schirdewan as an alternative first secretary.[306] Expelled from the central committee for 'factionalism' in February 1958, Wollweber was apparently threatened with execution if he did not engage in self-criticism.[307] He finally obliged in January 1959. After eight years' secluded retirement he died in 1967.

Gerhart Ziller was born in 1912 to a worker's family in Dresden. Trained as a mechanical engineer, he joined the Communist Youth Association in 1927 and the KPD in 1930. After being interned in Nazi concentration camps, he joined the SED in 1946. Appointed industry minister of Saxony in 1949, he served as GDR minister for mechanical engineering between 1950 and 1953. In 1953 he was elected to the central committee and assigned the job of economics secretary – a post he retained until his suicide on 14 December 1957.

Ziller did not fit the apparatchik mould. A sensitive and emotional character, he nurtured a passionate interest in art and culture.[308] Although a close friend of Schirdewan,[309] there seems to have been some personal tension with other Ulbricht critics. Wollweber regarded him as 'a hussar . . . always on the attack' – a kind of Ulbricht in reverse.[310] His relationship with Oelßner also seems to have been strained.[311] Although he was ambitious and, like Ulbricht, a workaholic,[312] there is no evidence to support the far-fetched assertion of one central committee member that he aspired to the job of first secretary.[313] Berger, who worked with Ziller in the 'planning and finance' department, remembers him as 'incompetent, volatile und wild'.[314] Ziller's style of working was certainly unorthodox. For example, he apparently hoped to ascertain the real conditions of the East German proletariat by spending a vacation in a factory disguised as an ordinary worker with false identification papers.[315] If such behaviour was eccentric, it may also have been symptomatic of a desire to repair the severed links between party and people.

The youngest member of the anti-Ulbricht opposition, Ziller might already have been a clandestine opponent in 1953. After the June uprising, he is reported to have told his friend, Fritz Selbmann: 'Comrade Ulbricht must go! That is the only salvation.'[316] Ziller believed the SED had much to learn from Khrushchev's denunciation of Stalin at the twentieth party congress. Addressing the central committee on 22 March 1956, he declared: 'this will and must also prompt us to review our own work in the party leadership and not to allow any violation of the norms when implementing our very complicated and important tasks.'[317] Shattered by Khrushchev's revelations, Ziller allegedly threatened to spark a debate over the personality cult, breaking the SED's taboo of silence on the issue. He is also reported to have voiced his discontent at meetings of the central committee secretariat.[318]

Apparently sympathetic to certain aspects of Schirdewan's political analysis,[319] Ziller wanted a discussion about the future direction of policy: 'We favour a clash of opinions (*Meinungsstreit*). Bloody hell, [it would be odd] if we didn't have different views on this or that issue and push them through!'[320] He regarded the growing exodus to West Germany as a manifestation of the failure to satisfy the material needs of the workers,[321] opposed the increase in work norms announced in October 1957[322] and, at a meeting with economic specialists, drew attention to 'evil symptoms of inefficiency and bureaucracy'[323] in the GDR. He refused to co-operate with Ulbricht's plans to restructure the state apparatus[324] and allegedly criticized the party training college for turning out 'Jesuits'.[325] His views on the German question are more difficult to ascertain. Apparently, he received a letter from conservative circles in Bonn[326] and may even have been invited to meet the CDU politician Friendensburg in Hamburg.[327] At the thirty-third central committee plenum in October 1957, Ulbricht refused to deliver the usual closing speech, dropping dark hints about an imminent purge in the leadership. Ziller apparently believed that he was next on Ulbricht's expulsion list.[328]

His opposition to the Ulbricht course climaxed at a meeting of the Wismut enterprise executive committee on 9 December 1957. Wismut AG was the GDR's main uranium plant and Ziller was on its board of directors. Under the influence of alcohol, he apparently predicted unprecedented conflicts at the thirty-fifth central committee plenum and claimed that Schirdewan, Oelßner, Selbmann and Grete Wittkowski were preparing to go public with their grievances: 'It is now do or die . . . we will go all out [to win]. We will not allow ourselves to be shot down, one by one. Either we go to the dogs, then we will be described as scoundrels (*Lumpen*), or we emerge as victors.'[329] He is also reported as saying that preparations were under way to depose Ulbricht as first secretary.[330] His alleged comments on the position of Khrushchev and the other communist leaderships in the Eastern bloc[331] corroborate Schirdewan's account.

Ulbricht used the events at Wismut to seize the initiative and allege the existence of a factional conspiracy. Schirdewan, however, is said to have blamed Ziller's outburst on the 'unhealthy' atmosphere in the party.[332] Oelßner agreed with this analysis, noting at a politburo meeting on 17 October 1957: 'Starting point of the affair is the oppressive atmosphere . . . no collective decision-making; instead personality cult, one-man rule, personal regime. Fear. Anxiety.

The issue is the complete evaluation of the twentieth party congress.'[333] Schirdewan believed that Ziller's drinks were deliberately mixed to provoke his unruly attack.[334] The latter shot himself on 14 December 1957, shortly after appearing before the politburo to account for his behaviour. He did so with the pistol allocated to all SED leaders to fend off 'counter-revolutionary' assassination attempts. In a suicide note addressed to Grotewohl, he criticized the lack of collective leadership and refused to engage in self-criticism.[335]

Excommunication awaited communist politicians who dared to challenge the prevailing orthodoxy. The logic of this iron law of Stalinist politics was too much for Ziller to bear. Defamed as a co-conspirator of the 'Schirdewan–Wollweber faction', he escaped the consequences of Ulbricht's retribution through suicide. The party, however, failed to draw any lessons from the tragedy. In Ziller's obituary it was stated simply: 'In a fit of depression, comrade Ziller took his own life.'[336]

Fritz Selbmann was born in 1899 in Hessen. A miner, he joined the Communist Party at the age of twenty-three. In the early 1930s, he was head of the district KPD in Upper Silesia and Saxony, before being elected to the *Reichstag* in 1932. The years from 1933 to 1945 were spent in concentration camps. After the war he was economics minister in Saxony, before being appointed deputy chairman of the German economics commission in 1948. Between 1949 and 1955, Selbmann was minister for industry, heavy industry and mining. Elected to the central committee in 1954, he was appointed deputy chairman of the council of ministers two years later.

Selbmann was the rising star of the technical intelligentsia. In February 1958 he was accused by Ulbricht of applying Western technocratic methods of industrial management to the socialist planned economy.[337] At the twenty-ninth central committee plenum, Selbmann rejected the economic plan as unrealistic and called for the correction of past failures.[338] His opposition to Ulbricht's reorganisation of the state apparatus was particularly stubborn. Rejecting Ulbricht's servile emulation of Khrushchev on this issue, he allegedly remarked 'what is being done now in the Soviet Union is out of the question for us.'[339] He opposed Ulbricht's idea of setting up an 'economics council'[340] to provide the economy with 'iron leadership.'[341] Convinced that the so-called 'decentralization project' would achieve the opposite result to that intended, he favoured granting greater independence to individual factory managements instead.[342]

Selbmann's critique was not confined to economic matters, however. At the twenty-ninth central committee plenum he seemed to warn the party that failure to implement the resolutions of the twentieth party congress might result in a 'Hungarian scenario.'[343] In his final statement of self-criticism to the politburo on 9 March 1959, he admitted to having harboured misgivings about the personality cult and violations of 'Leninist norms' in the SED.[344] It is also possible that he favoured slowing the tempo of socialist development in deference to the goal of national reunification. Challenging Selbmann at the thirty-third central committee plenum, one member of the central committee attested to a tendency among the 'technical intelligentsia' to adopt a pragmatic attitude on this issue. Many were apparently concerned that further steps towards socialism might exacerbate the split with West Germany.[345] Selbmann also argued for increased contact with industrial managers in the Federal Republic.[346] The assertion of one historian that Selbmann shared Oelßner's views on the collectivization of agriculture is open to question.[347] In a statement to the party leadership shortly after the thirty-fifth central committee plenum, Selbmann stated that while Oelßner's concept warranted discussion in summer 1956, its unfavourable results in Poland rendered it untenable.[348] He also denied allegations that he favoured a more conciliatory stance towards the students and the 'Harich group' in 1956.[349]

At the meeting of the Wismut enterprise executive committee in December 1957, Selbmann is said to have seconded Ziller's attack on Ulbricht. In an obvious allusion to the latter's attitude to Stalin, Selbmann claimed that – unlike others – he had never 'bowed' to the Soviet dictator. Most telling of all, however, was his alleged attack on those who had spent the war in Moscow: 'I was not in the emigration, I was locked up; but in the concentration camp with comrade Schirdewan [I] did political work under the most difficult conditions. Others spoke from comfortable positions over the radio to the soldiers in the trenches.'[350] If this highlights the existence of residual resentment between former concentration camp inmates and those who had spent the war in Moscow, Neumann's contention that the former intended 'taking over the leadership'[351] is exaggerated. As Selbmann himself indicated, these groups were no longer definable factions in the SED leadership.[352]

Although Selbmann would probably have favoured Schirdewan over Ulbricht in any leadership contest, he was well aware of his friend's limitations. In a statement to the politburo after the thirty-sixth central committee plenum in June 1958, he drew attention to Schirdewan's poor grasp of economics.[353] His evaluation on this point is supported by Berger and Wollweber.[354] After initial resistance, Selbmann engaged in self-criticism in March 1959. Despite his disagreements with Ulbricht, however, the SED could ill-afford to lose his talents. Although expelled from the central committee and relieved of his duties as deputy prime minister, he was appointed deputy chairman of the state planning commission – a position he held until 1961. In that year he was appointed deputy chairman of the economics council and in 1964 became chairman of the state planning commission's committee of scientific-technological services. He spent the last years of his life writing novels and died on 26 January 1975.

There were other critical voices in the central committee between 1956 and 1958. Those of Grete Wittkowski, Paul Wandel, Kurt Hager and Otto Buchwitz deserve a special mention.

Margarete Wittkowski was one of the few women to reach the summit of SED politics. Born in 1910 to a middle-class family of Jewish descent, she studied economics in Germany and Switzerland before entering the Jewish youth movement. In 1932 she joined the KPD before fleeing to Britain. Whilst in England she worked closely with the British communist Harry Pollit. On her return to Berlin in 1946, she co-founded the newspaper *Die Wirtschaft* before joining the staff of the embryonic German economics commission in 1947. As head of the commission's state planning office, Dr Wittkowski worked closely with Bruno Leuschner to lay the foundations of the planned economy. When Ulbricht emulated Stalin's purge of 'zionist conspirators' in 1951, she was demoted to the post of chairman of consumer co-operatives. Shortly after Stalin's death she was transferred back to the state planning commission.[355] Elected to the central committee in April 1954, she was appointed deputy minister for trade and provisions and first deputy to the chairman of the state planning commission.

Wittkowski was a persistent critic in the central committee between 1956 and 1958. Apart from opposing Ulbricht's economic policies,[356] she also sought to encourage a more open and wide-ranging debate in the leadership. At the twenty-sixth central committee plenum on 22 March 1956, Wittkowski criticized Ulbricht for mishandling the Stalin issue and for failing to brief central committee members on the resolutions of the twentieth party congress.[357] She went on to demand a little 'glasnost' in central committee discussions.[358] Wittkowski did not confine herself to criticism of the leadership, however. In a speech to the twenty-ninth central committee plenum in November 1956, she declared that the bureaucratic behaviour of many functionaries was discrediting the party and government.[359]

More explosive was Wittkowski's appeal for a new *Deutschlandpolitik*. Interpreting the refusal of West German workers to protest against the banning of the KPD as an indictment of SED policy, she went on to dismiss Ulbricht's initiative to set up an 'all-German Council' as a sham.[360] Proclaiming that there were 'two German states but only one German working class', Wittkowski called for 'new forms of struggle for the reunification of Germany and against the Adenauer government'. This meant pursuing rapprochement with the SPD and DGB (the West German Trade Union Federation). According to Wittkowski, the working class in Germany had never been so powerful. In the East it had seized state power; in the West it was represented by an increasingly influential SPD. Wittkowski believed that the party should take advantage of this situation to negotiate agreements on issues ranging from disarmament to the nationalization of industry. Her assertion that the SPD and DGB were socialist organizations with which one could do business was a repudiation of Stalinist dogma. Her appeal to former 'western émigrés' to foster their European contacts would have been unthinkable a few years before. Finally, she recommended establishing a permanent central committee commission under the chairmanship of former social democrat Otto Buchwitz to advise the leadership and draw up concrete proposals.[361] Ulbricht rejected Wittkowski's appeal out of hand. While the latter emphasized the unity of the German working class, the former blamed the SPD for its schism. The 'reformist' nature of its leadership, he declared, rendered the party a counter-revolutionary threat and rapprochement a dead letter. In Ulbricht's view, the SED had already conceded too much by granting an amnesty to imprisoned social democrats. The majority of those released, he said, were 'criminals.'[362]

For her role in the anti-Ulbricht opposition, Wittkowski was relegated to the post of an ordinary deputy to the chairman of the state planning commission. She also failed to win re-election to the central committee at the fifth party congress in July 1958. But, like Selbmann, her talents were soon redeployed elsewhere. In 1961 she was appointed to the council of ministers as Grotewohl's deputy for trade, supplies and agriculture.[363]

Born in 1905 to a working-class family in Mannheim, Paul Wandel was trained as a machine technician before joining the christian youth movement.[364] After transferring to the Socialist Youth Association in 1919, he joined the KPD in 1923. He emigrated to the Soviet Union a decade later. After joining the CPSU, he worked for the Comintern school and lectured at Moscow's Lomonosov University. He subsequently became political secretary to Wilhelm Pieck. On his return to Berlin in 1945, he was assigned the chief editorship of the KPD's *Deutsche Volkszeitung* and the post of president of the central administration for education. Joining the SED in 1946, he was elected to the party executive and then to the central committee. He was minister for education in the period 1949 to 1952, and central committee secretary for culture and education between 1953 and 1957. Considered to be a devoted supporter of Ulbricht until 1956, his subsequent conflict with the first secretary was a measure of the crisis afflicting the SED leadership.

As central committee secretary for culture and education, Wandel was especially well placed to observe the alienating effects of Ulbricht's policies on the intelligentsia. The harassment of a cultural elite already reeling under the impact of the twentieth party congress was depriving the GDR of its best artists, writers and actors. Believing that the only way to halt this trend was to adopt a less sectarian attitude, Wandel rejected the complacent SED dogma that the 'petit-bourgeois intelligentsia' was predestined to 'vacillate.'[365] When Wandel was relieved of his functions at the thirty-third central committee plenum in October 1957, the poet Johannes R. Becher said a few words in his defence: 'I must say that . . . . at a very difficult time, comrade Wandel helped us a great deal. I do not regard it as an error, that [he] did great work in the . . . strengthening of writers, who had broken down . . . under the impact of events. That is not an error . . . that is caring for the people.'[366] Wandel also refused to follow Ulbricht in unequivocally condemning the Italian communist leader Palmiro Togliatti[367] and the reformist Hungarian philosopher Georg Lukacs (despite his membership of the 'counter-revolutionary' Nagy government).[368]

So great was the Ulbricht family's disdain for the intelligentsia that his wife, Lotte, allegedly refused to shake hands with 'bourgeois' professors.[369] Wandel, by contrast, did not see 'bourgeois' intellectuals as an homogenous group bent on destroying socialism. Working with artists, writers and professors accustomed to a different socio-political milieu did not mean forcing them to change their opinions. As he put it in 1992: 'It was necessary to proceed more cautiously . . . There was also a progressive bourgeoisie.'[370] When Paul Fröhlich, SED first secretary in *Bezirk* Leipzig, ordered the arrest of the two novelists

Erich Loest and Gerhard Zwerenz in 1957, Wandel dispatched a sharply worded telegram of protest. The priority now, he said, was to 'hold on to the young intelligentsia of the party.'[371] Although in 1992 Wandel conceded that Harich and Janka had been treated unjustly,[372] his attitude in 1956 is more difficult to ascertain.

But Wandel's critique was not confined to cultural and educational matters. In his speech to the twenty-ninth central committee plenum, he pointed to widespread popular disaffection with the SED and appealed for 'a new relationship with the working class.' This meant increased consultation prior to policy decisions and the abolition of special privileges for party leaders. Wandel hoped that one day the SED would be able to rely on 'proletarian fists' rather than the state security forces to ward off counter-revolutionary activity. Ulbricht, he declared, had failed to provide a clear answer about how to go about achieving this goal. The masses, Wandel admitted, were not yet convinced that socialism was better than capitalism.[373]

Wandel's alleged ambivalence towards the *Jugendweihe*[374] (a new socialist confirmation ceremony in which fourteen year olds were given adult status) might have been a reflection of his concern for Church sensibilites. Hager accused him of replacing Ulbricht's introduction to the book *Weltall, Erde, Mensch* (distributed at the *Jugendweihe* service) with a piece written by an Austrian academic.[375] Furthermore, he was criticized for publishing his own alternative (*Unser Deutschland*) which barely mentioned the need to inculcate socialist values into the young.[376] According to Ulbricht, he also tried to prevent dissemination of atheist propaganda in the army.[377]

Expelled from the central committee secretariat at the thirty-third central committee plenum, Wandel was accused of neglecting the 'struggle for socialist culture' and sabotaging party education policy.[378] He had apparently betrayed his lack of enthusiasm for the new ten-class polytechnic schools by stalling on implementing the relevant resolutions. The one-sided emphasis on technical education was seen as unjust in that it imposed unreasonable demands on the less able and disadvantaged those with other talents [379] Members of the central committee were only informed of the decision to fire Wandel during Ulbricht's closing speech. The politburo was therefore prevented from debating the issue, the central committee was presented with a *fait accompli* and Wandel was denied the opportunity of defending himself.[380] Reluctantly, he engaged in self-criticism.[381] Shortly afterwards he was banished to China where he served as ambassador until 1961. He then served as deputy foreign minister of the GDR between 1961 and 1964, before being appointed president and vice-president of the League for Friendship among Peoples. In 1992, Wandel forcefully condemned Ulbricht's dictatorial style of leadership.[382] He died in 1995.

Born in 1912, Kurt Hager became a journalist before joining the KPD in 1930. He worked illegally for the party in Germany until 1936, then fought in the Spanish Civil War before emigrating to France and England. After 1945 he headed the party instruction and propaganda sections in the SED party executive and central committee. A professor at East Berlin's Humboldt University after 1949, he was elected a candidate member of the central committee a year later. In 1952 he was put in charge of a new department for 'science and universities' and, after 1954, became a full member of the central committee. In 1955 he was appointed central committee secretary for science and culture.

Kurt Hager delivered some of the most passionate speeches in the central committee between 1956 and 1958. Concerned that bureaucracy, 'dogmatism' and the personality cult were damaging relations between party and people, he defended the interests of the student rebels and welcomed the rise of Gomulka in Poland. At the twenty-sixth central committee plenum, Hager contested Ulbricht's claim that there was no personality cult in the SED.[383] In July 1956, he complained that the party was divesting socialism of its humanist appeal, thereby alienating many workers from the Republic. He rounded on party 'dogmatists' who refused to acknowledge a role for social democrats, trade unionists, christians and certain sections of the bourgeoisie in the struggle for 'peace, democracy and social justice.' Even in West Germany, he insisted, there were democratic rights and freedoms worth defending.[384]

With regard to the students, Hager felt that proper consideration should be given to their demands. The desire for more democracy and co-determination, he declared, was perfectly compatible with socialism.[385] Himself a witness to events in Poland, Hager commended the 'healthy revolutionary spirit' in the PUWP. However, as Hager himself admitted, the real issue was not Poland but the GDR: 'Is everything in order in the relationship between the party and people? And is everything as it should be in the party itself?'[386] Despite almost being expelled from the leadership in 1956–57,[387] Hager was rewarded for helping to discredit Wandel and for supporting Ulbricht at the thirtieth central committee plenum.[388] Elected a candidate member of the politburo in July 1958, he achieved full membership status five years later. In 1994, he characterized his own role in the anti-Ulbricht opposition as 'opportunist' and dismissed suggestions that Schirdewan offered any genuine political alternative.[389]

Otto Buchwitz was born in Breslau as son of a metalworker in 1879. After joining the SPD in 1898, he worked as a weaver and then as a miner. After serving as secretary of the German Association of Textile Workers' between 1907 and 1914, he was elected to the Prussian parliament in 1921 and to the *Reichstag* in 1924. After the Nazi seizure of power, he emigrated to Denmark where he worked illegally as a journalist. In 1940 he was sentenced to eight years' imprisonment for conspiring to commit high treason. He rejoined the social democrats in 1945 as a fervent campaigner for union with the KPD. Elected to the SED's party executive and central committee, he was chairman of Saxony's parliament until 1952. Thereafter (mainly due to old age but also because of his social democratic past) he was demoted to carrying out largely ceremonial duties.

Buchwitz was distressed by the harassment and marginalization of former social democrats in the SED. He was particularly perturbed by the practice of eavesdropping on party members with an SPD background. Addressing the thirtieth central committee plenum in early 1957, he declared: 'I know the sins of the Social Democratic Party leaders . . . But do I have to put on a penitential robe until the end of my life, because I was once a member of the SPD? . . . I have said to myself: Damn it all, what else must you do in the party, for it to show you trust?'[390] Buchwitz also complained that students at the party training college were being interrogated on their reasons for joining the SPD and not the KPD in 1945.[391] Since even former Nazis were no longer required to divulge former political allegiances when applying for party membership, this vividly illustrates the depth of communist antipathy towards former social democrats. Ulbricht, however, dismissed Buchwitz's protests as inappropriate and emphasized the need for vigilance in party ranks.[392]

Buchwitz also bemoaned the 'lack of solidarity' among party members. To give back the ordinary party worker a 'sense of belonging', he suggested consulting with them more frequently.[393] He also lambasted the FDJ's official history of the Socialist Youth movement for giving a distorted picture of the organization's history.[394] Ulbricht, however, had no time for historical objectivity. Claiming that the book was ideal for the education of East Germany's youth, he declared his opposition to portraying the history of the revolutionary labour movement as if it only consisted of internal struggles and failures. He then proceeded to lecture Buchwitz on the need to tolerate other people's opinions.[395] In November 1956, Wittkowski had called for a permanent commission chaired by Buchwitz to examine ways of fostering contacts with the SPD.[396] Buchwitz seemed sympathetic to the idea, suggesting that it might be possible to engage some social democrat members of the *Bundestag* in dialogue.[397] Such ideas were premature, however, and it was not until 1970 that the two parties agreed to talk to each other.

Other critical voices were occasionally raised in the period of uncertainty after the twentieth party congress of the CPSU. Otto Schön (secretary to the office of the politburo) urged the SED to interfere less in the affairs of the bloc parties and mass organizations.[398] Professor Wolfgang Steinitz, vice-president of the GDR's Academy of Sciences and national prize holder, censured the politburo for refusing to sanction a more open discussion in the party.[399] Otto Winzer, once a close confidant of Ulbricht, observed that internal party democracy was becoming a mere 'formality.'[400] Karl Mewis reminded the FDJ of its obligation to safeguard the interests of other parties in its new guise as a 'socialist' youth organization.[401]

Neither was the anti-Ulbricht opposition confined to the politburo and central committee. According to Fröhlich, sections of the SED apparatus were also infected – he singled out the academic and agriculture departments in particular. He also reported the view of many party intellectuals that Ulbricht should resign to help pave the way for German reunification.[402] These observations were corroborated by the results of an investigation carried out after the thirty-fifth central committee plenum. 'Revisionist' and 'opportunist' tendencies were discerned in support for freedom of the press, a slower tempo of socialist development, 'ideological coexistence' in cultural affairs and a degree of autonomy for the state apparatus.[403] Apparently, some FDGB functionaries even favoured granting a non-political role to the trade unions.[404]

An indication of the strength of the anti-Ulbricht opposition was that twenty-one of the central committee's eighty-nine full members and sixteen of its forty-four candidate members lost their seats at the fifth party congress in July 1958.[405]

Notes

1 Gomulka led the Polish CP in the immediate postwar period but was expelled for opposing tenets of the Stalinization process (e.g. the collectivization of agriculture) and championing a 'special Polish road to socialism.' He was re-elected first secretary of the PUWP at the 8 CC plenum on 20 October 1956 – a post he retained until his downfall in 1970.

2 According to Schirdewan, Ulbricht 'dreaded the possibility of a second 17 June'. Taped interview with Karl Schirdewan, 12.10.92.

3 W. Otto, 'Ernst Wollweber: Aus Erinnerungen. Ein Porträt Walter Ulbrichts', *BzG*, 3 (1990), 350–78; pp. 363–4. Wollweber (1953–55 state secretary, 1955–57 minister for state security) dictated this document to his wife Erika in October 1964. Ten years later she handed it to party leader Erich Honecker. Karl Schirdewan (taped interview, 12.10.92) and Grotewohl (interview with Kurt Hager, 6.4.94) were apparently more sympathetic to Gomulka's rise in Poland. After Rakosi's fall in summer 1956, Ulbricht warned the Hungarian communists that attempts to instigate reform would end in counter-revolution. His predictions were devastatingly accurate. See C. Stern, 'Der meistgehaßte, meistunterschätzte Mann. Walter Ulbricht – was dem DDR-Gründer gelang, wo der Staatratsvorsitzende scheiterte', *Der Spiegel*, 20 (10.5.71), 34–49; p. 46.

4 SAPMO-BArch, ZPA, NL 182/893. 'Die ideologischen Unklarheiten in der Partei und bei der Bevölkerung. Aus den Berichten der Sekretäre für Agitation und Propaganda der 14 Bezirksleitungen zusammengestellt (Anlage zum Brief an alle Mitglieder und Kandidaten des Zentralkomitees vom 22. Juni 1956 zur Vorbereitung der 28. Tagung des ZK).'

5 SAPMO-BArch, ZPA, IV 2/11/v801. Merker's letter to Grotewohl, 24 .8.56.

6 In July 1956, the CC passed a resolution implying that the accusations against Merker had been justified, only the punishment too harsh. There was no hint of rehabilitation or readmittance to the party (see SAPMO-BArch, ZPA, IV 2/1/164.) Faced with Merker's protests (see SAPMO-BArch, ZPA, IV 2/11/v801, Merker's letter to Grotewohl, 24.8.56), Ulbricht tried to buy time. First, he told Merker to regard his release from prison as 'rehabilitation' (see SAPMO-BArch, ZPA, NL 102/27, Ulbricht's letter to Merker, 7.9.56). Then, instead of rescinding Merker's expulsion from the SED at the 29 plenum in November 1956, he asked the CC to 'empower' the PB to draft a future resolution to this effect (SAPMO-BArch, ZPA, IV 2/1/168). When the PB finally approved Merker's readmission to the party on 29 December 1956 it was not even reported in the press.

7 SAPMO-BArch, ZPA, NL 102/27. Merker's draft statement, 8.12.56. See also SAPMO-BArch, ZPA, IV 2/11/v801. Merker's letter to Matern, 6.12.56.

8 According to Harich, Janka frequently commended Merker as 'a suitable German

Gomulka' during meetings at the Aufbau publishing house. Taped interview with Wolfgang Harich, 2.10.92.

9 Apart from Harich and Janka, two other dissident intellectuals attended this meeting: the chief editor of *Sonntag*, Heinz Zöger and his colleague Gustav Just. Along with Manfred Hertwig (editor-secretary of the *Deutschen Zeitschrift für Philosophie*), radio commentator Richard Wolf and research assistant Bernhard Steinberger, they received long prison sentences for membership of the 'Harich–Janka group'. All were members of the SED.

10 Harich's reform programme ('Über die Aufgaben der SED im Kampf für die Festigung ihrer Reihen, für die sozialistische Demokratisierung der DDR und für die friedliche Wiedervereinigung Deutschlands auf der Grundlage der Demokratie, des Sozialismus, der nationalen Souveränität und Unabhängigkeit und der Freundschaft mit allen Völkern') is mistakenly classified under Schirdewan's name in the SED archive (SAPMO-BArch, ZPA, NL 182/893), leading one American historian [A. James McAdams, *Germany Divided. From the Wall to Reunification* (Princeton, 1993), pp. 42–3] to cite Schirdewan as its author – something the latter refutes (taped interview, 12.10.92) See also typed statement from Harich to Grieder, 2.10.92. The manifesto has since been published in W. Harich, *Keine Schwierigkeiten mit der Wahrheit* (Berlin, 1993), pp. 112–60. Ulbricht distributed a copy to all PB members on 17 December 1956 (SAPMO-BArch, ZPA, J IV 2/202/7).

11 Taped interview with Harich, 2.10.92.

12 *Ibid.*

13 SAPMO-BArch, ZPA, IV 2/11/v801. Harich's testimony under interrogation, 11.2.57.

14 SAPMO-BArch, ZPA, IV 2/11/v801. 'Betr. Paul Merker. Zeitzeuglichen Vernehmung' (Harich's testimony).

15 *Ibid.* Merker's protestation of loyalty to the party line in a draft statement, 8.12.56 (see SAPMO-BArch, ZPA, NL 102/27) should be interpreted as an attempt to avoid the fate of Harich and Janka who had just been arrested. In December 1956 the SED was still paying lip service to the fight against 'dogmatism' and had yet to declare war on 'revisionism'.

16 SAPMO-BArch, ZPA, NL 102/27. Merker's rough draft of a statement, 8.12.56.

17 SAPMO-BArch, ZPA, IV 2/11/v801. 'Betr. Paul Merker. Zeitzeuglichen Vernehmung' (Merker's testimony).

18 SAPMO-BArch, ZPA, NL 102/27. Merker's draft statement, 8.12.56.

19 Taped interview with Harich, 2.10.92. Corroborated in Merker's draft statement, 8.12.56 (SAPMO-BArch, ZPA, NL 102/27).

20 Taped interview with Harich, 2.10.92. See also SAPMO-BArch, ZPA, IV 2/11/v801: 'Betr. Paul Merker. Zeitzeuglichen Vernehmung' (Harich's testimony).

21 SAPMO-BArch, ZPA, IV 2/11/v801. Harich's testimony under interrogation, 11.2.57.

22 W. Janka, *Schwierigkeiten mit der Wahrheit* (Reinbek bei Hamburg, 1989), p. 103.

23 SAPMO-BArch, ZPA, IV 2/11/v5280/2. Dahlem's letter to PB and CC, 23.9.56.

24 C. Stern, *Porträt einer bolschewistischen Partei. Entwicklung, Funktion und Situation der SED* (Köln, Berlin-West, 1957), p. 231.

25 SAPMO-BArch, ZPA, NL 90/303. Dahlem's letter to Ulbricht, 17.2.57.

26 SAPMO-BArch, ZPA, NL 90/303. Dahlem's letter to Ulbricht and Pieck, 25.1.55. This was the successor organisation to the VVN (Dahlem's power base before its dissolution in February 1953).

27 SAPMO-BArch, ZPA, NL 90/303. Dahlem's letter to Ulbricht, 17.2.57.

28 SAPMO-BArch, ZPA, IV 2/11/v5280/2. In July 1956 (before the events in Poland and Hungary) Dahlem allegedly described Ulbricht as the 'best and most capable member of the party leadership for the job of first secretary'. See 'Bericht über Mitgliederversammlung im Staatssekretariat für Hochschulwesen am 20.7.56', dated 24.7.56.

29 SAPMO-BArch, ZPA, NL 90/303. Dahlem's letter to Ulbricht and Pieck, 25.1.55.

30 *Ibid.*

31 SAPMO-BArch, ZPA, NL 90/303. Dahlem's letter to Ulbricht, 17.2.57.

32 SAPMO-BArch, ZPA, IV 2/11/v5280/2. 'Bericht über Mitgliederversammlung im Staatssekretariat für Hochschulwesen am 20.7.56', dated 24.7.56.

33 SAPMO-BArch, ZPA, IV 2/11/v5280/2. Dahlem's letter to Ulbricht, 18.3.56.

34 SAPMO-BArch, ZPA, IV 2/1.01/315. Minutes of CC youth commission, 10.12.56.

35 *Ibid.*

36 SAPMO-BArch, ZPA, IV 2/11/v5280/2. Dahlem's letter to Grotewohl and Schirdewan, 9.3.57.

37 SAPMO-BArch, ZPA, IV 2/1.01/315. Minutes of sitting of CC youth commission, 10.12.56.

38 *Ibid.*

39 *Ibid.*

40 SAPMO-BArch, ZPA, J IV 2/2/513. PB meeting, 17.11.56.

41 Wollweber, 'Aus Erinnerungen', p. 364.

42 See SAPMO-BArch, ZPA, NL 90/303. Dahlem's letter to Ulbricht, 17.2.57 and to Grotewohl, 22.2.57.

43 SAPMO-BArch, ZPA, NL 90/303. Dahlem's letter to Grotewohl, 6.7.56.

44 SAPMO-BArch, ZPA, IV 2/1/157.

45 SAPMO-BArch, ZPA, IV 2/1/161. Hans Kiefert's speech to 28 CC plenum, 27.–29.8.56.

46 SAPMO-BArch, ZPA, NL 90/303, Dahlem's letter to Ulbricht, 17.2.57. See also SAPMO-BArch, ZPA, IV 2/11/v5280/2, ('Bericht über Mitgliederversammlung im Staatssekretariat für Hochschulwesen am 20.7.56', dated 24.7.56) in which Dahlem recalls a 'demonstration' in his favour during a ceremony to decorate Ulbricht with the Hans-Beimler Medal.

47 SAPMO-BArch, ZPA, J IV 2/2/512.

48 Taped interview with Harich, 2.10.92.

49 SAPMO-BArch, ZPA, IV 2/1/193. See Dahlem's speech to 35 CC plenum.

50 C. Stern, *Ulbricht. A political biography* (London, 1965), p. 170.

51 SAPMO-BArch, ZPA, IV 2/1/193.

52 H. Blumberg, 'Franz Dahlem. Nachgelassenes. Ausgelassenes. Über einen Prozess und die Schwierigkeiten seiner richtigen Beurteilung', *BzG*, 1 (1990), 17–25; p. 23.

53 SAPMO-BArch, ZPA, J IV 2/202/7. Harich's testimony under interrogation, 11.2.57.

54 SAPMO-BArch, ZPA, IV 2/11/v5280/2. Dahlem's letter to Ulbricht, 31.10.58.

55 SAPMO-BArch, ZPA, IV 2/11/v5280/2. Dahlem's letter to Ulbricht, 1.8.65.

56 SAPMO-BArch, ZPA, J IV 2/2–1544. Dahlem's letter to Honecker, January 1975.

57 SAPMO-BArch, ZPA, NL 102/65. Dahlem's letter to Grete Merker, 5.3.80.

58 See also: P. Grieder, 'Eine unabhängige britische Sicht auf die Konflikte im SED-Politbüro zwischen 1956/1958' in T. Klein, W. Otto, P. Grieder, *Visionen, Repression und Opposition in der SED (1949–1989)* (Berlin, 1996).

59 O. Harbauer, 'Den Kampf mit Ulbricht gewagt', *Freiheit* (16.2.90), 9.

60 W. Ulbricht, 'Über den XX. Parteitag der Kommunistischen Partei der Sowjetunion', *ND* (4.3.56), 4.

61 Schirdewan recalls the reaction of many comrades to the Stalin revelations: 'We were so sad and full of consternation. We could not comprehend it at all.' Taped interview with Schirdewan, 23.11.92.

62 'Der zaudernde Rebell. Karl Schirdewan und die SED der 50er Jahre', *RIAS Berlin* (Beitrag von Manfred Rexin für die Sendereihe 'Themen der Zeit', 18.8.91, 18.35–19.30 Uhr).

63 'Die leninistische Geschlossenheit unserer Partei', *ND* (29.4.56), 3–4; p. 3.

64 Interview with Schirdewan, 9.7.94.

65 'Die leninistische Geschlossenheit unserer Partei', pp. 3–4. Apparently, the final version was not as radical as the original draft rejected by Ulbricht. Even the revised edition could only be published when the latter went away on holiday. Interview with Schirdewan, 9.7.94.

66 H. Lippmann, *Honecker and the new politics of Europe* (London, 1973), pp. 177–8.

67 ' "Die Führung lag in Moskau" M. Schumann und W. Dreßen im Gespräch mit Karl Schirdewan', *Niemandsland, Tugendterror*, 11/12 (1992), 305–26; p. 321.

68 SAPMO-BArch, ZPA, NL 215/112 'Mündliche Stellungnahme im Politbüro am 11.1.5[8]'. See also SAPMO-BArch, ZPA, NL 215/112, 'Politbüro 17.12.57'.

69 Interview with Schirdewan, 25.9.92.

70 SAPMO-BArch, ZPA, J IV 2/2A-532. PB meeting 10.11.56: 'Entwurf. Bericht des Politbüros über seine Tätigkeit seit dem 28. Plenum des Zentralkomitees vor dem 29. Plenum des Zentralkomitees'. See also Schirdewan's speech to 3 party conference of SED in *Protokoll der Verhandlungen der III. Parteikonferenz der Sozialistischen Einheitspartei Deutschlands*, I (Berlin-Ost, 1956), 305–20; p. 317.

71 SAPMO-BArch, ZPA, IV 2/1/191. Honecker's report to 35 CC plenum. SAPMO-BArch, ZPA, J IV 2/2/512. PB meeting 10.11.56.

72 Taped interview with Schirdewan, 23.11.92.

73 Taped interview with Schirdewan, 12.10.92. In a statement to the PB on 5.1.58, Oelßner accused Ulbricht of imitating Stalin's tactic of using expert commissions to undermine the elected leadership. (SAPMO-BArch, ZPA, NL 215/112, 'Erklärung an das Politbüro des Zentralkomitees der SED', 5.1.58). In 1957 Ulbricht used this method to amend the economic plan, revise the sugar programme and establish guidelines for restructuring the state bureaucracy. See SAPMO-BArch, ZPA, IV 2/1/192, Oelßner's speech to 35 CC plenum.

74 SAPMO-BArch, ZPA, NL 215/112. 'Diskussion PB, 29.12.56'.

75 SAPMO-BArch, ZPA, NL 215/112. 'Diskussion PB, 29.12.56'. There is no evidence, however, that Oelßner regretted his inauspicious role in defeating the Zaisser–Herrnstadt opposition of 1953. On the contrary, he would have 'done the same again'. SAPMO-BArch, ZPA, NL 215/112. 'PB Sitzung vor dem 28. Plenum'.

76 SAPMO-BArch, ZPA, NL 215/112. 'Mündliche Stellungnahme im Politbüro am 11.1.5[8]'.

77 SAPMO-BArch, ZPA, NL 215/112. 'Diskussion PB 29.12.56'.

78 Interview with Alfred Neumann, 16.10.92.

79 Taped interview with Schirdewan, 12.10.92.

80 *Ibid.*

81 See K. Schirdewan, *Aufstand gegen Ulbricht. Im Kampf um politische Kurskorrektur, gegen stalinistische, dogmatische Politik* (Berlin, 1994), pp. 86–7.

82 'Die leninistische Geschlossenheit unserer Partei', p. 3. In a letter of protest to Ulbricht in September 1956, Dahlem quoted from this article to demonstrate the incomplete nature of his own rehabilitation. See SAPMO-BArch, ZPA, IV 2/11/v5280/2. Dahlem's letter to PB and CC, 23.9.56.

83 SAPMO-BArch, ZPA, NL 215/112. 'Erklärung im Politbüro', 3.7.56.

84 *Ibid.*, and G. Bretschneider, K. Libera, R. Wilhelm, 'Karl Schirdewan: Fraktionsmacherei oder gegen Ulbrichts Diktat? Eine Stellungnahme vom 1. Januar 1958', *BzG*, 4 (1990), 498–512; p. 504.

85 SAPMO-BArch, ZPA, NL 215/112. 'Mein Vorschlag für Bericht Pol. Büro an 28. Plenum'.

86 SAPMO-BArch, ZPA, NL 215/112. 'Erklärung im Politbüro', 3.7.56.

87 SAPMO-BArch, ZPA, J IV 2/2/486. Ulbricht's reply of 7.9.56 to Oelßner's 'Erklärung im Politbüro', 3.7.56.

88 V. Falin, *Politische Erinnerungen* (München, 1993), p. 335. In the 1950s, Valentin Falin was member of an 'information committee' advising Soviet leaders on policy towards Germany. Had Pieck been well enough to participate in political life after the summer of 1956, Ulbricht would not necessarily have been able to count on his wholehearted support. Wollweber testifies to considerable tension between the two men. See Wollweber, 'Aus Erinnerungen', p. 360. His account was confirmed by Schirdewan (taped interview 12.10.92). Oelßner successfully mobilized Pieck to prevent Ulbricht from criticizing him at a CC plenum in 1954–55. SAPMO-BArch, ZPA, NL 215/112, 'Mündliche Stellungnahme im Politbüro am 11.1.195[8]'.

89 SAPMO-BArch, ZPA, NL 215/112. 'PB Sitzung vor 28. Plenum'.

90 *Ibid.*

91 SAPMO-BArch, ZPA, NL 215/112. 'Politbüro 11.1.58'.

92 *Ibid.*

93 Taped interview with Harich, 2.10.92.

94 SAPMO-BArch, ZPA, NL 215/112. 'Politbüro, 11.1.58'.

95 SAPMO-BArch, ZPA, NL 215/112. 'Politbüro 17.XII. 1957'.

96 SAPMO-BArch, ZPA, NL 215/112. 'Politbüro 11.1.58'.

97 SAPMO-BArch, ZPA, NL 215/112: 'Zur Lage in der Partei'. Oelßner in PB meeting, 30.12.56. See also Schirdewan's written statement to the PB of 1.1.58 in Bretschneider et al., 'Fraktionsmacherei', pp. 510–11.

98 SAPMO-BArch, ZPA, NL 215/112. 'Zur Lage in der Partei', PB meeting, 30.12.56.

99 Schirdewan in conversation with Wollweber on 11.1.57, reported in Wollweber, 'Aus Erinnerungen', p. 373. Wollweber's testimony is confirmed in Schirdewan's written statement to the PB of 1.1.58. See Bretschneider et al., 'Fraktionsmacherei', p. 511.

100 Bretschneider et al., 'Fraktionsmacherei', p. 510.

101 Hanna Wolf (CC member, close confidant of Ulbricht and director of the party training college 'Karl Marx') dismissed the phenomenon as an inevitable by-product of all revolutions. During the period of Jacobin dictatorship in France, she declared, the ruling classes had also emigrated – many of them just over the border to Koblenz! SAPMO-BArch, ZPA, IV 2/1/185, speech to 33 CC plenum, 16.–19.10.57.

102 SAPMO-BArch, ZPA, J IV 2/2A-532, PB meeting 10.11.56. Schirdewan's draft report to 29 CC plenum.

103 SAPMO-BArch, ZPA, NL 215/112. 'Politbüro 17.XII.1957'.

104 SAPMO-BArch, ZPA, NL 215/112. 'Zur Lage in der Partei, 30.12.56'.

105 SAPMO-BArch, ZPA, NL 215/112. 'Politbüro 11.1.58'.

106 SAPMO-BArch, ZPA, NL 215/112. 'Politbüro 17.XII.1957'. See also SAPMO-BArch, ZPA, IV 2/1/185. Hanna Wolf's speech to 33 CC plenum, 16.–19.10.57: 'I can remember a few years ago comrade Matern saying to me that these people would earlier have pushed off to the capital cities of south-eastern Europe – Warsaw, Budapest, Bucharest, etc. Today, however, these are cities one can no longer push off to – they belong to the socialist camp!'

107 SAPMO-BArch, ZPA, NL 215/112. 'Politbüro 11.1.58'. Wolfgang Berger, private aide to Ulbricht until 1971, is still steeped in the Stalinist view that the refugees were traitors to socialism. According to Berger, the 'longing for freedom' was no reason for leaving the GDR. 'Freedom' did not exist as a concept at this time. Most fled the country for less than noble reasons – to escape punishment for war crimes or to participate in the crass consumerism of the FRG. Interview with Wolfgang Berger, 27.11.92.

108 SAPMO-BArch, ZPA, NL 215/112. 'Politbüro 17.XII.1957'. The Berlin Wall was eventually built to stem the migrant flood. Construction began on 13 August 1961.

109 SAPMO-BArch, ZPA, IV 2/1/162.

110 SAPMO-BArch, ZPA, IV 2/1/192. Cited in Walter Buchheim's speech to 35 CC plenum.

111 SAPMO-BArch, ZPA, NL 215/112. 'PB Sitzung vor 28. Plenum'.

112 SAPMO-BArch, ZPA, NL 215/112. 'Zur Lage in der Partei 30.12.56'. The 'Petöfi club' was a group of Hungarian intellectuals concerned to further the cause of de-Stalinization in 1956.

113 See 'Arbeiterkomitees. Instruktion aus Polen', *Der Spiegel*, 5 (30.1.57), 16.

114 SAPMO-BArch, ZPA, NL 62/29.

115 Taped interview with Schirdewan, 23.11.92.

116 Bretschneider et al., 'Fraktionsmacherei', p. 503.

117 Taped interview with Schirdewan 23.11.92. According to Schirdewan, Warnke changed his mind after a long talk with Ulbricht.

118 According to Fritz Schenk (adviser to Leuschner in the state planning commission) Leuschner tried to avoid political conflict whenever possible. He was, however, close to tears when Ulbricht shelved plans for worker participation in industry. See F. Schenk, *Mein doppeltes Vaterland* (Würzburg, 1989), p. 181.

119 SAPMO-BArch, ZPA, IV 2/1/193. Wolfgang Steinke's speech to 35 CC plenum.

120 D. Borkowski, *Erich Honecker. Statthalter Moskaus oder deutscher Patriot?* (München, 1987), p. 248. After 1945, Borkowski worked closely with Honecker in the FDJ. A supporter of the 'Schirdewan–Wollweber group', he spent two years in solitary confinement between 1960 and 1962.

121 SAPMO-BArch, ZPA, IV 2/1/193. Ulbricht's closing speech to 35 CC plenum.

122 See P. Skyba, 'Die FDJ im Tauwetter – Tauwetter in der FDJ', in H. Gotschlich (ed.), '*Links und links und Schritt gehalten . . .*' Die FDJ: Konzepte – Abläufe – Grenzen (Berlin, 1994), pp. 206–26.

123 L. Röllecke, 'Es herrschten Personenkult, politische Arroganz', *Berliner Morgenpost* (19.–20.4.92), 52. See also Schirdewan, *Aufstand gegen Ulbricht*, pp. 121–2.

124 SAPMO-BArch, ZPA, J IV 2/2/557. PB meeting 3.9.57: 'Die sozialistische Erziehung der Jugend und die Aufgaben der Grundorganisationen der Partei'.

125 SAPMO-BArch, ZPA, IV 2/1/193.

126 SAPMO-BArch, ZPA, IV 2/1/191. Honecker's report to 35 CC plenum. See also SAPMO-BArch, ZPA, NL 77/51. Text of a letter sent out to all SED grassroots organ-

izations, February 1958: 'Comrade Schirdewan was of the opinion that it was enough to hold an ideological debate with the stirred up students . . . Against his will, however, the party leadership took the appropriate security measures and mobilized the workers' militia. . .'

127 SAPMO-BArch, ZPA, IV 2/1.01/315. Schirdewan's closing speech to CC youth commission, 10.12.56.

128 SAPMO-BArch, ZPA, IV 2/1.01/315. Honecker's speech to CC youth commission, 10.12.56.

129 SAPMO-BArch, ZPA, IV 2/1.01/315. Schirdewan's closing speech to CC youth commission, 10.12.56.

130 Interview with Neumann, 16.10.92.

131 SAPMO-BArch, ZPA, J IV 2/2A-532, PB meeting 10.11.56. Draft report to 29 CC plenum.

132 SAPMO-BArch, ZPA, J IV 2/2/514.

133 SAPMO-BArch, ZPA, IV 2/1/193. Ulbricht's closing speech to 35 CC plenum.

134 Accused of 'neglecting the necessary struggle against enemies of the German Democratic Republic', Haid was reprimanded and relieved of his post at the 36 CC plenum (10.–11.6.58). See SAPMO-BArch, ZPA, IV 2/1/201.

135 SAPMO-BArch, ZPA, IV 2/1/193. Ulbricht's closing speech to 35 CC plenum.

136 Taped interview with Schirdewan, 12.10.92. See also Schirdewan's letter to CPCC chairman, Walter Eberlein, 27.11.89, SAPMO-BArch, ZPA, IV 2/11/v5142.

137 Taped interview with Schirdewan, 12.10.92.

138 SAPMO-BArch, ZPA, IV 2/1/191. Matern's speech to 35 CC plenum.

139 SAPMO-BArch, ZPA, IV 2/1/191. Honecker's report to 35 CC plenum. In his two speeches to the same plenum, Schirdewan admitted having warned against a return to 'old methods'. See SAPMO-BArch, ZPA, IV 2/1/191 and SAPMO-BArch, ZPA, IV 2/1/193.

140 SAPMO-BArch, ZPA, NL 76/82. Matern's speech to conference of district party activists in Dresden, 13.2.58. Matern accused Schirdewan of attempting to extend the policy of 'coexistence' to domestic affairs.

141 See Bretschneider et al., 'Fraktionmacherei', p. 511.

142 SAPMO-BArch, ZPA, IV 2/1/162. Oelßner's speech to 28 CC plenum. Oelßner took the unusual step of taking his objections to the CC where he initially received a sympathetic hearing.

143 *Ibid.*

144 SAPMO-BArch, ZPA, NL 215/112. 'Zur Lage in der Partei 30.12.56'.

145 H. Weber, *DDR. Grundriß der Geschichte 1945–1990* (Hannover, 1991), p. 87.

146 SAPMO-BArch, ZPA, NL 215/112. PB meeting, 4.12.56.

147 SAPMO-BArch, ZPA, BPA, IV 2/2/113.

148 SAPMO-BArch, ZPA, IV 2/1/185. Speech to 33 CC plenum.

149 Stern, *Ulbricht*, p. 207.

150 Weber, *DDR*, p. 87.

151 SAPMO-BArch, ZPA, IV 2/1/192. Oelßner's speech to 35 CC plenum.

152 SAPMO-BArch, ZPA, IV 2/1/193. Ulbricht's closing speech to 35 CC plenum.

153 SAPMO-BArch, ZPA, NL 215/112. 'Erklärung zur Behandlung des Volkswirtschaftsplanes 1958 und des 2. Fünfjahrplanes 1958–1960', 10.12.57. Oelßner noted sardonically that 'for the sake of peace and quiet' the statement was not submitted.

154 SAPMO-BArch, ZPA, NL 215/112. Oelßner's 'Erklärung an das Politbüro des Zentralkomitees der SED', 5.1.58.

155 Bretschneider et al., 'Fraktionsmacherei', p. 504. Schirdewan claims to have regarded the policy of turning the GDR into a 'socialist display window' as doomed from the start. Taped interview with Schirdewan, 12.10.92.

156 SAPMO-BArch, ZPA, IV 2/1/165. Leuschner's speech to 29 CC plenum.

157 Taped interview with Schirdewan, 12.10.92.

158 SAPMO-BArch, ZPA, IV 2/1/192. Oelßner's speech to 35 CC plenum.

159 *Ibid.*

160 *Ibid.*

161 *Ibid.*

162 F. Oldenburg, *Konflikt und Konfliktregelung in der Parteiführung der SED 1945/46–1972* (Köln, 1972), p. 58.

163 SAPMO-BArch, ZPA, J IV 2/2A/599. PB meeting 18.12.57. See also SAPMO-BArch, BPA, IV – 2/2/113. Ulbricht's closing speech to conference of district party activists in Berlin, 17.2.58. SAPMO-BArch, ZPA, IV 2/1/193. Ulbricht's closing speech to 35 CC plenum.

164 SAPMO-BArch, ZPA, J IV 2/2A/599. PB meeting, 18.12.57.

165 SAPMO-BArch, ZPA, NL 215/112. 'Politbüro, 11.1.58'.

166 Interviews with Schirdewan, 25.9.92 and 9.7.94.

167 SAPMO-BArch, ZPA, IV 2/1/191.

168 H. Grüber, *Bevollmächtigt zum Brückenbau: Heinrich Grüber. Judenfreund und Trümmerprobst. Erinnerungen, Predigten, Berichte, Briefe* (Leipzig, 1991), p. 88.

169 M. Gerlach, *Mitverantwortlich: Als Liberaler im SED-Staat* (Berlin, 1991), p. 88. In a taped interview on 12.10.92, Schirdewan confirmed and clarified Gerlach's account. He apparently favoured granting the bloc parties the right to engage in free debate and practice opposition in the *Volkskammer*. These reforms would have been implemented within the contours of existing political structures.

170 Schirdewan and Gerlach became acquainted in Leipzig in 1952, where the former was SED first secretary and the latter deputy mayor. They also worked together on the national council of the National Front.

171 SAPMO-BArch, ZPA, J IV 2/2A/532. PB meeting 10.11.56: Draft report to 29 CC plenum. Schirdewan's success in ensuring inclusion of this passage in the final version of his report (see SAPMO-BArch, ZPA, IV 2/1/165) only shows the willingness of Ulbricht and his allies to pay lip service to policies they had no intention of implementing.

172 Interview with Neumann, 16.10.92.

173 Interview with Berger, 27.11.92.

174 W. Erfurt, *Moscow's policy in Germany. A study in contemporary history* (Esslingen, 1959), p. 68.

175 *Ibid.*, pp. 66, 99, 102.

176 Weber, *DDR*, p. 297.

177 *Ibid.*, p. 297.

178 Taped interview with Schirdewan, 12.10.92.

179 *Ibid.*

180 Erfurt, *Moscow's policy in Germany*, p. 66.

181 See Weber, *DDR*, p. 297.

182 J. Schecter, V. Luchkov (eds), *Khrushchev remembers. The glasnost tapes* (Boston, 1990), pp. 69–70.

183 Taped interview with Schirdewan, 12.10.92.

184 Cited in Erfurt, *Moscow's policy in Germany*, pp. 75–6.

185 SAPMO-BArch, ZPA, IV 2/1/191. Honecker's report to 35 CC plenum. See also Ebert's speech to conference of district party activists in Berlin, 17.2.58, SAPMO-BArch, BPA, IV 2/2/113.

186 *Protokoll der Verhandlungen der III. Parteikonferenz der Sozialistischen Einheitspartei Deutschlands* (Berlin-Ost, 1956), 305–20; pp. 309, 312–14.

187 'Die leninistische Geschlossenheit unserer Partei', p. 3.

188 According to Jänicke, Schäffer used the meeting to float the idea of an all-German confederation based on the Benelux model. Referendums would be held to determine the precise constitutional arrangements. See M. Jänicke, *Der dritte Weg. Die antistalinistische Opposition gegen Ulbricht seit 1953* (Köln, 1964) pp. 81–2. See also Weber, *DDR*, pp. 93–4. Falin claims that Schäffer met with Markus Wolf and his *Stasi* colleagues, but was unable to hold discussions with leading East German politicians. See Falin, *Politische Erinnerungen*, p. 331. Wolf provides new information about the meeting in his memoirs: M. Wolf, *In eigenem Auftrag. Bekenntnisse und Einsichten* (München, 1991), pp. 150–2.

189 SAPMO-BArch, ZPA, J IV 2/2A-532. Schirdewan's draft report to 29 CC plenum.

190 See Honecker's report to 35 CC plenum, SAPMO-BArch, ZPA, IV 2/1/191.

191 See Erich Mielke's speech to 5 party congress, July 1958 in *Protokoll des V. Parteitages der Sozialistischen Einheitspartei Deutschlands* (Berlin-Ost, 1959) I, 547–56; p. 553.

192 SAPMO-BArch, ZPA, J IV 2/2/520. PB, 29.12.56. 'Über die Wiedervereinigung Deutschlands zu einem friedliebenden und demokratischen Staat'.

193 Ulbricht interviewed in February 1958. Cited in Erfurt, *Moscow's policy towards Germany*, pp. 97–8.

194 The doctrine, proclaimed in December 1955, according to which the FRG denied full diplomatic recognition to any state (apart from the Soviet Union) which recognized the GDR.

195 *Ibid.*, p. 97.

196 SAPMO-BArch, BPA, IV 1 2/2/113. Ulbricht's closing speech to conference of district party activists in Berlin, 17.2.58.

197 SAPMO-BArch, ZPA, NL 76/82. Matern's speech to conference of district party activists in Dresden, 13.2.58.

198 In 1992, Schirdewan heavily criticized Ulbricht for imposing one-sided preconditions on the West. Ulbricht's demand that the FRG demilitarize, for example, should have been matched by a commitment to do likewise in the GDR. Taped interview with Schirdewan, 12.10.92.

199 SAPMO-BArch, ZPA, NL 76/82. Matern's speech to conference of district party activists in Dresden, 13.2.58.

200 Taped interview with Schirdewan, 12.10.92.

201 'Schirdewan hielt die Pläne Schäffers für annchmbar', *Die Welt, Unabhängige Zeitung für Deutschland*, Ausgabe B, 5 (7.1.59), 2.

202 Taped interview with Schirdewan, 12.10.92.

203 *Ibid.*

204 M. Lemke, 'Als Wehner "irgendwie mit der SED ins Gespräch kommen" wollte', *Die Zeit* (23.7.93), p. 8.

205 Grotewohl to Ulbricht, 22.2.57. Cited in F. Stempel, 'Erinnerung an Otto Grotewohl. Zu dessen 100. Geburtstag am 11. März 1994', *Utopie Kreativ*, 41/42 (March–April 1994), 154–65; pp. 158–9.

206 Taped interview with Schirdewan, 12.10.92.

207 SAPMO-BArch, ZPA, J IV 2/2A-543. PB meeting 15.1.57. Draft of theses for KPD party congress: 'Der Weg der Bundesrepublik zu Frieden, Freiheit, sozialen Fortschritt und nationaler Wiedervereinigung'. The SED PB passed a resolution rejecting the document. See SAPMO-BArch, ZPA, J IV 2/2/522. PB meeting, 15.1.57.

208 SAPMO-BArch, ZPA, J IV 2/2A-543. 'Stellungnahme zum Entwurf der Disposition für die Thesen der KPD' (H. Matern, P. Verner, M. Spangenberg).

209 According to Bauer, Fisch (a member of the *Bundestag*) was shortlisted as one of the main defendants in the planned show trial of German communists in East Berlin between 1950 and 1952. See 'Ich bin kein Lump, Herr Mielke!', *Der Spiegel*, 5 (30.1.57), 30–7; p. 34. Since he was present at the PB meeting on 15 January 1957, it is likely that Fisch submitted the draft policy declaration on behalf of the KPD. See SAPMO-BArch, ZPA, J IV 2/2/522.

210 After the 20 party congress of the CPSU, the PCI had distanced itself from Moscow and begun to emphasize its commitment to an 'Italian road to socialism'. Their leader, Palmiro Togliatti, criticized Khrushchev for concentrating his attack on Stalin rather than analysing the deeper causes of bureaucratic degeneration. He also appealed for 'polycentrism' in the world communist movement, i.e. an end to Moscow's hegemony. L. Kolakowski, *Main currents of Marxism. Its origin, growth and dissolution*, Vol. 3 (Oxford, 1978), p. 463.

211 BStU, 10993. 'Kurze Information über die Politbürositzung am 11. Januar 1958'.

212 Schirdewan stresses the importance of his war-time experiences in determining his political outlook and testifies to 'terrible tensions' between those who had sought sanctuary in the Soviet Union, those who had emigrated to the West and those who had remained in Germany. The first group had been 'morally corrupted' by their experiences. Taped interview with Schirdewan, 12.9.92.

213 Taped interview with Schirdewan, 23.11.92.

214 SAPMO-BArch, ZPA, NL 215/112. 'Erklärung an das Politbüro des Zentralkomitees der SED', 5.1.58.

215 Interview with Berger, 4.12.92. Berger dismisses claims that Schirdewan offered an alternative to Ulbricht, insisting that he resembled 'a big company chief' more than 'a great democrat.' He remembers Schirdewan as 'rough and ruthless . . . 90 per cent of department heads were afraid of Schirdewan'. Paul Wandel's wife remembers Schirdewan differently: 'Schirdewan was more human and democratic than Ulbricht.' Interview with the Wandels, 30.11.92.

216 Interview with Schirdewan, 25.9.92.

217 Member of CPSU presidium. Replaced Malenkov as premier in 1955. He initially played the role of Khrushchev's close partner in policy but as the leadership struggle intensified he made his availability as an alternative leader evident. In 1957 he threw his support behind Khrushchev's usurpers.

218 SAPMO-BArch, ZPA, IV 2/1/193. Ulbricht's closing speech to 35 CC plenum.

219 SAPMO-BArch, ZPA, IV 2/1/192. Wolf's speech to 35 CC plenum.

220 SAPMO-BArch, ZPA, IV 2/1/192. Rau's speech to 35 CC plenum.

221 SAPMO-BArch, ZPA, NL 215/112. 'PB 29.12.56'.

222 SAPMO-BArch, ZPA, NL 215/112. Rau at PB meeting on 4.12.57.

223 Schirdewan in conversation with Wollweber on 11 November 1957, reported in Wollweber, 'Aus Erinnerungen', p. 374.
224 Taped interview with Schirdewan, 23.11.92.
225 SAPMO-BArch, ZPA, IV 2/1/192.
226 'Der zaudernde Rebell'.
227 Schirdewan, *Aufstand gegen Ulbricht*, p. 122.
228 Schirdewan in conversation with Wollweber on 11.11.57 reported in Wollweber, 'Aus Erinnerungen', p. 374. Pushkin's stance is confirmed by new archival evidence from Moscow. See TsKhSD (Moscow Center for the Preservation of Contemporary Documentation): Rolik ('microfilm role') 8873, Fond ('collection of documents') 5, Opis ('inventory') 49, Delo ('file') 76. 'Report to CPSU CC from Ju. Andropov, chairman of department of CC of CPSU responsible for links with the Communist and Workers' Parties of the socialist countries, 30.1.58'. Copy of document handed to the author by Schirdewan during an interview, 9.7.94.
229 Falin, *Politische Erinnerungen*, p. 335.
230 Wollweber, 'Aus Erinnerungen', p. 375.
231 'Der zaudernde Rebell'.
232 SAPMO-BArch, ZPA, J IV 2/2A/3196. Ulbricht's letter to Hans Rodenberg, 23.10.71. Rodenberg, a personal friend of the SED first secretary, was an actor by profession and member of the GDR's council of state. One historian's conclusion that Ulbricht gained the Soviet leader's backing by slavishly duplicating his every initiative from 'decentralization' of the economy to maize plantation therefore requires qualification. See Jänicke, *Der dritte Weg*, p. 239.
233 Secretary of agitation and propaganda in Berlin's district leadership of the SED until 1953. A supporter of a 'third way' between capitalism and communism, Brandt fled to West Germany after the defeat of the anti-Ulbricht opposition in 1958. During a visit to West Berlin in 1961 he was kidnapped by the *Stasi* before being condemned to thirteen years' imprisonment. He was released in 1964 after sustained international protest.
234 H. Brandt, *Ein Traum, der nicht entführbar ist. Mein Weg zwischen Ost und West* (München, 1967), p. 328. See also Stern, 'Der meitsgehaßte, meistunterschätzte Mann', p. 44: 'In 1956 Ulbricht's overthrow in East Berlin was agreed. Yet the rebels were deposed, not the SED leader'.
235 Taped interview with Schirdewan, 12.10.92.
236 SAPMO-BArch, ZPA, NL 90/699. Grotewohl's handwritten notes of Khrushchev's meeting with the SED delegation in the Kremlin (29.1.58). Confirmation in taped interview with Schirdewan, 12.10.92: 'The Soviets defended me until the last moment.'
237 C. Stern, 'Wie stark ist Ulbricht?', *SBZ-Archiv* (10.3.58), 65–7; p. 66. See also A. Mitter, S. Wolle, *Untergang auf Raten. Unbekannte Kapitel der DDR-Geschichte* (München, 1993), p. 272; Lippman, *Honecker*, pp. 177, 180; Jänicke, *Der dritte Weg*, p. 239; Oldenburg, *Konflikt und Konfliktregelung*, p. 60
238 See Bretschneider et al., 'Fraktionsmacherei' and SAPMO-BArch, ZPA, NL 215/112. 'Erklärung an das Politbüro des Zentralkomitees der SED', 5.1.58.
239 BStU, 10993. 'Kurze Information über die Politbürositzung am 11. Januar 1958'. Honecker, Stoph, Ebert, Matern, Rau, Neumann, Warnke, Leuschner and Mückenberger supported Ulbricht. According to Schirdewan, Rau was no natural ally of Ulbricht but, like Ebert ('ambitious') and Mückenberger ('without stature'),

was reluctant to join the opposition after the trauma of 1953. Taped interview with Schirdewan, 12.9.92.

240 BStU, 10993. 'Kurze Information über die Politbürositzung am 11. Januar 1958'. New archival evidence from Moscow suggests Grotewohl still believed this when the SED delegation arrived at the Kremlin. See TsKhSD (Moscow Center for the Preservation of Contemporary Documentation): Rolik ('microfilm role') 8873, Fond ('collection of documents') 5, Opis ('inventory') 49, Delo ('file') 76. 'Report to CPSU CC from Ju. Andropov, chairman of department of CC of CPSU responsible for links with the Communist and Workers' Parties of the socialist countries, 30.1.58'. Copy of document handed to the author by Schirdewan during an interview, 9.7.94.

241 SAPMO-BArch, ZPA, NL 215/112. 'Politbüro 11.1.58'.

242 BStU, 10993. 'Kurze Information über die Politbürositzung am 11. Januar 1958'. See also SAPMO-BArch, ZPA, J IV 2/2A-606 and SAPMO-BArch, ZPA, NL 215/112, 'Politbüro 11.1.58'.

243 SAPMO-BArch, ZPA, J IV 2/2/577. PB 31.1.58.

244 SAPMO-BArch, ZPA, J IV 2/2/569. PB 3.12.57.

245 Taped interview with Schirdewan, 12.10.92.

246 SAPMO-BArch, ZPA, J IV 2/2/578. PB meeting, 1.2.58.

247 Taped interview with Schirdewan, 23.11.92.

248 See Oelßner's speech to 35 CC plenum, SAPMO-BArch, ZPA, IV 2/1/192.

249 SAPMO-BArch, ZPA, IV 2/2/579.

250 ' "Die Führung lag in Moskau" ', p. 323.

251 Taped interview with Schirdewan, 23.11.92.

252 *Ibid.*

253 Taped interview with Schirdewan, 23.11.92.

254 'Der zaudernde Rebell' and 'Den Kampf mit Ulbricht gewagt', *Freiheit* (16.2.90), 9. See also SAPMO-BArch, ZPA, IV 2/11/v5142, Schirdewan's letter to CPCC chairman Werner Eberlein, 27.11.89.

255 Taped interview with Schirdewan, 23.11.92.

256 *Ibid.*

257 'Erklärung des Genossen Karl Schirdewan', *NW*, 18 (1959), pp. 1237–8.

258 SAPMO-BArch, ZPA, NL 90/295. Oelßner's statement of self-criticism, 4.9.59.

259 Taped interview with Schirdewan, 23.11.92.

260 See resolution of CPSU CC cited in 'Zur Diskussion über den XX. Parteitag der KPdSU und die 3. Parteikonferenz der SED', *ND* (8.7.56), 3.

261 Interview with Schirdewan, 9.7.94.

262 Copy of the original from the private collection of Schirdewan handed to the author, 12.10.92.

263 Taped interviews with Schirdewan on 12.10.92 and 23.11.92.

264 Wollweber, 'Aus Erinnerungen' p. 358. It is also interesting to note his rejection of the allegations made against Zaisser.

265 SAPMO-BArch, ZPA, IV 2/1/191. See Honecker's report and Matern's speech to 35 CC plenum.

266 R. Engelmann, S. Schumann, 'Der Ausbau des Überwachungsstaates. Der Konflikt Ulbricht-Wollweber und die Neuausrichtung des Staatssicherheitsdienstes der DDR 1957', *VfZ*, 2 (1995), 341–78; p. 355.

267 SAPMO-BArch, ZPA, J IV 2/202/4/1. Bruno Beater's account (dated 15.2.57) of a conversation with Wollweber on 10.2.57.

268 Engelmann, Schumann, 'Der Ausbau des Überwachungsstaates', p. 354.

269 *Ibid.*, pp. 353–4.

270 *Protokoll der III. Parteikonferenz der Sozialistischen Einheitspartei Deutschlands*, II (Berlin-Ost, 1956), 947–58; p. 956.

271 SAPMO-BArch, ZPA, IV 2/1/165. Wollweber's speech to 29 CC plenum.

272 SAPMO-BArch, ZPA, IV 2/1/170. Wollweber's speech to 30 CC plenum.

273 Wollweber, 'Aus Erinnerungen', p. 367.

274 SAPMO-BArch, ZPA, IV 2/1/170.

275 *Ibid.* See also Wollweber's speech to the 3 party conference of the SED in *Protokoll der Verhandlungen der III. Parteikonferenz der Sozialistischen Einheitspartei Deutschlands*, pp. 949–50.

276 Cited in Engelmann, Schumann, 'Der Ausbau des Überwachungsssstaates', p. 347.

277 SAPMO-BArch, ZPA, IV 2/1/177. PB's report to 32 CC plenum, 10.–12.7.57, presented by Ebert.

278 Wollweber, 'Aus Erinnerungen', p. 372.

279 *Ibid.*, pp. 364–5.

280 SAPMO-BArch, ZPA, J IV 2/2/527.

281 Cited in Engelmann, Schumann, 'Der Ausbau des Überwachungsstaates', p. 346.

282 SAPMO-BArch, ZPA, IV 2/1/166.

283 SAPMO-BArch, ZPA, JIV 2/2/519. PB meetings 18/19/20.12.56.

284 SAPMO-BArch, ZPA, IV 2/1/171. Ulbricht's closing speech to 30 CC plenum.

285 See J. von Flocken, M. F. Scholz, *Ernst Wollweber. Saboteur, Minister, Unperson* (Berlin, 1994), pp. 142–64.

286 E. Wollweber, 'Schutz der Arbeiter-und-Bauern-Macht, Sache aller Bürger in der DDR', *ND* (21.12.56). Cited in Jänicke, *Der dritte Weg*, p. 83.

287 See also SAPMO-BArch, BPA, IV 2/2/113. Ulbricht's speech to conference of district party activists in Berlin, 17.2.58.

288 Wollweber, 'Aus Erinnerungen', p. 372.

289 *Ibid.*, p. 377.

290 *Ibid.*, pp. 370–1.

291 *Ibid.*, p. 372.

292 SAPMO-BArch, ZPA, IV 2/1/191. Honecker's report to 35 CC plenum.

293 See Wollweber, 'Aus Erinnerungen', p. 376.

294 *Ibid.*, p. 375.

295 According to one witness, Wollweber's home was bugged on Honecker's orders. Borkowski, *Erich Honecker*, pp. 248–9.

296 Published in Engelmann, Schumann, 'Der Ausbau des Überwachungsstaates', pp. 355–6.

297 SAPMO-BArch, BPA, IV 2/2/113. Ulbricht's speech to conference of district party activists in Berlin, 17.2.58.

298 Wollweber, 'Aus Erinnerungen', p. 371.

299 SAPMO-BArch, ZPA, IV 2/1/177. PB report presented by Ebert to 32 CC plenum, 10.–12.7.57.

300 Engelmann, Schumann, 'Der Ausbau des Überwachungsstaates', p. 375.

301 SAPMO-BArch, ZPA, JIV 2/2/562.

302 P. Sudoplatov, A. Sudoplatov, J. L. Schecter, L. P. Schecter, *Special tasks. The memoirs of an unwanted witness – a Soviet spymaster* (London, 1995), p. 25.

303 SAPMO-BArch, ZPA, IV 2/1/156.

304 SAPMO-BArch, ZPA, J IV 2/2/570. PB meeting, 10.12.57.
305 Engelmann, Schumann, 'Der Ausbau des Überwachungsstaates', pp. 354–5.
306 SAPMO-BArch, ZPA, IV 2/1/191. Matern's speech to 35 CC plenum.
307 'Der zaudernde Rebell'.
308 SAPMO-BArch, ZPA, IV 2/1/191. Schirdewan's speech to 35 CC plenum.
309 *Ibid*.
310 Wollweber, 'Aus Erinnerungen', p. 374.
311 BStU, 10993, Otto Last's testimony to SED leadership, 20.10.57. Last was head of the state security department at Wismut.
312 *Ibid*.
313 SAPMO-BArch, ZPA, IV 2/1/201. Rudi Kirchner's speech to 36 CC plenum, 10.–11.6.58.
314 Interview with Berger, 4.12.57. According to Gerhard Schürer (chairman of the state planning commission in the 1960s) Ziller was somewhat unstable and prone to sudden outbursts of rage. Interview with Gerhard Schürer, 5.11.92.
315 BStU, 10993. Last's testimony to SED leadership, 20.10.57.
316 SAPMO-BArch, ZPA, IV 2/1/191. Matern's speech to 35 CC plenum. Selbmann himself acknowledged that Ziller made these remarks (speech to 35 CC plenum, SAPMO-BArch, ZPA, IV 2/1/193).
317 SAPMO-BArch, ZPA, IV 2/1/156.
318 BStU, 10993. Last's testimony to SED leadership, 20.10.57.
319 Wollweber, 'Aus Erinnerungen', p. 374. See also Schirdewan, *Aufstand gegen Ulbricht*, pp. 122, 135.
320 SAPMO-BArch, ZPA, IV 2/1.01/343. 'Tagung mit den Wissenschaftlern auf ökonomischen Gebiet' (undated).
321 SAPMO-BArch, ZPA, IV 2/1/156. Ziller's speech to 26 CC plenum.
322 SAPMO-BArch, ZPA, IV 2/1/185. Ziller's speech to 33 CC plenum.
323 SAPMO-BArch, ZPA, IV 2/1.01/343. 'Tagung mit den Wissenschaftlern auf ökonomischen Gebiet' (undated).
324 SAPMO-BArch, ZPA, NL 113/27. Selbmann's 'Erklarung', 6.7.58.
325 SAPMO-BArch, ZPA, IV 2/1/192. Hanna Wolf's speech to 35 CC plenum.
326 Interview with Schirdewan, 9.7.94.
327 BStU, 10993. Last's testimony to SED leadership, 20.10.57. The invitation was discussed in the PB on 11.1.58. SAPMO-BArch, ZPA, NL 215/112. See also SAPMO-BArch, ZPA, IV 2/11/v520. Notes from PB meeting, 13.12.57.
328 SAPMO-BArch, ZPA, IV 2/1/193. Ziller's remarks as reported by Wandel in speech to 35 CC plenum.
329 BStU, Mielke Bestand. Ordner 879. Last's testimony to SED leadership, 11.12.57.
330 BStU, Mielke Bestand. Ordner 879. Ulbricht's letter to Khrushchev, 14.12.57. Ulbricht was quoting Ziller's remarks as reported by the deputy general director for cadres at the Wismut plant, Mr Schröder.
331 BStU, Mielke Bestand. Ordner 879. Last's testimony to party leadership, 11.12.57.
332 SAPMO-BArch, ZPA, IV 2/1/192. Cited in Stoph's speech to 35 CC plenum.
333 SAPMO-BArch, ZPA, NL 215/112.
334 Interview with Schirdewan, 12.10.92.
335 Ziller's suicide note, 13.12.57. Document from the private collection of Schirdewan handed to the author, 23.11.92.
336 SAPMO-BArch, ZPA, J IV 2/2/570. PB meeting, 13.–14.12.57.

337 SAPMO-BArch, ZPA, IV 2/1/193. Ulbricht's closing speech to 35 CC plenum. See also SAPMO-BArch, ZPA, IV 2/1/171. Ulbricht's closing speech to 30 CC plenum.

338 SAPMO-BArch, ZPA, IV 2/1/165.

339 SAPMO-BArch, ZPA, IV 2/1/185. Karl Mewis's speech to 33 CC plenum, 16.–19.10.57.

340 Proposed at the 30 CC plenum, 30.1.–1.2.57. Set up on 12 April 1957 to co-ordinate economic policy.

341 SAPMO-BArch, ZPA, IV 2/1/171. Selbmann's speech to 30 CC plenum.

342 SAPMO-BArch, ZPA, IV 2/1/185. Selbmann's speech to 33 CC plenum.

343 SAPMO-BArch, ZPA, IV 2/1/165.

344 SAPMO-BArch, ZPA, NL 113/27.

345 SAPMO-BArch, ZPA, IV 2/1/185. Karl Mewis's speech to 33 CC plenum.

346 Jänicke, *Der dritte Weg*, p. 88.

347 Oldenburg, *Konflikt und Konfliktregelung*, p. 58.

348 SAPMO-BArch, ZPA, NL 113/27. Undated draft of statement by Selbmann to SED PB shortly after 35 CC plenum.

349 SAPMO-BArch, ZPA, NL 113/27. Selbmann's statements to party leadership on 6.7.58 and after 36 CC plenum (undated).

350 BStU, Mielke Bestand. Ordner 879. Last's testimony to party leadership, 11.12.57. After initial denials, Selbmann admitted making this remark in an undated draft of a statement to the party leadership shortly after the 35 CC plenum. See SAPMO-BArch, ZPA, NL 113/27.

351 Interview with Neumann, 16.10.92.

352 SAPMO-BArch, ZPA, IV 2/1/191. Selbmann's speech to 35 CC plenum.

353 SAPMO-BArch, ZPA, NL 113/27. Selbmann's draft statement of self-criticism to party leadership after 36 CC plenum (undated).

354 Interview with Berger, 4.12.92. Wollweber, 'Aus Erinnerungen', p. 374.

355 F. Schenk, 'Grete Wittkowski und ihr neues Amt', *SBZ-Archiv*, 5 (March 1961), 73–4; p. 73.

356 Jänicke, *Der dritten Weg*, p. 92.

357 SAPMO-BArch, ZPA, IV 2/1/156.

358 *Ibid*. She reiterated these remarks at the 35 CC plenum. SAPMO-BArch, ZPA, IV 2/1/193.

359 SAPMO-BArch, ZPA, IV 2/1/165.

360 *Ibid*. Speech to 29 CC plenum. In his closing speech, Ulbricht rejected Wittkowski's comments. SAPMO-BArch, ZPA, IV 2/1/166.

361 SAPMO-BArch, ZPA, IV 2/1/165. Wittkowski's speech to 29 CC plenum.

362 SAPMO-BArch, ZPA, IV 2/1/166. Ulbricht's closing speech to 29 CC plenum.

363 Schenk, 'Grete Wittkowski und ihr neues Amt', p. 73.

364 Stern, *Porträt einer bolshewistischen Partei*, p. 314.

365 SAPMO-BArch, ZPA, IV 2/1/166. Wandel's speech to 29 CC plenum.

366 SAPMO-BArch, ZPA, IV 2/1/186. Becher's speech to 33 CC plenum.

367 Bretschneider et al., 'Fraktionsmacherei', p. 508. See also D. Reinert, J. Emendörfer, 'Ein Widersacher des mächtigen "Ersten"', *Berliner Zeitung* (10.–11.2.90), 9.

368 SAPMO-BArch, ZPA, IV 2/1/166. Wandel's speech to 29 CC plenum.

369 Paul Wandel's wife in interview, 30.11.92.

370 Interview with Wandel, 30.11.92.

371 Oldenburg, *Konflikt und Konfliktregelung*, p. 62.

372 Interview with Wandel, 30.11.92.
373 SAPMO-BArch, ZPA, IV 2/1/166.
374 'Das 33. Plenum des Zentralkomitees der SED. Enthüllung eines Geheimprotokolls', *APZ*, B IL (18.12.57), 837–51; p. 846. See speeches by Hager and Ulbricht.
375 SAPMO-BArch, ZPA, IV 2/1/186. Hager's speech to 33 CC plenum.
376 SAPMO-BArch, BPA, IV 2/2/113. Ulbricht's speech to conference of district party activists, Berlin, 17.2.58.
377 *Ibid.*
378 SAPMO-BArch, ZPA, NL 77/51. 'Über Fragen des 35. Plenums des ZK' (letter signed by Ulbricht sent to out all SED grass roots organizations in February 1958). See also Reinert, Emendörfer, 'Ein Widersacher des Mächtigen "Ersten" ', 9.
379 See Jänicke, *Der dritte Weg*, pp. 127–8.
380 See Bretschneider et al., 'Fraktionsmacherei', pp. 508–9.
381 See 'Das 33. Plenum', pp. 846–7.
382 Interview with Wandel, 30.11.92.
383 SAPMO-BArch, ZPA, IV 2/1/156.
384 SAPMO-BArch, ZPA, IV 2/1/163. Hager's speech to 28 CC plenum.
385 SAPMO BArch, ZPA, IV 2/1/165. Hager's speech to 29 CC plenum.
386 *Ibid.*
387 Interview with Hager, 1.12.92.
388 SAPMO-BArch, ZPA, IV 2/1/170.
389 Interview with Hager, 6.4.94.
390 SAPMO-BArch, ZPA, IV 2/1/170.
391 *Ibid.*
392 SAPMO-BArch, ZPA, IV 2/1/171. Ulbricht's closing speech to 30 CC plenum.
393 SAPMO-BArch, ZPA, IV 2/1/170. Buchwitz's speech to 30 CC plenum.
394 *Ibid.*
395 SAPMO-BArch, ZPA, IV 2/1/171. Ulbricht's closing speech to 30 CC plenum.
396 SAPMO-BArch, ZPA, IV 2/1/165.
397 SAPMO-BArch, ZPA, IV 2/1/167. Buchwitz's speech to 29 CC plenum.
398 SAPMO-BArch, ZPA, IV 2/1/163. Schön's speech to 28 CC plenum.
399 SAPMO-BArch, ZPA, IV 2/1/162. Steinitz's speech to 28 CC plenum.
400 SAPMO-BArch, ZPA, IV 2/1/156. Winzer's speech to 26 CC plenum.
401 SAPMO-BArch, ZPA, IV 2/1/166. Mewis's speech to 29 CC plenum.
402 SAPMO-BArch, ZPA, IV 2/1/162. Fröhlich's speech to 28 CC plenum.
403 SAPMO-BArch, ZPA, NL 77/51. 'Entschließung der Delegiertenkonferenz der Parteiorganization beim ZK der SED vom 24. und 25. April 1958' (Parteiinternes Material). See also SAPMO-BArch, BPA, IV 2/2/113. Ulbricht's closing speech to conference of district party activists in Berlin, 17.2.58.
404 SAPMO-BArch, ZPA, NL 77/51. 'Über Fragen des 35. Plenums des ZK' (letter signed by Ulbricht sent out to all SED grass roots organizations in February 1958.)
405 Oldenburg, *Konflikt und Konfliktregelung*, p. 68.

4

The fall of Ulbricht

Ulbricht has traditionally been presented as a dogmatic Stalinist whose removal from office was the prerequisite to the adoption of more flexible policies, particularly with regard to relations between the two German states. This view is now in need of revision. From the early 1960s, Ulbricht underwent a metamorphosis from incorrigible Stalinist to fanatical technocrat. He was the driving force behind Eastern Europe's first economic reform programme and mitigated the worst aspects of state repression. Contrary to previous interpretations, he also worked for dialogue with the West German SPD and rapprochement with Bonn. However, his aim to 'overtake' the Federal Republic by forcing the pace of the 'scientific-technological revolution' caused serious economic difficulties in 1970. An innovator in the ideological field, he propagated the GDR as a model for socialism and obstructed Allied negotiations over West Berlin. His determination to pursue this agenda without recourse to Moscow led to his being replaced by Erich Honecker in May 1971. This chapter is divided into three sections: the first devoted to Ulbricht's economic reforms, the second to his foreign policy and the third to his removal as first secretary.[1]

Ulbricht and economic reform

Shortly after building the Berlin Wall, Ulbricht allegedly remarked: 'Now we must rethink everything.'[2] Whether or not he said exactly this, he clearly did set out to redefine the GDR's domestic agenda after the final cementing of the division of Germany on 13 August 1961.[3] Sealing the open border with the West meant that the SED could no longer blame all its problems on the Federal Republic. It also removed the safety-valve of emigration, underlining the need for reform if popular unrest was to be avoided. On the other hand, it helped stabilize the country, reducing the leadership's fear of experiments.

In his report to the sixth party congress of the SED in January 1963, Ulbricht berated out of date, bureaucratic, over-centralized structures and set out the basic principles of what was to become the 'New Economic System' (NES). Factory managers would be granted a degree of autonomy within the context of a less rigid five-year plan; a more flexible pricing system would take account of market values; profit would become an important measure of economic success; material incentives would be introduced to encourage higher productivity; limited worker participation would be sanctioned through 'production committees'; private and semi-state-owned businesses would be granted security of tenure and allowed to merge; the SED apparatus would be circumscribed and non-party experts given a stake in economic decision-making. The aim was to make the central planning agencies more efficient by relieving them of the tasks of 'petty tutelage'.[4]

The 'New Economic System of Planning and Management' proclaimed in June 1963 represented more than a pragmatic attempt to placate an alienated population by improving living standards. Nor was it merely the product of the Berlin Wall, the 1960–62 economic crisis or the rapid recovery in West Germany. The rejection of Stalin's over-centralized command economy following the twentieth party congress of the CPSU in 1956 meant that it became possible to consider alternatives. Ulbricht had recognized the importance of the 'scientific-technological revolution' and had begun to adjust to post-Stalin realities. In the late 1950s he set up a commission accountable to the politburo charged with the task of examining new approaches to the economy. One of its members, Herbert Wolf (who later became deputy chairman of the state planning commission) remembers it as a forum where experts could freely speak their mind without fear of reprisals.[5] These wide-ranging discussions marked the beginning of a decisive shift in East German economic strategy. Unlike Lenin's new economic policy of 1921–28 (conceived as a temporary retreat from socialism), the NES was conceived as a socialist advance, designed to enhance the system's long-term viability as an alternative to capitalism.

Observers sometimes assumed that Khrushchev was using the GDR as an experimentation ground for his own projects[6] or that Ulbricht was following the prevailing line in Moscow.[7] It was not until 9 September 1962, however, that the Soviet economist, Yevsei Libermann, published his famous article in *Pravda* calling for greater use of 'economic' rather than 'administrative' instruments.[8] In the end, thoroughgoing economic reform failed to materialize in the USSR and Khrushchev seems to have had misgivings about the East German project.[9] If we are to believe the retrospective testimonies of those involved, the NES owed more to the initiative of Ulbricht than hitherto believed. As one of his close advisers, Wolfgang Berger, put it: 'before this important decision there was no prior checking or confirmation in Moscow'.[10] This account was supported by Gerhard Schürer who, unlike Berger and Wolf, never classified himself as a supporter of the reforms. According to him 'Khrushchev tolerated but did not support the NES.'[11]

In the early 1960s the SED leader surrounded himself with a new breed of economic experts. There was a radical overhaul in personnel as 'old communists' were replaced by younger, flexible and more qualified functionaries.[12] This generational change had profound consequences for SED policy during the 1960s.

According to one contemporary report, 'old communists' were informing their western contacts that Ulbricht was surrounding himself with 'opportunist young people' and threatening to 'betray the old ideas of the KPD'.[13] Apart from Ulbricht, the main advocates of economic reform in the politburo were Günter Mittag and Erich Apel. Together with Ulbricht's chief aides, Herbert Wolf and Wolfgang Berger, they should be regarded as the founding fathers of the NES.

Günter Mittag was born in 1926 in Stettin. A railway inspector who served in Hitler's airforce, Mittag joined the SED in 1946 before joining the central committee staff in 1951. Head of the transport and communications department of the central committee between 1953 and 1958, he was then awarded a doctoral degree before becoming a candidate member of the central committee and secretary of the politburo's economics commission in 1958. Elected a full member of the central committee in 1962, he became deputy chairman and secretary of the economics council in 1961. A year later he was appointed central committee secretary for the economy – a position he held until October 1973. He was elected a candidate member of the politburo in January 1963, achieving full membership status in September 1966. Mittag quickly gained a reputation as a ruthless advocate of the reforms.

Erich Apel was born in 1917 in Thuringia. A mechanical engineer by profession, he was deployed by the Nazis during the war to work on a rocket project in Peenmünde. Transferred to the Soviet Union in 1946 to work as a chief engineer, he returned in 1952 to join the SED and begin his steep climb through the GDR state apparatus. Only three years later, Apel was appointed minister for mechanical engineering. He soon became convinced of the need for reform, noting in a memo that the state apparatus had become 'too cumbersome and too complicated in its mechanisms'.[14] Elected a candidate member of the central committee in 1958, he became a full member two years later. Before being elected a candidate member of the politburo, he headed its economics commission between 1958 and 1961. After serving as a secretary of the central committee, he became chairman of the state planning commission in 1963. Emphasizing the need to make the reforms comprehensible to the East German population, he instructed his staff to draft proposals 'not in the style of a directive, but in plain, popular language'.[15]

As one of the main protagonists of economic reform, Apel worked hard to gain a foothold in world markets. Between 1962 and 1965, trade with the USSR decreased from 49.3 per cent of East Germany's total foreign trade to 43.4 per cent. Whereas in 1963, trade with the Soviet bloc had amounted to 78 per cent of the total, this had fallen to 73.7 per cent by 1966.[16] In February 1964 Apel wrote in *Neues Deutschland*: 'Our sights are definitely set on world standards. If . . . the Soviet Union achieves a world record, then we shall model ourselves on that pattern; if West Germany or Japan achieves a similar distinction, then we shall follow their example.'[17] For many older communists, this undisguised plea for a more pragmatic relationship with the Soviet Union was tantamount to heresy.

Claus Krömke (one of Mittag's senior aides directly involved in planning the

NES proposals) recalls the initial mood of optimism among supporters of reform. Certainly the economic benefits were undeniable. As levels of technological investment, productivity and industrial output rose, East Germans were rewarded with improved supplies of consumer goods and a shorter working week. It was not long, however, before the reforms ran up against resistance in the party.[18] According to Krömke, the issue which really polarized the debate was the role 'profit' should play in the communist system.[19] Primary sources tell us little about the positions of individual politburo members and we are therefore compelled to rely on the retrospective testimonies of those who waged the day-to-day battles. Wolf, Berger and Schürer broadly agree in their identification of the opponents and proponents of reform. According to Berger, there was no clear majority for the NES in the politburo.[20]

Wolf is more suited than most to make judgements in this respect because he was charged with the task of briefing politburo members on economic matters during the 1960s. Apart from Ulbricht, Apel and (until 1970) Mittag, Wolf identifies Halbritter, Kleiber and Jarowinsky as those most favourably disposed towards the reforms. Those clearly opposed were apparently Honecker, Fröhlich, Norden, Verner, Ewald, Neumann and Grüneberg.[21] While Honecker eschewed making any positive comment on the reforms in the early 1960s,[22] Neumann allegedly complained to Wolf about the 'revisionist' character of the NES programme.[23] As chairman of the economics council between 1961 and 1965, he opposed the use of profit as a performance indicator. Hager too was a sceptic, although in 1992 he claimed to have been a keen supporter.[24] Neither was former social democrat Friedrich Ebert enthusiastic. Ulbricht's old ally Matern was ambivalent.[25] Grotewohl was too ill to play any significant role and, according to Berger, 'did not understand the NES'.[26] His successor as prime minister, Willi Stoph, was also sceptical and by the end of the decade a diehard opponent.[27] Schürer admitted to having adopted a reserved attitude and classified Sindermann and Verner among the doubters.[28]

It is interesting to compare these testimonies with the influential analysis of the sociologist Peter Christian Ludz who, writing in the 1960s, assigned SED leaders to specific 'groups' or 'factions'. In one study, politburo members are sorted into four such categories: First, 'flexible and diversified functionaries between the ages of fifty and sixty' (Honecker, Stoph, Hager, Verner, Sindermann, Axen); second, 'younger functionaries who represent the technocrats and experts in the politburo' (Mittag, Jarowinsky, Halbritter, Ewald, Grüneberg, Kleiber); third, those significant simply for their 'firm faithfulness to Ulbricht' (Ebert, Matern, Warnke, Mückenberger, Müller); fourth 'older, particularly inflexible functionaries who represent the 'purist, dogmatic wing' (Fröhlich, Neumann, Norden).[29] In another study, Ludz divides the politburo into three groups: First the 'experts' (Mittag, Jarowinsky, Ewald, Halbritter, Kleiber, Müller); second the 'dogmatists' (Honecker, Fröhlich, Verner, Neumann, Norden, Axen); third the 'middlemen' (Ulbricht, Stoph, Sindermann and Hager).[30]

These analyses differ somewhat from the characterizations of Wolf, Berger and Schürer. Apart from being inconsistent (Honecker is defined as both a 'dogmatist' and a 'flexible' functionary) they neglect the central role of Ulbricht as the main apostle of reform. If Ulbricht had been a 'middleman' he might never have been deposed in 1971. The SED leader was overthrown not because of his 'centrism' but because of his reforming zeal. A typology which puts Hager, Sindermann and Stoph in the same group as Ulbricht must be flawed because these three functionaries were prime movers in the conspiracy to unseat him. Such categories, while still useful as a general guide, tend to gloss over the complexities of communist high politics in East Germany. They ignore a number of factors which influence political behaviour such as personal ambition (very important in explaining Mittag's later *volte-face*), petty rivalries and hatreds (for example, between Mittag and Neumann)[31] and Soviet misgivings (possibly a factor in the willingness of Halbritter, Jarowinsky, Müller, Kleiber and other so-called 'technocrats' to collaborate in dismantling the reforms after 1970). Mittag's assertion that a 'concrete faction of dogmatists'[32] set out to obstruct and then bury the reforms not only fails to do justice to political mutations inside the politburo, it is a disingenuous attempt to deny his own role in the drama.

With Leonid Brezhnev's ascension to power in 1964, the Soviet Union entered a prolonged period of conservative retrenchment. In the long run, this did not augur well for Ulbricht's economic reform programme.[33] Looking back on a visit to East Germany of that year, Brezhnev complained to Honecker about Ulbricht's arrogance in proselytizing his own model of socialism.

> [He] simply put my delegation to one side . . . forced me into a small room and went on at me about everything that was wrong in our country and exemplary in yours. It was hot. I sweated. He took no notice. I remember only that he wanted to dictate to me how we should work and how we should govern. I couldn't get a word in edgeways. His showed his total arrogance there, his disregard for the ideas and experiences of others. Have the S[oviet] U[nion], the CPSU, the Soviet people not changed the world?[34]

Nonetheless, the GDR continued to enjoy some room for manoeuvre on this issue. In Moscow on 10 September 1966, Brezhnev told Ulbricht that the future of the NES was a matter for the SED.[35] A year earlier the Soviet prime minister, Aleksei Kosygin, had announced a programme of economic reform for the USSR. Brezhnev's opposition to any significant restructuring, however, ensured that it remained very limited in scope.[36]

On 3 December 1965, the chairman of the GDR's state planning commission, Erich Apel, committed suicide. Since the primary sources shed no light on his motives we are compelled to rely on circumstantial evidence and the retrospective testimonies of close colleagues. It is probably no coincidence that he shot himself in his office one hour before the GDR signed a less than favourable agreement with the Soviet Union tying its trade more closely to the east. This, however, may have been the final straw rather than the fundamental cause. Although disappointed, Apel had in fact achieved significant improvements to the accord. Talking to Schürer on the telephone just minutes before taking his life, he had allegedly expressed satisfaction with its provisions.[37] Another factor might have been that the conservatives in the leadership were on the attack and highly critical of his work. On 1 December, his economic plan for the year 1966 had been rejected by the politburo,[38] and he was due to give an account of himself to the central committee a few days later. Although there seems to be a consensus that he was not about to be sacked as chairman of the state planning commission, Apel probably sensed that his political future was not as secure as it could have been. Having been accused by the West German press of helping to conscript concentration camp inmates for the manufacture of the V2 rocket during World War Two,[39] he might no longer have felt assured of Ulbricht and Mittag's unequivocal support.[40] Apparently, Apel was an extremely ambitious man who found defeats difficult to bear.[41] Schürer, who succeeded him as chairman of the state planning commission, dismisses talk of a sinister KGB plot as sensationalism.[42] Neither were there any obvious personal reasons for his suicide.[43] It would seem, therefore, that his reasons were political. Of one thing we can be certain: Apel's death was a blow to the economic reform programme. For many, the charismatic head of the state planning commission had become a personification not only of the NES, but of hopes for more openness in the GDR.[44] His successor, by contrast, responded to the new climate of Brezhnevite conservatism by attempting to apply the brakes. In March 1967 he allegedly warned Wolf against forcing the pace of reform.[45]

When Ulbricht launched phase two of the NES at the eleventh central committee plenum in December 1965, it was on a more centralized basis,[46] reflecting the growing strength of the conservatives in the leadership. Nonetheless, the first secretary emphasized the need to reduce the remit of central planning agencies; to increase the independence of territorial organs and factory management; to introduce more flexibility into the pricing system; to increase trade union autonomy, worker consultation and management accountability[47] and to expand the system of material incentives.[48] The third and final phase of reform was inaugurated at the seventh party congress of the SED in April 1967. It was now rechristened the 'Economic System of Socialism' (ESS).[49] Once again, Ulbricht inveighed against outdated 'administrative' practices and emphasized the need to make greater use of 'economic' and 'regulatory' instruments.[50] Central planners were instructed to concentrate on promoting the 'locomotives' of scientific-technological development (computing, electronics, petrochemistry) leaving additional scope for autonomy in the 'non-structure-determining sectors'.[51] Particularly striking was his acceptance of 'the market' as an important variable in the economic equation.[52]

According to a twenty-six page critique of Ulbricht's economic policy written shortly after his downfall and signed by Honecker, Ulbricht wanted to go much further in reducing central planning, even proposing its replacement with a system of 'self-regulatory' mechanisms.[53] Whether or not this is true, he certainly did favour enabling factories to claim compensation from agencies which imposed harmful decisions.[54] He also promoted the idea of a 'socialist commercial bank' to provide credit for industry[55] and came close to endorsing the concept of bankruptcy.[56] In the late 1960s, Ulbricht propagated the idea of a 'socialist human community' which eschewed class conflict and offered the hope that different social groups could coexist in harmony. By 1971 he was being accused of encouraging the 'capitalist sector' and granting a special status to private and partly state-run businesses.[57] Ulbricht wanted to preserve these enterprises[58] and insisted that the new constitution drafted in 1968 include a clause giving them security of tenure.[59] Honecker, however, had them all nationalized,[60] deleting the heretical clause from a revised constitution.[61]

In September 1967 Ulbricht used the centenary celebrations of Karl Marx's *Das Kapital* to debunk the view (enunciated by Marx, Engels and Lenin) that the period of transition from socialism to communism was of relatively short historical duration. Instead, he proclaimed 'the developed social system of socialism' – an autonomous socio-economic formation.[62] The concept enabled Ulbricht to present certain essential rudiments of his economic reforms (for example 'profit') as positive features of the 'socialist' system rather than as discredited vestiges of an earlier capitalist era. Since the USSR had already announced the transition to communism, this did not go down well in the Kremlin. According to Neumann, Honecker was emboldened by the critique of Soviet ideologists to oppose Ulbricht on this issue.[63] The 'developed social system of socialism' was elaborated in a massive textbook entitled *The political economy of socialism and its application in the GDR* published in 1969. Ulbricht himself wrote the introduction and Mittag also contributed. Its presentation of the GDR as a 'model' worthy of emulation (it was translated into numerous languages, including Russian, Japanese and Chinese) apparently displeased the Soviets.[64]

The first secretary also initiated a less repressive style of government in the 1960s. Between 1963 and 1965 Ulbricht presided over a cultural thaw, an easing of restrictions on travel to West Germany and the beginnings of a dialogue between party and population. In 1963 important legislation on the family and educational reform was put to public debate. The party structure was decentralized according to the 'production principle'[65] and a new statute was promulgated, containing 'additional' safeguards against the violation of 'Leninist norms'.[66] There was condemnation of 'dogmatism', 'heartless bureaucracy' and 'sectarianism'[67] and greater emphasis was placed on the role of the 'bourgeois' parties in the decision-making process.[68] A communiqué of 21 September granted East German youth a degree of independence[69] and a 'workers' and farmers' inspectorate' was set up to oversee the proper implementation of party and state directives.[70] In 1964 Ulbricht announced a new electoral law enabling voters to choose between individual candidates (thus abolishing the system of *en bloc* voting).[71] There was also less interference in the work of the churches.[72] Significantly, it was Honecker and not Ulbricht who launched the swingeing attack on East Germany's cultural elite at the eleventh central committee plenum in December 1965.[73] Reference was made to the 'further development' of 'social-ist democracy' at the seventh party congress in April 1967[74] and, later that year, Ulbricht warned against confusing democratic centralism with 'bureaucracy' and 'sterility'.[75] The new constitution of 1968 was submitted first to public debate and then to a plebiscite.[76]

One of the main accusations levelled at Ulbricht was his tendency to neglect the politburo and party apparatus as decision-making forums in favour of con-sultation with academic and technological experts.[77] At a politburo meeting after his downfall, he was accused of undermining the authority of his colleagues by seeking advice from extra-party organizations.[78] Ulbricht defended himself by stressing the need for wide consultation before policies were decided.[79] Proposals drawn up by a working group of Ulbricht's advisers (chaired by Herbert Wolf) in preparation for the eighth party congress in 1971 were con-ceived as contributions to the 'developed social system of socialism'. Among other things, they foresaw a greater role for the elected representatives and par-liamentary committees. There were also attacks on 'heartless bureaucracy'[80] and heavy emphasis on popular participation, consultation and accountability.[81] The declared aim was to 'enhance the effectiveness of socialist democracy'.[82] These proposals were based on the premise that, as society became more complex and the population more educated, the political system would evolve to a qualita-tively higher level. The main manifestation of this would be the way in which the SED exercised its 'leading role'. In a speech to district leaders in Leipzig on 21 November 1971, Ulbricht said that the challenge for the party was to establish friendly relations with all sections of the East German population.[83] Lower eche-lons of the political hierarchy were to be granted greater autonomy so that deci-sions could be made at the 'appropriate' level.[84] As Berger put it, Ulbricht strove for 'a better division of labour within the system'.[85] Whether Ulbricht's propo-sals were practical or even meaningful must remain speculative. That his col-leagues felt threatened by them cannot be disputed. Many of Wolf's proposals apparently corresponded with the basic views of the first secretary.[86]

Ulbricht, however, remained an implacable opponent of 'liberalization'.[87] Indeed, his advisers took special care to emphasize the irreconcilable conflict between 'liberalization' and 'socialist democracy'. Although Ulbricht instructed the working group to reconsider the role of the party in the political system,[88] there is no evidence to support Wolf's supposition that he might eventually have been willing to consider a return to the competitive multiparty system of 1946.[89] It was Ulbricht, after all, who enshrined the SED's 'leading role' in the new con-stitution of 1968.[90] At the eleventh central committee plenum in December 1965, he had poured scorn on the idea of an opposition party in the GDR.[91] For all his reforming zeal, there is no reason to assume that Ulbricht was capable of chang-ing his mind on this issue.[92]

The eventual abandonment of economic reform should be seen in the context of the invasion of Czechoslovakia which fuelled an anti-reform backlash after

1968.[93] During a private conversation with Honecker in Moscow on 20 August 1970, Brezhnev appeared to issue a warning: 'What is important is that the GDR has a structure like the S[oviet] U[nion] and other socialist countries, otherwise we will get into difficulties . . . The GDR is not only your concern, she is the concern of us all.'[94] Ulbricht, however, continued to popularize the 'East German model' of socialism. Next day, Ulbricht addressed a joint delegation of Soviet and East German leaders. Stressing the need to cultivate 'our own structure', he berated the Soviet Union's 'huge apparatus' and appealed for 'the development of socialist ideology'. He then stunned his audience by emphasizing the GDR's 'independence' from the USSR: East Germany, he insisted, was 'not Belorussia'.[95] In a politburo meeting over a year later, the central committee secretary responsible for relations with other communist parties, Hermann Axen, criticized Ulbricht for these remarks: 'You should have seen the comrades' faces! I wanted to fall through the floor. That was a sign of national arrogance. In the past your attitude to the Soviet Union had always been beyond reproach (*klar*) and now a sentence like that!'[96]

Ulbricht's determination to set unrealistic economic targets between 1968 and 1971 played into the hands of those who wanted to jettison the reforms. Obsessed with the need to force the pace of the 'scientific-technological revolution' in key sectors, Ulbricht demanded that the five-year plan be revised upwards. In a letter to Brezhnev in April 1969, Ulbricht bewailed the fact that East German productivity levels lagged behind those of the Federal Republic by some 20 per cent and set the unrealistic target of increasing the rate by a minimum of 10 per cent a year. Only in this way, he believed, could the GDR increase its influence over West Germany and prevent Bonn from 'provoking military conflicts'. Such a policy assumed, however, that the Soviet Union was able and willing to provide additional resources.[97] Ulbricht's slogan 'we must overtake without catching up' (*Überholen ohne Einzuholen*')[98] was rejected in Moscow.[99] Ulbricht apparently became increasingly irritated with what he perceived as Soviet inertia on this issue, criticizing the USSR and other socialist countries for failing to recognize the 'age of the computer'.[100] An indication of his obsession was his alleged insistence that East German ambassadors and diplomats be required to know as much about economics as international relations.[101]

This ceaseless campaign for technological advance in certain key industries was beyond East Germany's means and led to serious economic instability in 1970–71. A small country bereft of raw materials, retarded by the communist system, compelled to rely on insufficient Soviet investment and still recovering from the effects of war and division could only sustain such a burden by neglecting other sectors of the economy and reducing living standards. Yet this was precisely what Ulbricht proposed. In his closing speech to the fourteenth central committee plenum in December 1970, he condemned the 'consumerist' standpoint and spoke of the need for sacrifice if the country was to keep pace with the 'scientific-technological revolution'.[102]

The reforms were also discredited by Ulbricht's growing fetish for 'system-theory' analysis which often obfuscated the real problems and complicated their resolution. In 1992 Krömke recalled Ulbricht's obsession with heuretics and cybernetics.[103] Constantly bombarded with such ideas by his advisers, Ulbricht began to lose touch with reality. Further economic disruption was caused by the severe winters of 1969 and 1970. While the mood in the party and population became increasingly hostile,[104] Ulbricht is said to have ignored the warnings of his Warsaw Pact comrades.[105]

On 8 September 1970, with Ulbricht and most of his aides away on vacation,[106] Honecker called a meeting of the politburo to instigate an unprecedented attack on the ESS. Apart from measures to mitigate imbalances in the economy, the resulting resolution significantly strengthened the powers of the central planning agencies. Also discernible are the seeds of Honecker's 'consumer socialism' which shifted the emphasis away from scientific-technological projects towards improvements in living standards.[107] Wolf's conclusion that it amounted to an alternative programme[108] is borne out by the evidence. The resolution (drafted on 3 September and confirmed in the politburo five days later) was signed by Mittag and Stoph. Mittag is therefore exposed as a turncoat, refuting his claim that he defended the ESS its dying days.[109]

In order to present Ulbricht with a *fait accompli*, the resolution of 8 September was immediately published in *Neues Deutschland* and the council of ministers instructed to draw up guidelines for implementation. The Soviets had already expressed their support[110] and Ulbricht returned to find himself isolated. Even so, he denounced the *volte-face* and tried to prevent the council of ministers from putting it into effect.[111] Neither could the SED leader conceal his rage at Honecker's role in the affair.[112] It was probably to ensure his colleagues' loyalty in the face of Ulbricht's opposition that Honecker convened another politburo meeting on 20 October 1970. With the first secretary absent again, the council of ministers and central committee secretariat were instructed 'to take all necessary steps to ensure exact implementation'.[113]

Ulbricht was now powerless to prevent the dismantling of his economic strategy. A prisoner of his own politburo, he looked on helplessly as the chairman of the state planning commission, Gerhard Schürer, was delegated the task of drafting a new five-year plan. Honecker is reported to have given him the following advice over what to do with Ulbricht's counter-proposals: 'forget the nonsense'.[114] Without any debate, the reforms were effectively scrapped at the fourteenth central committee plenum between 9 and 11 December 1970. In his closing address, however, Ulbricht emphasized the link between the 'scientific-technological revolution', the ESS and the 'developed social system of socialism'.[115] On 12 December 1970, the politburo passed a resolution banning publication of the speech.[116] The objections of certain colleagues (Honecker, Stoph, Mittag, Sindermann, Halbritter and Verner) were in the form of letters of complaint addressed to Ulbricht personally. Honecker proposed suppressing the speech, on the grounds that it advanced two different strategies.[117] Sindermann's comments are perhaps the most telling of all: 'If [it] is published, all those in the central committee with different views will speak out!'[118] Mittag gave the most detailed exposition of his objections. Not only did he scold Ulbricht for ignoring the resolution of 8 September, he accused him of insufficient loyalty to the Soviet Union. Co-operation with Moscow, he said, was about much more than procuring raw materials for the GDR. It was about Marxist–Leninism and proletarian internationalism.[119]

Despite this defeat, Ulbricht refused to surrender. In a speech to the fifteenth central committee plenum on 28 January 1971, he condemned moves to draft a more balanced economic plan, citing the need to keep pace with the 'scientific-technological revolution'. There was also a reference to 'the formation of the developed social system of socialism with its centrepiece, the economic system of socialism.' Since 1967, he said, significant progress had been made in combining 'central planning of the key social processes' with increased autonomy for industry and local state organs. Finally, he spoke of the 'socialist human community' and the need to further develop 'socialist democracy'.[120] The claims of Ulbricht's opponents in the politburo that the first secretary continued to oppose official policy after the fourteenth central committee plenum[121] can therefore be confirmed. In January 1971, the politburo rejected a draft resolution drawn up by Ulbricht for the eighth party congress.[122] On 15 March, the latter is said to have criticized Honecker's domestic programme. Apparently, he also incited his aides to draw up alternative proposals.[123]

But Ulbricht was fighting a lost cause. Instead of economic reform, the population was bought off with promises of better housing and higher living standards financed by Western loans. Although the clock could not be turned back entirely, the ESS was barely mentioned at the eighth party congress of the SED between 15 and 19 June 1971. Its textbook *The political economy of socialism and its application in the GDR* was ignored and, in September 1972, withdrawn from the bookshops altogether.[124] References to the 'social system of socialism', 'economic system of socialism' and 'socialist human community' were removed from the 1974 constitution.[125]

Ulbricht, foreign policy and the German question

Following the conventional wisdom, one historian has characterized Ulbricht's foreign policy and *Deutschlandpolitik* in the 1960s as an 'all-encompassing anti-détente strategy that admitted of little flexibility or willingness to compromise'.[126] New primary sources, however, tell a different story. Although the SED leader initially moved to block West German attempts to establish diplomatic relations with her East European neighbours (forming the so-called 'iron triangle' of the GDR, Poland and Czechoslovakia in 1967)[127] this did not prevent him from pursuing his own policy of rapprochement with Bonn.

At the seventh central committee plenum in December 1964, Ulbricht suggested that the SPD's nomination of Willy Brandt as candidate for chancellor and the possible reorientation of West Germany on the Swedish model might offer an opportunity to improve relations. Honecker, by contrast, emphasized the dangers of such an approach, highlighting 'uncertainties' in the East German population over the character of the two German states.[128] On 7 February 1966, Ulbricht wrote to Brandt (apparently without the prior knowledge or consent of Moscow[129]) to propose talks.[130] Four days later, the SED central committee published an open letter to the delegates of the SPD party congress suggesting that the two parties agree a united action programme as a way of promoting negotiations between the GDR and Federal Republic. This, it was hoped, would eventually pave the way for a peace treaty and German reunification.[131] On 19 March, the SPD party executive sent a reply rejecting the SED's proposals and suggesting that members of the two parliaments be allowed to discuss their views openly in both German states.[132] Writing to Brandt on 25 March, Ulbricht welcomed the fact that contact had been established[133] and enclosed a second open letter from the SED central committee mooting the idea of a 'speaker exchange'.[134]

The primary sources reveal Ulbricht as both the initiator and main proponent of dialogue with the SPD.[135] After a speech by one of Brandt's aides proclaiming 'change through rapprochement' (known as *Ostpolitik*) in 1963, other politburo members were apparently less enthusiastic.[136] Kurt Hager claims to have endorsed the reported verdict of the East German foreign minister, Otto Winzer, that *Ostpolitik* was 'aggression in felt slippers'.[137] Differences over the speaker exchange can be discerned from the discussion at the twelfth central committee plenum in April 1966. Ulbricht criticized the tendency of many in his party to attack the SPD rather than the CDU and eagerly endorsed the dialogue.[138] He was backed by Franz Dahlem, an enthusiastic supporter of rapprochement in the 1950s.[139] Honecker and others adopted more sceptical positions.[140] If Ulbricht acquiesced in the resolution postponing the speaker exchange, his motives were quite different from those of the politburo critics. While they wanted to prevent it from taking place at all, for Ulbricht it was a question of when rather than if.[141] At the beginning of June, the SPD would stage its party congress in Dortmund. Only then would the SED be in a position to exert maximum influence.

The SPD party congress began moving towards the idea of forming a Grand Coalition government with the CDU and its Bavarian sister party, the CSU. Hopes that West German social democracy might split asunder and that its left wing would reject the CDU/CSU in favour of an alliance with the SED were therefore receding. Despite this, Ulbricht seemed determined to press ahead with his rapprochement strategy.[142] On 22 June he sent a confidential letter to Brandt reaffirming his interest in the speaker exchange and pressing for a preparatory meeting. But he also warned against the mutual trading of insults and proposed that representatives of the two parties first hold secret talks to discuss ways of achieving peaceful coexistence and confederation.[143] Those close to the first secretary appear to have genuinely believed in the practicability of a confederation between two German states rooted in different social systems.[144] Berger avers that Ulbricht's aim in this regard was to strengthen the GDR by facilitating economic co-operation with Bonn.[145] Seen from this angle, the Berlin Wall and restrictions on freedom of movement were not so much East German obstacles as West German excuses: 'After all', as Wolf put it, 'a wall can have doors!'[146]

On 28 June, the politburo decided to call off the speaker exchange. The reason given was the SPD's support for a motion in the *Bundestag* temporarily waiving the liability of SED representatives to prosecution under West German law.[147] The implicit reassertion of Federal jurisdiction over citizens of the GDR was used as an excuse to cancel the dialogue. That it was nothing *more* than an excuse is plain enough. First, the law proclaiming Federal jurisdiction over the GDR was already in force when Ulbricht made his offer of talks with the SPD. Second, the granting of temporary exemption from Federal jurisdiction guaranteed safe passage to all representatives of the SED taking part in the exchange. Third, the excuse would never have been used had the majority of politburo members been genuinely interested in pursuing rapprochement. After all, the SED refused to recognize the legitimacy of Allied travel agents in West Berlin, yet accepted their visas when necessary. Fourth, the law of safe passage was only used to call off the dialogue five days after its adoption by the Federal parliament on 23 June. The SED had never made it clear that the speaker exchange depended on this law *not* being adopted (had they done so the SPD might have voted against it). Ulbricht himself scolded Brandt over the issue in his letter of 22 June and, four days later, declared the impossibility of holding a speaker exchange so long as it remained in force. Yet his remarks were not disseminated until 28 June – a day after Brandt had rejected Ulbricht's offer of secret negotiations on peaceful coexistence and confederation.[148] Only now (and probably under pressure from Moscow[149]) did Ulbricht agree to cancel the exchange.

In Moscow on 10 September 1966, Ulbricht told Brezhnev that the exchange of letters had helped forge a popular movement against the Vietnam War and proposed emergency legislation[150] in West Germany. Determined to prevent the formation of a Grand Coalition in Bonn,[151] he withheld his support from the campaign to topple Ludwig Erhard as chancellor, claiming that he was more interested in reducing tensions.[152] On 18 November, Ulbricht sent the Soviet leader a draft report outlining party policy in the run-up to the next central committee plenum. Advocating official negotiations with the SPD leadership, strong emphasis was laid on the need for co-operation with the West German trade union movement, sections of the intelligentsia and the 'humanist bourgeoisie'.[153] Four days later, Ulbricht wrote to Brandt appealing for a 'normalization' of relations between the SED and SPD. He also called for an alliance of forces against 'neofascism' and 'social reaction'.[154] Brandt, about to become foreign minister in Kiesinger's Grand Coalition, was unimpressed and sent the letter back. Ulbricht, however, refused to be discouraged. When he met the deputy Soviet foreign minister Vladimir Semyonov on 17 January 1967, he declared himself in favour of continuing the dialogue[155] – a view reiterated to the seventh party congress three months later.[156] Ulbricht also proposed writing to the new Federal chancellor to offer negotiations over a treaty banning nuclear weapons from German territory.[157]

What were Ulbricht's reasons for pursuing this agenda? After all, in the 1950s he had nearly always opposed rapprochement. Yet now, despite the SPD's adoption of a non-Marxist programme at Bad Godesberg in 1959, Ulbricht was keen to enter into dialogue. Addressing the twelfth central committee plenum in April 1966, he welcomed the fact that over half the SPD's candidates for the Federal elections had spoken out against nuclear weapons and the proposed emergency laws. The problem in West Germany, he said, was not so much the Bad Godesberg programme as the fact that it was not being implemented.[158]

According to Hager, the reason is to be found in Ulbricht's status as an 'old communist'. Having lived through the debilitating divisions of 1918–33 and the subsequent disaster of the Third Reich, he was determined that history should not repeat itself.[159] Although Ulbricht does seem to have been concerned by the rise of the neo-Nazi NPD in West Germany at this time,[160] the theory fails to explain both his determination to continue pursuing rapprochement after the NPD's decline and his rejection of dialogue in the 1950s. It also ignores the attitude of 'old communists' such as Honecker and Hager.[161] Ulbricht's conversion must be seen in the context of the changed international situation after the building of the Berlin Wall, the apparent strength and stability of the GDR, the increasing popularity of the West German SPD and the beginnings of *Ostpolitik*. The impossibility of jamming all radio and television signals from the West probably also persuaded Ulbricht that a more offensive 'peace strategy' was required. Above all, he was determined to seize the initiative on the 'national question'. Like Brandt, he was determined to gain a foothold in the 'other Germany'. He wanted to promote his own model of socialism and sincerely believed in the prospect of German reunification under communist auspices. The possibility that he pursued co-operation with the SPD as a way of promoting the 'scientific-technological revolution' (and thereby his economic reforms)[162] should not be excluded. The GDR, its borders protected, was likely to benefit from a policy of détente and increased trade with the West. In Moscow on 2 December 1969, Brezhnev complained to Ulbricht about East Germany's 'tendency' to develop economic ties with the Federal Republic.[163]

It was probably a sign of Ulbricht's waning influence that his long cherished proposals for German confederation were quietly dropped at the seventh party congress in April 1967. At a meeting of the central committee secretariat in January of that year, one politburo member had openly admitted: 'There is no partner in West Germany either for a confederation or for reunification'.[164] On 2 February the state secretariat for all-German affairs was renamed the secretariat for West German affairs. A new citizenship law was introduced eliminating all references to a single German citizenship[165] and Kiesinger's offers to establish formal contacts[166] were rejected. Some party leaders even went so far as to omit the D (for *Deutschland*) when referring to the SPD.[167] The seeds of Honecker's later policy of *Abgrenzung* ('separation') were already being sown. Ulbricht, however, in his address to the seventh party congress, took special care to refute the increasingly held view that Germany was permanently divided:[168] 'The imperialists have divided Germany. The working class of the two German states will reunite it.'[169]

The Prague Spring of 1968 was the most serious threat to the cohesion of the Soviet bloc since the Hungarian revolution of 1956. The unprecedented attempt by the Communist Party of Czechoslovakia (CPC) to realize 'socialism with a human face' was brutally crushed by Warsaw Pact tanks less than eight months after it began.[170] New primary sources enable us to view the traditional interpretation of Ulbricht – as one of Alexander Dubcek's most implacable enemies, Brezhnev's chief lackey and diehard proponent of military intervention – in a different light.

Ulbricht apparently infuriated his politburo colleagues by rejoicing in the downfall of Antonin Novotny as CPC first secretary on 5 January 1968 and unashamedly supporting Dubcek during his first two months in power. During a trip to Prague in February of that year, Ulbricht allegedly advised Novotny's successor to purge the 'dogmatists' from the leadership and replace them with a younger generation of 'technocrats'.[171] Ulbricht's intention was certainly not to encourage Czechoslovakia to pursue political liberalization but to persuade the country to follow the GDR in promoting economic reform.[172] Two months after the invasion, Ulbricht could still find words of praise for the 1967 Richta Report (*Civilization at the Crossroads*) in which leading Czechoslovak ideologists propagated a new approach to socialism in the age of the 'scientific-technological revolution'.[173] His alleged remarks must also be interpreted in the context of his poor relationship with Novotny, whom Ulbricht regarded as an incorrigible 'dogmatist'. Not only had the Czechoslovak leader impeded the process of economic reform in his country, he had followed Khrushchev's lead in proclaiming the 'transition to communism'. Berger recalled how Ulbricht derided this last decision: 'How can they begin to build communism when workers still have to queue to buy meat?'[174]

It did not take long for Ulbricht to realize that Dubcek was 'falling under the influence of right wingers'[175] in the CPC presidium. But this did not stop Ulbricht from believing that he could prevail on the Czechoslovak leader to abandon both the 'dogmatists' and 'revisionists' and establish a position somewhere between the two. At the Dresden conference of Soviet bloc leaders on 23 March, he advised Dubcek's delegation to formulate the CPC Action Programme[176] in such a way that it distanced itself 'from both the dogmatic and revisionist viewpoints'.[177]

Between 14 and 15 July 1968, the leaders of the Warsaw Pact nations (with the exception of Czechoslovakia) met in Warsaw to discuss the situation in Prague. Ulbricht proposed dispatching an open letter to demand the reversal of the liberalization process. His proposal was adopted. Only Todor Zhivkov of Bulgaria openly championed a military solution.[178] Determined to act as mediator between Prague and Moscow (and to assert the 'independence' of East

German foreign policy), Ulbricht apparently tried to arrange a meeting with Dubcek shortly after publication of the Warsaw letter but was forced to drop the idea after objections from politburo colleagues.[179] On 3 August the leaders of the Soviet Union, Bulgaria, Czechoslovakia, Hungary, Poland and the GDR held emergency talks in Bratislava. The resulting 'Bratislava declaration' amounted to a temporary reprieve for the Czechoslovaks.[180]

Ulbricht believed the 'Bratislava declaration' sent a clear message to West German 'revanchists' that 'counter-revolution' in Czechoslovakia was off the agenda.[181] It was on this basis that Ulbricht called a special session of the East German parliament on 9 August to propose that his government immediately exchange high-level representatives with Bonn[182] with the aim of concluding a renunciation-of-force agreement.[183] The Federal Republic was expected to relinquish the Hallstein Doctrine and its claim to sole representation but, significantly, Ulbricht did not make full recognition of his regime a prerequisite. To the surprise of many listeners, Ulbricht also raised the possibility of trade talks with West Germany. This unexpected proposal was not linked to any of the above preconditions and was reaffirmed on 16 August when the GDR officially informed Bonn of its interest in beginning ministerial negotiations in late August or early September. Both initiatives were shelved as a result of the invasion of Czechoslovakia.[184]

It soon became clear that the CPC had no intention of sanctioning an end to the reform process. On 12 August, only eight days before the invasion, Ulbricht met with Dubcek in Karlovy Vary. Contemporaries suspected that the talks were part of a deliberate camouflage strategy,[185] or that Ulbricht triggered the decision to invade by relaying to the Soviets a negative account of his consultations with the CPC.[186] In a politburo meeting three years later, however, the former first secretary was blamed for 'damaging' the East German leadership on this issue.[187] In 1992, Berger claimed that Ulbricht had used every opportunity to render military invasion unnecessary.[188] The other Warsaw Pact leaders made no further attempt to negotiate with Dubcek, but Ulbricht made an eleventh-hour bid to bring the Czechoslovak leader to his senses.[189]

What was Ulbricht's aim in arranging this last minute *tête-à-tête* and why was he apparently so concerned to de-escalate the crisis? The answer may not only lie in the SED leader's inflated sense of self-importance. It is just possible that Ulbricht, torn between a desire to promote rapprochement with Bonn and the necessity to end the reform experiment in Prague, saw no alternative to exerting personal pressure on Dubcek. Significantly, the joint communiqué released after the conclusion of the Karlovy Vary talks welcomed the initiative of the *Volkskammer* 'to guarantee European security and normalize relations between the two German states'.[190] The first secretary might also have been worried about the consequences of military intervention for his economic reform programme. At a press conference the next day, Ulbricht lectured his hosts on the superiority of the East German economic system and reaffirmed the desirability of diplomatic relations between the GDR and Federal Republic.[191] Until 18 August the

SED chose to play down its differences with the CPC and emphasize points of agreement instead.[192] After the invasion, Ulbricht flaunted the Karlovy Vary initiative at the expense of the Moscow protocol (which kidnapped CPC leaders were forced to sign in the Kremlin on 27 August).[193]

The final decision to invade was taken at a gathering of East bloc leaders in the Kremlin on 18 August.[194] Contrary to previous assumptions, divisions of the GDR's People's Army (NVA) do not seem to have been included in the force which crossed Czechoslovakia's borders on the night of 20 August.[195] According to Hager and other top party functionaries, Ulbricht supported the invasion but opposed the deployment of GDR troops.[196] Shortly before he died in 1990, former politburo member Horst Sindermann (first secretary of the SED in Halle responsible for a large section of border territory extending to Karlovy Vary in the north) explained the reasoning behind the decision. Direct participation would have evoked memories of Hitler's *Wehrmacht* invasion, unleashing a tidal wave of anti-German feeling: 'Blind as we were to many things, we at least saw that clearly at the time.'[197] According to Sindermann, the issue was not discussed in the SED politburo[198] – a testimony supported by Neumann.[199]

None of this is to suggest that Ulbricht refused to support the invasion or that the GDR did not provide other forms of moral, technical and military assistance.[200] All accounts concur that Ulbricht was a hard line opponent of the Prague Spring.[201] At the eighth central committee plenum on 23 August, he endorsed military intervention as a logical consequence of the CPC's betrayal of communist principles.[202] According to Neumann, the Czechoslovak reformers had no support in the upper echelons of the SED: 'there were no prerequisites for that – the whole experiment was too bizarre.'[203] Schürer, however, recalled 'heated debates on the fringes of the central committee'.[204]

A quarter of a century later, many former SED functionaries were still unwilling to condemn the invasion of an allied country undertaken in 1968. Berger described Dubcek as a 'counter-revolutionary',[205] Schürer regarded the military intervention as an 'unfortunate necessity'.[206] Neumann justified it as a defence of socialist and therefore East German strategic interests and dismissed the epithet 'red imperialism' as an 'enemy concept'. Dubcek, he said, 'looked on the left but drove to the right'.[207]

Ulbricht's determination to follow his own instincts rather than those of the Kremlin brought him into conflict with Brezhnev on a number of other occasions. When Romania unilaterally established diplomatic relations with West Germany in 1967, Ulbricht had to be restrained from engaging in an open polemic with Nikolai Ceausescu.[208] Relations with Gomulka deteriorated sharply in 1969–70[209] as a result of Ulbricht's tendency to propagate the GDR as a 'socialist model' for other countries. In August 1970, Brezhnev told Honecker of his unhappiness at the SED's tendency to disparage the 'achievements' of its communist neighbours.[210] Ulbricht also forged an independent policy towards China. By refusing to follow the other Warsaw Pact states in unequivocally condemning Beijing, he infuriated his Kremlin patrons and alienated politburo colleagues.[211]

The 28 September 1969 marks a turning point, not only in the development of democracy in West Germany, but in the evolution of inter-German relations. In the elections to the sixth federal parliament, the SPD and Free Democrats (FDP) won 224 and thirty seats respectively, giving them the chance to form a coalition with a majority of twelve. Three weeks later on 21 October, Willy Brandt became chancellor of a new Social Democratic–Liberal (SPD–FDP) government, thus bringing to an end two decades of conservative rule. Walter Scheel, the FDP leader, was appointed deputy chancellor and foreign minister. The coalition was pledged to pursue reform at home and *Ostpolitik* abroad. A new era had begun.

Ulbricht, in contrast to his politburo colleagues, welcomed the change of government in Bonn as an historic opportunity for the GDR to pursue a strategy of German–German rapprochement. The politburo met to consider his proposals (in the form of a speech planned for the twelfth central committee plenum) on 18 November 1969. Discerning 'a few positive starting points' in Brandt's domestic programme, Ulbricht declared his desire to end the Cold War and build a new relationship based on peaceful coexistence.[212] His proposal to establish a network of social, economic and political contacts between the two German states as a way of encouraging 'a good-neighbourly exchange of experiences' aroused the ire of his politburo colleagues (for whom it probably smacked of confederation by the back door) and was deleted from the speech.[213] Many years later, Hager criticized Ulbricht for 'harbouring illusions' about the SPD.[214]

On 1 December the SED leadership was called to Moscow to formulate a common policy towards the new SPD–FDP coalition in Bonn. Ulbricht decided to pre-empt the Kremlin consultations with a personal letter to Brezhnev outlining his own agenda. Describing the election of a new government as 'progress' (a word Brezhnev later took issue with[215]), Ulbricht proposed writing to Brandt to express the hope that their governments could now work together for peace. This meant empowering Stoph to begin negotiations with the Federal Republic (FRG) over disarmament and a renunciation-of-force agreement.[216] Ulbricht also enclosed a draft treaty 'for the establishment of equal relations on the basis of non-discrimination between the governments of the GDR and FRG' in which he expressed a willingness to drop demands that the Federal Republic accord full diplomatic recognition to East Germany. Rather than 'embassies', he proposed that the two countries merely exchange 'missions'.[217] This is significant because it refutes the claim that Ulbricht's 'maximalist' demands held up initial moves towards German–German rapprochement.[218]

Undeterred by the negative attitude of his politburo colleagues, the first secretary wrote a speech for the Kremlin talks duplicating the positions he had adopted in both the draft central committee speech and letter to Brezhnev.[219] Shortly before departing for Moscow, Ulbricht, Stoph, Honecker and others held a meeting to argue out their differences. Ulbricht interpreted the SPD–FDP victory as a significant change in German politics and argued that it was the

SED's duty to help Brandt fulfil his election promises. Honecker, by contrast, lambasted the SPD as the smiling face of imperialism.[220]

Ulbricht repeated his heretical views in Moscow, this time irritating his hosts as well as his politburo colleagues. Apparently, Brezhnev refused to consider Ulbricht's proposals, concentrating instead on those drawn up by Honecker and Stoph. The first secretary's policy of 'quickly penetrating' West Germany was categorically rejected as was his offer to forgo full diplomatic recognition.[221] At this stage the Soviet leadership was clearly uninterested in permitting rapprochement between the two German states, regarding the election of an SPD–FDP government in Bonn with deep suspicion.[222] Addressing East European heads of government on 4 December, Brezhnev dismissed any suggestion that Brandt wanted to fundamentally alter Bonn's policy.[223] Two days earlier, Brezhnev had forbidden Ulbricht from entering into any correspondence with Brandt, insisting that the SED's task was not to 'help' but to 'unmask' the new Federal chancellor.[224]

Back in Berlin between 12 and 13 December 1969, the SED leadership convened for its twelfth central committee plenum. While Stoph, Honecker and others attacked West Germany's new government,[225] Ulbricht is said to have remained stubbornly committed to achieving an accommodation.[226] On 18 December he wrote to the West German president, Gustav Heinemann, proposing talks over his draft treaty on equal relations. As Brezhnev demanded, Ulbricht withdrew his concessions on full diplomatic recognition. On 12 February 1970, Stoph was instructed to invite Brandt to the GDR. Preparations for the first long-awaited and highly emotional encounter got underway on 2 March and seventeen days later (on 19 March 1970) they met in the East German town of Erfurt. The Brandt–Stoph summit had been called to lay the foundations of a treaty between East and West Germany. Yet, apart from the mutual affirmation 'never again may war originate from German soil', nothing concrete was achieved. Furthermore (and to the chagrin of his hosts) Brandt received a hero's welcome in Erfurt.

The second Brandt–Stoph summit meeting was scheduled for 21 May 1970 in the West German town of Kassel.[227] Six days before, on 15 May, Brezhnev met with Honecker in Moscow to discuss tactics. The latter was standing in for Ulbricht who was on a health cure in the Soviet Union. Concerned that Brandt had managed to steal the limelight in Erfurt, the Soviet leader resolved that Kassel would be the last such encounter. Stoph's task would be to ignore Brandt's agenda of establishing inter-German ties and instead concentrate on reaping propaganda capital for the SED. All the emphasis would be placed on obtaining full international recognition for the GDR and membership of the United Nations. Once it became clear that Brandt was unwilling to discuss on the SED's terms, the talks would be indefinitely postponed.[228]

It was Brezhnev's greatest fear that the GDR and Federal Republic might independently establish a special relationship based on an expansion of inter-German ties. In May 1970 he instructed Honecker to 'expose' such ideas as 'hostile' to socialism.[229] Yet the fostering of such links was precisely what Ulbricht had in mind. According to Neumann, he wanted to negotiate with Brandt personally.[230] During the Kassel meeting one of the West German secret intelligence services apparently picked up a telephone conversation between Stoph and Ulbricht during which the latter pushed for an agreement with the SPD.[231] Stoph, greeted by right-wing demonstrators, willingly carried out the politburo brief and rendered the summit a failure. Two months later in Moscow, Brezhnev expressed bafflement at Ulbricht's desire for rapprochement with Bonn.[232]

Ulbricht was determined to restart the GDR–FRG negotiations as soon as possible and, following his return from the Soviet Union in early June 1970, decided to defy the ban on further talks (euphemistically labelled a 'pause for reflection') imposed by Brezhnev and Honecker at Kassel.[233] In a draft copy of his closing speech to the thirteenth central committee plenum, Ulbricht proposed that the SED drop its insistence on full diplomatic recognition of the GDR and enter a 'third round' of talks with the SPD. These remarks were censored from the speech, only to reappear in *Neues Deutschland* a few days later.[234] At the plenum itself, Ulbricht criticized those who accused Brandt of refusing to relinquish the 'claim to sole representation' and reminded his audience that Bonn was about to sign renunciation-of-force agreements with Moscow and Warsaw. He also warned against exaggerating the influence of the extreme right over the middle classes in the Federal Republic.[235] According to Wolf, Ulbricht believed that German reunification (and the dismantling of the Berlin Wall) would occur within a relatively short period of time.[236] Ulbricht's own remarks at the June plenum would appear to support this view. Incredibly, he felt confident enough to predict national reunification under communist auspices within 'a few decades',[237] whereas Honecker deleted all references to this theme from the 1974 constitution.[238]

A few weeks later and without any prior consultation with Soviet or SED leaders,[239] Ulbricht chose, once again, to violate the politburo resolution that made further talks with the SPD conditional on full international recognition. In Rostock on 16 July, Ulbricht made a speech stipulating that the length of the pause for reflection depended only on the time the West German government needed to sign a treaty with the Soviet Union outlawing the use of force.[240] Shortly thereafter, Ulbricht travelled to Moscow to present a second draft treaty omitting the demand for full diplomatic recognition. As one politburo member later recalled, it was rejected out of hand by both Brezhnev and the other members of the SED delegation.[241]

Although Brezhnev was not yet ready to permit rapprochement between the two German states, he had endorsed détente between West Germany and the USSR. In Moscow on 12 August 1970, the Soviet Union signed a non-aggression treaty with the Federal Republic. Contrary to the claims of most historians,[242] the SED first secretary supported this accord. Writing to Brezhnev on 2 June 1970, Ulbricht praised the Moscow Treaty for transforming relations between the Soviet Union and West Germany. Ratification, he declared, would also improve the relationship between the two German states and secure peace in Europe. The task for the SED, he said, was now to conclude a comparable agreement with the Federal Republic[243] and support the Brandt–Scheel government in Bonn.[244] He set out his plans in a resolution drafted for the fourteenth central committee plenum.[245] Ulbricht's desire for German–German rapprochement in the summer of 1970 was obviously not shared by the majority of his politburo comrades because the relevant passage was deleted from the draft and replaced by one emphasizing the GDR's status as a member of the socialist bloc.[246]

The full extent of Brezhnev's disillusionment with Ulbricht became clear when Honecker visited him in Moscow on 28 July 1970. In a private conversation, the Soviet leader expressed his displeasure at Ulbricht's determination to pursue rapprochement with the Federal Republic. There was, he insisted, no difference between the SPD's Willy Brandt and the CSU's Franz Josef Strauß – both supported capitalism and both wanted to liquidate the GDR. The SED leader's attempts to link the two German states to a common national culture were to be resisted at all costs.[247] Dismayed by Ulbricht's insubordination, Brezhnev warned, 'We held on to the CSSR [the Czechoslovakian Soviet Socialist Republic] . . . it will also not be possible for him to rule without us . . . After all, we have troops in your country.'[248]

Three weeks later Brezhnev was host to a delegation of SED leaders in Moscow. Once again, he took Honecker aside to convey his deep anxiety over Ulbricht's *Deutschlandpolitik*. After indirectly accusing the first secretary of harbouring 'illusions' about the SPD and neglecting the KPD, he forbade any further steps towards German–German rapprochement. That, he said, would play into the hands of Brandt, Strauß and the West German bourgeoisie.[249] Ulbricht's attempts to foster links with the Federal Republic raised the spectre of German unity and for this reason were abhorrent to the Soviet leader: 'Germany does not exist anymore. That is a good thing. There is the socialist GDR and the capitalist Federal Republic. That is the way things are . . . The future of the GDR lies in the socialist community. We have our troops in your country. That is good and they will remain there'.[250]

Ulbricht, however, remained convinced that the establishment of friendly relations between the GDR and Federal Republic was in Soviet as well as German interests. Addressing the SED and CPSU delegations on 21 August, Ulbricht insisted that the election of an SPD-led government in Bonn offered an historic opportunity to achieve peaceful coexistence in Europe. If this opportunity was missed, he warned, neither the German nor the Soviet people would forgive them. He warmly endorsed the Moscow Treaty as an important weapon in the fight against West German 'revanchism', 'militarism' and 'neo-Nazism' and as a means of exerting ideological influence on social democrats. Dialogue with the SPD, he said, was definitely worth pursuing given that the majority of its members 'favoured capitalism but opposed the Vietnam War'.[251] The first secretary clearly had no intention of yielding to Soviet demands. On the contrary, he had raised the stakes. No doubt fearing an attempt by Ulbricht to mobilize support for his policies, Brezhnev forbade any discussion of this issue in the SED politburo and central committee.[252]

Brezhnev, other Warsaw Pact leaders and the majority of SED politburo members feared the potentially destabilizing consequences of German–German rapprochement for communist rule in Eastern Europe. Since Honecker was responsible for both the party organization and questions of national security, he hardly needed reminding that false hopes would be aroused if Ulbricht continued to press for closer ties with the Federal Republic. According to a report presented to the politburo on 15 September 1970, Brandt's *Ostpolitik* was being enthusiastically endorsed by thousands of former social democrats, many of whom were now members of the SED.[253] Reports such as these were probably staple ingredients of Ulbricht's strategy. First they showed that co-operation with Brandt enjoyed support among ordinary party members; second that unless the SED opted for rapprochement it would be eclipsed by the SPD as the party of German unity. Significantly, Ulbricht would later be taken to task for his frequent descriptions of the SED as a party of 'communists and social democrats'.[254]

In a letter to Ulbricht of 21 October 1970, Brezhnev characterized the SPD's *Ostpolitik* as an attempt to undermine the stability of the GDR. His support for the SED's emerging policy of *Abgrenzung* ('policy of separation')[255] meant nothing less than putting the whole theme of national reunification, not to mention the fostering of inter-German ties, on hold. Such a policy was a repudiation of Ulbricht's strategy towards West Germany.[256] Ulbricht, however, remained as recalcitrant as ever. In December 1970 a reference to the controversial Rostock speech the previous July had to be taken out of his address to the fourteenth central committee plenum.[257] He then contravened official SED policy by alluding to the virtues of an all-German confederation and reminding his audience that the SED had reaped certain rewards after making similar proposals in 1957.[258] One is bound to ask why Ulbricht should have felt it necessary to elaborate on the confederation proposals of the 1950s during a central committee plenum in the early 1970s, especially since the policy had been dropped a few years earlier. It is possible to interpret his remarks as an appeal to put confederation back at the heart of the GDR's *Deutschlandpolitik*. Ulbricht's careful distinction between 'federation' and 'confederation'[259] is also informative because it supports Berger's claim that the SED leader saw confederation as a way of strengthening the GDR as a separate, economically viable state.[260] As if taking up the gauntlet thrown down by Ulbricht, Mittag used his speech to deride the idea of inter-German co-operation. Instead, he endorsed a policy of ever increasing economic, political and ideological separation.[261]

In the closing months of 1970, Axen's 'strategic working group for foreign policy' began formulating proposals for an alternative strategy towards West Germany. Whereas Ulbricht continued to emphasize the need for a 'special relationship' with the Federal Republic, Axen demanded the 'foiling' of all plans for inter-German relations, claiming that the estrangement of the two German states was an inevitable and perpetual process.[262] Whereas Ulbricht argued for partnership with the SPD, Axen asserted that it was the SED's first duty to support the communists.[263]

Although powerless to prevent the dismantling of his *Deutschlandpolitik* agenda, Ulbricht used his speech to the fifteenth central committee plenum in January 1971 to issue one last appeal for co-operation with 'realistic forces in the Federal Republic that shy away from nuclear confrontation and armed imperialist aggression in Europe as a way of conducting politics'.[264] He never relinquished his vision of German–German rapprochement and apparently planned to campaign for it at the eighth party congress later in the year.[265] Two weeks after deposing Ulbricht as party leader in May 1971, Honecker travelled to Moscow to sound the final death knell of his predecessor's *Westpolitik*. Promising never to forget that the GDR owed its existence to the USSR's victory over fascism, he ruled out any further talks with the SPD.[266]

Once Brezhnev became willing to sanction German–German détente, Honecker began to steal some of Ulbricht's clothes. Unlike his predecessor, however, he combined rapprochement with his 'policy of separation' (*Abgrenzung*) designed to point up political and cultural differences with the Federal Republic. GDR institutions were renamed to disassociate them from any notion of a shared German culture. A new class of citizens was created – the so-called 'secret carriers'. These were prominent political figures, state officials, scientists and soldiers who by virtue of their positions were banned from interacting with Westerners.[267] In the revised constitution of 1974, the GDR was no longer defined as 'a socialist state of the German nation'[268] but as 'a socialist state of workers and farmers'.[269] The clause pledging the 'gradual rapprochement of the two German states until their unification on the basis of democracy and socialism' was also deleted.[270]

According to the former Soviet ambassador to West Germany, Valentin Falin, Honecker's obsession with *Abgrenzung* soon became a bone of contention. When Brezhnev finally permitted the two German states to sign a treaty regulating their relations on 21 December 1972, Honecker apparently began voicing the same fears he had expressed in 1969–70.[271] Negotiations between Bonn and East Berlin had started on 27 November 1970[272] while Ulbricht was still leader. The fact that it took them more than two years to reach an agreement is a reflection of Brezhnev and Honecker's initial lack of enthusiasm. Although economic ties with and dependence on West Germany increased after 1971, it is wrong to cite this as an example of Honecker's flexibility compared to Ulbricht.[273] In the run-up to the eighth party congress of the SED, the Soviets had to restrain Honecker from overindulging in ritual condemnation of the West German government.[274] There is a certain irony in the fact that, while Ulbricht did not hold official talks with a single West German leader, Honecker went on to visit the Federal Republic and become a world statesman.

The status of West Berlin (which lay on the territory of the GDR) was another source of conflict between Ulbricht and the Kremlin. Clinging to his utopia of a

Germany united under socialism, Ulbricht was determined that the 'West Berlin question' be resolved in the GDR's favour. Any agreement which prolonged or safeguarded Western occupation rights was therefore anathema. The Kremlin, however, was concerned to preserve rather than change postwar realities. An international crisis over West Berlin threatened to destabilize the status quo and jeopardize moves towards East–West détente.

In 1967, Ulbricht informed the Soviets that he would soon no longer tolerate a situation whereby West Berlin was accorded a special status on the territory of East Germany. Furthermore, the resolution of this conflict was a matter for the GDR and West Berlin, not the Allies (who only had the right to be consulted). In his reply, Brezhnev expressed doubts about the wisdom of the GDR's position, warning that such confrontational language could be interpreted as an attempt to intensify the conflict over West Berlin in the near future. Furthermore, he scolded, such talk was incompatible with the treaties of friendship and mutual assistance between socialist countries which recognized West Berlin as a special political unit.[275] Ulbricht's bold assertion that the GDR and the West Berlin Senate could resolve the question on their own (while taking some account of Allied interests) was also dismissed as a possible violation of international treaty obligations.[276]

The Quadripartite Accord signed on 3 September 1971[277] was conspicuously contradictory with regard to FRG rights in West Berlin. On the one hand it stipulated that West Berlin was not a 'constituent part of the Federal Republic', on the other that its ties with the West were to be 'maintained and developed'. Lambasting attempts to 'partially demolish' East German sovereignty by subjecting it to 'four-power control', Ulbricht went so far as to demand the blockading of transit routes and supply lines linking West Berlin with the Federal Republic.[278] Only after the replacement of Ulbricht as SED leader did the four-power negotiations over Berlin begin to make progress.

Ulbricht's foreign policy and *Deutschlandpolitik* in the period 1966 to 1971 were expressions of his desire to establish the GDR as a strong and self-confident German state. This inevitably brought him into conflict with Moscow. Honecker, by contrast, was initially concerned to stress the GDR's status as a satellite of the Soviet Union.[279] These differences in attitude were reflected in the constitutions of 1968 and 1974. While Ulbricht was content to assert 'all-round co-operation and friendship' with the USSR,[280] Honecker declared the GDR 'forever and irrevocably allied' with the Soviet Union.[281]

The end of the Ulbricht era, 1970–73

By 1970, Ulbricht had become Eastern Europe's longest-serving communist leader. He was, however, 'unwilling to stand down'.[282] Hager's admission in 1992 contradicts the version he propagated as Honecker's ideology chief until 1989, whereby Ulbricht resigned of his own volition due to old age and ill health. The veteran communist was indeed old and sick but he was far from incapacitated.[283]

It has always been claimed that Ulbricht chose Honecker to succeed him. According to one contemporary observer, this was because he 'was the only politburo functionary who offered a reasonable guarantee that his own policy would be continued'.[284] Yet as we have seen, Honecker opposed economic reform and rapprochement with the SPD. Apparently, the first secretary was increasingly worried by Honecker's poor grasp of economic issues and began leaning towards Mittag as an alternative successor.[285] Mittag's denials[286] are, of course, predictable given that he turned against Ulbricht in 1970–71. Neumann affirmed that, whatever his attitude to Mittag, Ulbricht was determined to prevent Honecker taking over as SED leader.[287] Interviewed in 1990, the latter made two striking admissions. First, that Ulbricht was initially reluctant to stand down; second, that he wished to replace him as his deputy.[288]

If Neumann is to be believed, Honecker began behaving like a 'leader-in-waiting' after 1967, organizing an anti-Ulbricht campaign behind the scenes and refusing to state his real views in politburo meetings.[289] Apparently, he was supported at an early stage by Stoph, who had borne a grudge against the first secretary ever since his removal as defence minister in 1960.[290] Honecker's manoeuvring apparently provoked an angry response from Ulbricht in the summer of 1970.[291] At a politburo meeting on 7 July 'the working methods of the politburo and central committee secretariat' were discussed[292] – a veiled but unmistakeable reference to Ulbricht's style of leadership. The severity of the conflict can perhaps be gauged by the decision to postpone discussion of party policy and other related questions pending talks with the Soviet leadership at the end of September. Over the year as a whole, the central committee met only twice (instead of the customary four times), reflecting the SED leadership's lack of clear direction.

On 28 July 1970, Honecker met with Brezhnev in Moscow. Dismayed by Ulbricht's insubordination, Brezhnev raised the possibility of installing Honecker as first secretary instead. Ulbricht would retain his place in the politburo and continue as chairman of the council of state, although the option of purging him from the leadership altogether was left open. To enable Moscow to be kept abreast of developments, Honecker was instructed to report back every two days and, if necessary, immediately.[293] If this was a signal to Honecker to begin making preparations for Ulbricht's departure, Brezhnev set no timetable and seemed prepared to let matters take their course.

Three weeks later, the first secretary travelled to Moscow with other politburo colleagues. After a private talk with Ulbricht, Brezhnev emerged to inform the waiting delegations that he had every confidence in the SED leader.[294] Instead of bringing down the curtain on Ulbricht's career, Brezhnev had declared party unity the top priority. For the moment at least, Ulbricht had been granted a reprieve. The Soviet leader had gone back on his word and it was down to Honecker to convince him of his error.

Ulbricht's refusal to support the abandonment of his economic strategy in September 1970 brought the leadership question back to the fore. Herbert Wolf recalled Ebert demanding Ulbricht's resignation at a politburo meeting that autumn.[295] Neumann avers that his own name was put forward by Ulbricht as a candidate for the succession. Apparently, he turned down the offer (which had not been discussed with him beforehand) and today believes that it was a tactical manoeuvre to warn off Honecker. This did not prevent the latter accusing Neumann of aspiring to become first secretary in 1970–71.[296]

On 21 January 1971, thirteen members of the SED politburo[297] (Axen, Grüneberg, Hager, Honecker, Mittag, Sindermann, Stoph, Verner, Mückenberger, Warnke, Jarowinsky, Lamberz, Kleiber) signed a secret letter to Brezhnev appealing for support in securing Ulbricht's resignation.[298] Given that eight of the twenty-one members (Ebert, Ewald, Halbritter, Matern, Müller, Neumann, Norden, Ulbricht) did not sign, one observer's claim that Honecker 'had the politburo behind him'[299] is untenable. New light is shed on the balance of forces in the SED leadership, qualifying Ludz's theory of power struggle between three clearly defined factions ('experts', 'dogmatists' and 'middlemen'). The letter proves three things. First, Ulbricht's downfall was the result of a conspiracy. Second, the majority of politburo members were involved. Third, the initiator was Honecker rather than Brezhnev.

Why did seven members (excluding Ulbricht) not add their names to the others? Matern was on his deathbed and can therefore be discounted. Given Honecker's later identification of him as a key supporter,[300] it is probably fair to conclude that he would have signed had he been well enough to do so. In 1992, Neumann used the terms 'factionalism' and 'conspiracy' to describe Honecker's initiative. While conceding that he had differences of his own with Ulbricht,[301] he claims to have withheld his signature on grounds of 'personal honour' and 'loyalty to the SED'. Had he known at the time who the signatories were he would have alleged violation of party statute and brought the matter before the central committee.[302] Ebert too – despite a poor personal relationship with Ulbricht[303] – would never have contemplated signing such an 'ignominious letter'.[304] Müller and Halbritter were apparently 'more inclined to support Ulbricht than Honecker',[305] while Norden was known to be an ally of the latter. Ewald, a candidate-member, was probably not deemed important or reliable enough to be consulted.

In the letter Ulbricht was accused of violating politburo resolutions, setting his own political agenda and putting himself on a pedestal with Marx, Engels and Lenin. His 'technocratic' leanings were singled out for attention as was his tendency to insult and mishandle colleagues. He was also admonished for using the council of state to undermine politburo authority. The letter ended with an appeal for Soviet help in securing Ulbricht's resignation before the eighth party congress later in the year.[306] On 8 February 1971, Ulbricht and his wife travelled to Moscow for a health cure. On arrival Ulbricht held talks with Brezhnev. He remained in the USSR for another five weeks, meeting the Soviet leader again on 15 March. For the moment at least, Brezhnev had decided to take no action on the SED politburo's appeal because throughout his stay Ulbricht was accorded all the honours traditionally bestowed on a first secretary. Twenty years later, Honecker claimed that Ulbricht had telephoned him from the USSR at the beginning of March to offer his resignation.[307] This account (designed to portray the resignation as an act of consent) is undermined by the historical evidence. In fact, the decision to depose Ulbricht was probably not taken until early April.

Meanwhile in Berlin, Honecker made some secret notes for a planned conversation with Brezhnev at the twenty-fourth party congress of the CPSU between 30 March and 9 April. Honecker wanted to force the SED leader from office at the sixteenth central committee plenum to be held shortly afterwards. Ulbricht would be allowed to remain chairman of the council of state and an ordinary member of the politburo.[308] Since Honecker did not even permit his secretary to write up a fair copy of these notes it is reasonable to see them as another twist in the unfolding conspiracy. They also confirm Neumann's testimony that Honecker had to exert pressure on Brezhnev to win his consent for the plan.[309]

On 16 February 1971, the SED politburo held a meeting to designate its delegation for the twenty-fourth party congress of the CPSU. Ulbricht was nominated leader. His proposals for the central committee's report to the eighth party congress of the SED were also approved. They concentrated on the need to strengthen 'socialist democracy' and 'socialist government' during the formation of the 'developed social system of socialism'.[310] Obviously frustrated by his failure to secure Ulbricht's resignation, Honecker called an emergency meeting of the politburo for 26 March. The first secretary himself did not attend. There was only one item on the agenda: Ulbricht's 'state of health'. The meeting had only one purpose: to prevent Ulbricht's attendance at the CPSU party congress.[311] By forcing him to remain in Berlin, Honecker hoped to lead the SED delegation to Moscow, persuade Brezhnev to depose Ulbricht and vaunt himself as the new first secretary. Ulbricht would later express outrage at these tactics.[312] To shield himself against possible repercussions, Honecker demanded that the other politburo members pledge their unconditional support.[313] Ulbricht, however, rejected the resolution and headed the SED delegation to Moscow.

On 31 March Ulbricht addressed the twenty-fourth party congress of the CPSU. The only Soviet bloc leader apart from Ceausescu not to condemn China, he launched into an exposition of the East German model of socialism, reminding his audience that he had met Lenin personally in 1922. Lenin, he said, had advised Russian comrades to learn from their German counterparts. Between 3 and 4 April there was a change of protocol. While the rest of his colleagues travelled to the provinces, Ulbricht remained in Moscow. Furthermore, the delegation's order of precedence suddenly changed. The SED leader's name was not even listed. On 12 April Brezhnev received Ulbricht and Honecker together in the Kremlin. Ulbricht was told to resign as first secretary, although he would be allowed to remain in the politburo and continue as chairman of the council of state.[314] Yet even now Ulbricht laid down conditions. He would only agree to this if also elected 'honorary chairman of the SED'.[315] This ceremonial post had to be especially created to guarantee a smooth transition of power. Ulbricht was deluding himself, however, if he planned to use it to undermine Honecker's position. The post was abolished on the death of its first chairman.

The first politburo meeting after the SED delegation's return from Moscow was held on 15 April. In Ulbricht's absence Honecker took the chair and was nominated to deliver the report on the twenty-fourth party congress to the sixteenth central committee plenum.[316] During a conference of district leaders on 16 and 17 April, a minor member of the Berlin delegation was charged with the task of openly attacking Ulbricht's views on the national question and the 'socialist human community'.[317] With Honecker away, Ulbricht chaired his last full meeting of the politburo on 20 April.[318] The following day at the SED's twenty-fifth anniversary celebrations he made his final speech as party leader. The CPSU's official congratulation telegram named Pieck and Grotewohl as founders of the SED – Ulbricht was not even mentioned.[319] A week later, on 27 April, the politburo met to approve Ulbricht's resignation and Honecker's appointment as first secretary.[320] This was confirmed at the sixteenth central committee plenum on 3 May.

The first politburo meeting of the Honecker era ushered in a new style of leadership. Determined to remedy Ulbricht's practice of neglecting the politburo as a decision-making forum, a resolution was passed to raise its status. The role of first secretary was also more clearly defined. Werner Krolikowski and Harry Tisch, both close associates of Honecker, were appointed first secretary for Dresden and Rostock respectively.[321] A week later, Honecker was in Moscow for talks with Brezhnev. Before passing on Ulbricht's 'comradely greetings', Honecker reassured his hosts: 'Everything is now in its right place . . . The situation is good, it is stable.'[322]

One of the first casualties of Honecker's takeover was his predecessor's agenda for the eighth party congress in June 1971. Ulbricht's keynote speech on the 'fully developed social system of socialism' was dropped as were those on 'the future development of the socialist state' and 'the role and tasks of the SED in the fully developed social system of socialism'.[323] The main themes were now *Abgrenzung* and 'the unity of social and economic policy'. Ulbricht was assigned the task of delivering the opening address. In the weeks immediately preceding the congress, Carl-Heinz Janson was nominated head of a central committee working group for the Berlin delegates' conference. Mittag instructed him to report on Ulbricht's activities. The latter, who was leader of the central committee deputation, apparently used the proceedings to proselytize technocratic 'system-theory' ideas on planning and management which contradicted the new party line.[324]

The first draft of Ulbricht's opening address to the eighth party congress (which contained references to the 'socialist human community' and 'developed social system of socialism') was rejected by the politburo on 1 June 1971 and the task of composing a new draft entrusted to a working group of Grüneberg, Norden, Ulbricht and Verner.[325] On 3 June Norden wrote to Honecker asking to be excused from that day's meeting of the central committee secretariat so that he could write Ulbricht's speech.[326] On 8 June (a week before the proceedings got under way) it was finally approved by the politburo.[327] This sheds new light on Ulbricht's reasons for staying away from the congress. Reeling from the after-effects of his unceremonious removal as SED leader, Ulbricht was not going to deliver a speech dictated by his politburo colleagues.

Illness was the official reason given for Ulbricht's non-attendance at the party congress on 15 June and there is no reason to doubt the authenticity of the doctors reports: 'In the late evening of 14 June 1971 comrade Ulbricht suffered acute circulation troubles, that did not regress despite the undertaking of therapy . . . We therefore felt obliged, early on 15 June 1971, to order that comrade Ulbricht . . . remain strictly confined to bed.'[328] This report is corrobo-rated by another, dated 19 July, describing Ulbricht's condition as 'serious'.[329] There is no evidence that politburo members exaggerated Ulbricht's illness to prevent him from attending the congress.[330] In fact, Ulbricht was severely repri-manded by his colleagues for failing to appear.[331]

The fallen SED leader may have been ill but this was not the only reason for his absence. After all, Pieck had been virtually incapacitated when he attended party congresses in the late 1950s. According to Neumann, Ulbricht stayed away for two reasons: first illness, and second his treatment at the hands of Brezhnev and Honecker.[332] A further indication of Ulbricht's fury is the behaviour of his wife Lotte. Although she attended the congress, she refused to applaud Brezhnev's speech (which was rapturously received by the other delegates) and walked out before the end of the proceedings.[333] From the congress lectern, Honecker alluded to his predecessor's unwillingness to respect the norms of 'collective leadership'[334] and Harry Tisch poured scorn on the 'technocratic' discourse of the Ulbricht era.[335] The congress also endorsed a new central committee. Of the fifteen members who lost their seats, most were directly involved in economic and indus-trial management. The majority of the new recruits came from the party appara-tus and almost none from the economic agencies.[336]

Within only a few months, relations between Ulbricht and his comrades in the leadership were at an all-time low. On 26 October 1971, Honecker convened an extraordinary session of the politburo which lasted from ten in the morning until six in the evening. There was only one item on the agenda: the behaviour of Walter Ulbricht. The stenographic verbatim minutes from this meeting reveal two things: First, the extent of Ulbricht's opposition to the new party line and to Honecker personally; second, the nature of the SED's campaign to discredit him. In a letter to Brezhnev shortly beforehand, Honecker accused his predecessor of holding conversations with hospital doctors and visitors during which he criti-cized the politburo, first secretary and resolutions of the eighth party congress.[337]

The SED politburo exploited Ulbricht's illness to isolate him politically. Not only was he denied access to his own medical records,[338] but information about his health condition was released into the public domain without his prior knowledge or permission.[339] Enraged by this breach of confidentiality, Ulbricht threatened not only to prosecute the doctors concerned[340] but to bring the matter before parliament and the central committee.[341] These threats provoked the anger of his colleagues. As one of Honecker's key allies Werner Krolikowski put it: 'You should not harbour any illusions. We would then have to put the question of your behaviour before the central committee . . . We are also prepared to put this question before the working class.'[342]

Ulbricht's complaint that he had been banished from public life[343] is certainly borne out by the evidence. On 24 June 1971 he was sacked as chairman of the national defence council and replaced by Honecker. Section six of the *Volkskammer's* standing orders stipulated that it was the responsibility of the incumbent chairman to propose his successor before formally handing over the seals of office in an official parliamentary ceremony. In Ulbricht's case, the point did not even reach the agenda. The politburo also withheld a letter from Ulbricht to his Leipzig constituents in the run-up to the *Volkskammer* elections and banned any mention of his name during the GDR's twenty-second anniversary celebrations in October. In a determined effort to strip him of any remaining vestiges of power, it was decreed that the council of state could no longer publish its own legislative report. Ulbricht was indignant.[344] His colleagues, however, saw things differently, saying that it was about time the council of state began operating according to the constitution rather than as a 'super government'.[345] Ulbricht regarded the campaign against him not only as a personal insult but as a dangerous attempt to sow seeds of division within the party: 'All those who did not believe that I resigned voluntarily have been confirmed in their opinion', he stated.[346] The former first secretary told the politburo in no uncertain terms that he intended to remain chairman of the council of state until well into the 1980s and would no longer tolerate the official campaign against him: 'I have enough character', he said, 'not to put up with everything'.[347]

Personal animosity helped poison the atmosphere in 1971. Resentments suppressed for years were suddenly given free rein. Stoph assailed Ulbricht's 'bad character', Ewald and Hager took him to task for arrogance and egocentricity. Norden bitterly recounted his experiences with Ulbricht over the past twelve months. Mückenberger refused to indulge in 'digging up the past' on grounds of 'politeness'.[348] Not a single politburo member could bring himself to visit Ulbricht in hospital at this time.[349]

However, the conflicts were also political. As Stoph put it: 'It is not a question here of health or illness. Given everything that we now know, it must be presumed that he disagrees with certain resolutions of the central committee and eighth party congress.'[350] Stoph's remarks were echoed by Lamberz, among others: 'There are certainly principal differences here in assessing the policies of the GDR . . .'[351] Ulbricht's formula of the 'developed social system of socialism' had already been attacked at the eighth party congress in June. Together with the concept of the 'socialist human community', it was officially repudiated by Hager on 14 October. In a speech to social scientists in Berlin, Hager proclaimed an 'intensification of the class struggle' and derided Ulbricht's ideological innovations.[352] Significantly, the deposed SED leader had not even been consulted about the change in policy.[353] Ulbricht was also held personally responsible for the parlous economic situation.[354]

Faced with political extinction, Ulbricht mounted a spirited defence of both his reputation and his policies. This entailed defying the Honecker leadership and inciting colleagues to do likewise.[355] Krolikowski took Ulbricht to task for implying that Honecker's days as party leader were numbered,[356] but it was Halbritter who posed the question directly: 'Do you want to see a new first secretary elected?'[357] Ulbricht's attack on Honecker had the opposite effect to that intended, resulting in the entire politburo closing ranks against him. Horst Sindermann seemed to speak for everyone when he said that the party would never accept a reversal of the resolutions of the sixteenth central committee plenum. Ulbricht's distrust of Honecker, he declared, could trigger a process leading to the division of the party.[358] Mittag, Krolikowski and Grüneberg even went so far as to ask whether Ulbricht should not also be replaced as chairman of the council of state.[359] Ebert reminded Ulbricht of the Zaisser–Herrnstadt case in the 1950s, hinting darkly that a similar fate might also be in store for him.[360]

Stung by the campaign against him, the deposed SED leader apparently turned on the entire politburo, dismissing its members as 'thickheads'.[361] He is also reported as telling a friend that he would not allow himself to be handled in the same way as Khrushchev. During the same conversation he allegedly branded Günter Mittag a 'traitor'.[362] When questioned about this in the politburo on 26 October he claimed to have used another word with a similar meaning.[363] According to notes ascribed to Krolikowski, Mittag had narrowly escaped expulsion from the politburo after Honecker's accession to power.[364] He was now trying to ingratiate himself with the new leader and this must be borne in mind when assessing his savage attack on Ulbricht at this politburo meeting. The fallen first secretary, he declared, was engaging in factional activity. He had worked with 'lies and defamations', operating according to the motto 'divide and rule'. That had brought him success in the past, but not any more. What was required was an immediate undertaking from Ulbricht that he would refrain from further acts of intrigue and slander.[365] These remarks should be contrasted with those of Neumann who was less harsh in his criticism and even offered some words of comfort.[366]

Faced with such a united front, Ulbricht had no choice but to engage in self-criticism.[367] Honecker then read out a resolution condemning Ulbricht's behaviour and imposing draconian restrictions on his work schedule. Banned from carrying out official duties until 15 November 1971, Ulbricht was prevented from making any political appearances in the run-up to the *Volkskammer* elections (scheduled for 14 November). Thereafter, his work load was restricted to three to four hours every three days and the length of his speeches to fifteen minutes. The resolution won unanimous approval.[368]

Relations between Ulbricht and his politburo colleagues continued to deteriorate as the campaign against him intensified. Traces of the 'Ulbricht cult' were removed wherever possible. His name was dropped from the title of the German

Academy of Jurisprudence and Political Science, and East Berlin's Walter Ulbricht Stadium was rechristened the Stadium on Chausseestraße.[369] Ulbricht's anticipated work on the national question was postponed and his history of the German labour movement censored. The party programme launched in 1963 was also revised.[370] His ambitious plans to write two books – one devoted to the problems of socialist architecture and the other to the history of the international working class – were rejected by the politburo.[371] The council of state, such a powerful body during the 1960s, atrophied. On 23 November 1971, Ulbricht felt moved to write Honecker a curt memo demanding that, as chairman, he at least be provided with a political adviser and personal consultant.[372] In 1972, he was excluded from official celebrations to commemorate the twenty-third anniversary of the GDR and the fifty-fifth anniversary of the Soviet Union.[373]

In March 1972 Ulbricht was asked by the committee for Soviet–Bulgarian friendship to write an article in memory of the late Bulgarian communist leader Georgi Dimitrov, who would have been celebrating his ninetieth birthday that year. He took advantage of the opportunity to remind his readers that he had met Lenin personally at the fourth congress of the Comintern in the early 1920s.[374] Fearing a ban on publication, he sent the article direct to Sofia. On 17 March, Ulbricht received a letter demanding its immediate submission to the politburo.[375] The only member of the SED leadership to have worked closely with Dimitrov, Ulbricht had not even been consulted about the commemoration plans. Furthermore, he had only been allowed to publish one article over the previous twelve months.[376]

On 15 June 1972 the GDR and the Federal Republic began talks on a general framework treaty to redefine the relationship between the two German states.[377] Perhaps mindful of difficulties with Honecker over how best to respond to Brandt's *Ostpolitik* and recalling the fallen SED leader's own desire for rapprochement with Bonn, Brezhnev sent Ulbricht a birthday telegram paying tribute to his role in helping to bring about détente in Europe.[378] Elated, Ulbricht dashed off a memo to Honecker requesting publication of the telegram in the press. Honecker, however, was determined to prevent his predecessor stealing the limelight and, with Soviet support, turned the request down.[379]

As chairman of the council of state, Ulbricht continued to exert some influence on East German foreign policy. Regarding relations with African states he occasionally used his position to challenge the party line. When he received the interior minister of the People's Republic of Yemen on 17 May 1972, Ulbricht ignored his official brief and made a point of criticizing the GDR's ministry of foreign affairs for failing to live up to its treaty obligations.[380] Accrediting the Ugandan ambassador on 12 April 1973, Ulbricht praised Tanzania as a model worthy of emulation by other African states, even though the country was under the ideological influence of China and had extremely poor relations with Uganda.[381]

The former first secretary seems to have been placed under effective surveillance by the SED. Many of those who conversed with him during his summer vacation in July–August 1972 reported their impressions to Honecker in writing. In a letter of 26 July, Harry Tisch gave an account of a meeting with Ulbricht during which the latter had allegedly complained about Honecker's 'vanity' and the treatment meted out to him by politburo colleagues. In a clear reference to the Honecker camarilla, Ulbricht was quoted as saying that he wanted to consult with other members of the politburo, but not with those from the central council of the FDJ. Ulbricht's grievances were obviously political as well as personal because, according to Tisch, 'Ulbricht began to develop all the old theories about the scientific-technological revolution . . . as if there had been no eighth party congress.'[382] Once Ulbricht had been cast into the political wilderness, old ghosts returned to haunt him. On 1 September 1972, Honecker was informed of a conversation during which Ulbricht had apparently expressed alarm over further moves to rehabilitate Franz Dahlem.[383]

Ulbricht continued to regard the GDR as a model for other Soviet bloc countries. According to a report from the SED's second district secretary in Ribnitz-Damgarten (addressed to Honecker and dated 30 June 1972), Ulbricht used a speech to a dinner of senior Soviet and East German officials on 9 June to cast doubt on the industrial and agricultural policies of the USSR.[384] On another occasion, Ulbricht dilated at considerable length on the need to get to grips with the 'scientific-technological revolution'. Drawing attention to the existence of a new 440 megawatt nuclear reactor in Ludwigshafen, West Germany, Ulbricht proposed the construction of a similar reactor in the GDR.[385]

Even in the last few months of his life, Ulbricht found the energy to criticize certain aspects of party policy. On 7 November 1972, Ulbricht wrote to Honecker demanding that the first point be struck from that day's politburo agenda.[386] The issue seems to have been East Germany's relationship to the Federal Republic.[387] Although it is unclear precisely what was at stake, Ulbricht expressed concern that the proposed discussion might endanger the policy of peaceful coexistence.[388] Matters came to a head in December 1972 when the campaign to hold Ulbricht personally responsible for the country's economic ills intensified. In a letter to Brezhnev, Ulbricht related how, on 7 December, Honecker had called an emergency meeting of the politburo to prevent him from addressing the central committee. The subject of his speech was to have been the economy. Although there was nothing in the preparatory draft which contradicted the party line,[389] Verner and Sindermann demanded that Ulbricht take personal responsibility for the crisis.[390] The latter's response was to blame factors beyond the party's control: devastation suffered during the war, national division, the economic sanctions of the West, the shortage of raw materials and the inevitable acceleration of the 'scientific-technological revolution'.[391]

In his letter to Brezhnev, Ulbricht demanded that the politburo end its campaign against him.[392] Complaining that the conflicts of recent months had 'cost him a few years of his life',[393] Ulbricht resolved to take an extended health cure in March–April 1973. It was to be his last. Meanwhile the campaign to discredit him continued unabated. On 23 January of that year, Honecker announced plans to publish a new biography of KPD leader Ernst Thälmann, scrapping the 1971 edition before it could even reach the bookshops.[394] That the new biography would present Ulbricht in a less than favourable light was a foregone conclusion and it was probably this which prompted Ulbricht to write a letter of protest on 2 February.[395] As can be seen from the politburo resolutions, the letter provoked a heavy-handed response. The 1971 edition was shredded and Ulbricht condemned in the strongest possible terms.[396]

The next few months saw a dramatic deterioration in Ulbricht's health condition. By April he was no longer able to give advance notice of attendance at politburo meetings. Although he pleaded to be kept up to date with political developments, this seems to have been denied him.[397] The man who had dominated East Germany for a quarter of a century was not even allowed to celebrate his eightieth birthday with guests of his own choosing. The task of drawing up a guest list was transferred to the 'protocol office'.[398]

On 24 July 1973 Ulbricht suffered a stroke from which he never recovered. He died a week later on 1 August 1973. There was then a lengthy disagreement over what to do with his remains.[399] One and a half months later, toppled by the system he had done so much to create, Ulbricht was buried alongside other 'communist heroes' in the cemetery at Friedrichsfelde. Over the next few years Ulbricht became an unperson. His words were removed from books and articles, his name from stamps, posters and museums. In the communist ancestral portrait gallery in Pieck's home town of Guben, GDR history was reduced to a decade. Next to Pieck's portrait, Honecker hung his own. Ulbricht had been consigned to the dustbin of history. The SED coined the term *Wende* ('turnabout') to mark the passing of his era.[400]

Notes

1 See also P. Grieder, 'The overthrow of Ulbricht in East Germany: A new interpretation', *Debatte. Review of Contemporary German Affairs*, 6: 1 (May 1998), 8–45.
2 Interview with Alfred Neumann, 23.10.92.
3 See also W. Berger, 'Fünf Jahre neues ökonomisches System', *ND* (6.6.68), 4.
4 W. Ulbricht, 'Das Programm des Sozialismus und die geschichtliche Aufgabe der Sozialistischen Einheitspartei Deutchlands', in *Protokoll der Verhandlungen des VI. Parteitages der Sozialistischen Einheitspartei Deutchlands,* I (Berlin-Ost, 1963), 28–250.
5 Interview with Herbert Wolf, 13.10.92.
6 H. Apel, 'Economic reforms in East Germany. A comment', *POC*, 3 (May–June 1966), 59–62; p. 60. See also T. A. Baylis, ' "Perfecting" the planning mechanism: The politics of incremental reform in the GDR', in D. L. Bahry, J. C. Moses, *Political implications of economic reform in communist systems. Communist dialectic* (New York, 1990), 295–321; p. 299.
7 C. Stern, *Ulbricht. A political biography* (London, 1965), pp. 210, 214.
8 Cited in G. Leptin, M. Melzer, *Economic reform in East German industry* (Oxford, 1978), p. 9. Among other things, the article suggested using profit or a special profit

indicator as a means of evaluating enterprise activity and calculating bonuses for the workforce.

9 SAPMO-BArch, ZPA, J IV 2/2A/3196. Ulbricht's letter to member of council of state, Hans Rodenberg, 23.10.71. Ulbricht admitted to having had fierce disagreements with Khrushchev over economic policy in the GDR. This letter comes from a remarkable collection of documents (also classified as SAPMO-BArch, ZPA, J NL 2/32) bound in synthetic leather and entitled *Dokumente*. The collection was apparently put together by Honecker for distribution in the PB in February 1989. The fascinating material on the fall of Ulbricht suggests that Honecker may have been using it to warn off a potential challenge to his own leadership. Once the volumes had been studied by PB members they were collected in and, with the exception of a few copies, shredded. Ulbricht repeated his comments about Khrushchev's attitude to the NES in a PB meeting on 26.10.71. See SAPMO-BArch, ZPA, J IV 2/2/1360, Bd. 1. Ulbricht's relationship with Khrushchev was apparently so strained that by 1964 (when the latter was deposed in a coup) they were barely on speaking terms (SAPMO-BArch, ZPA, J IV 2/2A/3196. Ulbricht's letter to Rodenberg, 23.10.71). See also 'Ulbricht. Edel auf dem Grabstein', *Der Spiegel*, 40 (30.9.64), 68–81; p. 80.

10 W. Berger, 'Zu den Hauptursachen des Unterganges der DDR', *Weißenseer Blätter*, 4 (1992), 26–37; p. 31. See also W. Berger, 'Als Ulbricht an Breshnew vorbei regierte', *ND* (23.–24.3.91), 13: 'The necessary decisions . . . had to be taken off our own bat.' Berger's testimony is supported by Wolf (interviewed, 13.10.92).

11 Interview with Gerhard Schürer, 5.11.92.

12 See Ulbricht, 'Das Programm des Sozialismus', p. 234. This trend is analysed in detail by P. C. Ludz. See *Parteielite im Wandel. Funktionsaufbau, Sozialstruktur und Ideologie der SED-Führung* (Köln-Opladen, 1968) and *The German Democratic Republic from the sixties to the seventies. A socio-political analysis* (Massachusetts, 1970).

13 'SED. "Lustiges Leben" ', *Der Spiegel*, 44 (28.10.64), 56–9; p. 56. For more detail on the nature and extent of 'old communist' group identity, see the doctoral dissertation of Catherine Epstein 'The "Old Communists" in the German Democratic Republic, 1945–1989' (Harvard University, forthcoming).

14 Cited in J. Roesler, 'Die Phraseologen mußten den Technologen weichen', *ND* (16.–17.2.91), 13.

15 *Ibid*.

16 I. Spittmann, 'East Germany: the swinging pendulum', *POC*, 4 (July–August 1967), 14–20; p. 16.

17 Cited in *ibid*.

18 Interview with Claus Krömke, 11.12.92. See also H. Wolf, 'Entgegnung zum Beitrag "Phraseologen mußten Technologen weichen". Wie war das mit dem Neuen Ökonomischen System?' *ND* (2.–3.3.91), 13; and G. Mittag, *Um jeden Preis. Im Spannungsfeld zweier Systeme* (Berlin, Weimar, 1991), pp. 136–7, 140, 144, 146–7, 190–2.

19 Interview with Claus Krömke, 11.12.92.

20 Interview with Berger, 7.10.92.

21 Interview with Wolf, 3.11.92.

22 F. Oldenburg, *Konflikt und Konfliktregelung in der Parteiführung der SED 1945/46–1972* (Köln, 1972), pp. 70–1.

23 Interview with Wolf, 3.11.92.

24 Interview with Kurt Hager, 1.12.92. His verdict on the NES thirty years later: 'a hopeful solution'. According to Berger, however, Hager attempted to block introduction of the ten-class polytechnic secondary school in 1964. The curricula of these schools were heavily biased in favour of scientific and technological subjects. Interview with Berger, 14.12.92.

25 Interview with Wolf, 13.10.92.

26 Interview with Berger, 7.10.92.

27 Interview with Wolf, 13.10.92.

28 Interview with Schürer, 19.10.92.

29 Ludz, *GDR*, pp. 48–50.

30 P. C. Ludz, 'The SED leadership in transition', *POC*, 3 (May–June 1970), 23–31; pp. 25–31.

31 See C. Janson, *Totengräber der DDR. Wie Günter Mittag den SED-Staat ruinierte* (Düsseldorf, Wien, New York, 1991), pp. 27–8. In 1992, Neumann railed against his former colleague in the council of national economy, branding him an 'immoral swine' and a 'Western spy'. Already in 1962, Neumann had advised Ulbricht to expel Mittag from the economic council. Interview with Neumann, 23.10.92. Allegations that Mittag was a 'Western spy' were repeated by Wolf (interviewed, 3.11.92) and Manfred Uschner (interviewed, 8.12.92). Schürer was, however, more sceptical (interviewed, 5.11.92). There are three problems with these allegations: (1) At the time of writing they cannot be substantiated; (2) nobody knows precisely what is meant by the term 'Western spy'; (3) they play into the hands of those who blame the GDR's economic debacle on the fact that *Nachmittag* (a German pun meaning 'after Günter Mittag' and 'afternoon') never came.

32 ' "Es reißt mir das Herz kaputt". Spiegel-Gespräch mit dem ehemaligen DDR-Wirtschaftslenker Günter Mittag über seine Politik und seine Fehler', *Der Spiegel*, 37 (9.9.91), 88–104; p. 96.

33 Herbert Wolf claims to have viewed the coming of Brezhnev with foreboding. In a private statement written on 8 February 1965 (four months after the coup against Khrushchev) Wolf predicted that the new climate of 'conservatism' might mark the beginning of the end for the communist movement. Document read to the author in interview with Wolf, 13.10.92.

34 SAPMO-BArch, ZPA, J NL 2/32. Record of conversation between Honecker and Brezhnev in Moscow, 28.7.70.

35 SAPMO-BArch, ZPA, J IV 2/201/735.

36 See K. W. Ryavec, *Implementation of Soviet economic reforms. Political, organizational and social processes* (New York, 1975).

37 Interview with Schürer, 19.10.92.

38 Janson, *Totengräber der DDR*, pp. 52–3. Neumann's verdict on Apel's economic plan: 'like a girl with a beautiful body, long legs and a hump on her back'. Cited in interview with Schürer, 19.10.92.

39 *Ibid.*

40 See Janson, *Totengräber der DDR*, p. 53.

41 Interview with Schürer, 19.10.92.

42 Interview with Schürer, 5.11.92. Schürer related an interesting episode shortly after the 1989 revolution when he was visited by the son of one of Apel's former colleagues who claimed knowledge of the man responsible for Apel's death. The visitor produced a photograph of Apel with a KGB man in the background, purported to be

the assassin. Schürer dismissed the claim as nonsense – 'part of the fashionable habit of blaming everything on the MfS and its Russian patrons'. The man apparently produced no sound evidence to support his allegations.

43 Interview with Schürer, 19.10.92.
44 Roesler, 'Die Phraseologen'.
45 Berger, 'Als Ulbricht an Breshnew vorbei regierte'.
46 H. Weber, *DDR. Grundriß der Geschichte 1945–1990* (Hannover, 1991), p. 120.
47 In October 1966 'social councils' (representing qualified people from all walks of life) were set up to oversee factory managements.
48 SAPMO-BArch, ZPA, IV 2/1/337. Ulbricht's report to 11 CC plenum: 'Probleme des Perspektivplanes bis 1970'.
49 W. Ulbricht, 'Die gesellschaftliche Entwicklung in der DDR bis zur Vollendung des Sozialismus', in *Protokoll der Verhandlungen des VII. Parteitages der Sozialistischen Einheitspartei Deutschlands*, I (Berlin-Ost, 1967), 25–287.
50 *Ibid.*, pp. 158–9.
51 *Ibid.*, pp. 142–4, 146–50, 155. See also the council of state resolution, 22.4.68 – 'on further measures for the development of the economic system of socialism'. Cited in Leptin, Melzer, *Economic reform*, pp. 98–9. The decision to centrally plan key industries was interpreted by some Western commentators as a partial reversal of the reforms. See *ibid*. Such an interpretation is contradicted by Ulbricht's speech and underestimates the new powers granted to enterprises in the non-priority sectors. Interviews with Berger, 19.7.94 and Wolf, 14.7.94.
52 Ulbricht, 'Die gesellschaftliche Entwicklung', p. 155. For a path-breaking study of the reforms in practice, see J. Kopstein, *The politics of economic decline in East Germany, 1945–1989* (Chapel Hill, 1997).
53 SAPMO-BArch, ZPA, J IV 2/2A/3196. 'Zur Korrektur der Wirtschaftspolitik Walter Ulbrichts auf der 14. Tagung des ZK der SED 1970'. The denunciatory nature of this document (probably compiled by Mittag's office after Ulbricht's downfall) renders it unreliable.
54 Ulbricht, 'Die gesellschaftliche Entwicklung', p. 158.
55 *Ibid.*, p. 160.
56 *Ibid.*, p. 161. According to Carl-Heinz Janson, member of the CC apparatus closely involved in planning and implementing the reforms, Ulbricht openly defended the concept during preparatory discussions. Janson, *Totengräber der DDR*, pp. 35–6.
57 SAPMO-BArch, ZPA, J IV 2/2A/3196, 'Zur Korrektur'.
58 Ulbricht, 'Das Programm des Sozialismus', p. 115.
59 Article 14, Section 2, 1968 constitution, *Verfassungen deutscher Ländern und Staaten von 1816 bis zur Gegenwart* (Berlin, 1989), pp. 495–518; p. 501.
60 The nationalization of the private and semi-state-owned companies was approved at the 6 CC plenum in July 1972.
61 See Article 14, revised constitution of 1974, *Verfassungen*, pp. 519–40; p. 523.
62 W. Ulbricht, 'Internationale wissenschaftliche Session: 100 Jahre "Das Kapital". Die Bedeutung des Werkes "Das Kapital" von Karl Marx für die Schaffung des entwickelten gesellschaftlichen Systems des Sozialismus in der DDR und den Kampf gegen das staatsmonopolistische Herrschaftssystem in Westdeutschland', *ND* (13.9.67), 3–6.
63 Interview with Neumann, 6.4.94.
64 Interview with Krömke, 11.12.92.

65 Ulbricht, 'Das Programm des Sozialismus', pp. 233–4, 245. This entailed setting up 'offices' at local, district and national level to lead the work of party organizations in industry and agriculture. Staffed by highly qualified professionals rather than SED apparatchiks, these organs limited the remit of the PB and reduced the power of Honecker's CC secretariat. In 1967–68, at Honecker's instigation, the 'production principle' was effectively disbanded.

66 Ulbricht, 'Das Programm des Sozialismus', p. 240.

67 *Ibid.*, pp. 235, 240, 242.

68 *Ibid.*, p. 244.

69 'SED. ' "Lustiges Leben" ', p. 56.

70 Ulbricht, 'Das Programm des Sozialismus', p. 181. Ulbricht stressed the need for more rigorous activity by 'independent' control organs. See *ibid.*, p. 234.

71 As Ulbricht put it: 'the transition from the dictatorship of the proletariat to a "people's state" has already begun.' 'SED. "Lustiges Leben" ', p. 59. There were, however, more than enough safeguards to ensure that the SED's 'leading role' remained intact.

72 D. Childs, *The GDR: Moscow's German ally* (London, 1988 edn), pp. 71, 92.

73 According to Schürer and Berger, Ulbricht adopted a more conciliatory stance on this issue. Interviews with Schürer, 19.10.92 and Berger, 19.7.94. There was no blistering attack on the GDR's cultural elite in Ulbricht's two speeches to the 11 CC plenum. See SAPMO-BArch, ZPA, IV 2/1/336–337.

74 Ulbricht, 'Die gesellschaftliche Entwicklung', pp. 95, 102.

75 Ulbricht, ' "Das Kapital" ', p. 6.

76 After public consultation, clauses protecting freedom of conscience and worship were nominally added to the draft constitution, as was a passage granting members of parliament immunity from prosecution. In this first plebiscite in the history of the GDR, the numbers of those who withheld their approval or refused to participate were unusually high compared to parliamentary elections: 94.5 per cent of those entitled to vote supported the constitution; in East Berlin the figure was 90.9 per cent. According to Neumann, Ulbricht and Honecker disagreed over the text of the constitution. Interview with Neumann, 23.10.92.

77 SAPMO-BArch, ZPA, J IV 2/2A/3196. 'Zur Korrektur'. See also Janson, *Totengräber der DDR*, p. 54.

78 SAPMO-BArch, ZPA, J IV 2/2/1360, Bd. 1. Gerhard Grüneberg in PB meeting, 26.10.71. This was one of the rare occasions when verbatim minutes were taken.

79 SAPMO-BArch, ZPA, J IV 2/2/1360, Bd. 1. Ulbricht in PB meeting, 26.10.71.

80 SAPMO-BArch, ZPA, J IV 2/202/402. 'Hauptproblem der Entwicklung der sozialistischen Staatsmacht und der sozialistischen Demokratie im Prognosezeitraum 1971–80'.

81 *Ibid.* See also SAPMO-BArch, ZPA, J IV 2/202/403. 'Gruppe Innenpolitik (Überarbeiter Auszug aus der Prognose). Stand: Februar 1971.' Sub-heading: 'How can the socialist state be further perfected and made ever more transparent for the whole people?'

82 SAPMO-BArch, ZPA, J IV 2/202/403. 'Gruppe Innenpolitik'.

83 SAPMO-BArch, ZPA, J NL 2/32. Ulbricht's speech to SED district leadership in Leipzig, 21.11.70. The speech was censored (see Honecker's preparatory notes – probably compiled in February/March 1971 – for a conversation with Brezhnev at the 24 party congress of the CPSU, SAPMO-BArch, ZPA, J IV 2/2A/3196).

According to Neumann, Honecker ordered the tape-recording of Ulbricht's remarks so that they could be used against him in Moscow. Interview with Neumann, 23.10.92.

84 Interview with Wolf, 13.10.92.

85 Interview with Berger, 27.11.92.

86 SAPMO-BArch, ZPA, J IV 2/2A/3196. 'Zur Korrektur'. Wolf was forced to take back his material as 'misconceived and useless'.

87 See SAPMO-BArch, ZPA, J IV 2/202/403. 'Gruppe Innenpolitik'.

88 H. Wolf, *Hatte die DDR je eine Chance?* (Hamburg, 1991), p. 43: 'with the forma-tion of . . . the "developed social system of socialism", Ulbricht was unequivocally positioning himself to prepare the political system, including the role of the party, for a more effective development of democracy . . .' According to Wolf, Ulbricht had recognized by 1971 that the GDR was 'pushing against the limits of its social system'. Interviews with Wolf, 13.10.92 and 3.11.92.

89 Interviews with Wolf, 13.10.92 and 3.11.92.

90 Article 1, 1968 constitution, *Verfassungen*, p. 495.

91 SAPMO-BArch, ZPA, IV 2/1/338. Ulbricht's closing speech to 11 CC plenum, 18.12.65.

92 Some of Ulbricht's closest advisers, however, may have been more favourably dis-posed. Wolf, for example, recalled a conversation with the East German economist Fritz Behrens in early 1966 during which the idea of founding a 'Socialist People's Party' was mooted. Modelled on the inter-war Socialist Worker's Party (which attempted to combine democratic features of the SPD with the revolutionary tra-ditions of the KPD) the party would have been granted an opposition role within the Democratic Bloc, enabling it to work with the SED for 'democratic renewal'. Both men expressed their support for the idea but, given the prevailing political climate at the time, did not pursue it any further. There is no way of corroborat-ing Wolf's testimony because Behrens is dead and the notes made at the meeting were apparently lost or stolen. Interviews with Wolf, 13.10.92 and 3.11.92; tele-phone conversation, 26.10.92. Wolf is now a member of the SED's successor party, the PDS, and calls himself a 'democratic socialist'. Elected to the *Bundestag* in 1990, he sat on its *Enquete-Kommission* charged with the task of reassessing the history of the GDR.

93 Childs, *GDR*, p. 161. See also Berger, 'Hauptursachen', p. 34.

94 SAPMO-BArch, ZPA, J NL 2/32. Record of conversation between Honecker and Brezhnev in Moscow, 20.8.70.

95 SAPMO-BArch, ZPA, J IV 2/2A/1396. Record of Ulbricht's remarks to SED and CPSU delegations, 21.8.70.

96 SAPMO-BArch, ZPA, J IV 2/2/1360, Bd. 1. PB meeting, 26.10.71.

97 SAPMO-BArch, ZPA, J IV 2/202/346, Bd. 12. Ulbricht's letter to Brezhnev, 18.4.69.

98 Ulbricht's speech announcing the policy (whereby the GDR would sustain such momentous economic growth that it would 'overtake' the FRG without stop-ping long enough to 'catch up') was published in *Die Wirtschaft*, 9 (26.2.70), pp. 8–9.

99 SAPMO-BArch, ZPA, J NL 2/32. Record of conversation between Honecker and Brezhnev in Moscow, 20.8.70.

100 SAPMO-BArch, ZPA, J IV 2/2A/3196 'Zur Korrektur'.

101 Interview with Berger, 27.11.92.

102 SAPMO-BArch, ZPA, IV 2/1/415. See also SAPMO-BArch, ZPA, J IV 2/2A/3196, 'Zur Korrektur'.

103 Interview with Krömke, 11.12.92. Schürer too was disparaging of such concepts, dismissing them as 'crazy'. Interview with Schürer, 19.10.92.

104 SAPMO-BArch, ZPA, IV A 2/5/15. Report from Werner Walde (first secretary of SED district leadership in Cottbus) to Ulbricht, 13.11.70.

105 SAPMO-BArch, ZPA, J IV 2/2A/3196, 'Zur Korrektur'.

106 Only ten of the politburo's twenty members and candidate members were present. SAPMO-BArch, ZPA, J IV 2/2/1300, PB meeting, 8 Sept. 1970.

107 SAPMO-BArch, ZPA, J IV 2/2/1300. 'Resolution analysing the implementation of the plan in the first half of 1970'.

108 Wolf, *Hatte die DDR je eine Chance?*, p. 42.

109 Mittag, *Um jeden Preis*, pp. 142–3.

110 Interview with Neumann, 23.10.92. See also letter of SED PB to Brezhnev, 21.1.71. SAPMO-BArch, ZPA, J IV 2/2A/3196.

111 SAPMO-BArch, ZPA, J IV 2/2/1360, Bd. 1. Mittag in PB meeting, 26.10.71. His testimony is supported by other speakers. See also SAPMO-BArch, ZPA, J IV 2/2A/3196, 'Zur Korrektur'

112 SAPMO-BArch, ZPA, J IV 2/2/1360, Bd. 1. Halbritter in PB meeting, 26.10.71. See also SAPMO-BArch, ZPA, J IV 2/2A/3196, 'Zur Korrektur'.

113 SAPMO-BArch, ZPA, J IV 2/2A/1.471. PB meeting, 20.10.70. 'Information about important results in the development of the national economy, September 1970'.

114 Interview with Schürer, 19.10.92.

115 SAPMO-BArch, ZPA, IV 2/1/415.

116 SAPMO-BArch, ZPA, J IV 2/2/1317.

117 SAPMO-BArch, ZPA, IV 2/1/415. Honecker's letter to Ulbricht.

118 SAPMO-BArch, ZPA, IV 2/1/415. Sindermann's letter to Ulbricht.

119 SAPMO-BArch, ZPA, IV 2/1/415. Mittag's letter to Ulbricht.

120 SAPMO-BArch, ZPA, IV 2/1/420. According to Honecker's preparatory notes for a conversation with Brezhnev at the CPSU party congress in Moscow, Ulbricht's speech 'was a compromise and met with incomprehension and disapproval in the party'. These notes were probably composed in February/March 1971. SAPMO-BArch, ZPA, J IV 2/2A/3196.

121 SAPMO-BArch, ZPA, J IV 2/2A/3196, 'Zur Korrektur'.

122 SAPMO-BArch, ZPA, J IV 2/2A/3196, Honecker's preparatory notes for a planned conversation with Brezhnev, February/March 1971.

123 SAPMO-BArch, ZPA, J IV 2/2A/3196, 'Zur Korrektur'.

124 G. Naumann, E. Trümpler, *Von Ulbricht zu Honecker. 1970 – ein Krisenjahr der DDR* (Berlin, 1990), pp. 47–8.

125 Compare articles 9 and 18 of the 1968 and 1974 constitutions, *Verfassungen*, pp. 495, 500, 501, 520, 522, 523.

126 M. Sodaro, *Moscow, Germany and the West from Khrushchev to Gorbachev* (London, 1991), p. 165. See also A. J. Nicholls, *The Bonn Republic. West German democracy, 1945–1990* (London, 1997), pp. 229, 231; P. Pulzer, *German politics, 1945–1995* (Oxford, 1995), p. 116. These accounts tally with the perceptions of contemporaries. See C. Stern, 'Der meistgehaßte, meistunterschätzte Mann. Walter Ulbricht – was dem DDR-Gründer gelang, wo der Staatsratsvorsitzender scheiterte',

Der Spiegel, 20 (10.5.71), 34–49; H. Weber, 'Walter Ulbricht überlebte sich selbst' (August 1973) in H. Weber *Aufbau und Fall einer Diktatur. Kritische Beiträge zur Geschichte der DDR* (Köln, 1991), 126–8, p. 128; A. Grosser, *Geschichte Deutschlands seit 1945. Eine Bilanz* (München, 1977), p. 389.

127 T. Garton Ash, *In Europe's name. Germany and the divided continent* (London, 1993), pp. 55–6.

128 Compare Ulbricht's speech to 7 CC plenum (*ND*, 6.12.64) with that of Honecker (*ND*, 5.12.64). Cited in H. Lippmann, *Honecker and the new politics of Europe* (London, 1973), pp. 197–8.

129 Interview with Hager, 6.4.94.

130 SAPMO-BArch, ZPA, J IV 2/202/88/1.

131 Sodaro, *Moscow*, p. 83. More sensational still was the offer to include other parties in the dialogue. See 'Offener Brief des Zentralkomitees der Sozialistischen Einheitspartei Deutschlands an die Delegierten des Dortmunder Parteitages der SPD und an alle Mitglieder und Freunde der Sozialdemokratie in Westdeutschland (7 February 1966)', *Dokumente der Sozialistischen Einheitspartei Deutschlands. Beschlüsse und Erklärungen des Zentralkomitees sowie seines Politbüros und seines Sekretariats*, XI (Berlin-Ost, 1969), 14–26; pp. 24–5. See also 'Antwort des Zentralkomitees der Sozialistischen Einheitspartei Deutschlands auf die "Offene Antwort" des Parteivorstandes der SPD an die Delegierten des Dortmunder Parteitages der SPD und an alle Mitglieder und Freunde der Sozialdemokratie in Westdeutschland (25 March 1966)', *ibid.*, 32–47; p. 46. At the beginning of April Manfred Gerlach, general secretary of the GDR's Liberal Democratic Party, proposed to hold talks with the leader of the West German Free Democrats (FDP), Erich Mende.

132 Cited in Sodaro, *Moscow,* p. 83.

133 SAPMO-BArch, ZPA, J IV 2/202/88/1.

134 Sodaro, *Moscow*, p. 83; Weber, *DDR*, p. 310.

135 SAPMO-BArch, ZPA, IV A 2/2.028/14. Ulbricht's letters to PB member Albert Norden, 31.3.66 and 2.4.66.

136 Interview with Hager, 1.12.92. In a speech at the Evangelical Academy in Tutzing on 15 July 1963, Egon Bahr proclaimed the SPD's new policy of *Ostpolitik*. It was not until 1969, however, (when the SPD–FDP coalition came to power in Bonn) that it was fully implemented.

137 Interview with Hager, 1.12.92. Winzer allegedly made this famous remark in response to Bahr's Tutzing speech. Garton Ash, *In Europe's name*, p. 204.

138 SAPMO-BArch, ZPA, IV 2/1/342. Ulbricht's speech to 12 CC plenum, 27.–28.4.66. As early as December 1965 he had called for restraint when criticizing SPD positions. See SAPMO-BArch, ZPA, IV 2/1/337. Ulbricht's report to 11 CC plenum.

139 SAPMO-BArch, ZPA, IV 2/1/342. Dahlem's speech to 12 CC plenum.

140 SAPMO-BArch, ZPA, IV 2/1/342 and ZPA, IV 2/1/343, see speeches of Honecker, Hoffmann, Matern and Norden.

141 SAPMO-BArch, ZPA, IV 2/1/342.

142 SAPMO-BArch, ZPA, J IV 2/2–1060. PB meeting, 1.6.66: 'The information about comrade Ulbricht's comments concerning continuation of the campaign for an exchange of views between SED and SPD is taken note of.' A week later Ulbricht instructed the CC's Western department to begin work on another letter to 'members of the SPD, workers, farmers and intellectuals in the Federal Republic'. See SAPMO-BArch, ZPA, J IV 2/2–1061. PB meeting, 7.6.66.

143 SAPMO-BArch, ZPA, J IV 2/2/1064. This would seem to cast doubt on the contemporary view that Ulbricht's offer of dialogue with the SPD was merely a propaganda stunt. See, for example, 'Die zweite Phase des Dialogs. Argumentation der SED nach der Absage des Redneraustausches', *SBZ-Archiv*, 14 (July 1966), 211–13; p. 212.

144 Ulbricht had first mooted the idea in early 1957. See also Ulbricht, 'Das Programm des Sozialismus', p. 249; and SAPMO-BArch, ZPA, IV 2/1/342. Ulbricht's closing speech to 12 CC plenum, April 1966.

145 Interview with Berger, 14.12.92. See also Berger, 'vorbei regierte'.

146 Interview with Wolf, 13.10.92.

147 SAPMO-BArch, ZPA, J IV 2/2/1064. PB meeting, 28.6.66. See also SAPMO-BArch, ZPA, J IV 2/202/88/1. Letter from SED leadership to Brandt, 30.6.66. SED representatives could have been prosecuted for shooting GDR refugees as they fled to the West.

148 I. Spittmann, 'Die Niederlage im Redneraustausch', *SBZ-Archiv*, 13 (July 1966), pp. 193–4.

149 Interview with Hager, 6.4.94. There is nothing in the primary sources to corroborate or contradict Hager's testimony. It is significant, however, that the speaker exchange was called off shortly before the summit of Soviet and East European leaders in Bucharest. Spittmann's implication that Moscow was the dynamic force behind the dialogue is undermined both by Hager's testimony and the new evidence pertaining to Ulbricht's position. See Spittmann, 'Die Niederlage', p. 194.

150 The rise of political non-conformism (particularly on the left) in the FRG at this time persuaded some politicians in Bonn that new legislation was required to protect the liberal democratic order.

151 The Grand Coalition was formed on 1.12.66. Dr Kurt Georg Kiesinger (CDU) became chancellor; Willy Brandt (SPD) foreign minister and deputy chancellor.

152 SAPMO-BArch, ZPA, J IV 2/202/735.

153 SAPMO-BArch, ZPA, J IV 2/202/1. ' "Zu einigen wichtigen Aspekten der Lage", 17. November 1966'.

154 SAPMO-BArch, ZPA, J IV 2/202/88/1. Ulbricht's letter to Brandt, 22.11.66.

155 SAPMO-BArch, ZPA, J IV 2/201/1094. Record of conversation between Ulbricht and Semyonov, 17.1.67.

156 Ulbricht, 'Die gesellschaftliche Entwicklung', pp. 72–3.

157 SAPMO-BArch, ZPA, J IV 2/201/1094. Record of conversation between Ulbricht and Semyonov, 17.1.67.

158 SAPMO-BArch, ZPA, IV 2/1/342.

159 Interview with Hager, 6.4.94.

160 For more detail on the NPD, see Nicholls, *The Bonn Republic*, pp. 188–9.

161 According to Ludz, 'young technocrats' were more likely than 'old communists' to support improved relations between the two German states. Ludz, *GDR*, pp. 47–8, 50.

162 Berger, 'vorbei regierte'. See also S. Bollinger, 'Die DDR kann nicht über Stalins Schatten springen. Reformen im Kalten Krieg – SED zwischen NÖS und Prager Frühling', *Hefte zur DDR-Geschichte*, 5 (Berlin, 1993), p. 47.

163 SAPMO-BArch, ZPA, J IV 2/2A/3196. Record of Brezhnev's remarks during meeting with SED delegation.

164 Hermann Axen, cited in A. James McAdams, *Germany divided. From the Wall to reunification.* (Princeton, 1993), p. 76.

165 Weber, *DDR.*, p. 310. The 'law concerning GDR state citizenship' was promulgated on 20.1.67.
166 In his government declaration of 12.4.67 the new Federal chancellor proposed '16 possibilities' for a relaxation of tensions between East and West Germany. Advocating the extensive development of 'human, economic and spiritual ties' with 'our compatriots in the other part of Germany', Kiesinger still refused to utter the syllables 'GDR', let alone recognize its existence.
167 McAdams, *Germany divided*, p. 77.
168 Ulbricht, 'Die gesellschaftliche Entwicklung', p. 68. He also proposed that the two German governments start negotiating to reduce tensions.
169 *Ibid.*, p. 69. In what must have been an indication of his misgivings about the emerging policy, Ulbricht told Semyonov that it was 'not easy' to temper the SED's all-German rhetoric and described attempts to do so as 'a huge ideological undertaking'. Semyonov, by contrast, commended the new party line. See SAPMO-BArch, ZPA, J IV 2/201/1094. Record of a conversation between Ulbricht and Semyonov, 17.1.67. According to the Soviet diplomat Juli Kwizinski, Ulbricht was increasingly angered by Semyonov's enthusiasm for *Abgrenzung*. See W. S. Semjonow, *Von Stalin bis Gorbatschow. Ein halbes Jahrhundert in diplomatischer Mission 1939–1991* (Berlin, 1995), p. 394.
170 When Antonin Novotny was toppled from power on 5.1.68, he was succeeded by a little known Slovak called Alexander Dubcek. The reform process initiated shortly thereafter quickly gained momentum, culminating in the invasion of Czechoslovakia by Soviet and Warsaw Pact troops on the night of 20 August.
171 SAPMO-BArch, ZPA, J IV 2/2 A/3196. 'Zur Korrektur'.
172 SAPMO-BArch, ZPA, IV 2/1/385. Ulbricht's speech to 8 CC plenum, 23.8.68.
173 Bollinger, 'Reformen im Kalten Krieg', p. 20.
174 Interview with Berger, 7.10.92.
175 *Ibid.*
176 On 5.4.68 the CC of the CPC adopted an Action Programme setting out its plans for reform.
177 Cited in L. Prieß, M. Wilke, 'Die DDR und die Besetzung der Tschechoslowakei am 21. August 1968', *APZ*, B36 (28.8.92), 26–34; p. 30.
178 *Ibid.*, p. 31. The letter contained an oblique but ominous warning: 'the determined defence of the socialist order in Czechoslovakia is our task as well as yours'.
179 SAPMO-BArch, ZPA, J IV 2/2/1360, Bd. 1., Axen in PB meeting, 26.10.71.
180 The declaration contained three phrases which served to obfuscate rather than clarify the positions of the two sides. The first promised that each Communist Party 'would creatively solve the problems of further socialist development'; the second restated the principle of 'equality, preservation of sovereignty, national independence, [and] territorial inviolability'; but the third declared that the 'support, protection and strengthening' of Soviet bloc nations were the 'joint international duty' of all. See J. Hochman (ed.) *Hope dies last. The autobiography of Alexander Dubcek* (London, 1993), p. 170.
181 SAPMO-BArch, ZPA, IV 2/1/382, Ulbricht's speech to 7 CC plenum, 7.8.68.
182 In 1968 the SPD had proposed that the two German states exchange plenipotentiaries ('General-Bevollmächtigte') as a step towards improving relations. Chancellor Kiesinger, however, always insisted that contacts with East Germany stop short of official recognition (de facto or de jure). By taking up the SPD's proposal in his speech

of 9 August, Ulbricht hoped to drive a wedge between Brandt and Kiesinger who were still Grand Coalition partners at this time.

183 See Ulbricht's explanation in his speeches to 7 CC plenum, 7.8.68 (SAPMO-BArch, ZPA, IV 2/1/382) and 8 CC plenum, 23.8.68 (SAPMO-BArch, ZPA, IV 2/1/385).

184 Other historians have provided very different (but, given the paucity of primary sources, necessarily speculative) interpretations of Ulbricht's initiative. According to Sodaro 'the most plausible explanation seems to be that the SED chief floated the trade negotiation proposal in order to exert pressure on Moscow to invade Czechoslovakia'. Sodaro, *Moscow*, p. 122. McAdams claimed that the Bratislava agreement had isolated those calling for immediate intervention, forcing Ulbricht to don 'the uncharacteristic pose of a moderate, seemingly accommodating himself to a less than optimal situation'. A. James McAdams, *East Germany and détente. Building authority after the Wall* (Cambridge, 1985), p. 88. Moreton speculated that Ulbricht was under pressure from 'technocrats' and 'pragmatists' inside the SED. E. Moreton, *East Germany and the Warsaw alliance* (Colorado, 1978), p. 83. As we have seen, Ulbricht was the GDR's leading economic reformer and hardly needed to be pressured into taking radical initiatives. Wolfe suspected that, for a brief period after the Bratislava talks, the USSR considered establishing closer ties with Bonn as a way of sidetracking an improved West German – Czechoslovak relationship, and that Ulbricht's initiative must be seen in this context. T. Wolfe, *Soviet power and Europe, 1945–1970* (Baltimore, London, 1970), p. 416. This does not concord well with Axen's testimony below (see note 187). Others argued that the decision to invade had already been taken by 9 August and that Ulbricht's gesture was designed to trick the West into thinking that the crisis was over (a view refuted by documents recently discovered in Soviet archives; see note 194).

185 Cited in I. Spittmann, 'Die SED im Konflikt mit der CSSR', *DA*, 6 (September 1968), 663–9; p. 668. Preparations for a possible invasion had been underway for some time. The military presence on Czechoslovakia's borders (camouflaged as Warsaw Pact manoeuvres) had been increasing since the middle of June. During July and early August it escalated further.

186 *Ibid.*, p. 669. Also referred to in K. Dawisha, *The Kremlin and the Prague Spring* (London, 1984), p. 279.

187 SAPMO-BArch, ZPA, J IV 2/2/1360. Axen in PB meeting, 26.10.71.

188 Interview with Berger, 7.10.92.

189 According to an article in *ND* a week after the invasion, the talks represented 'a further attempt to induce the CPC leadership to implement the Bratislava declaration in the struggle against bourgeois ideology and anti-socialist forces'. 'Die ständige Eskalation der antisozialistischen und konterrevolutionären Entwicklung in der CSSR – eine Dokumentation', *ND* (25.8.68). Cited in P. Probst, 'Nach der Invasion', *DA*, 6 (September 1968), 669–71; p. 671.

190 Spittmann, 'Die SED', p. 668.

191 *Ibid.*

192 *Ibid.*

193 See 'Der Standpunkt der Deutschen Demokratischen Republik', *ND* (30.6.68). Cited in Probst, 'Nach der Invasion', p. 671.

194 W. Wolkow, 'Sowjetische Parteiherrschaft und Prager Frühling 1968', *APZ*, B 36 (28.8.92), 11–17; p. 16. Volkov's analysis is based on documents discovered in the former Soviet foreign ministry. See also Horst Sindermann's interview with *Der*

Spiegel 19 (7.5.90). Cited in W. Rehm, 'Neue Erkenntnisse über die Rolle der NVA bei der Besetzung der CSSR im August 1968', *DA*, 2 (5.3.91), 173–85; pp. 175–6.

195 R. Wenzke, 'Zur Beteiligung der NVA an der militärischen Operation von Warschauer-Pakt-Streitkräften gegen die CSSR 1968. Einige Ergänzungen zu einem Beitrag von Walter Rehm', *DA*, 11 (1991), 1179–86; p. 1185: 'It can be deduced from archive materials deposited in Potsdam and from questioning those involved at the time, that no NVA combat troops in the form of divisions or regiments marched directly into Czechoslovakia.'

196 Interview with Hager, 6.4.94. His testimony is supported by Berger (interviewed 7.10.92), Wolf (interviewed 13.10.92), Schürer (interviewed 5.11.92) and Neumann (interviewed 23.10.92). See also Rehm, 'Neue Erkenntnisse', p. 183; and R. Wenzke, *Prager Frühling – Prager Herbst. Zur Intervention der Warschauer-Pakt-Streitkräfte in der CSSR 1968. Fakten und Zusammenhänge* (Berlin, 1990).

197 Sindermann interviewed by *Der Spiegel* 19 (7.5.90). Cited in Rehm, 'Neue Erkenntnisse', p. 176. Reports in July 1968 that Ulbricht offered Czechoslovakia the services of his own army and police force to crush the counter-revolution in Prague cannot be substantiated. See Dawisha, *Kremlin*, pp. 184–5.

198 Sindermann interviewed by *Der Spiegel* 19 (7.5.90). Cited in Rehm, 'Neue Erkenntnisse', p. 176.

199 Interview with Neumann, 23.10.92.

200 For more detail on the precise nature of this assistance, see Wenzke, 'Einige Ergänzungen', pp. 1185–6.

201 See Dawisha, *Kremlin*. See also the memoirs of contemporaries; e.g. Hochman, *Dubcek*, pp. 141, 162, 170–1; Z. Mlynar, *Night frost in Prague. The end of humane socialism* (London, 1980), pp. 153, 155–6, 161–2, 167, 174.

202 SAPMO-BArch, ZPA, IV 2/1/385.

203 Interview with Neumann, 23.10.92.

204 Interview with Schürer, 5.11.92.

205 Interview with Berger, 7.10.92.

206 Interview with Schürer, 5.11.92.

207 Interview with Neumann, 23.10.92.

208 SAPMO-BArch, ZPA, J IV 2/202/345, Bd. 11. Brezhnev's letter to Ulbricht, 8.4.67.

209 SAPMO-BArch, ZPA, J IV 2/2/1360, Bd. 1. Axen in PB meeting, 26.10.71. See also SAPMO-BArch, ZPA, J IV 2/2A/3196. Records of conversations between Brezhnev and Honecker, 15 May, 28 July and 20 August 1970.

210 SAPMO-BArch, ZPA, J IV 2/2A/3196. Record of conversation between Honecker and Brezhnev, 20.8.70.

211 SAPMO-BArch, ZPA, J IV 2/2/1360, Bd. 1. In the PB on 26.10.71, Axen accused Ulbricht of 'underestimating' the danger of Maoism and 'overestimating' the SED's role as broker between China and the Soviet Union.

212 SAPMO-BArch, ZPA, J IV 2/2A – 1.403, PB meeting 18.11.69. Draft of Ulbricht's speech to 12 CC plenum.

213 *Ibid.*

214 Interviews with Hager, 1.12.92 and 6.4.94.

215 SAPMO-BArch, ZPA, J IV 2/2A/3196. Meeting of Soviet and SED leaders in Moscow, 2.12.69.

216 SAPMO-BArch, ZPA, IV 2/202/346, Bd. 12. Ulbricht's letter to Brezhnev, 20.11.69.

217 *Ibid.*

218 See McAdams, *Germany divided*, pp. 88, 92 and Sodaro, *Moscow*, pp. 151, 164–5.

219 SAPMO-BArch, ZPA, J IV 2/2A-1.405. PB meeting, 28.11.69; draft of Ulbricht's speech to Moscow conference of Warsaw Pact leaders, 3.12.69.

220 SAPMO-BArch, ZPA, J IV 2/2A/3196. Record of meeting at leadership's retreat in Döllnsee.

221 SAPMO-BArch, ZPA, J IV 2/2/1360, Bd. 1. PB meeting, 26.10.71. According to Axen, the entire PB opposed Ulbricht on this issue. During the meeting with SED leaders on 2.12.69, Brezhnev took issue with Ulbricht's proposal to set up 'missions' rather than embassies. See SAPMO-BArch, ZPA, J IV 2/2A/3196.

222 This new evidence casts doubt on the traditional view espoused by Sodaro in *Moscow*, p. 151: 'When the [West German] election results . . . became known, the Soviet leaders were barely able to conceal their satisfaction . . . Ulbricht adopted a considerably less conciliatory stance, re-emphasizing his demands for de jure recognition and stiffening his terms for a rapprochement between the two German states . . .'

223 SAPMO-BArch, ZPA, IV 2/1/402. Moscow conference of Warsaw Pact leaders, verbatim minutes. According to Brezhnev, 'every new paragraph' of Brandt's programme 'cancelled out the one before'.

224 SAPMO-BArch, ZPA, J IV 2/2A/3196. Meeting with SED delegation, 2.12.69. Podgorny (second in the CPSU hierarchy) strongly supported Brezhnev's line, asserting that the SPD represented 'no improvement'.

225 SAPMO-BArch, ZPA, IV 2/1/404. See speeches of Honecker, Stoph, Hoffmann and Mielke to 12 CC plenum. *Stasi* chief Mielke alleged that the new government was more determined than its predecessors to destabilize the GDR. Stoph declared that the real watchword of the Brandt–Scheel government was 'continuity' not 'renewal'. McAdams's conclusion that suddenly 'everyone from Erich Honecker to Willi Stoph to Walter Ulbricht himself seemed to be transformed into thoughtful, if qualified, supporters of the new Social–Liberal coalition' is not sustained by the evidence (McAdams, *Germany divided*, p. 88).

226 SAPMO-BArch, ZPA, J IV 2/2/1360, Bd. 1. Axen in PB meeting, 26.10.71.

227 The talks in Erfurt and Kassel seem to have occurred largely as a result of Ulbricht's independent initiative. This view is supported by McAdams in *Germany divided*, p. 89.

228 SAPMO-BArch, ZPA, J IV 2/2A/3196. Record of conversation between Brezhnev and Honecker, 15.5.70.

229 *Ibid.*

230 Interviews with Neumann, 23.10.92 and 6.4.94.

231 Willy Brandt interviewed by Timothy Garton Ash, 2.10.91. I am very grateful to Mr Garton Ash for this information.

232 SAPMO-BArch, ZPA, J IV 2/2A/3196. Record of a conversation between Honecker and Brezhnev in Moscow, 28.7.70.

233 Stern's verdict that Ulbricht feared 'an accelerated relaxation of tensions' is therefore unfounded. See Stern, 'meistgehaßte', p. 49.

234 SAPMO-BArch, ZPA, J IV 2/2/1360, Bd. 1. Axen in PB meeting, 26.10.71. According to one historian, Ulbricht was sceptical about the negotiations because of the USSR's apparent willingness to accept less than full diplomatic recognition of the GDR by the FRG. See T. Neumann, *Die Maßnahme. Eine Herrschaftsgeschichte der SED* (Reinbek bei Hamburg, 1991), p. 145.

235 SAPMO-BArch, ZPA, IV 2/1/408. Ulbricht's closing speech to 13 CC plenum, 9.–10.6.70.

236 Interview with Wolf, 13.10.92. In Wolf's opinion, Ulbricht regarded the Berlin Wall as a necessary but temporary phenomenon. Honecker, however, had come to regard it as a more or less permanent feature of the German landscape.

237 SAPMO-BArch, ZPA, IV 2/1/409.

238 Revised constitution of 1974, *Verfassungen*, pp. 519–40. In January 1989, only months before the collapse of communism in Eastern Europe, Honecker prophesied that the Berlin Wall would still be standing in fifty or even one hundred years time. Quoted in McAdams, *Germany divided*, p. 3.

239 SAPMO-BArch, ZPA, J IV 2/2/1360, Bd. 1. Axen in PB meeting, 26.10.71.

240 W. Ulbricht, 'Den Rechtsblock in der Bundesrepublik gemeinsam schlagen!', *ND* (17.7.70). Cited in Lippmann, *Honecker*, pp. 213–14.

241 SAPMO-BArch, ZPA, J IV 2/2/1360, Bd. 1. Axen in PB meeting, 26.10.71. No member of the PB challenged Axen's account.

242 McAdams, *Germany divided*, p. 90; Sodaro, *Moscow*, p. 168; M. Fulbrook, *The Fontana history of Germany 1918–1990. The divided nation* (London, 1991), p. 208; J. Staadt, 'Obst, Gemüse und Abführmittel. Das bizarre Ende der Ära Ulbricht vor 25 Jahren', *FAZ*, (2.5.96), 102, p. 13. Contemporaries believed that through this treaty the Soviets had annulled the so-called 'Ulbricht-doctrine' according to which full West German recognition of the GDR was the condition for the normalization of Bonn's relations with the Eastern bloc. See I. Spittmann, 'Warum Ulbricht stürzte', *DA*, 6 (1971), 568–9. The evidence, however, does not support this claim. Fulbrook's assertion that Ulbricht was deposed because of his resistance to Moscow's favoured line of rapprochement with the West requires qualification. See M. Fulbrook, *Anatomy of a dictatorship. Inside the GDR 1949–1989* (Oxford, 1995), p. 36.

243 As Garton Ash correctly observes 'it was only after Walter Ulbricht was replaced by Erich Honecker . . . that these negotiations began to bear fruit.' Garton Ash, *In Europe's name*, p. 127. Initially, however, the chief obstacle to progress was Brezhnev, not Ulbricht. See also McAdams, *Germany divided*, p. 79: 'only the removal of Ulbricht himself could allow for the kind of breakthrough that was finally achieved with the negotiation of the inter-German treaty in the summer and early fall of 1972.'

244 SAPMO-BArch, ZPA, J IV 2/202/347, Bd. 13. Ulbricht's letter to Brezhnev, 2.6.70. In his reply of 24.6.70, Brezhnev ignored Ulbricht's appeal for a new relationship with the West German SPD (see SAPMO-BArch, ZPA, J IV 2/202/347, Bd. 13). Ulbricht reiterated his support for the Moscow Treaty and inter-German rapprochement in a speech to district leaders in Leipzig (subsequently censored) on 21.11.70; SAPMO-BArch, ZPA, J NL 2/32. According to the recently released memoirs of the Soviet ambassador to West Germany, Valentin Falin, it was Honecker who opposed the Moscow Treaty. V. Falin, *Politische Erinnerungen* (Munich, 1993), p. 187.

245 SAPMO-BArch, ZPA, J IV 2/202/347, Bd. 13. Draft resolution, August/September 1970.

246 SAPMO-BArch, ZPA, J IV 2/202/347, Bd. 13. New censored copy passed on to the Soviets.

247 SAPMO-BArch, ZPA, J IV 2/2A/3196. Record of conversation between Honecker and Brezhnev, 28.7.70.

248 *Ibid*.

249 SAPMO-BArch, ZPA, J IV 2/2A/3196. Record of a conversation between Honecker and Brezhnev, 20.8.70.

250 *Ibid.*
251 SAPMO-BArch, ZPA, J IV 2/2A/3196. Ulbricht's speech to SED and CPSU delega-tions, 21.8.70.
252 SAPMO-BArch, ZPA, J IV 2/2A/3196. Brezhnev's remarks to SED and CPSU delega-tions, 21.8.70.
253 SAPMO-BArch, ZPA, J IV 2/2A – 1.464. PB meeting, 15.9.70. 'Zwischenbericht über den Stand der Vorbereitung und Durchführung des Umtausches der Parteidokumente'.
254 SAPMO-BArch, ZPA, J IV 2/2/1360, Bd. 1. Hager in PB meeting 26.10.71.
255 SAPMO-BArch, ZPA, J IV 2/2A/3196. Brezhnev's letter to Ulbricht, 21.10.70.
256 Ulbricht apparently wanted an agreement with the SPD without *Abgrenzung*. Interview with Hager, 6.4.94.
257 SAPMO-BArch, ZPA, J IV 2/2A/3196. Honecker's preparatory notes (drafted February/March 1971) for conversation with Brezhnev at 24 CPSU Congress, April 1971.
258 SAPMO-BArch, ZPA, IV 2/1/415. Ulbricht's closing speech to 14 CC plenum.
259 *Ibid.*
260 Berger, 'vorbei regierte'.
261 SAPMO-BArch, ZPA, IV 2/1/415. Mittag's speech to 14 CC plenum.
262 SAPMO-BArch, ZPA, IV 2/2.035/11.
263 *Ibid.*
264 SAPMO-BArch, ZPA, IV 2/1/420.
265 Interview with Berger, 7.10.92.
266 SAPMO-BArch, ZPA, J IV 2/2A/1.514. PB meeting, 20.5.71. See 'information about the meetings of the party and government delegations of the USSR and GDR on 18 May 1971 in Moscow'.
267 McAdams, *Germany divided*, p. 102.
268 Article 1, 1968 constitution,*Verfassungen*, p. 495.
269 Article 1, revised constitution of 1974, *Verfassungen*, p. 519.
270 See Article 8, 1968 constitution, *Verfassungen*, p. 499 and Article 8, revised constitu-tion of 1974, *Verfassungen*, p. 521.
271 Falin, *Erinnerungen*, p. 186.
272 Garton Ash, *In Europe's name*, p. 620.
273 See McAdams, *Germany divided*, p. 105.
274 SAPMO-BArch, ZPA, J IV 2/202/1. Soviet comments on SED politburo's draft report for 8 party congress, June 1971 (two documents). Emphasizing the need for a more nuanced assessment of the SPD, the Soviets wanted more attention paid to forces willing to reach agreement with the communist bloc.
275 SAPMO-BArch, ZPA, J IV 2/202/345, Bd. 11. 'Bemerkungen zum Dokument der deutschen Freunde über die internationale Lage und die Außenpolitik der DDR'. Brezhnev's letter to Ulbricht, 8.4.67.
276 *Ibid.*
277 It was supplemented by an all-German transit agreement on 17.12.71.
278 SAPMO-BArch, ZPA, J IV 2/2A – 1.481, Bd. 1. PB meeting, 30.11.70. Draft copy of Ulbricht's speech to the political advisory committee of the Warsaw Pact states.
279 SAPMO-BArch, ZPA, J IV 2/2A/1.514. PB meeting, 20.5.71. See 'information about the meetings of the party and government delegations of the USSR and GDR on 18 May 1971 in Moscow'.

280 Article 6, 1968 constitution, *Verfassungen*, p. 498.

281 Article 6, revised constitution of 1974, *Verfassungen*, p. 521.

282 Interview with Hager, 1.12.92.

283 Berger recalled Ulbricht's enormous energy and appetite for work in 1970–71. Interview with Berger, 4.9.92.

284 Lippmann, *Honecker*, p. 217.

285 Interview with Berger, 4.9.92. Neumann recalled Berger informing him of Ulbricht's doubts about Honecker's ability to lead the party in the age of the 'scientific-technological revolution'. Interview with Neumann, 16.10.92. Contemporary witnesses testify to Mittag boasting about a conversation with Ulbricht during which the latter proposed to nominate him as successor. Naumann, Trümpler, *Von Ulbricht zu Honecker*, p. 53.

286 See P. Przybylski, *Tatort Politbüro. Honecker, Mittag und Schalk-Golodkowski*, Vol. 2 (Berlin, 1992), p. 46.

287 Interview with Neumann, 16.10.92.

288 R. Andert, H. Herzberg, *Der Sturz. Erich Honecker im Kreuzverhör* (Berlin, Weimar, 1991), p. 271.

289 Interview with Neumann, 23.10.92.

290 Interview with Neumann, 16.10.92. Stoph was forced to resign as minister of defence after revelations that he had fought for the Nazis in World War Two.

291 SAPMO-BArch, ZPA, J IV 2/2/1360, Bd. 1. Norden's recollections in PB meeting, 26.10.71. His remarks were corroborated by Hager and Sindermann.

292 SAPMO-BArch, ZPA, J IV 2/2A/1.453. PB meeting, 7.7.70.

293 SAPMO-BArch, ZPA, J IV 2/2A/3196. Record of conversation between Honecker and Brezhnev in Moscow, 28.7.70.

294 SAPMO-BArch, ZPA, J IV 2/2A/3196. Record of consultations between CPSU and SED delegations in Moscow, 21.8.70.

295 Interview with Wolf, 13.10.92.

296 Interview with Neumann, 16.10.92.

297 Przybylski incorrectly claims that fourteen out of the twenty-one members and candidate members signed. See P. Przybylski, *Tatort Politbüro. Die Akte Honecker*, Vol. 1, p. 110.

298 SAPMO-BArch, ZPA, J IV 2/2A/3196.

299 Przybylski, *Tatort Politbüro*, p. 110.

300 Andert, Herzberg, *Der Sturz*, p. 272.

301 One bone of contention was apparently Ulbricht's close co-operation with Mittag in compiling *The political economy of socialism and its application in the GDR*. Interview with Neumann, 16.10.92.

302 Interview with Neumann, 16.10.92.

303 By Ebert's own admission, his relationship with Ulbricht had never been very warm. SAPMO-BArch, ZPA, J IV 2/2/1360, Bd. 1. PB meeting, 26.10.71.

304 Interview with Neumann, 16.10.92.

305 *Ibid.*

306 SAPMO-BArch, ZPA, J IV 2/2A/3196.

307 Andert, Herzberg, *Der Sturz*, p. 272.

308 SAPMO-BArch, ZPA, J IV 2/2A/3196. Honecker's notes for a planned conversation with Brezhnev at 24 party congress of CPSU. Probably written at the end of February/early March 1971.

309 Interview with Neumann, 23.10.92.
310 SAPMO-BArch, ZPA, J IV 2/2/1325. PB meeting, 16.2.71.
311 SAPMO-BArch, ZPA, J IV 2/2/1332. Extraordinary PB meeting, 26.3.71.
312 SAPMO-BArch, ZPA, J IV 2/2/1360, Bd. 1. Ulbricht in PB meeting, 26.10.71.
313 SAPMO-BArch, ZPA, J IV 2/2/1332. Extraordinary PB meeting, 26.3.71.
314 Naumann, Trümpler, *Von Ulbricht zu Honecker*, p. 53. Also see Przybylski, *Die Akte Honecker*, p. 114.
315 See also Honecker's comments in Andert, Herzberg, *Der Sturz*, p. 272.
316 SAPMO-BArch, ZPA, J IV 2/2/1334. PB meeting, 15.4.71.
317 McAdams, *Germany divided*, p. 92.
318 SAPMO-BArch, ZPA, J IV 2/2/1335. PB meeting, 20.4.71.
319 W. Leonhard, *Das kurze Leben der DDR. Berichte und Kommentare aus vier Jahrzehnten* (Stuttgart, 1990), p. 145.
320 SAPMO-BArch, ZPA, J IV 2/2/1336. PB meeting, 27.4.71.
321 SAPMO-BArch, ZPA, J IV 2/2/1337. PB meeting, 11.5.71.
322 SAPMO-BArch, ZPA, J IV 2/2A/1.514. PB meeting, 20.5.71. 'Information über das Treffen der Partei- und Regierungsdelegationen der UdSSR und der DDR am 18. Mai 1971 in Moskau'.
323 Lippmann, *Honecker*, pp. 215–16.
324 Janson, *Totengräber der DDR*, pp. 56–7.
325 SAPMO-BArch, ZPA, J IV 2/2/1339. PB meeting, 1.6.71.
326 SAPMO-BArch, ZPA, IV A 2/2.028/3. Norden's letter to Honecker, 3.6.71.
327 SAPMO-BArch, ZPA, J IV 2/2/1340. PB meeting, 8.6.71.
328 SAPMO-BArch, ZPA, J IV 2/2/1360, Bd. 20. Doctors report, Berlin, 17.6.71.
329 SAPMO-BArch, ZPA, J IV 2/2/1360, Bd. 20. Doctors report, 19.6.71.
330 Przybylski, *Honecker, Mittag und Schalck-Golodkowski*, p. 32.
331 SAPMO-BArch, ZPA, J IV 2/2/1360, Bd. 1. See speeches of Tisch, Axen and Lamberz at PB meeting, 26.10.71.
332 Interview with Neumann, 23.10.92.
333 SAPMO-BArch, ZPA, J IV 2/2/1360, Bd. 1. Lamberz in PB meeting, 26.10.71.
334 *Protokoll der Verhandlungen des VIII. Parteitages der Sozialistischen Einheitspartei Deutschlands*, I (Berlin-Ost, 1971), p. 104.
335 *Ibid.*, p. 287.
336 P. Ludz, 'Continuity and change since Ulbricht', *POC*, 2 (March–April, 1972), 56–67; p. 66.
337 SAPMO-BArch, ZPA, J IV 2/2A/3196. Honecker's letter to CPSU leadership (precise date unknown, but contents suggest it was written shortly before PB meeting of 26.10.71).
338 SAPMO-BArch, ZPA, J IV 2/2/1360, Bd. 1. Ulbricht in PB meeting, 26.10.71.
339 See Ulbricht's letter of complaint to Brezhnev, 12.12.72. SAPMO-BArch, ZPA, J IV 2/2/1360, Bd. 20.
340 SAPMO-BArch, ZPA, J IV 2/2/1360, Bd. 1. Ulbricht and Stoph in PB meeting, 26.10.71.
341 SAPMO-BArch, ZPA, J IV 2/2/1360, Bd. 1. Ulbricht in PB meeting, 26.10.71.
342 SAPMO-BArch, ZPA, J IV 2/2/1360, Bd. 1. Krolikowski in PB meeting, 26.10.71.
343 SAPMO-BArch, ZPA, J IV 2/2/1360, Bd. 1. Ulbricht in PB meeting, 26.10.71.
344 *Ibid.*
345 SAPMO-BArch, ZPA, J IV 2/2/1360, Bd. 1. Axen in PB meeting, 26.10.71.

346 SAPMO-BArch, ZPA, J IV 2/2/1360, Bd. 1. Ulbricht in PB meeting, 26.10.71.

347 *Ibid.*

348 SAPMO-BArch, ZPA, J IV 2/2/1360, Bd. 1. Mückenberger in PB meeting, 26.10.71.

349 SAPMO-BArch, ZPA, J IV 2/2/1360, Bd. 1. Ulbricht in PB meeting, 26.10.71.

350 SAPMO-BArch, ZPA, J IV 2/2/1360, Bd. 1. Stoph in PB meeting, 26.10.71. Hager accused Ulbricht of merely paying lip service to the resolutions of the 8 party congress.

351 SAPMO-BArch, ZPA, J IV 2/2/1360, Bd. 1. Lamberz in PB meeting, 26.10.71.

352 Cited in K. W. Fricke, *Opposition und Widerstand in der DDR. Ein politischer Report* (Köln, 1984), p. 152.

353 SAPMO-BArch, ZPA, J IV 2/2/1360, Bd. 1. Ulbricht in PB meeting, 26.10.71.

354 SAPMO-BArch, ZPA, J IV 2/2/1360, Bd. 1. Stoph in PB meeting, 26.10.71.

355 SAPMO-BArch, ZPA, J IV 2/2/1360, Bd. 1. Axen and Stoph in PB meeting, 26.10.71.

356 SAPMO-BArch, ZPA, J IV 2/2/1360, Bd. 1. Krolikowski in PB meeting, 26.10.71.

357 SAPMO-BArch, ZPA, J IV 2/2/1360, Bd. 1. Halbritter in PB meeting, 26.10.71.

358 SAPMO-BArch, ZPA, J IV 2/2/1360, Bd. 1. Sindermann in PB meeting, 26.10.71.

359 SAPMO-BArch, ZPA, J IV 2/2/1360, Bd. 1. PB meeting, 26.10.71. See also Ulbricht's letter of complaint to Brezhnev, 12.12.72, SAPMO-BArch, ZPA, J IV 2/2/1360, Bd. 20: 'In 1972 there were systematic attempts to release me from my responsibilities as chairman of the council of state and to push comrade Ebert into my position.'

360 SAPMO-BArch, ZPA, J IV 2/2/1360, Bd. 1. Ebert in PB meeting, 26.10.71. His remarks were echoed by Axen.

361 SAPMO-BArch, ZPA, J IV 2/2/1360, Bd. 1. Mückenberger in PB meeting, 26.10.71;

362 SAPMO-BArch, ZPA, J IV 2/2A/3196. Honecker's letter to CPSU leadership (October 1971, precise date unknown). The alleged comments were apparently made in the course of a private conversation between Ulbricht and Rodenberg (member of CC and council of state) before being reported to Honecker by the latter. In a letter to Rodenberg dated 23.10.71, Ulbricht denied making the remarks (SAPMO-BArch, ZPA, J IV 2/2/3196).

363 SAPMO-BArch, ZPA, J IV 2/2/1360, Bd. 1. Ulbricht in PB meeting, 26.10.71. If we can rely on Halbritter, the word he had actually used was 'enemy'. SAPMO-BArch, ZPA, J IV 2/2/1360, Bd. 1. Halbritter in PB meeting, 26.10.71.

364 See 'Notiz Werner Krolikowskis "Über das Verhältnis von Erich Honecker und Günter Mittag" vom 12. November 1980'. Cited in Przybylski, *Honecker, Mittag und Schalck-Golodkowski*, pp. 353–7; p. 356: 'At first Erich Honecker had him on his expulsion list. And before the 8 party congress many comrades in the politburo (Stoph, Verner, Axen, Lamberz, Hager, Grüneberg, etc.) told Honecker that Günter Mittag did not belong in the politburo. Erich Honecker agreed with these comrades but played his special game, because he knew that Günter Mittag would be his unscrupulous servant. At his hunting lodge and in the presence of W. Stoph, Erich Honecker took Günter Mittag to task and presented him with the alternative: either break with W. Ulbricht and serve him or fly out of the politburo. After that Günter Mittag decided in favour of Honecker, but hypocritically continued to stand by Ulbricht during his final period as 1 secretary of the central committee.'

365 SAPMO-BArch, ZPA, J IV 2/2/1360, Bd. 1. Mittag in PB meeting, 26.10.71.

366 SAPMO-BArch, ZPA, J IV 2/2/1360, Bd. 1. Neumann in PB meeting, 26.10.71.

367 SAPMO-BArch, ZPA, J IV 2/2/1360, Bd. 1. Ulbricht in PB meeting, 26.10.71.

368 SAPMO-BArch, ZPA, J IV 2/2/1360, Bd. 1. PB meeting, 26.10.71. See also Ulbricht's

letter of complaint to Brezhnev, 12.12.72 (SAPMO-BArch, ZPA, J IV 2/2/1360, Bd. 20).

369 Fricke, *Opposition und Widerstand*, pp. 152–3.
370 Oldenburg, *Konflikt und Konfliktregelung*, p. 81.
371 SAPMO-BArch, ZPA, J IV 2/2/1360, Bd. 1. PB meeting, 26.10.71.
372 SAPMO-BArch, ZPA, J NL 2/32. Ulbricht's letter to Honecker, 23.11.71.
373 SAPMO-BArch, ZPA, J IV 2/2/1360, Bd. 20. Ulbricht's letter of complaint to Brezhnev, 12.12.72.
374 SAPMO-BArch, ZPA, J IV 2/2/1360, Bd. 20. W. Ulbricht, 'Georgi Dimitroff – der Begründer der neuen Strategie und Taktik der kommunistischen Weltbewegung'.
375 SAPMO-BArch, ZPA, J IV 2/2/1360, Bd. 20. Verner's letter to Ulbricht, 17.3.72.
376 SAPMO-BArch, ZPA, J IV 2/2/1360, Bd. 20. Ulbricht's letter to SED PB, 20.3.72.
377 Garton Ash, *In Europe's name*, p. 621.
378 SAPMO-BArch, ZPA, J IV 2/2/1360, Bd. 20. Brezhnev's letter to Ulbricht, 29.6.72.
379 SAPMO-BArch, ZPA, J IV 2/2/1360, Bd. 20. Ulbricht's letter to Honecker, 30.6.72.
380 SAPMO-BArch, ZPA, J IV 2/2/1360, Bd. 21. 'Bericht über ein Gespräch des Genossen Ulbricht mit dem Mitglied des Politbüros der NFO und Minister des Innern der Volksdemokratischen Republik Jemen, Mutee'a, am 17. Mai 1972'.
381 SAPMO-BArch, ZPA, J NL 2/32. 'Gespräch bei der Akkreditierung des Botschafters von Uganda, Herrn Ondoga, am 12.4.73'.
382 SAPMO-BArch, ZPA, J IV 2/2/1360, Bd. 21. Tisch's letter to Honecker, 26.7.72.
383 SAPMO-BArch, ZPA, J IV 2/2/1360, Bd. 21. Mewis's letter to Honecker, 1.9.72. Mewis was Dahlem's nephew.
384 SAPMO-BArch, ZPA, J IV 2/2/1360, Bd. 21. 'Information zur Veranstaltung mit sowjetischen Genossen im Gästehaus der Regierung in Dierhagen, 30. Juni 1972.'
385 SAPMO-BArch, ZPA, J IV 2/2/1360, Bd. 21. G. Zimmermann to Honecker. 'Information über das Gespräch mit Genossen Ulbricht und Gattin vom 22.8.72.'
386 SAPMO-BArch, ZPA, J IV 2/2A/3196. Ulbricht's letter to Honecker, 7.11.72.
387 SAPMO-BArch, ZPA, J IV 2/2A/1.636. PB meeting, 7.10.72. 'Beschluß zum Ergebnis der Verhandlungen zwischen Staatssekretär Genossen Dr M. Kohl und Staatsekretär E. Bahr.' Eventually discussed as point 4, Ulbricht's letter of protest was now point 1.
388 SAPMO-BArch, ZPA, J IV 2/2A/3196. Ulbricht's letter to Honecker, 7.11.72.
389 Ulbricht enclosed with his letter a typed-up copy of preparatory notes for the speech.
390 SAPMO-BArch, ZPA, J IV 2/2/1360, Bd. 20. Ulbricht's letter to Brezhnev, 12.12.72.
391 *Ibid.*
392 *Ibid.*
393 *Ibid.*
394 J. S. Davidovitch, *Ernst Thälmann. Seiten seines Lebens und Kampfes* (Berlin, 1971).
395 SAPMO-BArch, ZPA, J IV 2/2A/1659. Ulbricht's letter to PB, 2.2.73.
396 SAPMO-BArch, ZPA, J IV 2/2/1433. PB meeting, 6.2.73.
397 SAPMO-BArch, ZPA, J IV 2/2/1360, Bd. 20. Ulbricht's letter to PB, 24.5.73.
398 Leonhard, *Das kurze Leben der DDR*, p. 157.
399 A. McElvoy, *The saddled cow. East Germany's life and legacy* (London, 1993), p. 82.
400 Naumann, Trümpler, *Von Ulbricht zu Honecker*, p. 55.

Conclusion

Contrary to the image it liked to present of itself, the SED leadership between 1946 and 1973 was no monolith. During the late 1940s, there were disagreements over Stalinization, the type of socialist system suitable for Germany and ways to facilitate reunification with the Western zones. The 'national question' continued to be a controversial issue in the 1950s, which also saw arguments over Ulbricht's personality cult, the dictatorial leadership methods of the SED, the lack of internal party democracy, and sectarianism towards the bloc parties and mass organizations. But the main source of conflict was the tempo of socialist development, and this was reflected in different approaches to the economy, the Church, the peasantry, the bourgeoisie, the working class and the intelligentsia. The steady flight of refugees to the West persuaded some in the leadership that a more moderate brand of politics was required. Major issues of contention during the 1960s and early 1970s were economic reform and policy towards West Germany. After Ulbricht's overthrow in 1971, the Economic System of Socialism (ESS) was disbanded and plans for an immediate rapprochement with the Federal Republic shelved. Thereafter, negotiations with Bonn were linked to a policy of *Abgrenzung*, designed to stress ideological, political, socio-economic and cultural differences between the two German states.

Different shades of opinion on the German question must be placed in the context of Moscow's *Deutschlandpolitik* between 1946 and 1973. There can be little doubt that Stalin ultimately aimed to subjugate the whole of Germany to communist control. In the medium term, however, he worked for the creation of a united, 'democratic' and 'peace-loving' German state based on a radical interpretation of the Potsdam Agreement. This, according to the Soviet interpretation, meant placing draconian restrictions on monopoly capitalism. A separate GDR – although it was never ruled out – was considered the least favourable scenario. In return for German neutrality and Western economic assistance, Beria might have been prepared to sacrifice the GDR altogether. Whether or not this is true, the rest of the Soviet leadership firmly opposed such a policy. While Ulbricht's main priority between 1949 and 1961 was to consolidate the GDR as a separate socialist state, Ackermann, Dahlem, Grotewohl, Herrnstadt and

Schirdewan were concerned not to lose sight of the all-German perspective. Unlike Ulbricht and his close associates, they advocated a more active policy towards West Germany. From the mid-1950s on, the Soviet Union came to accept the existence of two German states. Given this situation, Ulbricht's conversion to inter-German dialogue during the 1960s initially aroused suspicions in the Kremlin.

Traditional assumptions about why Ulbricht was deposed in 1971 require revision. Until recently, he was viewed as an unreconstructed Stalinist determined to block moves towards détente in Europe. These were not, however, the reasons for his downfall. During the 1960s, he showed himself to be an innovative, creative but also extremely unrealistic leader prepared to adopt a high-risk strategy in pursuit of his goals. Both at home and abroad he revealed a remarkable ability to embrace new ideas and adapt to a changing environment. The verdict of one historian that, 'in many respects, Ulbricht was more conservative than Brezhnev'[1] is not borne out by the evidence. Unlike most communist leaders, Ulbricht became more inclined to experiment as he grew older.

Recognizing the importance of the 'scientific-technological revolution', Ulbricht significantly modified the Stalinist model of centralized command management after 1963. His pioneering programme of economic reform attempted to combine plan and market by circumscribing the central planning bureaucracy and granting factory managements a degree of autonomy. Profit and limited forms of private and semi-private ownership were also legitimized. His fanciful aim of 'overtaking' the Federal Republic led to serious economic problems which played into the hands of those in the leadership who wanted to jettison the reforms. Although willing to refine the political system and mitigate some of its worst features, Ulbricht never countenanced its democratization. With regard to foreign policy, his goal was to further the interests of the GDR and achieve the speedy reunification of Germany as a socialist state. Without waiting for Moscow, he pursued links with the SPD and rapprochement with Bonn. On the issue of West Berlin, however, he continued to adopt an intransigent attitude.

Ulbricht's policies during the 1960s must be seen in the context of the new situation in East Germany after the building of the Berlin Wall. Once the escape route to the West had been sealed, the GDR achieved stability and reform became a viable option. A combination of economic crisis, the need to placate an alienated population, the beginnings of a reform debate in the USSR and rising living standards in West Germany persuaded Ulbricht that a 'new economic system' was required. His policy of rapprochement with the SPD was partly a response to Brandt's *Ostpolitik*, partly an attempt to gain a foothold in the FRG. It might also have been prompted by economic considerations and by the rise of the neo-Nazi NPD in the Federal Republic. Much to the chagrin of the Soviet Union and other East bloc countries, he soon began propagating the GDR as a model for socialism in Europe.

The experiences of party leaders before 1945 influenced but did not determine their later political responses. Dahlem and Merker had emigrated to the West and this certainly exacerbated their disagreements with Ulbricht. On the other hand, Zaisser, Herrnstadt, Ackermann, Oelßner and Wandel had spent the war in Moscow, yet ended up opposing the first secretary; Schirdewan and Honecker were political prisoners in Nazi Germany, yet became bitter rivals; Neumann and Honecker supported Ulbricht in the 1950s, yet neither had emigrated to the Soviet Union; 'old communists' such as Ulbricht, Dahlem, Merker and Hager disagreed on certain issues. The former social democrats Mückenberger and Ebert eventually became obedient Stalinists, Grotewohl and Buchwitz adopted more moderate positions, Fechner went to prison and Gniffke fled to the West. Those who had spent the war in Moscow often regarded 'western émigrés' and former social democrats with deep suspicion. Even so, the cohesion of all these groups was weakened by the process of Stalinization.

Ludz's division of the SED leadership into 'technocrats', 'dogmatists' and 'middlemen' was influential in changing Western attitudes towards the GDR in the 1960s. In the light of the evidence, however, his analysis requires qualification. The so-called 'technocrats' were never a clearly definable entity and if some SED leaders supported the New Economic System (NES) more than others, Günter Mittag (putative head of the 'technocrat' group) was one of the prime authors of its destruction. Only Ulbricht defended the economic reforms to the last and he was labelled a 'middleman' along with Willi Stoph, one of his fiercest critics. Ultimately, none of these typologies do justice to the vicissitudes and complexity of communist high politics in the Ulbricht era.

Despite its reputation as Moscow's most reliable and dependent ally, the East German leadership enjoyed greater room for manoeuvre *vis-à-vis* the Kremlin than has generally been assumed. Although it is well known that the SED and CPSU differed on some issues, the nature and extent of these disagreements may surprise some historians. Ulbricht and Tiul'panov's policies in the Soviet zone, for example, did not always concur with Stalin's medium-term agenda for postwar Germany. In 1952, Ulbricht apparently persuaded a reluctant Soviet dictator to approve the 'accelerated construction of socialism' in the GDR. A year later, he ignored the Kremlin's advice to moderate his domestic policies. He also appears to have instigated the purge of Dahlem in May 1953 and Merker was kept in prison long after the Soviets had lost any interest in his case. Zaisser and Herrnstadt seemed unaware of the power struggle being waged in the Kremlin during the spring and early summer of 1953. Claims that they were associated with Beria were probably fabricated by Ulbricht. Having circumscribed the New Course, the latter went on to resist de-Stalinization. In 1958 he purged Schirdewan, disregarding Khrushchev's advice. He also clashed with the Soviet leader over maize plantation and the GDR's attempt to 'overtake' the Federal Republic. In 1959–60 he took the initiative in collectivizing East German agriculture.

The NES seems to have been the brainchild of the SED and Ulbricht nurtured it throughout the 1960s in the face of Moscow's increasing scepticism. His political, economic and ideological schemes after 1963, his 'developed social system of socialism', his 'socialist human community', his new *Deutschlandpolitik*, his stances on West Berlin, China and the Prague Spring all deviated from official Soviet policy. Ulbricht remained SED first secretary until May 1971, but in the end it was Honecker (backed by a majority of politburo colleagues) who obtained Brezhnev's permission to depose him.

This greater room for manoeuvre requires us to pay more attention to indigenous factors in explaining how and why the various oppositions were defeated. The 'Ulbricht factor' is particularly significant in this regard. Rejected by the majority of his politburo colleagues and still bereft of Kremlin backing three weeks after the June 1953 uprising, Ulbricht used all the weapons at his disposal to reverse the situation. Displaying the consummate skill of a shrewd political operator, he apparently persuaded the Soviets to back him. He then neutralized his opponents in the politburo before presenting the central committee with scapegoats for the 17 June debacle. Between 1956 and 1958, Ulbricht intimidated the opposition, playing its different members off against each other and preventing the full rehabilitation of unjustly condemned leaders. This time, however, his critics were in a minority. During the 1960s, Ulbricht became the inflexible proponent of flexible policies. He overestimated his ability to defy Moscow and his politburo colleagues, thus paving the way for his own downfall.

Ulbricht's critics themselves must bear a heavy responsibility for the defeats inflicted on them between 1946 and 1958. Ultimately, they all proved willing to sacrifice their principles on the altar of party discipline. The maintenance of party unity was the first commandment of Stalinist politics. As one member of the central committee put it in 1953: 'For us, party discipline is the ultimate freedom!'[2] At the fifteenth central committee plenum in July of that year, Zaisser and Herrnstadt refrained from challenging Ulbricht on the grounds that this would have split the party and harmed the Soviet Union.[3] Five years later, Herrnstadt accused the leadership of taking advantage of his communist discipline to deny him rehabilitation. Nonetheless, he promised to die 'saluting the party' as Zaisser had done.[4] In 1958, Fritz Selbmann spoke in a similar vein, declaring that he would 'chop himself into pieces' for the sake of the party.[5]

Loyalty to the SED, however, was only one side of the equation. Persecution, ostracism, imprisonment, perhaps even death awaited those who deviated from the official line. Rehabilitations, if they occurred at all, were half-hearted and there is no example of any purged SED leader being restored to his previous position. Herrnstadt cited fear as one of the reasons why he did not contest the resolutions of the fifteenth central committee plenum.[6] None of Ulbricht's critics engaged in opposition lightly – the potential consequences were too severe. For all their courage and tenacity in criticizing certain aspects of SED rule, Ulbricht's critics between 1950 and 1958 never challenged the Stalinist system itself. Instead, they wanted to reform it. Trapped in its culture of subservience, they cut themselves off from opposition lower down in the party and in the population at large.

Ulbricht destroyed his critics by accusing them of 'factionalism', the most heinous crime in the party's rule book. Contrary to the official SED version, however, the defeated oppositions examined above were rather loose, heterogeneous groupings. A lack of solidarity among their individual members helped Ulbricht consolidate his position. Grotewohl betrayed the former social democrats, Ackermann and Dahlem approved the expulsions of Gniffke and Merker. Schmidt, Ackermann and Jendretzky failed to support Zaisser and Herrnstadt who, in turn, helped destroy Fechner. Schirdewan condemned Dahlem, Dahlem condemned Schirdewan. Along with Oelßner, the latter was also instrumental in defaming Zaisser and Herrnstadt. Ulbricht was eventually deposed by a factional conspiracy in 1971. If his critics in the 1940s and 1950s had organized themselves in a similar fashion, their chances of deposing him would have been greater.

By comparison with purged communists in other Soviet bloc countries, disgraced SED leaders were treated relatively leniently. Although Merker and Fechner were sent to prison and some former social democrats to Siberia, show trials and executions did not in the end materialize. Zaisser and Herrnstadt were only expelled from the party. Ackermann, Schmidt, Jendretzky, Dahlem, Schirdewan, Wollweber, Oelßner, Wandel and Selbmann all remained inside the ranks of the SED.

In the early 1950s, preparations were under way to stage an East German show trial similar to those of Hungary, Bulgaria and Czechoslovakia. That it did not in the end take place can probably be attributed to five factors. First, the special status of the GDR within the communist bloc: The country still had an open border with the West and German reunification had not yet been ruled out. Second, the marked relaxation in Soviet policy following the death of Stalin. Third, the proclamation of the New Course in the GDR at Moscow's behest in June 1953. Fourth, the overthrow and execution of Beria, the Soviet interior minister whose agents had organized the purges across East-Central Europe. Fifth, the refusal of Merker and Dahlem to co-operate with attempts to frame them as 'imperialist agents'.

Claims that Ulbricht helped prevent the trial and execution of his rivals in the SED leadership are not supported by the evidence. A moderating influence may, however, have been exerted by Pieck, who intervened on behalf of Merker, Grotewohl, who spoke up for Ackermann, and Zaisser, who expressed misgivings about the Dahlem case. After 1953 there were no more show trials in East-Central Europe. The twentieth party congress of the CPSU in 1956 ensured that they remained a thing of the past.

Despite the straitjacket of Stalinist politics, conflict was a salient feature of the East German leadership under Ulbricht. There were a number of reasons for this. In the period until 1961, the communist system was in its formative years and the 'national question' still open. The GDR was in a state of continual crisis and this stimulated argument over the future direction of policy. Another factor was Ulbricht's style of leadership: During the 1940s and 1950s he repeatedly provoked criticism with his sectarian and dictatorial approach to government. In the

1960s, it was his determination to pursue his own agenda in defiance of the Kremlin and his politburo colleagues that aroused controversy.

From a post-1989 perspective one is bound to ask whether any of the defeated oppositions explored in this book could have built a better East Germany. The question is, of course, unanswerable. Other communist states which did introduce reforms ultimately fared no better. For the SED, however, such attempts were especially fraught with dangers due to the magnetism of the Federal Republic. They might always have triggered a revolution from below and the collapse of communist rule. Paradoxically then, Stalinism was both the lifeblood and the wasting disease of the GDR.

Notes

1 M. Sodaro, *Moscow, Germany and the West from Khrushchev to Gorbachev* (London, 1991), p. 28. Neumann's description of Ulbricht as an 'unimaginative apparatchik' also requires revision. T. Neumann, *Die Maßnahme. Eine Herrschaftsgeschichte der SED* (Reinbek bei Hamburg, 1991), p. 138.

2 SAPMO-BArch, ZPA, IV 2/1/120. Johannes R. Becher's speech to 15 CC plenum, 24.–26.7.53.

3 N. Stulz-Herrnstadt (ed.) R. Herrnstadt, *Das Herrnstadt-Dokument* (Reinbek bei Hamburg, 1990), pp. 158, 163.

4 SAPMO-BArch, ZPA, IV 2/4/392. Herrnstadt's letter to Ulbricht, 28.11.59. Also cited in V. Herrnstadt, 'Parteidisziplin hat Menschen kaputt gemacht', *Mitteldeutsche Zeitung* (27.4.90), 4.

5 SAPMO-BArch, ZPA, IV 2/1/193. Selbmann's speech to 35 CC plenum, 3.–6.2.58.

6 N. Stulz-Herrnstadt, *Das Herrnstadt-Dokument*, p. 158.

Appendix: short biographies

Short biographies of important characters whose lives are not summarized in the text

Axen, Hermann   Born March 1916 in Leipzig. Member of KJV, 1932. Jailed, 1935. Emigrated to France, 1938. Moved to USSR, 1939. Imprisoned in Vernet concentration camp (France) and Auschwitz, 1940–42. Co-founder of FDJ, 1946. Secretary of central council of FDJ until 1949. Member of CC and CC secretary for agitation, 1950. Second SED secretary for *Bezirk* Berlin, 1953–56. Chief editor of *ND*, 1956–66. Candidate member of PB, 1963; full member, 1970. After February 1966, CC secretary responsible for relations with fraternal parties. Expelled from party, December 1989. Died 1992.

Ebert, Friedrich   Born 1894 in Bremen. Son of the first president of Weimar Republic. Training as a printer. Member of SPD, 1913. Soldier, 1915–18. Editor of *Vorwärts* and *Sozialdemokratischer Pressedienst*, 1919–25. Member of *Reichstag*, 1928–33. Imprisoned for eight months, 1933. Under police surveillance until 1945. Soldier, 1939–40, then employed by *Reich* publishing board. Joined SPD, 1945. Member of CC, SPD 1945–46. Member of SED CS, 1947–49 and thereafter of PB. Member of PE, 1946–50 and thereafter of CC. Mayor of East Berlin, November 1948 – July 1967. Died 1979.

Fechner, Max   Born 1892 in Berlin. Toolmaker. Member of SPD, 1910–17, 1922. Member of USPD, 1917–22. Editor of local government journal *Die Gemeinde*. Member of Prussian parliament, 1928–33. Concentration camp, 1933–34 and 1944. Chairman of CC, SPD, 1945. Deputy chairman of SED, 1946. Member of CS and PE, 1946–49. Member of CC, 1950–53. Minister of justice, 1949–53. Arrested after June 1953 uprising for defending the right to strike, expelled from SED and condemned to eight years in prison. Released, 1956. Readmitted to SED, 1958. Died 1973.

Grotewohl, Otto   Born 1894 in Braunschweig. Printer. Joined SPD, 1912. Soldier, 1914–18. For a short period member of USPD before rejoining SPD. Member of Braunschweig parliament, 1920–25. Minister of interior, education and justice in Braunschweig, 1921–23. Chairman of Braunschweig SPD, president of the *Land* insurance institute and member of *Reichstag,* 1925–33. After 1933 a merchant. Imprisoned for seven months in 1938–39. Chairman of SPD in Soviet zone, 1945–46. Played a key role in unification of SPD with KPD, 1946. With Pieck, chairman of SED, 1946–54. Member of CS and PE, 1946–48; of PB and CC, 1949–64. Prime minister of GDR, 1949–64. Died 1964.

Halbritter, Walter   Born 1927 in Aschersleben. Joined SED, 1946. Head of department in finance ministry, 1951–54. Head of department in planning and finance section of CC, 1954–61. Deputy minister of finance, 1961–63. Deputy chairman of state planning commission, 1963–65. Head of prices office in council of ministers, 1965. Member of CC, 1967. PB candidate member, 1967–73.

Harich, Wolfgang   Born 1923 in Königsberg as son of a writer. Philosophy student during war years. Joined SED, 1946, then theatre critic for *TR.* Professor of philosophy at Humboldt University, East Berlin, 1949. Chief editor of *Deutsche Zeitschrift für Philosophie,* 1949–56. Arrested and condemned to ten years' imprisonment in a show trial for treasonous activities against the GDR, 1956. Amnestied, 1964. Journalist and editor in East Berlin. Emigrated to Austria, 1979 then returned to GDR. Rehabilitated and acquitted by GDR supreme court, 1990. Attempted to found a new Communist Party in Germany, 1992. Chaired alternative *Enquete-Kommission* for the reappraisal of GDR history, 1993. Died 1995.

Honecker, Erich   Born 1912 in Saar as son of a miner. Trained as a roofer, 1927–29. Joined KPD, 1929. Secretary of KJV in Saarland, 1931. Member of illegal CC of KJV, 1934. Arrested, 1935. Sentenced to ten years' imprisonment, 1937. Freed from Brandenburg prison, 1945. Youth secretary of CC, KPD, 1945. Chairman of FDJ, 1946–55. Member of PE, 1946–50; and of CC, 1950–89. PB candidate member, 1950–58. CC secretary and full member of PB after 1958. First secretary of SED, 1971. From June 1971, chairman of national defence council. From November 1971 member and after 1976 chairman of the council of state. General secretary of SED, 1976. Stripped of all party and state functions, 24 October 1989. Expelled from SED, December 1989. Died 1994.

Janka, Walter   Born 1914 in Chemnitz. Apprenticeship as a typesetter. Leader of KJV in Erzgebirge, 1933. Arrested, 1933 and imprisoned until 1935. Officer in Spanish Civil War, 1936–39. Interned in France, 1939–41, then fled to Mexico. Returned to Germany, 1947. General director of DEFA, 1948–51. Head of *Aufbau* publishing house, 1952–56. Arrested, December 1956. Sentenced to five years' imprisonment in a show trial for participating in a 'counter-revolutionary conspiracy against the Ulbricht government', July 1957. Released from prison after international protests, 1960. Thereafter dramaturge for DEFA. Retired, 1972. Rehabilitated by SED, November 1989. Sentence quashed by GDR supreme court, 1990.

Jendretzky, Hans   Born 1897 in Berlin as son of a printer. Trained as a lock-smith. Member of USPD, 1919. Joined KPD, 1920. Member of Prussian parliament, 1928–32. Imprisoned, 1934–37; in concentration camp, 1937–38, then resumed work as a locksmith. Arrested again, 1944. Chairman of FDGB, 1946–48. Leader of Berlin SED, 1948–53. Member of SED PE, 1946–49, and of CC, 1950. PB candidate member, 1950. Relieved of all his functions in connection with Zaisser–Herrnstadt opposition and expelled from PB, 1953. Expelled from CC, 1954. Rehabilitated, 1956. Deputy interior minister, 1957–60. Member of CC, 1957–89.

Karsten, August   Born 1888 in Peine. Member of USPD, 1917–22. Joined SPD, 1922. Member of control commission, 1920–24. Member of *Reichstag*, 1920–33. Imprisoned for short periods, 1933–45. Member of SPD PE, 1945. Member of SED CS (responsible for party affairs) and PE, 1946–49. Then relieved of all party posts.

Lehmann, Helmut   Born 1882 in Berlin. Office worker. Member of central executive of office workers' associations, 1902. Joined SPD, 1903. Co-founder and chairman of society of Berlin apprentices and young workers, 1904. Full-time trade union official, 1907–14. Deputy chairman, then chairman of Germany's main health insurance association, 1914–33. Member of SPD resistance group after 1933. Condemned for attempted high treason, 1944. Member of SPD executive, 1945. Member of SED CS and PB, 1946–50. Responsible for employment, social security, health care, agriculture and resettlement. Thereafter in subordinate posts (president of 'people's solidarity'/chairman of GDR's central executive for social security). Member of PE and CC, 1946–59. Died 1959.

Matern, Hermann   Born 1893 in Magdeburg as son of a worker. A tanner until 1926. Joined SPD, 1911. Resigned from party after it voted for war credits, 1914. Member of USPD, 1918. Joined KPD, 1919. After 1926 secretary of KPD district leaderships in Magdeburg and East Prussia. Member of Prussian parliament, 1932. Arrested, 1933; escaped from prison, 1934, then emigrated to Czechoslovakia, Switzerland, Austria, France, Holland, Denmark, Norway and Sweden. Moved to Moscow, May 1941 where he helped found the NKFD. Headed group to Dresden, May 1945. Chairman of KPD in Saxony, 1945. Chairman of Berlin SED, April 1946. Member of PE and then SED CC, 1946–71. Chairman of CPCC, 1949–71. Member of CS and PB from 1946 until his death in 1971.

Meier, Otto   Born 1889 in Magdeburg. Employed as a trade official after training as a businessman. Joined SPD, 1911. Joined USPD, 1917. When right wing of USPD split off in 1922, returned to SPD, then member of Berlin's district executive. Editor, 1921–33. Member of Prussian parliament, 1921–33. Illegal party activity after 1933. Arrested, 1944. Member of SPD executive, 1945. Member of SED CS (responsible for culture, education and party instruction), 1946–50. Member of PE, 1946–50. Then lost all political influence. Died 1962.

Mielke, Erich Born 1907 in Berlin. Trained as a clerk. Joined KPD, 1925. Involved in murder of two police captains, 1931. Fled Germany. Fought in Spanish Civil War, 1936–39. Interned in France, 1940, then emigrated to USSR. Returned to Germany, 1945. With Zaisser, built up political police. Member of CC, 1950–89. State secretary in MfS, 1950–53 and 1955–57. Deputy state secretary in interior ministry, 1953–55. Minister for state security, 1957–89. PB candidate member, 1971; full member, 1976. Expelled from party, December 1989. Arrested, 1990.

Mückenberger, Erich Born 1910 in Chemnitz. Locksmith. Joined SPD, 1927. Illegal resistance activity, 1933. Arrested, 1934. In Sachsenhausen concentration camp until 1936. Sentenced to ten months' imprisonment, 1938. Member of German army punishment battalion, 1942–45. Rejoined SPD, 1945. First secretary of SED *Kreis* leadership in Chemnitz, 1946–48. Student at party training college, 1948. Second secretary of SED state leadership in Saxony, 1948–49. First secretary of SED state leadership in Thuringia, 1949–52. First secretary of SED district leadership in Erfurt, 1952–53. CC secretary for agriculture from 1953. Member of CC, 1950. Candidate member of PB, 1950; full member 1958–89.

Neumann, Alfred Born 1909 in Berlin. Carpenter. Member of workers' sport movement and 'Red Front Fighters' League'. Joined KPD, 1929. Illegal resistance activity in Berlin after 1933. Emigrated to USSR, end 1934. Fought in Spanish Civil War, 1936–38. Emigrated to France, 1938. Interned in France, 1939–40. Returned to Germany, 1941. Arrested and sentenced to eight years' imprisonment, 1942. Member of KPD, 1945. SED secretary in Berlin-Neukölln, 1946. Deputy mayor of East Berlin, 1951–53. First secretary of SED in East Berlin, 1953–57. PB candidate member, 1953–58, thereafter full member. Member of CC, 1950–89. Secretary of CC, 1957–61. Chairman of economics council, 1961. After 1965, minister for materials. Expelled from SED, January 1990.

Norden, Albert Born 1904 in Upper Silesia. Joined KPD, 1920 then editor of KPD newspapers. Emigration to France, 1933, then Czechoslovakia and America. Publisher of *Germany Today* in USA. Returned to Germany, 1946; member of SED. Chief editor of *Deutschlands Stimme*, 1948–49. Head of press section in GDR's bureau of information, 1949. Almost purged as western émigré, 1953. Government speaker at press conferences, secretary of committee for German unity, 1954. Member and secretary of CC after 1955. Member of PB, 1958. After February 1963, secretary and head of PB's agitation commission. Died 1982.

Pieck, Wilhelm Born 1876 in Guben. Carpenter. Member of SPD, 1895–1918. In World War One joined Spartacus League. Deserted from German army to neutral Holland, 1918. Co-founder of KPD and member of its CC, 1918. Arrested with Luxemburg and Liebknecht, 1919. Member of Prussian parliament, 1921–28. Member of *Reichstag*, 1928–33. After 1928, member of executive committee of Communist International. Emigration to France, 1933, then

USSR, 1939. Replaced Thälmann as chairman of KPD CC, 1935. Secretary of Comintern, after 1942 involved in NKFD. Chairman of KPD, 1945. Member of SED CS, PE, then PB and CC. With Grotewohl chairman of SED, 1946–54. President of GDR, 1949–60. Died 1960.

Rau, Heinrich Born 1899 in Stuttgart as son of a farmer. Press worker. Member of Spartacus League, 1916. Co-founder of KPD, 1919. Secretary of agriculture in KPD CC, 1920. Member of Prussian parliament, 1928–33. Imprisoned, 1933–35. Headed international agrarian institute in USSR, 1936–37. Commissar of international brigades in Spain, 1937–38. Interned in France, 1939. Transferred to Germany, 1942; in Mauthausen until 1945. Chairman of DWK, 1946–49. Member of PE and CC, 1949–58. PB member, 1950–58. Minister for economic planning, 1949. Chairman of state planning commission, 1950–53. Minister for mechanical engineering, 1953–55. Minister for foreign trade and intra-German trade, 1955–58. Died 1958.

Schmidt, Elli Born 1908 in Berlin. Dressmaker. Joined KPD, 1927. Active in district leadership of Berlin. Student at Lenin School in Moscow, 1932–33. Illegal activity for KPD in Germany, 1933–37. Emigrated to Czechoslovakia and France. Moved to USSR, 1940. Announcer for Radio Moscow, 1940–45. Head of women's secretariat in SED CC, 1945–49. Chairman of DFD, 1949–53. Member of CS and PB, 1946–53. Member of CC, 1950–54. Chairman of state commission for trade and supplies, 1953. Relieved of all party functions in connection with Zaisser–Herrnstadt case, July 1953. Head of German fashion institute, 1953–67. Rehabilitated, 1956. Died 1980.

Schürer, Gerhard Born 1921 in Zwickau as son of a worker. Trained as a machine fitter. Soviet captivity as wartime volunteer in antifascist camp. SED, 1948. Head of section in state planning commission, 1951. Studied at party training school in Moscow, 1955–58. Head of planning and finance section in SED CC, 1960–62. Member of CC from 1963. Member of economics commission of PB, 1960–62. Chairman of state planning commission from December 1965. Deputy chairman of council of ministers after 1967. Candidate member of PB, October 1973–89. Expelled from party, 1990.

Stoph, Willi Born 1914 in Berlin as son of a worker. Builder and site engineer. Joined KPD, 1931. Military service, 1935–37. Soldier during war. Head of building materials section of SED PE, 1946–47. Head of economic policy section of PE/CC, 1948–50. Member of CC secretariat, 1950–53. Member of CC after 1950. Member of PB after 1953. Interior minister, 1952–55. Minister of national defence, 1956–60. First deputy chairman of council of ministers, 1962–64. Succeeded Grotewohl as prime minister, 1964. Expelled from SED, December 1989.

Ulbricht, Walter Born 1893 in Leipzig as son of a tailor. Carpenter. Soldier, 1915–18. Member of SPD, 1912–19. Joined Spartacus League, 1918. Joined KPD,

1919. Member of KPD CC, 1923–24. Helped lead communist uprising in central Germany, 1923. Studied at Lenin School in Moscow. KPD representative in Comintern, 1926–27, 1938–43. Member of Saxony's parliament, 1926–28. Member of *Reichstag*, 1928–33. Member of KPD CC, 1927–45. Head of KPD in Berlin-Brandenburg, 1929. Sentenced to two years' imprisonment in a fortress for high treason, 1930. Secretary of KPD PB in exile after 1934. Emigrated to Paris and Prague, 1933–38. Political commissar in international brigades during Spanish Civil War, 1936–38. Emigrated to USSR, 1938–45. Helped found NKFD, 1943. Returned to Berlin as head of 'Ulbricht group', 1945. Deputy chairman of SED, 1946–50. Member of CS and PE from 1946, thereafter of PB and CC. General secretary / first secretary of SED, 1950–71. Chairman of national defence council, 1960–71. Chairman of council of state, 1960–73. Removed as first secretary, 1971. Honorary chairman of SED, 1971–73. Died 1973.

Bibliography

Manuscript sources

Berlin: 'Stiftung Archiv der Parteien und Massenorganisationen der DDR im Bundesarchiv, Zentrales Parteiarchiv' (SAPMO-BArch, ZPA)

SAPMO-BArch, ZPA, IV 2/1/ – Records of the SED party executive and central committee.

SAPMO-BArch, ZPA, IV 2/2.1/ – Records of the central secretariat.

SAPMO-BArch, ZPA, IV 2/2 – and SAPMO-BArch, ZPA, J IV 2/2 – Records of the SED politburo.

SAPMO-BArch, ZPA, IV 2/2A – and SAPMO-BArch, ZPA, J IV 2/2A – 'Working records' of the SED politburo.

SAPMO-BArch, ZPA, IV 2/201/1 – Office of the politburo.

SAPMO-BArch, ZPA, IV 2/1.01/75 – Conferences and discussions of the party executive and central committee.

SAPMO-BArch, ZPA, IV 2/4/ – Records of the central party control commission.

SAPMO-BArch, ZPA, IV 2/11/v801 – Paul Merker's cadre file.

SAPMO-BArch, ZPA, IV 2/11/v519 – Wilhelm Zaisser's cadre file.

SAPMO-BArch, ZPA, IV 2/11/v5280/ – Franz Dahlem's cadre file.

SAPMO-BArch, ZPA, IV 2/11/v5142 – Karl Schirdewan's cadre file.

SAPMO-BArch, ZPA, IV 2/11/v520 – Gerhart Ziller's cadre file.

SAPMO-BArch, ZPA, IV 2/11/v746 – Erich Gniffke's cadre file.

SAPMO-BArch, ZPA, J IV 2/202/ – Büro Walter Ulbricht.

SAPMO-BArch, ZPA, IV A 2/2.028/ – Büro Albert Norden.

SAPMO-BArch, ZPA, IV 2/2.035/ – Büro Hermann Axen.

SAPMO-BArch, ZPA, IV 2/2.022/ – Sekretariat Paul Merker.

SAPMO-BArch, ZPA, J IV 2/3/ – Records of the small secretariat.

SAPMO-BArch, ZPA, NL 36/ – Wilhelm Pieck *Nachlaß*.

SAPMO-BArch, ZPA, NL 90/ – Otto Grotewohl *Nachlaß*.

SAPMO-BArch, ZPA, NL 215/ – Fred Oelßner *Nachlaß*.

SAPMO-BArch, ZPA, NL 182/ – Walter Ulbricht *Nachlaß*.

SAPMO-BArch, ZPA, NL 102/ – Paul Merker *Nachlaß*.

SAPMO-BArch, ZPA, NL 62/ – Heinrich Rau *Nachlaß*.

SAPMO-BArch, ZPA, NL 113/ – Fritz Selbmann *Nachlaß*.

SAPMO-BArch, ZPA, NL 109/ – Anton Ackermann *Nachlaß*.

SAPMO-BArch, ZPA, NL 76/ – Hermann Matern *Nachlaß*.
SAPMO-BArch, ZPA, NL 77/ – Otto Schön *Nachlaß*.
SAPMO-BArch, ZPA, NL 101/ – Max Fechner *Nachlaß*.

Berlin: 'Stiftung Archiv der Parteien und Massenorganisationen der DDR im Bundesarchiv, Berlin Parteiarchiv' (SAPMO-BArch, BPA)

SAPMO-BArch, BPA, IV 2/2 – Records of the Berlin district party leadership.

Berlin: Der Bundesbeauftragte für die Unterlagen des Staatssicherheitsdienstes der ehemaligen Deutschen Demokratischen Republik (BStU). Stasi archive or 'Gauck Behörde'

BStU, 10993.
BStU, UA 192/56.
BStU, Mielke Bestand. Ordner 879.

Moscow Center for the Preservation of Contemporary Documentation (TsKhSD)

Private collections of documents
Documents from the private collection of Karl Schirdewan handed to the author, 23.11.92.

Printed sources

Published SED documents

'Das 33. Plenum des Zentralkomitees der SED. Enthüllung eines Geheimprotokolls', *APZ*, B IL (18.12.57), 837–51.
'Der neue Kurs und die Aufgaben der Partei', *Entschließung der 15. Tagung des Zentralkomitees der Sozialistischen Einheitspartei Deutschlands vom 24. bis 26. Juli 1953* (Berlin-Ost, 1953), 105–38.
Dokumente der Sozialistischen Einheitspartei Deutschlands. Beschlüsse und Erklärungen des Zentralkomitees sowie seines Politbüros und seines Sekretariats, Vol. 11, Berlin-Ost, 1969.
Grotewohl, O., 'Die gegenwärtige Lage und der neue Kurs der Partei', *Der Neue Kurs und die Aufgaben der Partei,* Berlin-Ost, 1953.
'Grundsätze und Ziele der Sozialistischen Einheitspartei Deutschlands', *Einheit*, 2 (March, 1946), 2–4.
Protokoll der Verhandlungen der I. Parteikonferenz der Sozialistischen Einheitspartei Deutschlands, Berlin-Ost, 1949.
Protokoll der Verhandlungen der II. Parteikonferenz der Sozialistischen Einheitspartei Deutschlands, Berlin-Ost, 1952.
Protokoll der Verhandlungen der III. Parteikonferenz der Sozialistischen Einheitspartei Deutschlands, Berlin-Ost, 1956.
Protokoll der Verhandlungen des II. Parteitages der Sozialistischen Einheitspartei Deutschlands, Berlin-Ost, 1947.
Protokoll der Verhandlungen des IV. Parteitages der Sozialistischen Einheitspartei Deutschlands, Berlin-Ost, 1954.

Protokoll der Verhandlungen des V. Parteitages der Sozialistischen Einheitspartei Deutschlands, Berlin-Ost, 1959.

Protokoll der Verhandlungen des VI. Parteitages der Sozialistischen Einheitspartei Deutschlands, Berlin-Ost, 1963.

Protokoll der Verhandlungen des VII. Parteitages der Sozialistischen Einheitspartei Deutschlands, Berlin-Ost, 1967.

Protokoll der Verhandlungen des VIII. Parteitages der Sozialistischen Einheitspartei Deutschlands, Berlin-Ost, 1971.

'Rechenschaftsbericht des Zentralkomitees der KPdSU (B) an den XIX. Parteitag', *Bericht des Sekretärs des ZK der KPdSU (B),* Berlin-Ost, 1952.

Party journals and newspapers

Einheit
Neuer Weg
Neues Deutschland
Tägliche Rundschau

Documents published since 1989

'Stalin and the SED leadership, 7 April 1952: "You must organize your own state"', *CWIHP Bulletin,* 4 (Fall, 1994), 35, 48.

Bretschneider, G., Libera, K., Wilhelm, R., 'Karl Schirdewan: Fraktionsmacherei oder gegen Ulbrichts Diktat? Eine Stellungnahme vom 1. Januar 1958', *BzG,* 4 (1990), 498–512.

Knoll, V., Kölm, L., *Der Fall Berija. Protokoll einer Abrechnung. Das Plenum des ZK der KPdSU Juli 1953. Stenographischer Bericht,* Berlin, 1993.

Malycha, A., ' "Hier stehe ich, ich kann nicht anders!" Rede Otto Grotewohls am 11. November 1945', *BzG,* 2 (1992), 167–84.

Malycha, A., 'Sozialdemokraten in der SED: Der "Fall" Ernst Thape', *BzG,* 3 (1993), 77–90.

Naimark, N., 'The Soviet occupation: Moscow's man in (East) Berlin', *CWIHP Bulletin,* 4 (Fall, 1994), 34, 45–48.

Ostermann, C. F., 'New documents on the East German uprising of 1953', *CWIHP Bulletin,* 5 (Spring 1995), 10–21, 57.

Ostermann, C. F., ' "This is not a politburo, but a madhouse". The post-Stalin succession struggle, Soviet *Deutschlandpolitik* and the SED: New evidence from Russian, German, and Hungarian archives', *CWIHP Bulletin,* 10 (March 1998), 61–110.

Otto, W., 'Dokumente zur Auseinandersetzungen in der SED 1953', *BzG,* 5 (1990), 655–72.

Stöckigt, R., 'Ein Dokument von großer historischer Bedeutung vom Mai 1953: "Über die Maßnahmen zur Gesundung der politischen Lage in der Deutschen Demokratischen Republik" ', *BzG,* 5 (1990), 648–54.

Weber, H., 'Kurt Müller, Ein historisches Dokument aus dem Jahre 1956. Brief an den DDR-Ministerpräsidenten Otto Grotewohl', *APZ,* B11 (9.3.90), 16–29.

Zimmermann, F., 'Brief von Otto Buchwitz an Berliner SPD-Funktionäre, 16. März 1946', *BzG,* 2 (1991), 235–8.

Books

Davidovitch, J. S., *Ernst Thälmann. Seiten seines Lebens und Kampfes,* Berlin, 1971.

Herrnstadt, R., *Die Entstehung der Klassen*, Berlin-Ost, 1965.

Kießling, W., *Allemania Libre in Mexico*. *Band 2: Texte und Dokumente zur Geschichte des antifaschistischen Exils (1941–46)*, East Berlin, 1974.

Merker, P., *Deutschland. Sein oder Nicht Sein?*, Vol 1, Mexico, 1944.

Steininger, R. (ed.), *Quellen zur Geschichte des Parlamentarismus und der Politischen Parteien. Die Ruhrfrage 1945/46 und die Entstehung des Landes Nordrhein-Westfalen. Britische, Französische und Amerikanische Akten*, Düsseldorf 1988.

Unserem Freund und Lehrer. J. W. Stalin zum 70. Geburtstag, Berlin, 1949.

Memoir sources

Andert, R., and Herzberg, W., *Der Sturz. Erich Honecker in Kreuzverhör*, Berlin, Weimar, 1990.

Bauer, L., ' "Die Partei hat immer Recht". Bemerkungen zum geplanten deutschen Rajkprozeß (1950)', *APZ*, B27 (4.7.56), 405–19.

Berger, W., 'Als Ulbricht an Breshnew vorbei regierte', *ND* (23.–24.3.91), 13.

Berger, W., 'Zu den Hauptursachen des Unterganges der DDR', *Weißenseer Blätter*, 1 (1992), 26 37.

Blumberg, H., 'Franz Dahlem. Nachgelassenes. Ausgelassenes. Über einen Prozess und die Schwierigkeiten seiner richtigen Beurteilung', *BzG*, 1 (1990), 17–25.

Brandt, H., 'Die sowjetische Deutschlandpolitik im Frühjahr 1953 aus der Sicht fortschrittlicher Kräfte in der SED', *Osteuropa*, 6 (June 1965), 369–77.

Brandt, H., *Ein Traum, der nicht entführbar ist. Mein Weg zwischen Ost und West*, München, 1967.

Djilas, M., *Conversations with Stalin*, London, 1962.

Falin, V., *Politische Erinnerungen*, München, 1993.

Gerlach, M., *Mitverantwortlich: Als Liberaler im SED-Staat*, Berlin, 1991.

Gniffke, E. W., *Jahre mit Ulbricht*. 2nd edn, Köln, 1990.

Gromyko, A., *Memories*, London, 1989.

Grüber, H., *Bevollmächtigt zum Brückenbau: Heinrich Grüber. Judenfreund und Trümmerprobst. Erinnerungen, Predigten, Berichte, Briefe*, Leipzig, 1991.

Harich, W., *Keine Schwierigkeiten mit der Wahrheit*, Berlin, 1993.

Hochman, J., (ed.) *Hope dies last. The autobiography of Alexander Dubcek*, London, 1993.

Janka, W., *Schwierigkeiten mit der Wahrheit*, Reinbek bei Hamburg, 1989.

Janka, W., *Spuren eines Lebens*, Berlin, 1991.

Janson, C., *Totengräber der DDR. Wie Günter Mittag den SED-Staat ruinierte*, Düsseldorf, Wien, New York, 1991.

Kantorowicz, A., *Deutsches Tagebuch*, Munich, 1959.

Kantorowicz, A., *Deutsches Tagebuch*, II, Munich, 1962.

Leonhard, W., *Die Revolution entlässt ihre Kinder*, 5th edn, Köln, 1992.

Lippmann, H., *Honecker and the new politics of Europe*, London, 1973.

Lippmann, H., *Honecker. Porträt eines Nachfolgers*, Köln, 1972.

Mittag, G., *Um jeden Preis. Im Spannungsfeld zweier Systeme*, Berlin, Weimar, 1991.

Mlynar, Z., *Night frost in Prague. The end of humane socialism*, London, 1980.

Otto, W., 'Ernst Wollweber: Aus Erinnerungen. Ein Porträt Walter Ulbrichts', *BzG*, 3 (1990), 350–78.

Resis, A. (ed.), *Molotov remembers. Inside Kremlin politics. Conversations with Felix Chuyev*, Chicago, 1993.

Schecter, J., Luchkov, V. (eds), *Khrushchev remembers. The glasnost tapes,* Boston, 1990.

Schenk, F., *Im Vorzimmer der Diktatur. 12 Jahre Pankow,* Köln–West Berlin, 1962.

Schenk, F., *Mein doppeltes Vaterland,* Würzburg, 1989.

Schirdewan, K., *Aufstand gegen Ulbricht. Im Kampf um politische Kurskorrektur, gegen stalinistische, dogmatische Politik,* Berlin, 1994.

Semjonow, W. S., *Von Stalin bis Gorbatschow. Ein halbes Jahrhundert in diplomatischer Mission 1939–1991,* Berlin, 1995. Translated from the Russian by Hilde and Helmut Ettinger.

Stempel, F., 'Erinnerung an Otto Grotewohl. Zu dessen 100. Geburtstag am 11. März 1994', *Utopie Kreativ,* 41/42 (March–April 1994), 154–65.

Stulz-Herrnstadt, N. (ed.), Herrnstadt, R., *Das Herrnstadt-Dokument. Das Politbüro der SED und die Geschichte des 17. Juni 1953,* Reinbek bei Hamburg, 1990.

Sudoplatov, P., Sudoplatov, A., Schecter, J. L., Schecter, L. P., *Special tasks. The memoirs of an unwanted witness – a Soviet spymaster,* London, 1995.

Wolf, H., 'Entgegnung zum Beitrag "Phraseologen mußten Technologen weichen". Wie war das mit dem Neuen Ökonomischen System?' *ND* (2.–3.3.91), 13.

Wolf, H., *Hatte die DDR je eine Chance?,* Hamburg, 1991.

Wolf, M., *In eigenem Auftrag. Bekenntnisse und Einsichten,* München, 1991.

Interview sources

' "Es reißt mir das Herz kaputt". Spiegel-Gespräch mit dem ehemaligen DDR-Wirtschaftslenker Günter Mittag über seine Politik und seine Fehler', *Der Spiegel,* 37 (9.9.91), 88–104.

Bouvrier, B. W., Schultz, H. P., '. . . *die SPD aber aufgehört hat zu existieren'. Sozialdemokraten unter sowjetischer Besatzung,* Bonn, 1991.

Harbauer, O., 'Den Kampf mit Ulbricht gewagt', *Freiheit* (16.2.90), 9.

Interviews with Wolfgang Berger, 4.9.92, 7.10.92, 4.12.92, 14.12.92, 27.11.92, 19.7.94.

Interviews with Kurt Hager, 1.12.92, 6.4.94.

Interview (taped) with Wolfgang Harich, 2.10.92.

Interview with Wolfgang Kießling, 15.9.92.

Interview with Claus Krömke, 11.12.92.

Interviews with Alfred Neumann, 16.10.92, 23.10.92, 6.4.94.

Interview with Wilfriede Otto, 28.11.92.

Interviews (taped) with Karl Schirdewan, 12.9.92, 12.10.92, 23.11.92. Untaped 25.9.92, 9.7.94.

Interviews with Gerhard Schürer, 5.11.92, 19.10.92.

Interview with Manfred Uschner, 8.12.92.

Interview with Paul Wandel, 30.11.92.

Interviews with Herbert Wolf, 13.10.92, 3.11.92, 14.7.94. Telephone conversation 26.10.92.

Neubert, H., 'Der Berija-Plan und ein chiffriertes Telegramm. Hermann Axen über die deutschlandpolitische Problematik im Jahre 1953 – Auszüge aus einem Gespräch mit Prof. Dr. Harald Neubert', *ND* (25.6.93), 3.

Reinert, D., Emendörfer, J., 'Ein Widersacher des mächtigen "Ersten" ', *Berliner Zeitung* (10.–11.2.90), 9.

Rexin, M., 'Der zaudernde Rebell. Karl Schirdewan und die SED der 50er Jahre', *RIAS Berlin* (Beitrag von Manfred Rexin für die Sendereihe 'Themen der Zeit', 18.8.91,

18.35–19.30 Uhr).

Röllecke, L., 'Es herrschten Personenkult, politische Arroganz', *Berliner Morgenpost* (19.–20.4.92), 52.

Schumann, M., Dreßen, W., ' "Die Führung lag in Moskau" M. Schumann und W. Dreßen im Gespräch mit Karl Schirdewan', *Niemandsland, Tugendterror,* 11/12 (1992), 305–26.

Willy Brandt interviewed by Timothy Garton Ash, 2.10.91.

Wolf, D. 'Messengers from Moscow', BBC2 television documentary directed and produced by Daniel Wolf, 10.00–11.00pm, 19.2.95.

Printed secondary works

Books

Arens, U., *Die andere Freiheit. Die Freiheit in Theorie und Praxis der Sozialistischen Einheitspartei Deutschlands,* München, 1976.

Bahry, D. L., and Moses, J. C. (ed.), *Political implications of economic reform in communist systems. Communist dialectic,* New York, 1990.

Baring, A., *Uprising in East Germany: June 17, 1953,* London, 1972.

Benser, G., *Die KPD im Jahre der Befreiung. Vorbereitung und Aufbau der legalen kommunistischen Massenpartei (Jahreswende 1944/1945 bis Herbst 1945),* Berlin, 1985.

Borkowski, D., *Erich Honecker. Statthalter Moskaus oder deutscher Patriot?,* München, 1987.

Brandt, P., Schumacher, J., Schwarzrock, G., and Sühl, K., *Karrieren eines Außenseiters. Leo Bauer zwischen Kommunismus und Sozialdemokratie 1912 bis 1972,* Berlin and Bonn, 1983.

Childs, D., *The GDR: Moscow's German ally,* 2nd edn, London, 1988.

D'Agnostino, A., *Soviet succession struggles. Kremlinology and the Russian question from Lenin to Gorbachev,* Massachusetts, 1988.

Dawisha, K., *The Kremlin and the Prague Spring,* London, 1984.

Erfurt, W., *Moscow's policy in Germany. A study in contemporary history,* Esslingen, 1959.

Fischer, A., *Sowjetische Deutschlandpolitik im Zweiten Weltkrieg 1941–1945,* Stuttgart, 1975.

Flocken, J. von, Scholz, M. F., *Ernst Wollweber. Saboteur, Minister, Unperson,* Berlin, 1994.

Fricke, K. W., *Opposition und Widerstand in der DDR. Ein politischer Report,* Köln, 1984.

Fricke, K. W., *Warten auf Gerechtigkeit. Kommunistische Säuberungen und Rehabilitierungen. Bericht und Dokumentation,* Köln, 1971.

Fulbrook, M., *Anatomy of a dictatorship. Inside the GDR, 1949–1989,* Oxford, 1995.

Fulbrook, M., *The Fontana history of Germany, 1918–1990. The divided nation,* London, 1991.

Gaddis, J., *We now know. Rethinking Cold War history,* Oxford, 1997.

Garton Ash, T., *In Europe's name. Germany and the divided continent,* London, 1993.

Grosser, A., *Geschichte Deutschlands seit 1945. Eine Bilanz,* 5th edn, München, 1977.

Hagen, M., *DDR – Juni 1953. Die erste Volkserhebung im Stalinismus,* Stuttgart, 1992.

Herf, J., *Divided memory. The Nazi past in the two Germanys,* London, 1997.

Jänicke, M., *Der dritte Weg. Die antistalinistischer Opposition gegen Ulbricht seit 1953,* Köln, 1964.

Kennedy-Pipe, C., *Stalin's Cold War. Soviet strategies in Europe, 1943 to 1956,* Manchester, 1995.

Kessler, M. (ed.), *Antisemitismus und Arbeiterbewegung. Entwicklungslinien im 20. Jahrhundert,* Bonn, 1993.

Klein, T., Otto, W., Grieder, P., *Visionen, Repression und Opposition in der SED (1949–1989),* Frankfurt/Oder, 1996.

Knight, A., *Beria. Stalin's first lieutenant,* Princeton, 1993.

Kocka, J., (ed.) *Historische DDR-Forschung. Aufsätze und Studien,* Berlin, 1993.

Kolakowski, L., *Main currents of Marxism. Its origin, growth and dissolution,* Vol. 3, Oxford, 1978.

Kopstein, J., *The politics of economic decline in East Germany, 1945–1989,* Chapel Hill, 1997.

Krisch, H., *The German Democratic Republic. The search for identity,* Colorado, 1985.

Laschitza, H., *Kämpferische Demokratie gegen den Faschismus. Die programmatische Vorbereitung auf die antifaschistisch-demokratische Umwälzung in Deutschland durch die Parteiführung der KPD,* Berlin, 1969.

Leonhard, W., *Das kurze Leben der DDR. Berichte und Kommentare aus vier Jahrzehnten,* Stuttgart, 1990.

Leonhard, W., *Kreml ohne Stalin,* Frankfurt, 1959.

Leptin, G., and Melzer, M., *Economic reform in East German industry,* Oxford, 1978. Translated from the German by R. A. Clarke.

Loth, W., *Stalins ungeliebtes Kind. Warum Moskau die DDR nicht wollte,* Berlin, 1994.

Loth, W., *The division of the world, 1941–1955,* London, 1988.

Ludz, P. C., *Parteielite im Wandel. Funktionsaufbau, Sozialstruktur und Ideologie der SED-Führung,* Köln-Opladen, 1968.

Ludz, P. C., *The German Democratic Republic from the sixties to the seventies. A socio-political analysis,* Cambridge, MA, 1970.

Mastny, V., *The Cold War and Soviet insecurity. The Stalin years,* Oxford, 1996.

McAdams, A. James, *East Germany and détente. Building authority after the Wall,* Cambridge, 1985.

McAdams, A. James, *Germany divided. From the Wall to reunification,* Princeton, 1993.

McCauley, M., *Marxism-Leninism in the German Democratic Republic. The Socialist Unity Party (SED),* London, 1979.

McCauley, M., *The German Democratic Republic since 1945,* London, 1983.

McElvoy, A., *The saddled cow. East Germany's life and legacy,* London, 1993.

Mitter, A., Wolle, S., *Untergang auf Raten. Unbekannte Kapitel der DDR-Geschichte,* München, 1993.

Moreton, E., *East Germany and the Warsaw alliance,* Colorado, 1978.

Müller-Enbergs, H., *Der Fall Rudolf Herrnstadt. Tauwetterpolitik vor dem 17. Juni,* Berlin, 1991.

Naimark, N., *The Russians in Germany. A history of the Soviet zone of occupation, 1945–1949,* London, 1995.

Naumann, G., Trümpler, E., *Von Ulbricht zu Honecker. 1970 – ein Krisenjahr der DDR,* Berlin, 1990.

Nekrassov, V., *Berija. Henker in Stalins Diensten. Ende einer Karriere,* Berlin, 1992.

Translated from the Russian by Barbara and Lothar Lehnhardt.

Neumann, T., *Die Maßnahme. Eine Herrschaftsgeschichte der SED*, Reinbek bei Hamburg, 1991.

Nicholls, A. J., *The Bonn Republic. West German democracy, 1945 1990*, London, 1997.

Oldenburg, *Konflikt und Konfliktregelung in der Parteiführung der SED 1945/46–1972*, Köln, 1972.

Przybylski, P., *Tatort Politbüro. Die Akte Honecker*, Vol. 1, Berlin, 1991.

Przybylski, P., *Tatort Politbüro. Honecker, Mittag und Schalk-Golodkowski*, Vol. 2, Berlin, 1992.

Pulzer, P., *German politics, 1945–1995*, Oxford, 1995.

Richert, E., *Das zweite Deutschland. Ein Staat, der nicht darf*, Frankfurt, Hamburg, 1966.

Richert, E., *Die DDR-Elite oder unsere Partner von Morgen?*, Reinbek bei Hamburg, 1968.

Richert, E., *Macht ohne Mandat*, Köln, Opladen, 1958.

Ryavec, K. W., *Implementation of Soviet economic reforms. Political, organizational, and social processes*, New York, 1975.

Skyba, P., 'Die FDJ im Tauwetter – Tauwetter in der FDJ?' in Gotschlich, H. (ed.), *'Links und links und Schritt gehalten . . .' Die FDJ: Konzepte – Abläufe – Grenzen*, Berlin, 1994.

Sodaro, M. J., *Moscow, Germany and the West from Khrushchev to Gorbachev*, London, 1991.

Spanger, H. J., *Die SED und der Sozialdemokratismus. Ideologische Abgrenzung in der DDR*, Köln, 1982.

Staritz, D., *Die Gründung der DDR. Von der sowjetischen Besatzungszone zum sozialistichen Staat*, II Munich, 1987.

Stern, C., *Porträt einer bolschewistischen Partei. Entwicklung, Funktion und Situation der SED*, Köln–West Berlin, 1957.

Stern, C., *Ulbricht. Eine politische Biographie*, Köln–West Berlin, 1963. Published in English translation, London, 1965.

Stößel, F. T., *Positionen und Strömungen in der KPD/SED 1945–54*, Köln, 1985.

Sywottek, A., *Deutsche Volksdemokratie. Studie zur politischen Konzeption der KPD 1935–46*, Düsseldorf, 1971.

Verfassungen deutscher Ländern und Staaten. Von 1816 bis zur Gegenwart, Berlin, 1989.

Weber, H., *Aufbau und Fall einer Diktatur. Kritische Beiträge zur Geschichte der DDR*, Köln, 1991.

Weber, H., *DDR. Grundriß der Geschichte 1945–1990*, Hannover, 1991.

Wenzke, R., *Prager Frühling – Prager Herbst. Zur Intervention der Warschauer-Pakt-Streitkräfte in der CSSR 1968. Fakten und Zusammenhänge*, Berlin, 1990.

Wolfe, T., *Soviet Power and Europe, 1945 1970*, Baltimore and London, 1970.

Articles

'Arbeiterkomitees. Instruktion aus Polen', *Der Spiegel*, 5 (30.1.57), 16.

'Der mit dem Bart muß weg', *Der Spiegel* (14.6.93), 65–9.

'Der Weg einer Tarnorganisation. Zur Auflösung der VVN in der Sowjetzone', *SBZ-Archiv*, 6 (20.3.53), 86–7.

'Die zweite Phase des Dialogs. Argumentation der SED nach der Absage des Redneraustausches', *SBZ-Archiv*, 14 (Juli 1966), 211–13.

'Dreimal gleiche Treue. Glückhafter Beginn', *Der Spiegel*, 3 (21.7.49), 6–7.

'Ein Generalplan der SED. Wie gesamtdeutsche Wahlen vorbereitet werden sollen', *SBZ-Archiv*, 10 (25.5.55), 147–9.

'Fäden zum Strick', *Der Spiegel*, 22 (27.5.53), 13–14.

'Für ehrliche Zusammenarbeit', *Der Spiegel*, 19 (9.5.94), 84–91.

'Ich bin kein Lump, Herr Mielke!', *Der Spiegel*, 5 (30.1.57), 30–7.

'Otto Grotewohl', *Der Spiegel*, 40 (30.9.64), 72.

'Säuberung. Neun befühlen ihren Hals', *Der Spiegel,* 36 (6.9.50), 5–6.

'Schirdewan hielt die Pläne Schäffers für annehmbar', *Die Welt, Unabhängige Zeitung für Deutschland*, Ausgabe B, 5 (7.1.59), 2.

'SED. "Lustiges Leben" ', *Der Spiegel*, 44 (28.10.64), 56–9.

'Ulbricht. Edel auf dem Grabstein', *Der Spiegel*, 40 (30.9.64), 68–81.

Apel, H., 'Economic reforms in East Germany. A comment', *POC*, 3 (May–June 1966), 59–62.

Baring, A., 'Volksarmee schaffen – ohne Geschrei', *FAZ* (25.9.91), 35.

Besymenski, L., '1953 – Berija will die DDR beseitigen', *Die Zeit*, 42 (15.10.93), 81–3.

Bollinger, S., 'Die DDR kann nicht über Stalins Schatten springen. Reformen im Kalten Krieg – SED zwischen NÖS und Prager Frühling', *Hefte zur DDR-Geschichte*, 5 (Berlin, 1993).

Braun, G., ' "Regierungsangelegenheiten" in Thüringen im Spannungsfeld von sowjetischer Deutschlandpolitik und SED-Kalkülen 1947', *BzG*, 34 (1992), 67–91.

Dietrich, G., 'Ein Mitbürger der Vergangenheit, Gegenwart und Zukunft. Anton Ackermann', *BzG*, 1 (1991), 107–15.

Engelmann, R., Schumann, S., 'Der Ausbau des Überwachungsstaates. Der Konflikt Ulbricht–Wollweber und die Neuausrichtung des Staatssicherheitsdienstes der DDR 1957', *VfZ*, 2 (1995), 341–78.

Garabiol, P., 'Berlin, 17 juin 1953. Une premiére tentative de réunification de l'Allemagne', *Revue d'histoire diplomatique*, 104 (1990), 57–75.

Grieder, P., 'The overthrow of Ulbricht in East Germany: A new interpretation', *Debatte. Review of Contemporary German Affairs* , 6: 1 (May 1998), 8–45.

Herf, J., 'East German communists and the Jewish Question: The case of Paul Merker', *Journal of Contemporary History* , 29 (1994), 627–61.

Herrnstadt, V., 'Parteidisziplin hat Menschen kaputt gemacht', *Mitteldeutsche Zeitung* (27.4.90), 12.

Jakob, W., 'Der Fall Dahlem', *SBZ-Archiv*, 10 (25.5.53), 145–7.

Kießling, W., ' "Ich wehrte mich gegen die Beschuldigung, ein Agent zu sein" ', *ND* (17.–18.8.91), 13.

Kießling, W., 'Im Widerstreit mit Moskau: Paul Merker und die Bewegung Freies Deutschland in Mexico', *BzG*, 3 (1992), 29–42.

Kießling, W., 'Paul Merker und der "Sozialismus der dummen Kerls" ', *ND* (1.12.92), 14.

Kießling, W., 'Zweikampf oder die Abstinenz von Demokratie. Memorial für Paul Merker (1. Februar 1894 bis 13. Mai 1969), *Utopie Kreativ* (January–February 1994), 114–23.

Larres, K., 'Neutralisierung oder Westintegration? Churchill, Adenauer, die USA und der 17. Juni 1953', *DA*, 6 (1994), 568–85.

Lemke, M., 'Als Wehner "irgendwie mit der SED ins Gespräch kommen" wollte', *Die Zeit* (23.7.93), 8.

Lippmann, H., 'Der 17. Juni im Zentralkomitee der SED; Vorgeschichte, Ablauf und Folgen' *APZ*, B24 (13.6.56), 369–76.

Ludz, P. C., 'Continuity and change since Ulbricht', *POC*, 2 (March–April 1972), 56–67.

Ludz, P. C., 'The SED leadership in transition', *POC*, 3 (May–June 1970), 23–31.

Malycha, A., 'Sozialdemokratische Vorstellungen in der SED in den Jahren 1946–1948', *BzG*, 3 (1990), 339–49.

Neumann, S., 'Die Tragödie des Gehorsams', *Die Weltbühne*, 34 (1990), 1080–2.

O'Doherty, P., 'The GDR in the context of Stalinist show trials and anti-Semitism in Eastern Europe 1948–54', *German History*, 3 (October 1992), 302–17.

Osten, W., 'Die Deutschlandpolitik der Sowjetunion in den Jahren 1952/53', *Osteuropa*, 1 (January 1964), 1–13.

Ostermann, C. F., 'The United States, the East German Uprising of 1953, and the limits of roll-back', *CWIHP. Woodrow Wilson International Center for Scholars*, Working Paper no. 11 (December 1994).

Otto, W., 'Expertise im Auftrag der Enquete-Kommission des Bundestages "Ausarbeitung von Geschichte und Folgen der SED-Diktatur in Deutschland". Thema: "Widerspruch und abweichendes Verhalten in der SED" ' (manuscript).

Otto, W., ' "Genossen, ich verstehe nicht . . ." Die Geschichte von Hans Schrecker und die Jagd nach einer "Slansky-Verschwörerbände" in der DDR', *Horch und Guck*, 5 (1993), 25–30.

Otto, W., Lauter, G., 'Wilhelm Zaisser: Zwischen Parteibefehl und Bannbulle', *Disput*, 12 (1993), 12–15.

Pfefferkorn, O., 'Anton Ackermann. Shdanows Schatten', *SBZ-Archiv*, 17 (5.9.53), 263–4.

Pfefferkorn, O., 'Franz Dahlem. Der letzte Revolutionär', *SBZ-Archiv*, 6 (20.3.53), 85–6.

Pfefferkorn, O., 'Fritz Ebert. "Der Oper-Bürgermeister" in Ostberlin', *SBZ-Archiv*, 9 (5.5.53), 137–8.

Pfefferkorn, O., 'Wilhelm Zaisser. Pankows Berija', *SBZ-Archiv*, 8 (20.4.53), 123–4.

Prieß, L., Wilke, M., 'Die DDR und die Besetzung der Tschechoslowakei am 21. August 1968', *APZ*, B36 (28.8.92), 26–34.

Probst, W., 'Nach der Invasion', *DA*, 6 (September 1968), 669–71.

Prokop, S., 'Ackermann-Legende?', *Die Weltbühne*, 27 (1990), 850–3.

Rehm, W., 'Neue Erkenntnisse über die Rolle der NVA bei der Besetzung der CSSR im August 1968', *DA*, 2 (5.3.91), 173–85.

Richter, J., 'Reexamining Soviet policy towards Germany in 1953', *Europe–Asia Studies*, 4 (1993), 671–91.

Roesler, J., 'Die Phraseologen mußten den Technologen weichen', *ND* (16/17.2.91), 13.

Rupieper, H. J., 'Zu den sowjetischen Deutschlandnoten 1952. Das Gespräch Nenni–Stalin', *VfZ*, 3 (July, 1985), 547–57.

Schenk, F., 'Grete Wittkowski und ihr neues Amt', *SBZ-Archiv*, 5 (March 1961), 73–4.

Spittmann, I., 'Die Niederlage im Redneraustausch', *SBZ-Archiv*, 13 (July, 1966), 193–4.

Spittmann, I., 'Die SED im Konflikt mit der CSSR', *DA*, 6 (September 1968), 663–9.

Spittmann, I., 'Warum Ulbricht stürzte', *DA*, 4 (1971), 568–9.

Spittmann, I., 'East Germany: the swinging pendulum', *POC*, 4 (July–August 1967), 14–20.

Staritz, D., 'Die SED, Stalin und der "Aufbau des Sozialismus" in der DDR', *DA*, 7 (July 1991), 686–700.

Stern, C., 'Der meistgehaßte, meistunterschätzte Mann. Walter Ulbricht – was dem DDR-Gründer gelang, wo der Staatratsvorsitzende scheiterte', *Der Spiegel*, 20 (10.5.71), 34–49.

Stern, C., 'Wie stark ist Ulbricht?', *SBZ-Archiv* (10.3.58), 65–7.

Stöckigt, R., 'Eine historische Chance wurde vertan . . .', *ND* (16.–17.6.90), 13.

Weber, H., 'Die DDR-Geschichtswissenschaft im Umbruch? Aufgaben der Historiker bei der Bewältigung der stalinistischen Vergangenheit', *DA*, 7 (1990), 1058–70.

Weber, H., 'Die Wandlung der SED und ihre Rolle im Parteiensystem 1945 bis 1950', *DA*, 2 (1993), 255–65.

Wenzke, R., 'Zur Beteiligung der NVA an der militärischen Operation von Warschauer-Pakt-Streitkräften gegen die CSSR 1968. Einige Ergänzungen zu einem Beitrag von Walter Rehm', *DA*, 11 (1991), 1179–86.

Wettig, G., 'Die beginnende Umorientierung der sowjetischen Deutschland-Politik im Frühjahr und Sommer 1953', *DA*, 5 (1995), 495–507.

Wettig, G., 'Die Deutschland-Note vom 10. März 1952 auf der Basis diplomatischer Akten des russischen Außenministeriums. Die Hypothese des Wiedervereinigungs-angebots', *DA*, 7 (1993), 786–805.

Wolkow, W., 'Sowjetische Parteiherrschaft und Prager Frühling 1968', *APZ*, B 36 (28.8.92), 11–17.

Unpublished dissertations

Harrison, H., 'The bargaining power of weaker allies in bipolarity and crisis: Soviet–East German relations, 1953–1961', PhD dissertation, University of Columbia (1993).

Spilker, D., 'The Socialist Unity Party of Germany (SED) and the German Question, 1944–53', University of Oxford (1998).

Index

Note: 'n.' after a page reference indicates the number of a note on that page.